Digital Sovereignty in the Global Data Economy:

Rights, Regulation, and Resistance

Muhammad Anshari
Universiti Brunei Darussalam, Brunei

Mohammad Nabil Almunawar
https://orcid.org/0000-0001-5296-2576
Universiti Brunei Darussalam, Brunei

Hazri Kifle
Universiti Brunei Darussalam, Brunei

IGI Global
Scientific Publishing
Publishing Tomorrow's Research Today

Vice President of Editorial	Melissa Wagner
Director of Acquisitions	Mikaela Felty
Director of Book Development	Jocelynn Hessler
Production Manager	Mike Brehm
Cover Design	Jose Rosado

Published in the United States of America by
IGI Global Scientific Publishing
701 East Chocolate Avenue
Hershey, PA, 17033, USA
Tel: 717-533-8845 | Fax: 717-533-7115
Website: https://www.igi-global.com E-mail: cust@igi-global.com

Library of Congress Cataloging-in-Publication Data

LCCN: 2026014693 (CIP Data Pending)
ISBN13: 9798260002889
Isbn13Softcover: 9798260002896
EISBN13: 9798260002902
British Cataloguing in Publication Data
A Cataloguing in Publication record for this book is available from the British Library.

Editorial Advisory Board and List of Reviewers

Editorial Advisory Board

List of Reviewers

Nurhadhinah Nadiah Ridzuan, *Universiti Brunei Darussalam, Brunei*
Sarbjit Kaur, *University of Delhi, India*
Triyo Supriyatno, *Universitas Islam Negari Maulana Malik Ibrahim, Indonesia*

Table of Contents

Detailed Table of Contents

as digital infrastructure control, data governance, AI sovereignty, and cybersecurity frameworks to explain how firms adapt to fragmented digital ecosystems. Furthermore, the chapter explores the role of sovereign cloud strategies, digital supply chain resilience, and cross-border governance in shaping corporate competitiveness. By linking geopolitical forces with corporate digital capabilities, the study provides a comprehensive framework for understanding how businesses achieve sustainable advantage in a multipolar digital economy.

This chapter examines transformation of sovereignty in the digtial age by a comparative analysis of major data governance regimes existing in the world. Comparison among European Union, United States, China, India, Brazil and Africa is analysed. The chapter develops upon the different types of sovereignty models among the states. It also demonstrates about the demonstrates about the digital sovereignty and its dependency on several factors. With the rise of technology corporations have become a quasi-sovereign actors which exercises functional authority over data and digital markets and its challenge to the traditional state dominance. The reassertion and role of the states through several mediums such as legislative framework, infrastructure development is also discussed.

This chapter examines the evolution of the digital economy by focusing on the emergence of Web 2.5 economy. The Web 2.5 economy is defined here as the eclectic embeddedness of blockchain-based decentralized technologies into the prevailing platform economy. Although the term "Web 2.5" is widely used in informatics and technology-oriented media, explicit references to "Web 2.5 economy" are absent from the economics and business literature. The chapter investigates the Web 2.5 economy as a necessary analytical category for studying emerging techno-economic and institutional formations within the digital economy. It conceptualizes the Web 2.5 economy as an organic component of platform capitalism and as a system of technological and institutional relations that constitutes a distinct state of play in the evolution of the digital economy. By providing conceptual grounding alongside empirical illustration, the chapter lays the foundation for future scholarly inquiry and offers a framework for more effective strategies, policies and governance.

This chapter addresses that analytical fragmentation by developing a comparative framework through which localization rules, AI governance instruments, and sovereignty claims are examined as mutually conditioning layers of digital statecraft rather than as isolated legal categories. A structured review of an uploaded Scopus corpus, which contained 139 records, was combined with a comparative analysis of India, Indonesia, Kenya, and Brazil, alongside official instruments issued by the African Union, UNESCO, the OECD, and NIST. The analysis demonstrates that broad territorial restrictions on data do not by themselves produce operational digital sovereignty; durable sovereignty is achieved when selective localization is aligned with data classification, compute and cloud capacity, risk-based AI governance, and interoperable cross-border transfer mechanisms.

The rapid rise of deepfake technologies has fundamentally challenged the reliability of digital information, raising urgent questions about who controls data, identity, and truth in the global data economy. This chapter analyzes deepfakes as a governance problem that reshapes power across digital systems. Using the Data Technology Platform Governance model, it explains how synthetic media operates through interconnected layers of data, artificial intelligence, platforms, and governance structures. The chapter argues that existing regulatory approaches remain fragmented and reactive, struggling to address the transnational and scalable nature of synthetic media. It highlights key risks, including violations of privacy, manipulation of digital identity, and erosion of trust in democratic processes. The chapter also examines emerging forms of resistance and concludes by emphasizing the need for coordinated and adaptive governance strategies that balance innovation with the protection of rights and public trust.

This chapter examines the shifting landscape of African cyber-jurisprudence, moving from the Malabo Convention (AU Convention on Cyber Security and Personal Data Protection) to the complex integration of the 2026 UN Convention Against Cybercrime. The central argument is that Africa faces a "double-edged fragmentation": the external friction between global geopolitical blocs and the internal lack of harmonization between African states. This chapter provides an ecosystem-level analysis of African cross-border cooperation, focusing on the transition from colonial-era Mutual Legal Assistance Treaties (MLATs) to modern, intelligence-led judicial cooperation. It further examines how jurisdictional fragmentation, mobile money ecosystems, and evidentiary challenges enable transnational cybercrime. The chapter concludes by assessing emerging threats posed by artificial intelligence and quantum computing, emphasizing the need for harmonized legal systems, institutional resilience, and collaborative governance to secure Africa's digital future.

This chapter examines the challenges of governing cross-border data flows within a fragmented global legal landscape with a focus on the tension between digital sovereignty and transnational data mobility. It argues that legal fragmentation is a structural feature of contemporary data governance, producing regulatory conflicts and reinforcing power asymmetries between states, corporations and individuals. The chapter analyses how state-led sovereignty strategies and societal as well as technological resistance seek to address these challenges but often reproduce underlying fragmentation. It then explores pathways toward more coherent governance through interoperability, institutional coordination and shared normative principles.

In doing so, it highlights the importance of aligning global data governance with broader commitments to inclusive development, accountability and the values reflected in the sustainable development goals.

Preface

OVERVIEW OF THE SUBJECT MATTER

Digital sovereignty has emerged as the organizing concept for answering that question. In its most general formulation, digital sovereignty refers to the capacity of actors whether individuals, states, or supranational entities to exercise meaningful control over their digital environments, including the data generated within them, the infrastructures through which it flows, and the algorithms that process it. This concept is not merely a technical or administrative concern; it is a fundamentally political one, touching on questions of autonomy, power, democracy, and justice in the information age.

This edited volume, Digital Sovereignty in the Global Data Economy: Rights, Regulation, and Resistance, brings together twenty-two scholarly contributions that approach digital sovereignty from multiple disciplinary vantage points, including law, political science, public administration, economics, computer science, Islamic jurisprudence, and international relations. The chapters span multiple scales of analysis, from the rights of individual data subjects navigating surveillance capitalism to the geopolitical dynamics shaping cross-border data flows among nations and blocs. Together, they constitute a rigorous, multi-perspectival examination of one of the defining governance challenges of our time.

THE TOPIC IN THE WORLD TODAY

The question of digital sovereignty has never been more urgent. Across the globe, governments, corporations, civil society organizations, and individual citizens are grappling with the consequences of a world in which data has become the primary resource of economic and political power. The Cambridge Analytica scandal exposed how personal data harvested from social media platforms can be weaponized for political manipulation. Mass surveillance revelations demonstrated how state intelligence agencies exploit digital infrastructure to monitor citizens and foreign governments alike. The proliferating deployment of algorithmic systems in hiring, credit scoring, criminal justice, and social service delivery has exposed the discriminatory potential of data-driven decision-making.

The rise of artificial intelligence has added new urgency and complexity to these debates. Generative AI systems are trained on vast datasets whose provenance and ownership are frequently unclear. AI-driven deepfakes challenge the epistemic foundations of democratic discourse. Algorithmic systems embedded in platform ecosystems exercise governance functions moderating speech, curating information, shaping public opinion without the accountability mechanisms that democratic theory demands of public institutions. This volume addresses all of these dimensions, situating scholarly analysis in the context of a rapidly evolving global reality.

TARGET AUDIENCE

This volume is designed for a broad academic and professional readership with an interest in the governance of the digital economy. It will be essential reading for scholars and graduate students in information science, law, political science, public administration, international relations, development studies, and Islamic studies who are engaged with questions of digital governance, data regulation, platform power, and technological sovereignty.

The book will also be of significant value to policymakers, regulatory practitioners, and civil society advocates who are working on data governance frameworks at national, regional, and international levels. Its multi-jurisdictional coverage encompassing contributions from scholars based in Southeast Asia, South Asia, the Middle East, Africa, Europe, and Latin America makes it particularly relevant for readers seeking perspectives that move beyond the dominant Euro-American axis of digital governance scholarship.

Business and technology professionals concerned with regulatory compliance, data strategy, and the geopolitical dimensions of digital infrastructure will likewise find this volume a valuable resource. The book assumes no prior technical expertise and is accessible to any reader with a background in social science, law, or the humanities.

DESCRIPTION OF CHAPTER CONTRIBUTIONS

The volume is organized across four thematic sections, each corresponding to a distinct layer of the multi-level framework for digital sovereignty that animates the book's intellectual architecture: the individual, the national, the regional, and the cross-border.

Chapter 1: Data Driven Governance and the Transformation of Public Policy Discourse

Data has become a key driver of governance and public policy in the digital age. Across areas such as health, climate, finance, and public administration, data is increasingly used to support faster and more efficient decision-making. This chapter examines how policymaking has shifted from policy-informed data to data-driven governance, where algorithms, datasets, and real-time analytics shape policy agendas and public discourse. It argues that those who collect and control data now influence which problems are recognised, which communities become visible to the state, and which solutions are considered possible. While data-driven policymaking may improve efficiency and evidence-based governance, it also raises concerns about democratic accountability, digital sovereignty, regulatory control, and the loss of human agency. The chapter explores these issues through the lens of rights, regulation, and resistance, particularly in developing and middle-income countries facing pressure to modernise governance systems.

Chapter 2: Digital Sovereignty and Media Regulation: Governing Journalism in Platform Ecosystems

This chapter explores the transforming role of the digital platforms in penetrating journalism and information governance in the platform age. It puts accents on the rising significance of digital sovereignty and media regulation in the context of the ability of global technology corporations to control news creation, distribution, and visibility. Social media have become significant mediators and construct social discourse based on algorithms and content management regulations. This brings issues concerning transparency, responsibility and security of the journalistic autonomy. The chapter also examines the current policy reactions such as platform regulation and data governance models both on global and national backgrounds. It states that platforms power requires regulation to promote effective media regulation, support public interest journalism and provide democratic regulation of information ecosystems.

Chapter 3: Cybersecurity Copilots and Digital Sovereignty in Security Operations Centers

This chapter examines the use of large language model (LLM) copilots in Security Operations Centers (SOCs) serving government and critical infrastructure and analyzes the sovereignty risks created by their adoption. It argues that copilots can improve alert triage, explanation, and incident reporting, but can also expose sensitive cyber-defense workflows to foreign jurisdiction, vendor dependence, opaque governance, and model-specific security vulnerabilities. Through a qualitative comparative policy analysis of the European Union, United States, United Kingdom, Singapore, and India, the chapter assesses the extent to which current AI and cybersecurity frameworks address SOC-specific risks. Its principal contribution is the SOC-LLM Governance Framework (SLGF), which differentiates among Fully Sovereign, Hybrid Sovereign, and Foreign Dependent deployment models and maps each to actionable controls for data handling, hosting, auditability, robustness testing, and exit feasibility.

Chapter 4: Corporate Digital Sovereignty Strategies and Geopolitical Positioning

This chapter examines the evolving concept of corporate digital sovereignty within the context of global geopolitical dynamics and technological transformation. It highlights how organizations increasingly navigate complex regulatory environments, data localization policies, and geopolitical tensions while maintaining operational efficiency and strategic autonomy. The discussion integrates key dimensions such as digital infrastructure control, data governance, AI sovereignty, and cybersecurity frameworks to explain how firms adapt to fragmented digital ecosystems. Furthermore, the chapter explores the role of sovereign cloud strategies, digital supply chain resilience, and cross-border governance in shaping corporate competitiveness. By linking geopolitical forces with corporate digital capabilities, the study provides a comprehensive framework for understanding how businesses achieve sustainable advantage in a multipolar digital economy.

Chapter 5: New Sovereigns States, Corporations And The Struggle Over Data

This chapter examines transformation of sovereignty in the digtial age by a comparative analysis of major data governance regimes existing in the world. Comparison among European Union, United States, China, India, Brazil and Africa is analysed. The chapter develops upon the different types of sovereignty models among the states. It also demonstrates about the demonstrates about the digital sovereignty and its dependency on several factors. With the rise of technology corporations have become a quasi-sovereign actors which exercises functional authority over data and digital markets and its challenge to the traditional state dominance. The reassertion and role of the states through several mediums such as legislative framework, infrastructure development is also discussed.

Chapter 6: The Emergence of Web 2.5 Economy: The Digital Economy Between Platforms and Protocols

This chapter examines the evolution of the digital economy by focusing on the emergence of Web 2.5 economy. The Web 2.5 economy is defined here as the eclectic embeddedness of blockchain-based decentralized technologies into the prevailing platform economy. Although the term "Web 2.5" is widely used in informatics and technology-oriented media, explicit references to "Web 2.5 economy" are absent from the economics and business literature. The chapter investigates the Web 2.5 economy as a necessary analytical category for studying emerging techno-economic and institutional formations within the digital economy. It conceptualizes the Web 2.5 economy as an organic component of platform capitalism and as a system of technological and institutional relations that constitutes a distinct state of play in the evolution of the digital economy. By providing conceptual grounding alongside empirical illustration, the chapter lays the foundation for future scholarly inquiry and offers a framework for more effective strategies, policies and governance.

Chapter 7: Data Localization, AI Governance, and Digital Sovereignty in Emerging Economies A Comparative Governance Framework

This chapter addresses that analytical fragmentation by developing a comparative framework through which localization rules, AI governance instruments, and sovereignty claims are examined as mutually conditioning layers of digital statecraft rather than as isolated legal categories. A structured review of an uploaded Scopus corpus, which contained 139 records, was combined with a comparative analysis of India, Indonesia, Kenya, and Brazil, alongside official instruments issued by the African Union, UNESCO, the OECD, and NIST. The analysis demonstrates that broad territorial restrictions on data do not by themselves produce operational digital sovereignty; durable sovereignty is achieved when selective localization is aligned with data classification, compute and cloud capacity, risk-based AI governance, and interoperable cross-border transfer mechanisms.

Chapter 8: Deepfakes and Digital Sovereignty: Governance Challenges of Synthetic Media in the AI-Driven Data Economy

The rapid rise of deepfake technologies has fundamentally challenged the reliability of digital information, raising urgent questions about who controls data, identity, and truth in the global data economy. This chapter analyzes deepfakes as a governance problem that reshapes power across digital systems. Using the Data Technology Platform Governance model, it explains how synthetic media operates through interconnected layers of data, artificial intelligence, platforms, and governance structures. The chapter argues that existing regulatory approaches remain fragmented and reactive, struggling to address the transnational and scalable nature of synthetic media. It highlights key risks, including violations of privacy, manipulation of digital identity, and erosion of trust in democratic processes. The chapter also examines emerging forms of resistance and concludes by emphasizing the need for coordinated and adaptive governance strategies that balance innovation with the protection of rights and public trust.

Chapter 9: African Digital Sovereignty, Cross Border Cybercrime and The Future of Networked Governance

This chapter examines the shifting landscape of African cyber-jurisprudence, moving from the Malabo Convention (AU Convention on Cyber Security and Personal Data Protection) to the complex integration of the 2026 UN Convention Against Cybercrime. The central argument is that Africa faces a "double-edged fragmentation": the external friction between global geopolitical blocs and the internal lack of harmonization between African states. This chapter provides an ecosystem-level analysis of African cross-border cooperation, focusing on the transition from colonial-era Mutual Legal Assistance Treaties (MLATs) to modern, intelligence-led judicial cooperation. It further examines how jurisdictional fragmentation, mobile money ecosystems, and evidentiary challenges enable transnational cybercrime. The chapter concludes by assessing emerging threats posed by artificial intelligence and quantum computing, emphasizing the need for harmonized legal systems, institutional resilience, and collaborative governance to secure Africa's digital future.

Chapter 10: Digital Sovereignty and Cross-Border Data Flows: Legal Fragmentation and Governance Challenges

This chapter examines the challenges of governing cross-border data flows within a fragmented global legal landscape with a focus on the tension between digital sovereignty and transnational data mobility. It argues that legal fragmentation is a structural feature of contemporary data governance, producing regulatory conflicts and reinforcing power asymmetries between states, corporations and individuals. The chapter analyses how state-led sovereignty strategies and societal as well as technological resistance seek to address these challenges but often reproduce underlying fragmentation. It then explores pathways toward more coherent governance through interoperability, institutional coordination and shared normative principles. In doing so, it highlights the importance of aligning global data governance with broader commitments to inclusive development, accountability and the values reflected in the sustainable development goals.

CONCLUSION: HOW THIS BOOK IMPACTS THE FIELD

Digital Sovereignty in the Global Data Economy: Rights, Regulation, and Resistance makes several distinctive contributions to the rapidly growing scholarship on data governance and digital sovereignty. First, it offers a genuinely multi-scalar framework spanning individual, national, regional, and cross-border levels of analysis that enables readers to appreciate both the internal logic of governance challenges at each level and the interconnections between them. This integrated perspective is essential for understanding why piecemeal regulatory responses so frequently fail to achieve their objectives.

Second, the volume brings together perspectives from the Global South that are frequently marginalized in dominant accounts of digital governance, which tend to center European and North American regulatory experiences. Contributors from Southeast Asia, South Asia, the Middle East, Africa, and Latin America bring insights rooted in their own regulatory contexts, complicating generalizations derived from the experience of established digital powers and enriching the conceptual vocabulary available for thinking about sovereignty, resistance, and governance innovation.

Third, the volume makes a serious attempt to engage with Islamic jurisprudential and ethical traditions as resources for data governance thinking. At a time when a significant proportion of the world's population is navigating digital governance challenges through frameworks shaped by Islamic values, the inclusion of Maqasid al-Shariah and Islamic stewardship frameworks represents an important contribution to the pluralism of the field.

Fourth, the thematic emphasis on resistance the 'R' in Rights, Regulation, and Resistance distinguishes this volume from treatments of digital sovereignty that focus exclusively on state regulatory authority. By attending to the resistance of civil society, communities, and individuals to data exploitation, and to the ambivalent relationship between state sovereignty claims and citizen protection, the volume offers a more complete and politically honest account of how power over data is actually contested and distributed.

Finally, by gathering contributions that span law, computer science, Islamic studies, political economy, environmental governance, and financial regulation, this volume models the interdisciplinary collaboration that effective data governance scholarship requires. No single discipline has the conceptual resources to address the full complexity of digital sovereignty; this volume demonstrates what becomes possible when scholars from diverse fields bring their expertise to bear on a shared set of questions.

The editors express their sincere gratitude to all contributing authors for the quality of their scholarship and the generosity with which they engaged with the editorial process. We thank the team at IGI Global for their support and professionalism throughout the production of this volume. We hope that the conversations these chapters generate will advance the development of governance frameworks that are adequate to the complexity, urgency, and human stakes of the global data economy — frameworks that protect individual rights, respect national sovereignty, enable beneficial data use, and resist the concentration of informational power in the hands of the few.

Muhammad Anshari
Universiti Brunei Darussalam, Brunei

Mohammad Nabil Almunawar
Universiti Brunei Darussalam, Brunei

Hazri Kifle
Universiti Brunei Darussalam, Brunei

Introduction

1. THE DATA REVOLUTION AND ITS DISCONTENTS

We live in an era defined by the exponential of explosion of data. Every digital transaction, every social media interaction, every sensor embedded in our homes, vehicles, and urban infrastructure generates streams of information that, in aggregate, constitute what we now call Big Data. The scale of this phenomenon is extraordinary. By 2030, the global datasphere is projected to over 600 zettabytes, a nearly fourfold increase from 2025 levels driven by the relentless expansion of generative AI and IoT ecosystems (IDC, 2024; Holon, 2025). Yet behind the debate of the *data economy* lies a question of deep legal, ethical, and political consequence: who, precisely, owns this data, and who has the right to decide how it is used?

This edited volume, *Digital Sovereignty in the Global Data Economy: Rights, Regulation, and Resistance*, is driven by that question and by the urgent need to subject it to rigorous academic analysis. The chapters gathered here approach digital sovereignty from multiple disciplinary such as law, political science, public health, economics, computer science, and international relations, and from multiple scales of analysis, ranging from the rights of individual data subjects to the geopolitical dynamics that shape cross-border data flows. The premise shared by all contributors is that data is not merely a technical artifact. Data is power: the power to profile, predict, push, exclude, surveille, and govern. Understanding who controls data, under what conditions, and to what ends is therefore one of the defining governance challenges of our time.

2. THE ANATOMY OF THE DATA OWNERSHIP PROBLEM

2.1 From Personal Data to Pervasive Data

The origins of contemporary debates about data ownership lie in a fundamental shift in how data is generated and collected. In earlier phases of digitisation, data was predominantly a by-product of deliberate, bounded transactions: a bank record, a medical file, a census return. The subject of the data and the institution holding it were typically known to one another, and regulatory frameworks, however flawed were constructed around this relationship. What has changed in the age of pervasive connectivity is the elimination of any meaningful boundary between the zones of data production and everyday life.

Two developments are particularly consequential. The first is the maturation of social media platforms as infrastructures of sociality. Users of these platforms do not merely communicate, they perform their identities, preferences, affiliations, and anxieties in environments specifically engineered to stimulate disclosure (Yusuf et al., 2026). The data generated is not incidental to platform use, it is the product that the platform harvests and monetises. Crucially, much of this disclosure is voluntary but not fully conscious. Users may understand in the abstract that their data is being collected, yet few appreciate the precision with which disaggregated data points can be combined to produce actionable profiles. Demographic information (age, gender, location), geographic movement patterns, and psychographic signatures (personality traits, values, emotional states) can all be inferred from apparently mundane digital traces such as a 'like', a search query, a pause over a video (Kosinski et al., 2013; Matz et al., 2017).

The second development is the rapid increase of Internet of Things (IoT) devices, which has shifted data generation from something people do to something that happens to them continuously and often invisibly. Smart meters, fitness trackers, connected vehicles, CCTV systems equipped with facial recognition, environmental sensors embedded in public space each of these devices is a persistent data-collection instrument. Unlike social media, IoT data collection frequently requires no active participation by the subject at all. The data subject may be entirely unaware that data is being generated, let alone how it is being stored, shared, or analysed. The aggregate effect of these two developments is what Shoshana Zuboff (2019) has termed 'surveillance capitalism': an economic logic in which the systematic extraction and commodification of behavioural data becomes the primary driver of value creation.

2.2 Third-Party Access and the Erosion of Informational Self-Determination

The foundational principle underlying most legal frameworks governing personal data is that data subjects should retain meaningful control over information relating to themselves. In practice, however, a complex digital ecosystem of third-party actors routinely accesses, aggregates, and exploits personal data in ways that lie far beyond the awareness or comprehension of data subjects.

Data brokers occupy a particularly consequential position in this digital ecosystem. These companies, some operating with minimal public visibility, purchase, aggregate, and resell personal data from hundreds or thousands of sources, constructing dossiers of extraordinary granularity. The commercial uses of such data range from targeted advertising to credit scoring and employment screening; the political uses include micro-targeted campaign messaging and the manipulation of electoral behaviour (Cadwalladr & Graham-Harrison, 2018). State actors, too, are significant consumers of commercially collected data, particularly where legal constraints on direct government surveillance can be circumvented by purchasing profiles assembled by private actors (Pasquale, 2015).

What unites these diverse actors is their capacity to exercise power over individuals through data, without those individuals' knowledge or meaningful consent. This asymmetry between the informational resources of large institutional actors and the practical ignorance of data subjects is the central problem that digital sovereignty frameworks seek to address.

3. DIGITAL SOVEREIGNTY: CONCEPT, CONTESTATION, AND COMPLEXITY

3.1 Defining the Concept

The concept of digital sovereignty, though now widely invoked, remains contested and underspecified. In its most general formulation, digital sovereignty refers to the capacity of actors whether individuals, states, or supranational entities to exercise meaningful control over their digital environments, including the data generated within them, the infrastructures through which it flows, and the algorithms that process it (Pohle & Thiel, 2020). This formulation is usefully capacious, but it obscures important distinctions between different registers at which sovereignty claims operate.

At the individual level, digital sovereignty intersects with established traditions of privacy rights and data protection, as codified in instruments such as the European

Union's General Data Protection Regulation (GDPR). At this level, the core claim is that individuals should have the right to know what data is held about them, to consent to its use, to access and correct it, and, under certain conditions, to require its deletion of the so-called *right to be forgotten*.

At the national level, digital sovereignty takes on a more explicitly political character, encompassing rights about states' rights to regulate digital infrastructure, to assert jurisdiction over data flows, and to protect what is increasingly framed as a strategic national resource. The Chinese concept of 'cyber sovereignty' represents one expression of this debate, as does the European Union's pursuit of technological sovereignty through instruments such as the European Data Strategy and the EU Data Act. These national-level frameworks are, however, frequently in tension with one another and with the logic of the global digital economy, which depends on the largely frictionless cross-border movement of data. At the regional and supranational level, digital sovereignty involves the negotiation of frameworks that can manage cross-border data flows while preserving the regulatory privileges of participating states.

3.2 Sectoral Complexity

A further complication is that the appropriate level of data sovereignty protection, and the mechanisms best suited to deliver it, vary extremely across sectors. In healthcare, the tension between data sovereignty and data utility is acute: patient data is deeply sensitive and attracts strong privacy protections, yet population-level health data is indispensable for epidemiological research, pandemic preparedness, and the development of personalised medicine. The challenge is to construct governance frameworks that protect individual rights without foreclosing the public benefits of health data use (Prainsack, 2017).

In the transport sector, the explosion of connected vehicles and intelligent transport systems generates continuous, fine-grained locational data that is simultaneously commercially valuable, operationally necessary, and capable of constituting a comprehensive record of individuals' movements. In national security contexts, tensions between sovereignty claims and the operational requirements of intelligence sharing have generated enduring friction, as illustrated by the diplomatic fallout from revelations of mass surveillance programmes. In financial services, the rise of open banking and fintech has created new pressures on traditional data protection frameworks, as regulatory innovation struggles to keep pace with technological change (Anshari et al.,2021).

These sectoral variations are not merely technical but they reflect deeper political and ethical disputes about the proper balance between individual rights, collective interests, commercial imperatives, and state prerogatives. Any adequate account of digital sovereignty must engage with this complexity, resisting the temptation to offer one-size-fits-all prescriptions.

4. DIGITAL SOVEREIGNTY ACROSS LAYERS: A MULTI-LEVEL FRAMEWORK

The figure below presents a conceptual framework for understanding digital sovereignty across four interconnected layers of analysis. This volume is organised around precisely this multi-layered architecture, which we believe is essential to capturing the full scope of the challenges at stake.

Figure 1. A multi-level framework for digital sovereignty

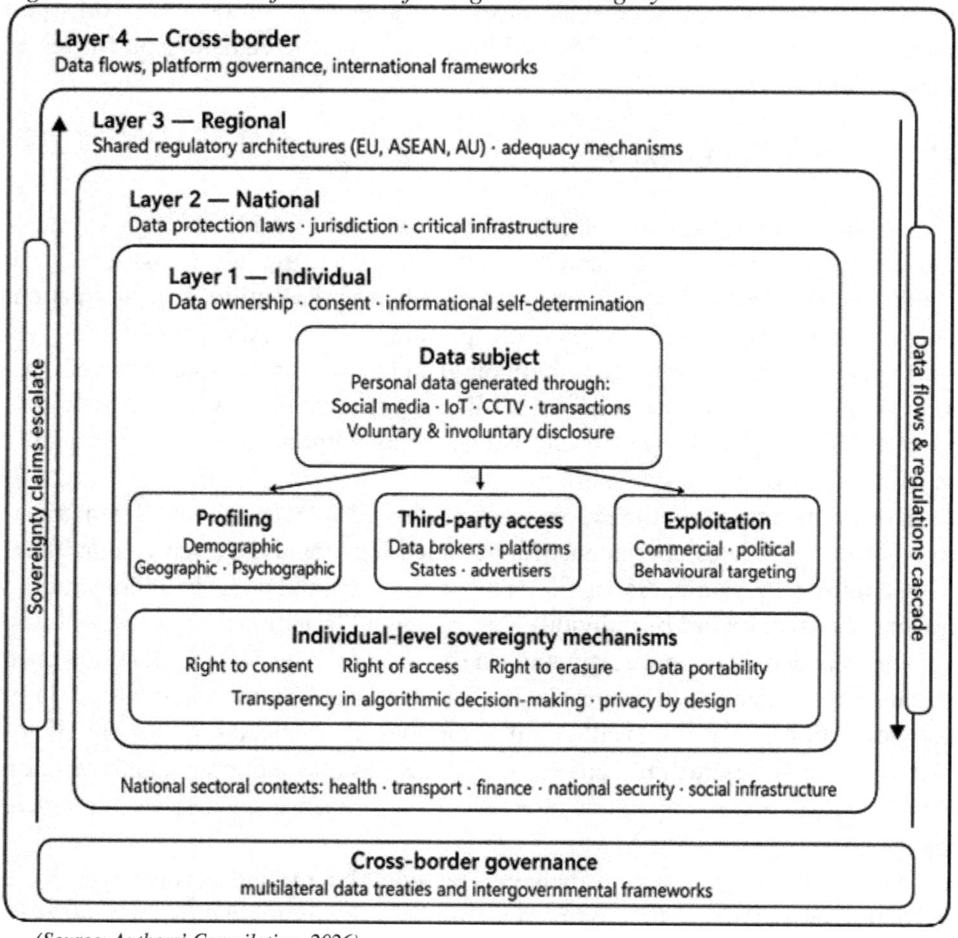

(Source: Authors' Compilation, 2026)

4.1 The Individual Layer

At the individual layer, digital sovereignty encompasses the rights of data subjects to control information pertaining to themselves. This includes rights to informed consent, data access, rectification, portability, and erasure. It also encompasses the right to meaningful transparency about algorithmic decision-making that affects individuals' life chances. The contributions in Part I of this volume examine how these rights operate in practice, assessing the extent to which existing legal frameworks deliver genuine empowerment or merely formal compliance.

4.2 The National Layer

At the national layer, digital sovereignty concerns the capacity of states to govern the data economy within their territorial jurisdiction to regulate the collection and use of data, to ensure that critical digital infrastructure is secure and resilient, and to protect the interests of their citizens against both private actors and foreign governments. The contributions in Part II examine national regulatory strategies across a range of jurisdictions, mapping the diverse approaches that states have adopted and analysing their relative effectiveness.

4.3 The Regional Layer

At the regional layer, digital sovereignty involves the construction of shared governance frameworks among states that share geopolitical, economic, or normative interests. The data governance architecture in ASEAN is emerging along with other regional contexts. The contributions in Part III examine these regional frameworks, attending both to their internal tensions and to their external implications for global data governance.

4.4 The Cross-Border Layer

At the cross-border layer, digital sovereignty confronts the fundamental challenge that data flows are inherently transnational, while regulatory authority remains anchored in territorial jurisdictions. This layer encompasses the negotiation of international data governance agreements, the management of jurisdictional conflicts, and the governance challenges posed by the activities of large digital platforms that operate across multiple regulatory environments. The contributions in Part IV examine these cross-border dimensions, engaging with debates about the prospects for effective multilateral data governance.

5. RESISTANCE AND THE POLITICS OF DIGITAL SOVEREIGNTY

While, Rights, Regulation, and Resistance signals our belief that digital sovereignty is not merely a technical or legal problem, but a political one. The distribution of power over data is not natural or inevitable. It is the product of choices about regulatory design, platform architecture, international negotiation, and, perhaps above all, the political mobilisation of those whose interests are at stake.

The theme of resistance runs through this volume in multiple registers. There is the resistance of states to the data sovereignty claims of other states that the geopolitical dimension of digital sovereignty disputes. There is the resistance of civil society organisations to the data practices of large platforms. A dimension that has produced significant regulatory reform in some jurisdictions. And there is the resistance of individuals, communities, and social movements to surveillance and profiling resistance that takes forms ranging from legal challenge to technical circumvention to political organising.

We do not assume that resistance is always progressive, or that its outcomes are always beneficial. The statement of national digital sovereignty can serve the interests of governance as readily as it can protect citizens from corporate surveillance. The chapters in this volume engage critically with these ambiguities, resisting the temptation to treat digital sovereignty as an unqualified good.

6. CONCLUSION

The convergence of mass IoT deployment, platform-mediated social life, and the commodification of behavioural data has created conditions in which the informational foundations of individual autonomy, democratic governance, and national security are simultaneously at risk. Existing regulatory frameworks, designed for an earlier technological moment, are struggling to keep pace. The concept of digital sovereignty offers a productive framework for analysing these challenges and for developing more adequate responses but only if it is used with precision and critical self-awareness. This volume does not offer a definitive account of digital sovereignty, and still less does it propose a single policy prescription. What it offers is a rigorous, multi-perspectival examination of the challenges at stake, conducted by scholars who bring diverse disciplinary, geographic, and political perspectives to bear on a problem that no single discipline or jurisdiction can resolve alone. We hope that the conversations generated by these chapters will contribute to the development of governance frameworks that are genuinely adequate to the complexity of the global data economy frameworks that protect individual rights, respect national sovereignty, enable beneficial data use, and resist the concentration of informational power in the hands of the few. The stakes of getting this right could not be higher. Data sovereignty is not an abstract philosophical question: it bears directly on who can speak, who can be heard, who can be excluded, and who can be governed without their knowledge or consent. It is, in the deepest sense, a question about the conditions of democratic life in a digital age.

Muhammad Anshari
Universiti Brunei Darussalam, Brunei

Mohammad Nabil Almunawar
Universiti Brunei Darussalam, Brunei

Hazri Kifle
Universiti Brunei Darussalam, Brunei

REFERENCES

Anshari, M., Almunawar, M. N., Masri, M., Hamdan, M., Fithriyah, M., & Fitri, A. (2021, November). Digital wallet in supporting green FinTech sustainability. In *2021 Third International Sustainability and Resilience Conference: Climate Change* (pp. 352-357). IEEE. DOI: 10.1109/IEEECONF53624.2021.9667957

Cadwalladr, C., & Graham-Harrison, E. (2018). Revealed: 50 million Facebook profiles harvested for Cambridge Analytica in major data breach. The Guardian.

Holon, I. Q. (2025). *The 2030 global data outlook: Intelligence, infrastructure, and the zettabyte era*. HolonIQ Intelligence.

IDC. (2024). Worldwide Global DataSphere forecast, 2024–2028: The AI-driven data explosion (Doc #US52375924). International Data Corporation.

Kosinski, M., Stillwell, D., & Graepel, T. (2013). Private traits and attributes are predictable from digital records of human behaviour. *Proceedings of the National Academy of Sciences of the United States of America*, *110*(15), 5802–5805. DOI: 10.1073/pnas.1218772110 PMID: 23479631

Matz, S. C., Kosinski, M., Nave, G., & Stillwell, D. J. (2017). Psychological targeting as an effective approach to digital mass persuasion. *Proceedings of the National Academy of Sciences of the United States of America*, *114*(48), 12714–12719. DOI: 10.1073/pnas.1710966114 PMID: 29133409

Pasquale, F. (2015). *The black box society: The secret algorithms that control money and information*. Harvard University Press. DOI: 10.4159/harvard.9780674736061

Pohle, J., & Thiel, T. (2020). Digital sovereignty. *Internet Policy Review*, *9*(4). Advance online publication. DOI: 10.14763/2020.4.1532

Prainsack, B. (2017). *Personalized medicine: Empowered patients in the 21st century?* New York University Press.

Yusuf, H., Fitri, A., & Razzaq, A. (2026). Using artificial intelligence for human-AI collaboration in knowledge management systems to improve organizational efficiency and learning. In *Driving Organizational Transformation Through Human-Robotic Collaboration* (pp. 35–48). IGI Global Scientific Publishing.

Zuboff, S. (2019). *The age of surveillance capitalism: The fight for a human future at the new frontier of power*. PublicAffairs.

Chapter 1
Data-Driven Governance and the Transformation of Public Policy Discourse

Muhammad Asfand Yar
http://orcid.org/0000-0002-1598-5629
Institute of Policy Studies, Universiti Brunei Darussalam, Brunei

Mahani Hamdan
http://orcid.org/0000-0003-3859-4433
Faculty of Military Studies, Universiti Brunei Darussalam, Brunei

Muhammad Anshari
http://orcid.org/0000-0002-8160-6682
Institute of Policy Studies, Universiti Brunei Darussalam, Brunei

Ayan Ullah Khan
http://orcid.org/0009-0003-1466-4991
School of Digital Sciences, Universiti Brunei Darussalam, Brunei

ABSTRACT

Data has become a key driver of governance and public policy in the digital age. Across areas such as health, climate, finance, and public administration, data is increasingly used to support faster and more efficient decision-making. This chapter examines how policymaking has shifted from policy-informed data to data-driven governance, where algorithms, datasets, and real-time analytics shape policy agendas and public discourse. It argues that those who collect and control data now influence which problems are recognised, which communities become visible to the state, and which solutions are considered possible. While data-driven policymaking may improve efficiency and evidence-based governance, it also raises concerns

DOI: 10.4018/979-8-2600-0288-9.ch001

about democratic accountability, digital sovereignty, regulatory control, and the loss of human agency. The chapter explores these issues through the lens of rights, regulation, and resistance, particularly in developing and middle-income countries facing pressure to modernise governance systems.

1. INTRODUCTION

This is the era of datafication, where data recognised as governance architecture, as an active instrument of government ad administration across sectors and scales. The algorithmic welfare, predictive policing, biometric identity, and real-time fiscal surveillance across the global from North to South, data systems are no longer merely policy managing tools, instead they provide landscape for policy contest, design, and legitimacy (Couldry & Mejias, 2019). The metaphors assigned to data as "new oil of digital economy" Toonders (2014), the "new gold", and infrastructure if fifth industrial revolution Schwab et al. (2011), are revealing and not merely verbal add-ons, instead they encrypt a specific understanding of data as a resource, rare, extractable, and valuable to those who keep it. These metaphors naturalize sporadic political economy in which data-rich corporations based in Global North and a small group of advanced technological nations collect structural advantages that transform directly into policymaking power (Mayer-Schönberger & Cukier, 2013).

In the prevalent era of digitisation, data integration in policymaking is trending, transforming the out-dated assumption-based practices to evidence-based policymaking and reshaping the dynamics of modern-day public policy discourse. This transformative paradigm shift compels the policy makers to detach the bureaucratic and incremental approaches and adopt sophisticated analytical tools for evidence-based policymaking, and data-informed decision-making. The advanced data science and analytics has unprecedent capacity to understand the complex social trends, analyse the patterns, and provides insights that assist the policymakers to formulate and design adaptive policy responses (Benoit, 2024).

The paradigm shift demands to embrace the extensive volume of transactional data and embed the methodologies of advanced data analytics across the entire policy cycle, from problem identification to evaluation by introducing predictive models for counterfactual analysis and by simulating potential policy options for on-going interventions, improvements, and changes to address the unintended challenges during implementation. The proliferation of data and AI navigates the policy discourse, revolutionize the policy sciences, and enhance the capacity of evidence-based policymaking (Guerrero & Margetts, 2024). The advanced technologies such as Govt-Tech, Legal-Tech, and Civic-Tech are overwhelmingly evolving governance and administration functions and revamp the policymaking process by inclusion of public participation.

In modern-day public governance systems, policy disputes are gradually increase over data systems like data regulatory, authority, hegemony, and sovereignty in modelling best evidence based on metrices, and indicators to categories public policy problems. Literature shows that indicators, and metrices are not enough to define, and describe policy reality, because metrices merely depends on comparative frames, setting priorities, and allocative decisions. In measurable and quantified governance, controlled indicator systems and data infrastructures gains the power to reshape the policy discourse, negating legislatures, and regulators (Beaumont & Sending, 2012; Yusuf et al., 2026).

This study covers the dynamics of data translation in policymaking through descriptive and normative lens. Descriptively, it tracks how data plays fundamental role in policy direction by determining which policy problems become legible to the government, which communities are entertained or not by government institutions, and which policy intrusions seem rational or feasible. Normatively, it explores the effects of this paradigm shift, argues that the design of data-driven policymaking challenge democratic obligation, and epistemic sovereignty, as the right of nations to produce, interpret, and execute generated knowledge from within their own social values and local context.

The chapter covers five sections, following a literature review both theoretical and empirical on data, power, and governance, summaries methodology supporting analysis. The thematic discourse analysis shows, data systems role in agenda-setting, community readability, and solution outlining in modern policymaking context. The discussion includes the findings within the broader geopolitical landscape of digital sovereignty, regulatory politics, and resistance. The conclusion evolves a normative claim to regain human agency in data-driven policymaking through ethical and regulatory frameworks, participatory data governance, and what the chapter calls epistemic justice in policymaking.

2. LITERATURE REVIEW

The interdisciplinary literature across political economy, public policy, data governance, and global health, gradually links on a shared ground, i.e., data is not merely a policy input, but architecture of governance with a power to set policy agendas, legitimacy, and reallocates governing authority through data infrastructures, metrics, indicators, and access control.

2.1 Data and Governance

Governance and information have a long relationship, since the 17th century, when the states had collected, manged, and used statistics as a tool to rule. The art and practice of governing people, through knowledge, categorisation, and normalisation, 'governmentality' (Foucault, 1991). Desrosières (1998) analysed this practice extensively by showing how statistical systems just not define social realism but create it dynamically, rendering publics readable to administrative power through the production of standardised categories.

The welfare states of 20th century ruled through bureaucratic discretions regulated by proficient norms, whereas, the digital welfare state governs increasingly through automated systems and render data into decisions with nominal human reflection. Though past statistical practices are significant, however, the emergence of algorithmic decision-making support systems that operationalise volume and velocity of data in real-time and at scale, often without meaningful human oversight, make it distinguishes modern data-driven policymaking (O'neil, 2017).

2.2 Algorithmic Policymaking

The term of "algorithmic policy architecture" describes the data collection approaches, methods, procedures, systems, analytical and predictive models, and automated decision support tools that are being introduced and applied in spheres of public policy, public administration, and governance. The algorithmic policy architecture encrypts specific norms about social problems and solutions, submitting options unseen and surely ignore the voices of marginalised communities whose lives do not adapt to design factors of governing data systems. Advocates of data-driven policymaking has a claim that it signifies and improves automation over intuition-based or politically motivated governance (Mayer-Schönberger & Cukier, 2013). Data-driven practices have reduced the corruption level, better target efficiency and enable rapid response to changing social conditions and programmes. AI-enabled techniques, ML predictive models, NLP tools, sentiment analysis, mobile data, and satellite imagery has replaced the traditional and costly surveys approaches used to identify social, economic, and poverty conditions, potentially enable more timely and accurate allocation of public resources (Jean et al., 2016).

The critics of data-enabled practices in policymaking raised ethical concerns of digital divide, social discrimination, and citizens privacy. Algorithmic policymaking in education, criminal justice, and credit systematically reproduce existing social inequalities, because they are trained on historical data that encodes past discrimination. A study depicts that automated eligibility systems for social welfare programmes in the United States effectively operated as tools to exclude poor and marginalised groups, denying services through algorithmic adjudication that offered no meaningful avenue for appeal or redress (Eubanks, 2018; Samiha et al., 2022). Longworth (2021) coined the notion of the 'New Jim Code' that defines how racial bias embed within edifices of digital technologies that seem neutral and objective.

2.3 Data Hegemony

The concept of "Data Hegemony" by extending Gramscian hegemony theory into digital governance domain, describes the process by which data actors attain data dominance over the global policy discourse not through obligation but applying soft power of data standards, interoperability frameworks, and the sheer pull of large volume of datasets. Data hegemony drives through inclusion and exclusion, i.e., by adding developing nations into global data systems. Data hegemony describes how dominant data actors apply a stabilise common sense of what counts as feasible evidence by controlling data flux, ethics, and explanatory frames. A trending knowledge has placed the dynamics of data hegemony within a broader geopolitical context, argus that global data on political economy replicates and extends comparable power structures to historic colonization (Couldry & Mejias, 2019). The term 'digital colonialism' has surfaced by Couldry and Mejias (2019) that define the systematic data extraction from peoples of the Global South for the benefits of technological corporations and governments based in the Global North, a process similar to the extraction of natural resources in earlier colonial establishments (Kwet, 2019). 'Data colonialism' describes the emerging social order in which humans and their social relations are assumed as raw material for datafication, a process that is not just economic but ontological, reshapes the terms on which individuals and communities understand their relationships with states and tech-corporations. Birhane (2020) claimed that the obligation of Western ML frameworks on African social context creates an epistemic form of colonialism, obliging categorised knowledge derived from specific cultural contexts.

2.4 Data Sovereignty

The concept of "epistemic sovereignty" as a dimension of digital sovereignty refers to capacity of governance system in a public state to produce, validate, and act on its own knowledge systems, free from structural dependence on peripheral made data frameworks. The notion of "digital sovereignty" has appeared as a significant framework that helps to understand mechanism by which states and communities seek to affirm control over data systems through which it is formed and explained (Pohle & Thiel, 2020). The states invoked digital sovereignty to justify the requirements of data localisation, operational checks on foreign technological companies, and the promotion of domestically controlled digital infrastructure. The loss of digital sovereignty occurs when a policy actor faces technical incapacity, economic pressures, institutional resistance, and relays on others designed data structures to deal with its own policy problems. The European Union's General Data Protection Regulation (GDPR) can be recognised partially as a claim of European digital sovereignty against the data practices of American tech-corporations (Hoofnagle et al., 2019). There is an immense pressure on developing and middle-income countries to adopt data-driven models for automation in policymaking, championed by international development institutions, tech-companies, and bilateral donors. The politics of digital sovereignty are particularly tense for middle-income countries as the adoption of externally designed data systems produce reliance and weaken local relevance and governance context (Taylor & Broeders, 2015).

3. METHODOLOGY

This chapter applies qualitative methodology, draws on thematic discourse analysis and theoretical synthesis across disciplinary fields international political economy, science and technology, and data studies. The methodological approach is informed by practices of policy studies, which treats policy texts, institutional arrangements, and data structures not as neutral items but set as power-laden meaning-making that reflects and replicate specific social interests and normative norms.

The analysis is designed around three themes, i.e., data power in agenda-setting, community legibility, and solution feasibility where, each theme signifies a diverse mechanism through which data systems exert integral dominance on policy discourse. These themes are examined through a series of comparative case illustrations drawn from contexts South Asia, Latin America, and sub-Saharan Africa. This comparative approach is intentionally cross-contextual, to explain both the global reach of data hegemony and the varied forms of resistance and adaptation that it meets. The aim of this study is descriptive and normative: to synthesise present empirical knowledge into an integrated critical framework capable to reveal the structural dynamics of data-driven policymaking across contexts, and to advance a normative argument about the conditions under which data governance can be rendered democratically accountable and epistemically just.

4. ANALYSIS

In the contemporary governance systems, data and policy relates to informed good decisions, i.e., data works as structural force that shapes measurable, and governable policy instruments. In case of macroeconomic policymaking, the indicators such as GDP growth rates, inflation, and tax to GDP ratios have replaced alternative welfare metrics like inequality-adjusted HDI's. The choice of dataset in this case is a policy choice. In macroeconomic governance, international data indicators are not based on neutral baselines, in fact they are items of political economy that form policy imagination, influence public narrative, and control whole fiscal flows. The literature on political economy depicts that globalisation has defective and biased economic data with technical errors of systematic falsification with tangible distributional significance. When these economic indicators and metrics move in transnational organizations normatively attached in Global North, the resulting policy discourse force out alternative paradigms such as informal economies, and ecological costs that are more relevant for developing nations (Linsi & Mügge, 2019).

A rapid advancement in digital data analytics has significantly transformed contemporary governance and political systems, where data from administrative resources serves as the primary driver to shape and direct the structure of policy discourse in addition to its role as evidence for policymaking. There is a global raising trend of data analytics and digital information system among policy circles not only to adopt data-driven policies, but with data framework, metrics, and algorithmic logic that are capable to define the very terms of policy debate, and to guide policy solutions, address policy challenges, identify alternatives, and evaluate outcomes based on data-driven insights. Modern data economy has changed the role of data, as primary architect of public policy rather than a by-product of social activity. Data systems support the structure of governance and work as governance architecture that can entrench irregular dependencies that often adopt external standard metrics, data regulations, and globally dominant data systems to translate policy into quantifiable actions. Data systems as policy systems, structures visible, governable, and comparable policy solutions (Pohle & Thiel, 2020).

In global health governance, the COVOD-19 pandemic determined with utter clarity that pandemic modelling data, collected and controlled by small number of government machineries, drove the full international policy response, while nations that have weak data infrastructure were left dependent, reactive, and epistemically negligible. In controlled governance systems, data is regulated by political actors to secure particular interests, and in these scenarios data hubs are being used to shape policy discourse. The COVID-19 has proven that data-driven projections can design and drive the global health policy by keeping local epistemological significances. The epistemic injustice literature on global health claims that who produces knowledge, for whom, and on what theoretical footings concern significantly for policy legitimacy, particularly when global data control is mainly collected, tailored, and validated in organizations based in Global North. The governance and politics of knowledge production and global data models create structural gaps and dependencies that make local policy actors incapable in defining policy problems and designing solutions (Bhakuni & Abimbola, 2021). Table 1, describes analytical value of different dimensions.

Table 1. Analytical lens of Data-Driven Governance, Source, Author Compilation, 2026

Dimensions	Analytical
Governance by indicators	Metrics and indictor's structure agendas, comparability, and authority.
Data Sovereignty	Extraction, ownership, and visibility reproduce inequality.
Data Hegemony	Observability asymmetries narrow regulatory options.
Algorithmic Policy	Models, funding, and publication pipelines shape policy legitimacy.
Global South state practice	Developing nations negotiate legibility, open data, and autonomy.

4.1 Data's Power to set as Agenda

The simplest way that data systems exercise power in policy discourse is through agenda-setting the capacity to define which social conditions are recognized as problems demanding policymaking attention, and which fall into invisibility. The present knowledge stands on classical agenda-setting theories developed to study mass media developing the analysis to consider how data indicators and metrics further set the government's agendas (Davis, 2012). The risk associated with data-driven policy agendas is, it undermines deliberative democratic process causes people's participatory deficit, raises ethical, transparency, and accountability challenges. The people are unable to contest a GDP growth competition or a credit-risk algorithm in a same way that they can participate in a legislative voting for welfare entitlement. This creates a technocratic boom, limits the legitimate space of political actors. The digital regulatory capture in multiple domains such as financial services, social media, and environmental compliance the regulated entities possess vast data resources to regulatory authority. This data asymmetry forms a soft regulatory capture, in which regulators become reliant on data systems with foreseeable consequences for the independence of effective governance.

The journey from complex, multidimensional development problems to quantifiable indicators did not simply similar to existing political consensus, it actively produced it, prioritising those aspects of poverty, health and education that could be measured through established data systems while marginalising those dimensions that stubbornly resisted its quantification. Davis (2019) noted, "indicators change the world not just by measuring it but also by producing new actors and relationships and identities". In domestic governance contexts, algorithmic systems perform similar agenda-setting power through categories they infuse and thresholds they implement. Welfare eligibility algorithms, trained on historical administrative data, encode past policy priorities as objective parameters, deciding which conditions constitute need, which behaviours confirm compliance and which individuals are deserving recipients (Eubanks, 2018). Such decisions rarely find their way into public or legislative debate; they are made at the behest of technical teams under conditions of limited accountability, with policy outcomes achieved through administrative processes that do not register as 'political' in normal terms.

As the capacity to collect and analyse data in real-time grows its agenda-setting power is increasingly amplified. Governments institutions and autonomous bodies are increasingly relied on flux of administrative data, social media monitoring, mobile phone metadata and satellite imagery to diagnose 'emerging problems' for which policy response is essential, sometimes before these problems are even named by communities affected by them. Furthermore, this anticipatory character of data-driven policy discourse radically shortens the time lag between problem recognition and policy response, thus pre-empting even slower forms of democratic deliberation within which policy priorities have historically been negotiated.

4.2 Community Legibility and the Politics of Visibility

A second way in which data systems exert constitutive power over policy discourse relates to 'legibility' and Scott (2020), defined it as "creation of administrative categories by which states make populations knowable and governable". Data systems do not just depend on social groups as they existed prior to data practices; these practices actively constitute the groups themselves by shaping what counts as membership, establishing thresholds for inclusion and exclusion.

India's Aadhaar biometric identification system, a modern case of data-mediated salience, launched in 2009 as a universal identification system, enrolled over a billion of India's residents in the first decade after its rollout, creating the world's largest biometric database (Masiero & Das, 2019). Similarly in Pakistan, the database of Benazir Income Support Program launched in 2010 with the support of World Bank, under National Socio-Economic Registry is a flagship programme. Supporters claimed that the data-platforms are helpful in removal of duplication and fraudulent claims to ensure cleaner service delivery of welfare benefits for targeted groups such as elderly persons, a rural women and agricultural workers. However, critics recorded systematic fraudulent claims and old age people with faded fingerprints, whose biometric data could not be matched against database system records leading to a denial of food rations and other essential services.

These two cases exemplify a dogged paradox of data-enabled policy and governance for the systems which are meant to make marginalised communities more legible to the state also tend to make them more vulnerable to exclusion by enshrining narrow definitions of identity, documenting certain ways of life. The dynamics in facial recognition systems, wherein algorithms trained primarily based on data from lighter-skinned faces show much higher rates of error when applied to darker ones resulting in patterns of misidentification which, if embedded into law enforcement or border control systems, lead to catastrophic outcomes for those communities. The politics of legibility are particularly acute in the developing world, where historical deficits in civil registration and administrative data infrastructure exert an impulse to pursue forms of rapid datafication that cannot be guaranteed to have been designed for local needs and rights frameworks. The accelerated global push to establish various donor-funded data systems in sub-Saharan Africa, including health management information systems, social protection registries and agricultural data platforms has been accompanied by increasing concern over the extent to which these systems reflect and encode the priorities and assumptions of external funders vs those of communities themselves (Couldry & Mejias, 2019).

4.3 Solution Feasibility and Technological Lock-In

The third mechanism in which data systems exert constitutive authority over policy discourse relates to the framing of solutions. A central insight of critical policy studies is that the framing of a problem shapes the set of possible solutions that seem technically feasible, politically viable or administratively rational. This aspect of policy discourse is shaped by data systems with remarkable power to exercise a great degree of influence; not only which interventions can be evaluated, monitored, and scaled in the existing data technology infrastructures after all. The hegemony the randomised controlled trial (RCT) method of evaluation has achieved in evaluating development interventions points to this fact. RCTs favour interventions where it is possible to impose an experimental design generally pinpointed, time-limited and quantifiable in terms of outcomes yielding weaker evidence for systematic, structural or process-oriented interventions that work through diffuse causal pathways and longer time horizons. Due to the increasingly high status of RCT evidence in hierarchies of evidence for international development policy, the methodological affordances offered by experimental data systems have influenced not just knowledge production concerning what makes effective interventions, but also which kinds of development efforts receive funding, are replicated and/or are actively institutionalized.

More broadly, the commitment to particular data architectures, be they national identification systems dedicated to monitoring citizens' compliance, health register systems for expanding biometric surveillance or fiscal data management systems, creates path dependencies that limit future policy options. Once a government has invested heavily in an integrated data infrastructure, the transitional technical and financial costs of alternative systems are too high, locking in place many of the policy assumptions enshrined within the data systems (Braun & Busch, 1999). Such technological lock-in is particularly damaging when data systems are purchased from commercial providers under proprietary licensing arrangements that preclude governments from modifying, auditing or exiting the system.

4.4 The Geopolitics of Data Hegemony

The forces of agenda-setting, legibility, and solutions-oriented feasibility described above do not function in a geopolitical vacuum. They are situated within and sustained by a global political economy wherein a select group of states and corporations excessively govern the design, implementation, and management of data systems around the world. This concentration of data power is what this chapter calls data hegemony: the structural dominance exercised by certain actors in the global data economy that translates into agenda-setting power not just within domestic policy systems, but also across those institutions and relationships of bilaterality that through which policymaking is negotiated and resourced at an international level.

The United States and China are the central poles of this geopolitical order contains continuous evolving tech-systems in the world's top technology corporations, alongside China with institutional capacity to re-direct data systems towards explicit governance targets at scale (Buisseret & Van Weelden, 2020). So, between these two poles, the European Union has tried to assert a regulatory identity of its own through the GDPR and more recently with the AI Act establishing European values of privacy, transparency, and human dignity as a basis for an alternative model for data governance that poses challenges to both American platform capitalism and Chinese state surveillance. This geopolitical competition produces a genuinely constrained landscape of choice for most of the world's states particularly in the Global South. Relying on foreign technology infrastructure for critical functions of public administration creates weaknesses that go beyond cyber security to the basic terms under which governments can govern. So when the algorithms underpinning a national social protection system are designed and maintained by a foreign corporation, the data architecture of the welfare state itself becomes an area of structural dependency (Kwet, 2019).

5. DISCUSSION

The developing nations like South Asian, sub-Saharan Africa, Latin America often under dominance of global standard data frameworks, where domestic policy discourse is conducted in metrics that do not reflect local relevance. Data hegemony works to limit policy imagination of developing nations that lacks in capacity to produce authoritative knowledge of their own terms. The developing nations with large populations are facing robust external pressures on policy settings while keeping balance with local data systems and governance models. In the case South Asian nations like India and Pakistan, where centralised data registration authorities for large scale identification have used to shape the power dynamics, and citizen clarity, raises concerns on data sovereignty, privacy, and welfare administration. Brazil, in Latin America, documents show the evolving approaches to data governance, as part of digitalisation, emphasises institutional design that value public accountability. In Kenya, research on digital identity and state–citizen relations focus on how data systems can replicate or deepen intergroup inequalities, making "being legible" a political issue rather than a purely administrative one.

5.1 Rights, Regulation, and Resistance

The analysis above shows a moderate account of the risks associated with data-driven policymaking, risks that are structural rather than incidental, and that fall disproportionately on communities and countries that are already marginalized within existing global power structures. Yet the picture is not one of simple or total domination. Across contexts, communities, civil society organisations, regulatory bodies, and states have developed a variety of strategies for contesting the terms on which data systems are deployed constituting what this chapter conceptualizes as a politics of digital resistance.

At the level of rights, there has been significant progress over the past decade in the explanation of a normative framework for data governance that centers individual and collective rights rather than instrumental efficiency. The GDPR's codification of data subject rights including rights of access, rectification, deletion, and automated decision-making formed an effective model that has been adapted in varying forms across jurisdictions from Brazil and South Africa to India and California (Hoofnagle et al., 2019). The emergent recognition of data rights as an aspect of human rights by treaty bodies and special procedures of the United Nations has further anchored this normative framework within the international human rights system.

However, rights-based frameworks alone cannot tackle the structural dynamics of data hegemonies. Individual data rights such as the right to access, correct or delete personal data do not tackle what is among the most critical collective aspects of data power: how systems of data formation create communities; how they influence political agendas and limit policy options at the systemic level. This limitation has given rise to interest in frameworks that extend beyond individual rights towards collective data governance, such as proposals for data trusts, community data ownership and participatory data governance as mechanisms of granting affected communities meaningful agency over the descent targets by which their lives are ordered (Birchall, 2017).

5.2 The Question of Epistemic Sovereignty

While the chapter focuses on data hegemony as a negative force, it also contends that the most contemporary and basic normative concern generated by this data domination is what it defines as a loss of epistemic sovereignty: communities or countries' ability to affect their own understanding, representation and action based on knowledge produced internally within its social and political framework. Epistemic sovereignty is separate but related to notions of data sovereignty and digital sovereignty. If data sovereignty worries about what jurisdictional force can do to affect data flows and storage, epistemic sovereignty is concerned with the more existential question of whose categories, what methods or interpretive frameworks inform the understanding of social reality that comes to ground policy decisions. Applied to the context of data-driven governance, epistemic sovereignty highlights how externally designed data systems displace but also actively delegitimize forms of knowledge, contextual, experiential, and relational through which communities have historically made sense and meaning out of their social worlds.

The developing and middle-income country implications are especially big. For states, the adoption of international data standards often appears as a technical necessity and condition of access to development financing for those seeking to modernise their systems of governance. But this adoption is hardly neutral: it involves the importation of classificatory frameworks, performance measures and algorithmic models that were designed for specific institutional and cultural contexts which may not well-fit with the social realities they are applied to (Birhane, 2020) & (Taylor & Broeders, 2015). Table 2, depicts the implications into time-based implementation of epistemic sovereignty.

Table 2. Implementation roadmap to strengthen epistemic sovereignty, Source Compilation, 2026

Time horizon	Priority actions	Illustrative emphasis
Short term	Open-data release rules, pilot data-sharing MoUs, sovereignty working groups, revised procurement templates.	Visible quick wins that improve observability and transparency.
Medium term	Legislative updates, interoperable data infrastructure, specialist training, South–South exchanges.	Institutional capacity-building and enforceable governance reforms.
Long term	Decentralized data governance, regional data ecosystems, and joint reform of global metrics and reporting regimes.	Structural reforms that embed enduring epistemic sovereignty.

5.3 Towards Democratic Data Governance

Reclaiming epistemic sovereignty in the context of data-driven governance requires interventions at multiple levels like technical, institutional, regulatory, and political. At the technical level, a concept of 'algorithmic governance from below' there is growing interest in the development of data systems designed to be locally modifiable, algorithmically transparent, and accountable to affected communities. The development of open-source data platforms that can be adapted to local contexts without dependence on proprietary systems represents one dimension of this agenda.

At the institutional level, the establishment of independent data governance bodies with the mandate and capacity to audit algorithmic systems, enforce data rights, and require impact assessments for high-risk data deployments represents a critical institutional infrastructure for democratic accountability. The European Union's AI Act, with its requirements for conformity assessments and post-market monitoring of high-risk AI systems, offers one model though critics have noted its limitations in relation to public sector AI systems and its inadequate provisions for collective redress.

At the regulatory level, confronting the structural dimensions of data hegemony will necessarily involve building new forms of multilateral frameworks for governance of data that are capable of amplifying the interests and needs of states from the Global South, while also establishing mechanisms to contest the power held by a small number technologically sophisticated states and corporations. The continuing negotiations around a UN Framework Convention on Artificial Intelligence are early efforts in this direction yet so far, the political will to convert normative aspirations into binding responsibilities is lacking

At the political level, reclaiming epistemic sovereignty involves cultivating something this chapter calls data literacy at scale: the ability of citizens civil society organisations, and elected representatives to critically engage the data systems and algorithmic processes through which public policy is increasingly made. This is not, above all else, a technical problem; it's a political and educational one that demands continuous investment in the public ability to analyze data, challenge algorithmic decisions and engage substantively in governing digital infrastructure. In modern measurable governance models, the controlled data systems have the power to shape policy discourse, supports the claim that quantification as data infrastructure is now the part of algorithmic policy architecture like in global health and macroeconomic governance.

6. CONCLUSION

This chapter has argued that data has become constitutive of policy discourse in the modern-day governance not just informing policy decisions but actively shaping which problems are recognized as legitimate, which communities are rendered visible to the state, and which solutions appear technically feasible. This constitutive role of data in policymaking is not politically neutral: it reflects and reproduces existing structures of power, both within and between nations, in ways that raise fundamental concerns about democratic accountability, regulatory capture, and the erosion of epistemic sovereignty.

The shift from policy-informed to data-driven policy represents a qualitative transformation in the governance structure, one that has proceeded with remarkable speed and with inadequate public deliberation about its implications. The communities most affected by algorithmic governance are frequently those with the least capacity to contest it: marginalized populations in wealthy countries who depend on automated welfare systems, and developing nations that lack the institutional infrastructure to audit and govern the data systems they have adopted in the name of modernisation.

The chapter identifies grounds for qualified optimism. The politics of digital resistance expressed through rights-based legal challenges, civil society advocacy, regulatory innovation, and community-led data governance are generating a growing range of tools and frameworks for contesting the terms on which data systems are deployed. The normative ambition of epistemic sovereignty, the right of communities and nations to produce and interpret knowledge from within their own contexts, offers a generative framework for articulating what democratic data governance might require, beyond the minimalism of individual data rights.

The central challenge is political as much as technical. Building the coalitions necessary to reshape the global data economy in the interests of democratic accountability and epistemic justice requires sustained engagement across disciplinary boundaries, institutional sites, and geopolitical divides. This chapter represents a contribution to that broader intellectual and political project one that will require the collective efforts of scholars, policymakers, civil society advocates, and affected communities if the promise of data-driven governance is to be redeemed rather than merely rationalized.

REFERENCES

Beaumont, P., & Sending, O. J. (2012). Governance by indicators and the re-politicisation of expertise. *Review of International Studies*, •••, 1–19.

Benoit, K. (2024). AI and data science for public policy. *LSE Public Policy Review*, *3*(3), 1. DOI: 10.31389/lseppr.115

Bhakuni, H., & Abimbola, S. (2021). Epistemic injustice in academic global health. *The Lancet. Global Health*, *9*(10), e1465–e1470. DOI: 10.1016/S2214-109X(21)00301-6 PMID: 34384536

Birchall, C. (2017). *Shareveillance: The dangers of openly sharing and covertly collecting data*. U of Minnesota Press. DOI: 10.5749/9781452958347

Birhane, A. (2020). Algorithmic colonization of Africa. *Script-ed*, *17*, 389.

Braun, D., & Busch, A. (1999). Public policy and political ideas.

Buisseret, P., & Van Weelden, R. (2020). Crashing the party? Elites, outsiders, and elections. *American Journal of Political Science*, *64*(2), 356–370. DOI: 10.1111/ajps.12457

Couldry, N., & Mejias, U. A. (2019). The costs of connection: How data is colonizing human life and appropriating it for capitalism. In *The costs of connection*. Stanford University Press.

Davis, K. (2012). *Governance by indicators: Global power through classification and rankings*. Oxford University Press. DOI: 10.1093/acprof:oso/9780199658244.001.0001

Davis, K. E. (2019). *Between impunity and imperialism: The regulation of transnational bribery*. Oxford University Press. DOI: 10.1093/oso/9780190070809.001.0001

Desrosières, A. (1998). *The politics of large numbers: A history of statistical reasoning*. Harvard University Press. Eubanks, V. Automating Inequality: How High-Tech Tools Profile, Police, and Punish the Poor. In: HeinOnline.

Eubanks, V. (2018). *Automating inequality: How high-tech tools profile, police, and punish the poor*. Macmillan+ ORM.

Foucault, M. (1991). *The Foucault effect: Studies in governmentality*. University of Chicago Press.

Guerrero, O. A., & Margetts, H. (2024). Are all policymakers data scientists now? data, data science and evidence in policymaking. *LSE Public Policy Review*, *3*(3), 9. DOI: 10.31389/lseppr.116

Hoofnagle, C. J., Van Der Sloot, B., & Borgesius, F. Z. (2019). The European Union general data protection regulation: What it is and what it means. *Information & Communications Technology Law*, *28*(1), 65–98. DOI: 10.1080/13600834.2019.1573501

Jean, N., Burke, M., Xie, M., Alampay Davis, W. M., Lobell, D. B., & Ermon, S. (2016). Combining satellite imagery and machine learning to predict poverty. *Science*, *353*(6301), 790–794. DOI: 10.1126/science.aaf7894 PMID: 27540167

Kwet, M. (2019). Digital colonialism: US empire and the new imperialism in the Global South. *Race & Class*, *60*(4), 3–26. DOI: 10.1177/0306396818823172

Linsi, L., & Mügge, D. K. (2019). Globalization and the growing defects of international economic statistics. *Review of International Political Economy*, *26*(3), 361–383. DOI: 10.1080/09692290.2018.1560353

Longworth, J. (2021). Benjamin Ruha (2019) Race After Technology: Abolitionist Tools for the New Jim Code. Medford: Polity Press. 172 pages. eISBN: 9781509526437. *Science & Technology Studies*, *34*(2), 92–94. DOI: 10.23987/sts.102639

Masiero, S., & Das, S. (2019). Datafying anti-poverty programmes: Implications for data justice. *Information Communication and Society*, *22*(7), 916–933. DOI: 10.1080/1369118X.2019.1575448

Mayer-Schönberger, V., & Cukier, K. (2013). *Big data: A revolution that will transform how we live, work, and think.* Houghton Mifflin Harcourt.

O'neil, C. (2017). *Weapons of math destruction: How big data increases inequality and threatens democracy*. Crown.

Pohle, J., & Thiel, T. (2020). Digital sovereignty. *Pohle, J. & Thiel.*

Samiha, Y. T., Handayani, T., Razaq, A., Fithriyah, M., Fitri, A., & Anshari, M. (2022, March). Implementation of Education 4.0 as sustainable decisions for a sustainable development. In *2022 International conference on decision aid sciences and applications (DASA)* (pp. 846-850). IEEE. DOI: 10.1109/DASA54658.2022.9765080

Schwab, K., Marcus, A., Oyola, J., Hoffman, W., & Luzi, M. (2011). Personal data: The emergence of a new asset class. An Initiative of the World Economic Forum, Scott, J. C. (2020). *Seeing like a state: How certain schemes to improve the human condition have failed.* yale university Press.

Taylor, L., & Broeders, D. (2015). In the name of development: Power, profit and the datafication of the global south. *Geoforum*, *64*, 229–237. DOI: 10.1016/j.geoforum.2015.07.002

Toonders, J. (2014). *Data is the new oil of the digital economy*. Wired, July.

Yusuf, H., Fitri, A., & Razzaq, A. (2026). Using artificial intelligence for human-AI collaboration in knowledge management systems to improve organizational efficiency and learning. In *Driving Organizational Transformation Through Human-Robotic Collaboration* (pp. 35–48). IGI Global Scientific Publishing.

Chapter 2
Digital Sovereignty and Media Regulation:
Governing Journalism in Platform Ecosystems

Azamat Ali
http://orcid.org/0000-0003-2931-2166
Lovely Professional University, India

ABSTRACT

This chapter explores the transforming role of the digital platforms in penetrating journalism and information governance in the platform age. It puts accents on the rising significance of digital sovereignty and media regulation in the context of the ability of global technology corporations to control news creation, distribution, and visibility. Social media have become significant mediators and construct social discourse based on algorithms and content management regulations. This brings issues concerning transparency, responsibility and security of the journalistic autonomy. The chapter also examines the current policy reactions such as platform regulation and data governance models both on global and national backgrounds. It states that platforms power requires regulation to promote effective media regulation, support public interest journalism and provide democratic regulation of information ecosystems.

1. INTRODUCTION

Digital transformation of journalism has essentially changed the production, distribution and consumption of news. The current developments in digital technologies, especially the internet and mobile communication, have facilitated the

DOI: 10.4018/979-8-2600-0288-9.ch002

dissemination of information to the rest of the world in faster and more convenient ways. The classical print and broadcast media have been in the process of moving towards the online platform, which enables journalists to post content in real time and which reach more people (Jamil, 2022). Other forms of transformation brought by this change include use of multimedia storytelling, data journalism, and interactive reporting. Consequently, journalism is now not bound by geographical or time limits. But newsroom practices have also changed with this change necessitating the journalists to adjust to news cycles, audience analytics, and digital tools. The increasing reliance on digital infrastructures has not only rendered journalism more alive, it has also exposed it to the force of technologies and economics (Krstic, 2024).

Ecosystems of platforms have also altered the makeup of the news production and distribution. Digital platforms more so, social media and search engines are now the main gateways where the audiences are receiving news. These sites are not merely passive distributors of content, but they actively determine the visibility by using algorithms to curate content. News houses are more and more dependent on the platforms to reach their audiences hence, providing some sort of interdependence between technology companies and journalism (Peters et al., 2022). This ecosystem focuses on the engagement metrics like clicks, shares, and views which can have an impact on the editorial decisions. Consequently, the contents of the news are usually shaped to platform dynamics at the expense of depth and accuracy. The concentration of information dissemination in several major platforms has also been an issue of concern in regards to the monopoly on the public sphere (Kristensen & Bro, 2024).

In this regard, the phenomenon of digital sovereignty has become highly important. Digital sovereignty is the capacity of states, institutions and individuals to have control over digital infrastructures, data and information flows. The digital age has made the management of the digital systems to be closely intertwined with the politics and economy of the digital age as data is a resource (Pierucci, 2025). Governments are also trying to put in place regulation systems to give the country control of data storage, online services and online information. This also encompasses the attempts to localize the data, control the cross-border data flows, and build the domestic technological capacity. Digital sovereignty also encompasses the protection of the right of citizens such as privacy, freedom of expression and access to information. The idea emphasizes the conflict between international digital networks and state control particularly when the platforms can be found in a variety of jurisdictions (Flonk et al., 2024).

Multinational technology companies pose major threats to journalism and politics. There is also the large power of companies like major social media and search engines in the process of formation of information ecosystems. They can control what we see, what is prioritized or repressed because they are in charge of algorithms, data and channels of distribution. This monopoly of power also brings up the issues of transparency and accountability because the decisions on the platform are typically determined by the proprietary systems that are not completely disclosed (Stockmann, 2023). Also, these companies run business models in which advertising revenues and user interaction take precedence over the values of public interest journalism. Global dominance may also hamper the effectiveness of the national governments to establish the rules since the companies usually move across the borders. This makes the field of journalism complicated where it is directed by the forces of the market and the platform governance structures (Nguyen & Hekman, 2024).

2. CONCEPTUAL FOUNDATIONS

2.1 Digital Sovereignty

Digital sovereignty describes the ability of a state, institution or community to control its digital infrastructure, data and technological systems. It has become a significant idea as a reaction to the increased hegemony of world digital networks and multinational technological companies. The internet at the beginning phase was in many ways considered as a borderless space, which allowed free flow of information across national borders. But with time, governments and policymakers came to realize that they have to assume dominance over the digital spaces to ensure national interests, economic stability, and the rights of citizens. This change has seen the development of the notion of digital sovereignty to become a real policy goal in most parts of the globe (Musiani, 2022). The development of digital sovereignty is also closely associated with the growth of the role of data as a strategic resource. Information is now one of the key factors in economic growth, government, and national security. Consequently, nations are trying to control the manner in which data is gathered, stored as well as the transfer. One of them is the presentation of laws that involve localizing the data, i.e. some sort of data must be stored within national borders. The governments are also investing in home digital infrastructure, including cloud services and communication networks to minimize the reliance on foreign technologies. These are to be used in order to enhance national control of digital systems and provide resiliency and security (Fratini et al., 2024).

One of the most prominent problems under the concept of digital sovereignty is the tension between national and transnational jurisdiction of digital infrastructures. As states attempt to regulate digital activities within their jurisdictions, digital platforms may cut across a number of jurisdictions. This gives problems in implementation of national laws as corporations can keep data in other countries or offer services worldwide. The issue of transnationalism in digital platforms makes it hard to create a clear regulatory power. It also creates concerns on the jurisdiction, accountability and state power boundaries within the digital realm (Gordon, 2024). Digital sovereignty is largely influenced by data ownership and governance. The issue of ownership of data, its accessibility, and how such data can be utilized are important questions in the establishment of control over digital systems. Data protection laws to protect personal information and promote responsible use of data are becoming increasingly popular among governments. Concurrently, there is an increasing awareness of the necessity to have clear and ethical data governance models. These frameworks seek to strike a compromise between innovation and economic growth and safeguarding individual rights. To ensure the attainment of trust in digital systems and upholding democratic values in the information age, effective data governance is required (Pierucci, 2025).

2.2 Media Regulation in the Digital Age

The regulation of media has greatly changed due to the emergence of digital technologies. The traditional media regulation was mainly on the print and broadcast media which had simple national boundaries. Regulatory frameworks were crafted to provide fairness, precision as well as accountability of the people. Regulatory bodies and governments came up with regulations in terms of licensing, content standards and ownership system. These systems were not quite stable and were premised on the fact that media institutions were easily identifiable and manageable (Flew & Martin, 2022). On the contrary, platform based regulation has new challenges, which are not similar to the traditional approaches. Digital platforms are not content creators but are significant in controlling the flow of information. This has brought confusion regarding the way they should be controlled. In comparison to traditional media organizations, the platforms have user generated content and they curate information through algorithms. This complicates the direct application of the existing regulatory structures. Consequently, policymakers are seeking alternative methods to regulate the activities of platforms, such as content regulation, use of data, and the transparency of the algorithms (Kokshagina et al., 2023).

It has also been changing state centric regulation into hybrid models of governance. Governments had been the main regulators of media systems in the past. Nonetheless, the regulation in the digital era presents various stakeholders, such as corporate entities, non-governmental organizations, and multilateral organizations. Policies Platforms may also create their own community policies and content moderation, which serve as types of internal regulation. Simultaneously, governments are bringing up legislation, which makes platforms responsible towards harmful material and fake news. This forms a co-regulatory system whereby both the government and the civil society have a role to play in governance (Haenig & Ji, 2024). The issue of regulation exists specifically in the cross-border digital spaces. The digital platforms are worldwide and thus it is hard to apply national regulations in a uniform manner. One may have acceptable content in one nation but in another country; it may be prohibited. This brings clashes among various legal frameworks and cultural values. Governments have challenges in making platforms responsible when they have their headquarters in different jurisdictions. Also, the issue of overregulation is mentioned, which may reduce the freedom of speech and creativity. The process of policymaking requires a compromise between regulation and the enforcement of the basic rights (Ziegert & Sotirov, 2024).

2.3 Platform Governance and Journalism

Platform governance is the term that describes the regulations, policies and practices by which online platforms control content, users and interactions. Platform governance is a vital concept in the news production, distribution and consumption within the context of journalism. The search engines and social media have taken over as key players in news ecosystem. They are the intermediaries between the news organizations and audiences. This has changed the conventional relationship between the journalists and the people since platforms are now shaping the way information is accessed and understood (Papaevangelou, 2023). The digital platforms play an important role in making news visible due to the algorithmic curation. Content is ranked, filtered, and recommended using algorithms that are based on the preferences and engagement patterns of the users. Although this has the potential to improve user experience as they can have access to personalized content, it is not without some concerns, including bias and lack of transparency. Algorithms can focus on sensational or popular material rather than on accurate and detailed reporting. It may result in the exaggeration of misinformation and the relegation of quality journalism. Algorithms, which are not transparent in regard to decision making, also render journalists and viewers incapable of comprehending how data is chosen and viewed (Lischka & Garz, 2023).

The journalistic practices are also directly influenced by platform policies. Platforms make decisions on what people can post, how it is to be posted, and the ability to monetize it. Such policies affect editorial choices because news companies tend to tailor content to the platform specifications. To illustrate, journalists can concentrate on the production of content that can result into greater involvement to become more visible on social media. Meanwhile, content moderation policies may result in the ban or limitation of some types of news content. This brings issues of censorship and boundaries of editorial freedom (Hastuti et al., 2025). Platforms and journalism are thus jointly defined as an opportunity and constraint relationship. The platforms can provide new ways of reaching out and allow new innovative forms of storytelling. They, however, also bring in new types of control which can influence the integrity and autonomy of journalism. The nature of media systems in the digital age is changing and platform governance is a necessary understanding in the analysis (Mellado et al., 2024).

3. PLATFORM POWER AND INFORMATION CONTROL

3.1 Algorithmic Mediation of News

The algorithmic mediation is at the center of influencing the form in which news is distributed and consumed in cyberspace. Digital platforms are based on algorithms to arrange high volumes of information and provide it to the user in a way that suits them. These algorithms understand the behavior of users, including clicks, likes, shares and viewing time to suggest the most likely content that a user would be interested in. This has led to a situation whereby news distribution is not only based on editorial judgment but the use of automated systems has become significant. This has changed how audience's consumption of news since personal feeds has been adopted in place of front page designs and planned broadcasts (Hastuti et al., 2025). Algorithms do not just impact the content that is shown, but also the frequency and salience of the content. Engaging contents are usually given priority and hence exaggerating sensational or emotional stories may occur. This poses a problem to the quality journalism where detailed reporting cannot be given prominence as compared to one that is made in such a way as to generate instant interest. The dependency on the engagement metrics may hence influence editorial practices and prompt the creation of content that satisfies the platform dynamics (Lundahl, 2022).

Algorithms also have a problem of bias, filter bubble, and echo chamber. There is no such thing as an algorithmic system that is neutral because it is created under certain assumptions and information input. Biases may arise when algorithms impose the preference over some content or opinion over another. Filter bubbles are caused by the users viewing information mostly biased towards their existing beliefs, and preventing different opinions. This is further supported by the existence of echo chambers, which build environments where the similar views are reproduced and enhanced. Such phenomena may decrease the critical interaction with information and lead to polarization in society (Makady, 2023).

3.2 Content Moderation and Editorial Authority

Platform governance is an important feature that implies content moderation and that is significant in the regulation of information flow. Digital platforms create rules and guidelines by which content of all kinds is permitted or forbidden. The enforcement of these rules is done both by automated mechanisms and human auditors. The content moderation practices are intended to deal with harmful content, including hate speech, the spread of misinformation and content that is unlawful. Nonetheless, when it comes to enforcing such practices, there are usually intricate choices regarding what is acceptable on what is not (Zeng & Kaye, 2022). The application of platform based content moderation has the potential to generate frictions with conventional concepts of editorial control in journalism. Journalists are educated to adhere to professional guidelines that stress on accuracy, fairness and the interest of the people. Nevertheless, platform policies can give more importance to other factors, including community safety or legality. This may lead to cases whereby the content that is considered as legitimate journalism is deleted or blocked on the platform since it does not conform to platform guidelines. As an example, news about sensitive issues can be reported as unsuitable or deceptive by the automated systems (Santos et al., 2025).

The moderation power being concentrated in the hands of the private companies causes the question of accountability and transparency. The platforms are important in determining what information is exposed to the masses, but their decision making process is not entirely publicized. Such a lack of transparency complicates the evaluation of the use of moderation practices that are applied equally and fairly. It also restricts the powers of journalists and media houses to question those decisions that impact on their content. The increased importance of platforms as sources of information has thus transformed the equilibrium of power between journalists and the tech companies (Van Dijck et al., 2023).

3.3 Economic Dependencies and Revenue Models

The digital media environment is dominated by the revenue models of advertising. Online platforms bring impressive revenues through the sale of targeted advertising, which is based on the user data. This has seen platforms take over the digital advertising industry, at the cost of conventional news organizations, in many cases. Newsrooms are being hit by the diminished revenues of the print and broadcast channels as advertisers redirect their expenditures to the platforms. This has caused financial strains that impact sustainability of journalism (Kim, 2024). The news organizations have been more reliant on audience reach and revenue generating platforms. A good number of media platforms depend on the traffic of the platform to get readers and earn advertisement revenues. It may affect editorial choices, where organizations may make decisions favoring content that gives them high performance on platforms. This in certain instances results in implementation of tactics like click based headlines or streamlined reports. Although these methods can make journalism more visible, they can also compromise the quality and richness of journalism (Li et al., 2022). Market concentration and competition have also been an issue with the prevalence of platforms within the advertising ecosystem. There are a few technology firms that have a significant portion of digital advertising revenue, and it is restrictive to the small media organizations. The result of this imbalance is a lack of diversity in the media space and the ability of independent journalism to flourish. The financial difficulties of the news organizations point to the necessity of new revenue patterns and governmental measures which allow sustainable journalism (Garganas, 2024).

3.4 Datafication and Surveillance Concerns

Datafication can be explained as the process of datafying different spheres of social life and turning it into a collectable, analyzable, and lucrative piece of data. Digital platforms are involved in a wide ranging data collection process and collect data on the behavior, preferences, and interaction of the users. This information is utilized to enhance services, customize the content, and advertise. Although data driven systems can come with advantages in its efficiency and customization, it has significant questions regarding privacy and surveillance (Flensburg & Lomborg, 2023). The personal information gathered and the use of such details by the platforms may result to more surveillance of individuals. Social networks tend to follow the activity of users in various devices and services, which builds a comprehensive profile, which can be utilized commercially and politically. The degree of such surveillance can cast some ethical doubts on the issue of consent and how much the user is aware of how his or her data is being utilized. Data collection practices are not always transparent and in most instances, this reduces the level of informed decision making by the users (Knorr & Pentzold, 2025).

Datafication also has implications to journalism and popular trust. Journalists depend on digital platforms to find their audiences, yet they also work in systems that focus on data driven engagement. This is able to shape the production and presentation of news because data analytics have become central to the editorial approaches. Meanwhile, the issues of surveillance and misuse of information may minimize the trust towards online platforms and the information that they provide. It can also be influenced by the feeling by the people that the news content is influenced by data driven incentives, and not editorial integrity, on the part of the journalism (Schaetz, 2024). The problem of privacy is a crucial one regarding datafication. To ensure that these issues are addressed, governments and regulatory agencies have come up with data protection laws that are used to facilitate the management of personal information in a manner that is responsible. Nevertheless, it is difficult to enforce such laws because online platforms are global. The data driven innovation has some advantages and some disadvantages and the question of the equilibrium between the two is a persistent issue in the digital age (Schaetz et al., 2025).

4. CHALLENGES TO JOURNALISTIC AUTONOMY

4.1 Transparency and Accountability Issues

The platform based media environment has now emerged as a significant issue regarding transparency and accountability. Digital platforms have their complicated algorithms to classify and distribute the news material, yet the operations of such algorithms are not fully revealed. This transparency of algorithms renders understanding of information selection, ranking, and presentation to be hard to journalists, researchers and the general population. The algorithms are run using data feeds and design options that are manipulated by the private firms. These operations are typically considered as confidential information, which restricts the external examination (Hastuti et al., 2025). Lack of transparency leaves the question of fairness and unbiased content distribution. Journalists do not necessarily understand how come that some stories become visible and some are hidden. This influences their audience coverage and the ability to assess the performance of their work. It also brings up the issue of possible biasness in algorithmic systems. The information on the functionality of algorithms is not easy to access, so it is hard to find out whether some opinions are being promoted or suppressed (Kuang et al., 2025).

Transparency is directly connected with accountability, but it has extra problems. Online platforms are now potent participants in the information ecosystem though they do not necessarily face the same regulation as traditional media organizations. The question of who is in charge is often obscured in the case of harmful content that is disseminated or journalistic content that has been blocked inappropriately. The platforms themselves can argue that they are not publishers but are intermediaries, and therefore they are not responsible directly of the content they are hosting (Dragomir & Túñez López, 2024). The complexity of holding the platforms responsible is a problem that is complicated by the operations of these platforms worldwide. The technology companies are found in various countries and this complicates the implementation of regulations by the government of the countries. Legal frameworks are different; different jurisdictions have different laws and a platform can be compliant and resistant to the same law. This poses weak points in accountability and constrains the efficacy of regulatory interventions. Civil society groups and independent researchers have tried to keep track of platform practices, but they usually have limited access to the data. Consequently, meaningful accountability is a complicated and unfixed challenge (Angus et al., 2024).

4.2 Threats to Editorial Independence

Independent editorial decision making is one of the pillars of journalism, although it is often questioned in platform based reporting. Digital platforms provide an impact on the distribution and news consumption and this impacts editorial decision making. News organizations are also dependent on platforms to reach out to audiences, which may influence the kind of content that they create. Editors can change their strategies to correspond to the platform algorithms and work on the topics and forms that have higher chances to be seen and engaged with (Kiberg et al., 2025). The power of platforms can result in minor editorial shifts. Journalists can highlight the stories, which have better chances of success on clicks, sharing, or comments. This may lead to the move towards investigative or public interest journalism to more audience friendly content. Some of the consequences of this strategy include increased visibility but less diversity and depth in the news coverage. The editorial judgment can be informed by platform metrics instead of the values of journalism (Mäder & Rinsdorf, 2023).

Another major issue in this regard is self-censorship. Media and journalists can prefer not to address some issues or state controversial positions because they are afraid of decreased popularity or even blocking their content. The policy on content moderation in platforms can result in confusion regarding what is acceptable, which makes journalist operate with a conservative mindset. This has the potential of curtailing critical reporting and diminishing the power accountability of journalism (Elsheikh et al., 2025). It is also content prioritization that contributes to editorial independence. Platforms decide the form of content that is advanced or suppressed on their algorithms. This affects the manner in which news organizations report their stories such as the use of headlines, images and format. Journalists can fit the content to satisfy the platform preferences, including producing a shorter article or more visual posts. Although these adaptations have the benefit of making access easier, depth and quality of reporting might be affected (McNally & Bastos, 2025). The increasing power of the platforms regarding the editorial processes concerned the independence of journalism. News organizations might lose their independence when decisions associated with editorial choices are influenced by other technological systems. It makes the relationship between journalism and platform driven distributions complex because it has to find the balance between its core values and platform requirements (Simon, 2022).

4.3 Misinformation, Disinformation, and Public Trust

The problem with misinformation and disinformation is one of the biggest obstacles in the platform based media ecosystems. False or misleading information that is exchanged with no intention of harm is called misinformation and the creation and the spread of fake information to mislead audiences are referred to as disinformation. This has been facilitated by the digital platforms where such content can easily spread and reach massively in a short time. The pace and size of information communication makes it harder to check truthfulness before communicated information is accessed by a huge number of people (Cennamo & Karanovic, 2025). Algorithms may also lead to the propagation of fake news by favoring the content that produces high interaction. False or sensational news usually gets more attention as compared to reporting of facts and could make it to be amplified. This brings about a situation where the misleading content fights credible journalism to be laid in the limelight. Users can be exposed to fake content on many occasions and this may affect their attitudes and assumptions (Plikynas et al., 2025).

The existence of misinformation and disinformation is a serious challenge to the journalists. The process of fact checking and verification takes time and resources and can be easily disseminated due to the false content with the least amount of effort. Journalists should strive to rectify the errors and give sound information, yet their works do not always reach the same audiences who are subjected to fake information. This can bring about an imbalanced information environment where there are both truth and falsehood (Aïmeur et al., 2023). These dynamics directly relate to the public trust toward journalism and the media houses. In cases where the viewer's receive a significant quantity of misleading or conflicting pieces of information, it may be hard to judge which ones are credible and others are not. This may cause discouragement of any kind of media, including professionally based journalism. A lack of trust is also weakened by the failure of platforms to deal with the dissemination of destructive materials in a proper manner (Thomson et al., 2022). Weaker impacts of trust destruction on the democratic societies are wider. The journalism is important in enlightening the general population and facilitating informed decision making. With a weakened trust of news, journalism becomes unable to play this role. The efforts of journalists, platforms, policymakers, and audiences should be used together to reduce the adverse effects of misinformation and restore citizens trust (Custodi et al., 2026).

5. POLICY RESPONSES AND REGULATORY FRAMEWORKS

5.1 Global Approaches to Platform Regulation

The emergence of digital platform regulation as a means of controlling information ecosystems has led to the creation of global strategies of platform regulation. There are a number of regulatory programs launched by governments and international bodies to handle issues associated with competition, content moderation, data protection, and accountability. These are the efforts meant to establish a more balanced relationship between platforms, users, and the institutions of the people. The regulative actions are usually aimed at transparency of the algorithmic operations, restricting the destructive content, and ensuring fair competition in the online market (Gawer, 2022). The European Union has been proactive in the regulation of platforms by means of elaborate legal frameworks. Policies like the Digital Services Act and the Digital Markets Act introduce specific liability to the platforms when it comes to how to handle the content of the platform, the safety of users, and the competition in the market. Such laws ask platforms to show more transparency concerning their algorithms and act against illegal content. The EU solution focuses on the rights of the users and accountability, as well as the safeguarding of the democratic value. It is also aimed at curbing the influence of major technology firms through the application of rules of competition (Kim & Ahn, 2025).

The United States, on the contrary, has historically enjoyed a more market focused platform regulation approach. The US law has been based on freedom of expression and innovation. Section 230 of the Communications Decency Act has been instrumental in influencing the governance of the platforms by providing platforms with immunity in the case of liability of the content posted. Nevertheless, there is an emergent controversy regarding the reform of this provision to overcome the problems of misinformation and accountability. Concerns regarding platform power and the necessity to maintain free speech are often struck in regulatory debates in the US (Montalbano, 2022). The Global South countries have varying problems and opportunities in regulating digital platforms. Most of these nations are creating their own similar regulatory frameworks to meet local interests, including misinformation, digital inclusion, and economic development. Among governments, there has been tightening of content and data controls in order to retain sovereignty over online spaces. But these policies may be influenced by resources and technological ability which are limited. The fact that the approaches are diverse in different parts of the world underlines the complexity of developing coherent global rules of platform regulation (Jiang, 2024).

5.2 National Digital Sovereignty Strategies

The national digital sovereignty plans are aimed at enhancing authority over digital infrastructure and data as well as online services within the territories of a country. Governments are becoming sensitive towards the need to reduce reliance on technology providers abroad. This has seen the formulation of policies that favor local digital industries and the growth of technological independence. Such strategies usually involve local data centre investment, cloud computing infrastructure and the communication network (Fratini et al., 2024). Policies depending on countries are different and depend on political, economical and technological circumstances. The emphasis on the stricter regulatory control of digital platforms is in some countries; meanwhile, other countries are more lenient. Indicatively, some governments demand platforms to be in accordance with the national laws with reference to content moderation and data storage. The purpose of these policies is to make sure that the digital activities would be consistent with national interests and legal frameworks. In other instances, governments to demand that platforms have local offices or representatives to help in the process of regulatory control (Misra et al., 2025).

The data localization laws are one of the main aspects of the strategies of digital sovereignty. These laws mandate that some form of data particularly the personal data or sensitive data should be stored and processed within the national boundaries. This aims at improving the security of data, and allowing governments to have more control over information. Localization of data may also be helpful in promoting investment within local economies by boosting their infrastructure. Nevertheless, these policies can escalate the cost of operation by the firms and make cross-border data transfer more difficult (Pierucci, 2025). Another significant feature of the national sovereignty strategies is control of digital infrastructure. Governments can control or create important infrastructure like telecommunications and internet services. This lessens the dependence on other service providers and boosts national security. Nevertheless, the attempts to exercise control over the digital systems might also bring some doubts regarding censorship and limitations of the freedom of speech. Openness and sovereignty are the major concerns that policymakers need to strike a balance on (Giannopoulou, 2023).

5.3 Data Governance Models

The models of data governance specify the process of data collection, management, sharing, and protection in digital ecosystems. The models are vital in making sure that the use of data is done in a responsible and ethical manner. Privacy laws and data protection frameworks are central in this framework of governance practices. Some regulations including General Data Protection Regulation in the European Union provide proper guidelines on data collection, consent, and user rights. Such frameworks are supposed to safeguard people against abuses of personal data and enhance data transparency (Lis et al., 2023). Privacy laws also mean that the organization informs the users on how their data is being collected and used. They also give people their rights to access their data, to make corrections, and to ask to be deleted. These can enhance the power of the user regarding the personal information and accountability to the data handlers. But the implementation of these legal provisions may prove difficult particularly when information crosses more than one jurisdiction (Koskinen et al., 2023).

Another important data governance issue is the role of the public and private control of data. The digital platforms, particularly the private companies, are also possessing huge volumes of user data, and they have a lot of control in the usage of such data. They can use their power to innovate and even grow economically, but their ability to control data creates issues of power concentration and accountability. Political administrations are interested in controlling the activities of the owners of personal data to be fair and safeguard the interests of people (Kuzio et al., 2022). Public ownership of information refers to using data in social and governmental agendas, including government services, research, and policy making. The government can gather and process data to enhance decision making and provision of services. Nevertheless, privacy, as well as ethical standards must also be honored in the process of public data collection. To establish a fair and sustainable digital environment, it is necessary to balance the role of the government and corporations in the regulation of the data (Hossin et al., 2023).

5.4 Co-regulation and Multi-stakeholder Governance

Multi-stakeholder governance and co-regulation have become significant strategies of curbing digital platforms. These are models that include governments, private firms, the civil society, and other stakeholders. Co-regulation, instead of being merely a regulation by the state, is a mix of the legal requirements with industry driven practices. Platforms can formulate their own policies and be in line with the government standards, which form a common responsibility system (Schneider, 2024). Co-operation among actors would make governance more adaptive and flexible. Governments can stipulate general regulation policy, and platforms are taking action to tackle such problems as content control and data safety. The role of civil society organizations is to defend the rights of users, monitor practices in the platforms, and offer independent control. This group strategy can enhance transparency and accountability. New forms of democratic governance of digital systems are aimed at making people more engaged and inclusive. The models are intended to engage the users and communities in making decisions regarding policies on the platforms. As an example, certain platforms have established oversight boards or consultations with the general public to provide feedback on content moderation practices. These efforts aim at increasing the legitimacy and trust in the systems of governance (Popiel, 2022).

The multi-stakeholder type of governance takes care of the global character of digital platforms too. International organizations and cooperation between countries are required because the fact that platforms work across the borders. Certain collaborative systems can be effective in aligning the regulations and solving common problems like misinformation, protection of personal data, and competition in the market. Nevertheless, political systems, cultural values, and economic priorities may present an obstacle to cooperation due to their differences (Shirkoohi & Mohiuddin, 2025). The emergence of co-regulation and multi-stakeholder frameworks implies the intricacy of the digital platform governance. The digital ecosystem is complicated, and it cannot be controlled by just one actor. It is important that the development of balanced and efficient regulatory frameworks should be done through shared responsibility and cooperation (Poyton, 2023).

6. IMPLICATIONS

Platform ecosystems undergo transformation with important implications on the practice and ethics of journalism. The journalists are facing an increasing need to learn to survive in digital settings where speed, visibility, and engagement with audiences have become the priority. This trend has an impact on reporting patterns, formats of content and editorial judgment. The issue of working within ethical dilemmas arises when reporters need to maintain the accuracy of their work and the interests of the public and the demands of platform algorithms and performance indicators. The need to remain professional, including through verification, objectivity, and accountability, is more difficult in rapid paced digital settings. The journalists have to also negotiate the aspects of content moderation, usage of data, and dependency on the platforms and maintain their independence (Paik, 2025).

The influence on the democratic processes and discourses is also significant. The digital platforms have become the focal point of political communication and debate. They allow participation and access to information by more people but also facilitate the propagation of misinformation and polarization. The exposure to various perspectives can be controlled with the help of algorithmic filtering and this influences informed decision making among citizens. Usually, the level of discussion might go down when sensational or deceptive information is hiked. The issues of integrity of the democratic systems and the role of journalism in promoting informed citizenship are brought up by these developments (Asimakopoulos et al., 2025).

The necessity of equal regulation that facilitates innovation and responsibility is increasing. An excessively high level of regulation can limit technological progress and freedom of speech, whereas the opposite is also possible because an excessively low amount of regulations can enable malicious activities. Digital innovation should not reduce the advantages of digital innovation because policymakers should develop structures that promote transparency, safeguard the rights of the user, and fair competition. This is a balance that is necessary to maintain a healthy media environment (Kim & Ahn, 2025).

The journalism of public interest is of fundamental importance in the ecosystem of platforms due to authentic and valid information. It helps in accountability, social awareness and democracy. Such journalism has to be supported with policy, sustainable funding models and reasonable practices of platforms that focus on the quality of content (Lindquist & Weltevrede, 2024). Cooperation between governments, platforms and civil society can be a key to the future of information governance in a digitalized world. The effective governance should respond to the issues of information, algorithms, and digital business worldwide and ensure the preservation of basic rights and democratic values (Bhanye & Shayamunda, 2025).

7. CONCLUSION, LIMITATION AND FUTURE DIRECTIONS

7.1 Conclusion

This chapter has discussed the increasing role of the digital platform in the field of journalism and information governance. It has demonstrated that the platform ecosystems are at the forefront when it comes to the production, distribution, and consumption of news. The discussion revealed the growing relevance of digital sovereignty in ensuring the control over the flows of data, infrastructure, and information. It also talked about the impact of platform governance on journalistic independence using the signals of algorithmic curation, content moderation, and economic attachments. New challenges are facing transparency, accountability and editorial independence with these developments. The chapter also explained how these factors of misinformation, data habits and power of the platforms can influence public trust and democratic discourse. It stressed the fact that although internet platforms give a chance to reach a broader audience with information, they also carry the dangers that undermine the standards of the journalism. Global and national policy reactions have been discussed in order to demonstrate how policy regulatory frameworks are shifting to deal with these challenges. The conclusions indicate that regulation needs to be implemented effectively to moderate the influence of the platform and the requirements of the public interest journalism. Enhancing accountability, safeguarding user rights and supporting a healthy competition is a key approach to achieving sustainable and democratic information ecosystem.

7.2 Limitations

In this study, there are some limitations to scope and approach. It is more concerned with conceptual and policy based analysis as opposed to the empirical inquiry. The discussion relies on broad tendencies and might not be able to reflect the regional or local differences in platform governance and media regulation. The differences between nations and cultural circumstances are accepted but not discussed in-depth. Moreover, some of the regulatory developments might develop outside the scope of this chapter since digital technologies are changing rapidly. The research also uses the secondary sources hence it might not be comprehensive enough in some parts.

7.3 Future Scope

The future study can examine how new technologies like artificial intelligence will impact on journalism and platform governance. It is necessary to discuss the impact of AI driven systems on the content creating, modifying, and spreading processes. The other area where further studies can deal is the comparative analysis of regulatory models in various regions. The changing aspect of the international digital policies offers the prospect of analyzing the emergent types of governance and collaboration. The long term study can examine how digital sovereignty will emerge in reaction to the technological change. Such dynamic will be relevant in the future in helping to sustain journalism and democratic communication.

REFERENCES

Aïmeur, E., Amri, S., & Brassard, G. (2023). Fake news, disinformation and misinformation in social media: A review. *Social Network Analysis and Mining*, *13*(1), 30. DOI: 10.1007/s13278-023-01028-5 PMID: 36789378

Angus, D., Hayden, L., Obeid, A. K., Tan, X. Y., Carah, N., Burgess, J., Parker, C., Andrejevic, M., Fordyce, R., Cellard, L., & Bagnara, J. (2024). Computational methods for improving the observability of platform-based advertising. *Journal of Advertising*, *53*(5), 661–680. DOI: 10.1080/00913367.2024.2394156

Asimakopoulos, G., Antonopoulou, H., Giotopoulos, K., & Halkiopoulos, C. (2025). Impact of information and communication technologies on democratic processes and citizen participation. *Societies (Basel, Switzerland)*, *15*(2), 40. DOI: 10.3390/soc15020040

Bhanye, J., & Shayamunda, R. (2025). The promise of civic-tech: digital technologies and transparent, accountable governance. In *Digitalisation and public policy in Africa: GovTech and CivicTech innovations* (pp. 93–122). Springer Nature Switzerland., DOI: 10.1007/978-3-031-75079-3_5

Cennamo, C., & Karanovic, J. (2025). Are Social Media Platforms a Threat to Democracy? An Ecosystem Governance Perspective. *Journal of Management Studies*. Advance online publication. DOI: 10.1111/joms.70044

Custodi, J., Trenz, H. J., & Moland, M. (2026). Countering Post-Truth: A Comparative Study of Journalists' Responses to Disinformation Challenges. *Journalism & Mass Communication Quarterly*, *103*(1), 114–133. DOI: 10.1177/10776990251393745

Dragomir, M., & Túñez López, M. (2024). How public service media are changing in the platform era: A comparative study across four European countries. *European Journal of Communication*, *39*(6), 608–624. DOI: 10.1177/02673231241290062

Elsheikh, D., Jackson, D., & Jebril, N. (2025). Journalism in transitional context: Societal hostility, self-censorship and the expansion of "one voice journalism". *Journalism Practice*, *19*(9), 1921–1939. DOI: 10.1080/17512786.2024.2308526

Flensburg, S., & Lomborg, S. (2023). Datafication research: Mapping the field for a future agenda. *New Media & Society*, *25*(6), 1451–1469. DOI: 10.1177/14614448211046616

Flew, T., & Martin, F. R. (2022). *Digital platform regulation: Global perspectives on internet governance*. Palgrave Macmillan., DOI: 10.1007/978-3-030-95220-4

Flonk, D., Jachtenfuchs, M., & Obendiek, A. (2024). Controlling internet content in the EU: Towards digital sovereignty. *Journal of European Public Policy, 31*(8), 2316–2342. DOI: 10.1080/13501763.2024.2309179

Fratini, S., Hine, E., Novelli, C., Roberts, H., & Floridi, L. (2024). Digital sovereignty: A descriptive analysis and a critical evaluation of existing models. *Digital Society : Ethics, Socio-Legal and Governance of Digital Technology*, *3*(3), 59. DOI: 10.1007/s44206-024-00146-7

Garganas, O. (2024). Digital video advertising: Breakthrough or extension of TV advertising in the new digital media landscape? *Journalism and Media*, *5*(2), 749–765. DOI: 10.3390/journalmedia5020049

Gawer, A. (2022). Digital platforms and ecosystems: Remarks on the dominant organizational forms of the digital age. *Innovation (North Sydney, N.S.W.)*, *24*(1), 110–124. DOI: 10.1080/14479338.2021.1965888

Giannopoulou, A. (2023). Digital identity infrastructures: A critical approach of self-sovereign identity. *Digital Society : Ethics, Socio-Legal and Governance of Digital Technology*, *2*(2), 18. DOI: 10.1007/s44206-023-00049-z PMID: 37200582

Gordon, G. (2024). Digital sovereignty, digital infrastructures, and quantum horizons. *AI & Society*, *39*(1), 125–137. DOI: 10.1007/s00146-023-01729-7

Haenig, M. A., & Ji, X. (2024). A tale of two Southeast Asian states: Media governance and authoritarian regimes in Singapore and Vietnam. *Asian Review of Political Economy*, *3*(1), 4. DOI: 10.1007/s44216-024-00024-6

Hastuti, H., Maulana, H. F., Lawelai, H., & Suherman, A. (2025). Algorithmic influence and media legitimacy: A systematic review of social media's impact on news production. *Frontiers in Communication*, *10*, 1667471. DOI: 10.3389/fcomm.2025.1667471

Hossin, M. A., Du, J., Mu, L., & Asante, I. O. (2023). Big data-driven public policy decisions: Transformation toward smart governance. *SAGE Open*, *13*(4), 21582440231215123. DOI: 10.1177/21582440231215123

Jamil, S. (2022). Digital transformation in journalism: Implications of media convergence for journalists' work in Pakistan's mainstream news media. In *Die digitale Transformation der Medien: Leitmedien im Wandel* (pp. 443-458). Wiesbaden: Springer Fachmedien Wiesbaden. DOI: 10.1007/978-3-658-36276-8_21

Jiang, M. (2024). Models of state digital sovereignty from the global south: Diverging experiences from China, India and South Africa. *Policy and Internet*, *16*(4), 727–738. DOI: 10.1002/poi3.427

Kiberg, H., Olsen, G. R., Krumsvik, A., Kalsnes, B., Kavtaradze, L., & Steensen, S. (2025). Navigating Platform Dependency: Four Strategic Approaches for Social Media News Publishing. *Journalism Studies*, •••, 1–19. DOI: 10.1080/1461670X.2025.2608960

Kim, H. Y. (2024). What's wrong with relying on targeted advertising? Targeting the business model of social media platforms. *Critical Review of International Social and Political Philosophy*, •••, 1–21. DOI: 10.1080/13698230.2024.2309047

Kim, J., & Ahn, S. (2025). The platform policy matrix: Promotion and regulation. *Policy and Internet*, *17*(1), e414. DOI: 10.1002/poi3.414

Knorr, C., & Pentzold, C. (2025). Making sense of "big data": Ten years of discourse around datafication. *Big Data & Society*, *12*(2), 20539517251330181. DOI: 10.1177/20539517251330181

Kokshagina, O., Reinecke, P. C., & Karanasios, S. (2023). To regulate or not to regulate: Unravelling institutional tussles around the regulation of algorithmic control of digital platforms. *Journal of Information Technology*, *38*(2), 160–179. DOI: 10.1177/02683962221114408

Koskinen, J., Knaapi-Junnila, S., Helin, A., Rantanen, M. M., & Hyrynsalmi, S. (2023). Ethical governance model for the data economy ecosystems. *Digital Policy. Regulation & Governance*, *25*(3), 221–235. DOI: 10.1108/DPRG-01-2022-0005

Kristensen, L. M., & Bro, P. (2024). News values in a digital age-Intra-media, inter-media, and extra-media platforms. *Journalism*, *25*(4), 819–836. DOI: 10.1177/14648849231165855

Krstic, A. (2024). Digital transformation of journalism and media in Serbia: What has gone wrong? *Journalism*, *25*(5), 1014–1030. DOI: 10.1177/14648849231151798

Kuang, Y., Zheng, J., Sun, M., & Xu, X. (2025). The Role of Algorithmic Fairness, Accountability, and Transparency in Shaping User Satisfaction on Digital Platforms: A Quantitative Study in China. *International Journal of Human-Computer Interaction*, •••, 1–17. DOI: 10.1080/10447318.2025.2546663

Kuzio, J., Ahmadi, M., Kim, K. C., Migaud, M. R., Wang, Y. F., & Bullock, J. (2022). Building better global data governance. *Data & Policy*, *4*, e25. DOI: 10.1017/dap.2022.17

Li, S. C., Chen, Y. C., Chen, Y. W., & Huang, Y. (2022). Predicting advertisement revenue of social-media-driven content websites: Toward more efficient and sustainable social media posting. *Sustainability (Basel)*, *14*(7), 4225. DOI: 10.3390/su14074225

Lindquist, J., & Weltevrede, E. (2024). Authenticity governance and the market for social media engagements: The shaping of disinformation at the peripheries of platform ecosystems. *Social Media + Society, 10*(1), 20563051231224721. DOI: 10.1177/20563051231224721

Lis, D., Gelhaar, J., & Otto, B. (2023). Data strategy and policies: The role of data governance in data ecosystems. In *Data governance: From the fundamentals to real cases* (pp. 27–55). Springer Nature Switzerland., DOI: 10.1007/978-3-031-43773-1_2

Lischka, J. A., & Garz, M. (2023). Clickbait news and algorithmic curation: A game theory framework of the relation between journalism, users, and platforms. *New Media & Society, 25*(8), 2073–2094. DOI: 10.1177/14614448211027174

Lundahl, O. (2022). Algorithmic meta-capital: Bourdieusian analysis of social power through algorithms in media consumption. *Information Communication and Society, 25*(10), 1440–1455. DOI: 10.1080/1369118X.2020.1864006

Mäder, A., & Rinsdorf, L. (2023). Constructive journalism as an adaptation to a changing media environment. *Journalism Studies, 24*(3), 329–346. DOI: 10.1080/1461670X.2022.2159859

Makady, H. (2023). To interact or not to interact with news posts: The role of algorithmic awareness & self-monitoring in Facebook news consumption. *Electronic News, 17*(4), 223–246. DOI: 10.1177/19312431231166933

McNally, N., & Bastos, M. (2025). The news feed is not a black box: A longitudinal study of facebook's algorithmic treatment of news. *Digital Journalism (Abingdon, England), 13*(7), 1209–1228. DOI: 10.1080/21670811.2025.2450623

Mellado, C., Blanchett, N., Stępińska, A., Mothes, C., Lecheler, S., Blanco-Herrero, D., & Zhao, X. (2024). Does news platform matter? Comparing online journalistic role performance to newspaper, radio, and television. *Digital Journalism (Abingdon, England), 12*(3), 376–399. DOI: 10.1080/21670811.2023.2191332

Misra, S., Barik, K., & Kvalvik, P. (2025). Digital sovereignty in the era of industry 5.0: Challenges and opportunities. *Procedia Computer Science, 254*, 108–117. DOI: 10.1016/j.procs.2025.02.069

Montalbano, K. (2022). Reimagining section 230 and content moderation: Regulating incivility on anonymous digital platforms. *Communication Law and Policy, 27*(3-4), 187–219. DOI: 10.1080/10811680.2022.2136442

Musiani, F. (2022). Infrastructuring digital sovereignty: A research agenda for an infrastructure-based sociology of digital self-determination practices. *Information Communication and Society, 25*(6), 785–800. DOI: 10.1080/1369118X.2022.2049850

Nguyen, D., & Hekman, E. (2024). The news framing of artificial intelligence: A critical exploration of how media discourses make sense of automation. *AI & Society, 39*(2), 437–451. DOI: 10.1007/s00146-022-01511-1

Paik, S. (2025). Journalism ethics for the algorithmic era. *Digital Journalism (Abingdon, England), 13*(4), 696–722. DOI: 10.1080/21670811.2023.2200195

Papaevangelou, C. (2023). The role of citizens in platform governance: A case study on public consultations regarding online content regulation in the European Union. *Global Media and China, 8*(1), 39–56. DOI: 10.1177/20594364221150142

Peters, C., Schrøder, K. C., Lehaff, J., & Vulpius, J. (2022). News as they know it: Young adults' information repertoires in the digital media landscape. *Digital Journalism (Abingdon, England), 10*(1), 62–86. DOI: 10.1080/21670811.2021.1885986

Pierucci, F. (2025). Sovereignty in the digital era: Rethinking territoriality and governance in cyberspace. *Digital Society : Ethics, Socio-Legal and Governance of Digital Technology, 4*(1), 27. DOI: 10.1007/s44206-025-00189-4

Plikynas, D., Rizgelienė, I., & Korvel, G. (2025). Systematic review of fake news, propaganda, and disinformation: Examining authors, content, and social impact through machine learning. *IEEE Access : Practical Innovations, Open Solutions, 13*, 17583–17629. DOI: 10.1109/ACCESS.2025.3530688

Popiel, P. (2022). Digital platforms as policy actors. In *Digital platform regulation: Global perspectives on internet governance* (pp. 131–150). Springer International Publishing., DOI: 10.1007/978-3-030-95220-4_7

Poyton, D. (2023). The role of regulation in facilitating new business models driven by digital platforms: Creating regulatory ecosystems. *International Review of Law Computers & Technology, 37*(3), 227–251. DOI: 10.1080/13600869.2022.2136934

Santos, A., Cazzamatta, R., & Napolitano, C. J. (2025). Holding platforms accountable in the fight against misinformation: A cross-national analysis of state-established content moderation regulations. *The International Communication Gazette, 87*(8), 729–750. DOI: 10.1177/17480485251348550

Schaetz, N. (2024). Journalism & audience datafication: How audience data practices shape inequity. *Digital Journalism (Abingdon, England), 12*(8), 1184–1204. DOI: 10.1080/21670811.2023.2171894

Schaetz, N., Lischka, J. A., & Laugwitz, L. (2025). Datafication of journalism: How data elites and epistemic infrastructures change news organizations. *Digital Journalism (Abingdon, England), 13*(4), 677–695. DOI: 10.1080/21670811.2023.2235601

Schneider, G. (2024). Stakeholder engagement in EU digital platform regulations: Ways forward and persisting gaps. In *Repositioning Platforms in Digital Market Law* (pp. 125–153). Springer Nature Switzerland., DOI: 10.1007/978-3-031-69678-7_6

Shirkoohi, S. M., & Mohiuddin, M. (2025). Developing sustainable global value chain: Role of multi-stakeholder collaborations and digitalization. *Cleaner Logistics and Supply Chain, 100271*, 100271. Advance online publication. DOI: 10.1016/j.clscn.2025.100271

Simon, F. M. (2022). Uneasy bedfellows: AI in the news, platform companies and the issue of journalistic autonomy. *Digital Journalism (Abingdon, England)*, *10*(10), 1832–1854. DOI: 10.1080/21670811.2022.2063150

Stockmann, D. (2023). Tech companies and the public interest: The role of the state in governing social media platforms. *Information Communication and Society*, *26*(1), 1–15. DOI: 10.1080/1369118X.2022.2032796

Thomson, T. J., Angus, D., Dootson, P., Hurcombe, E., & Smith, A. (2022). Visual mis/disinformation in journalism and public communications: Current verification practices, challenges, and future opportunities. *Journalism Practice*, *16*(5), 938–962. DOI: 10.1080/17512786.2020.1832139

Van Dijck, J., de Winkel, T., & Schäfer, M. T. (2023). Deplatformization and the governance of the platform ecosystem. *New Media & Society*, *25*(12), 3438–3454. DOI: 10.1177/14614448211045662

Zeng, J., & Kaye, D. B. V. (2022). From content moderation to visibility moderation: A case study of platform governance on TikTok. *Policy and Internet*, *14*(1), 79–95. DOI: 10.1002/poi3.287

Ziegert, R. F., & Sotirov, M. (2024). Regulatory politics and hybrid governance: The case of Brazil's Amazon Soy Moratorium. *Global Environmental Change*, *88*, 102916. DOI: 10.1016/j.gloenvcha.2024.102916

Chapter 3

Cybersecurity Copilots and Digital Sovereignty in Security Operations Centers

Ayan Ullah Khan
http://orcid.org/0009-0003-1466-4991
Universiti Brunei Darussalam, Brunei

Muhammad Asfand Yar
Universiti Brunei Darussalam, Brunei

Muhammad Anshari
http://orcid.org/0000-0002-8160-6682
Universiti Brunei Darussalam, Brunei

ABSTRACT

This chapter examines the use of large language model (LLM) copilots in Security Operations Centers (SOCs) serving government and critical infrastructure and analyzes the sovereignty risks created by their adoption. It argues that copilots can improve alert triage, explanation, and incident reporting, but can also expose sensitive cyber-defense workflows to foreign jurisdiction, vendor dependence, opaque governance, and model-specific security vulnerabilities. Through a qualitative comparative policy analysis of the European Union, United States, United Kingdom, Singapore, and India, the chapter assesses the extent to which current AI and cybersecurity frameworks address SOC-specific risks. Its principal contribution is the SOC-LLM Governance Framework (SLGF), which differentiates among Fully

DOI: 10.4018/979-8-2600-0288-9.ch003

Sovereign, Hybrid Sovereign, and Foreign Dependent deployment models and maps each to actionable controls for data handling, hosting, auditability, robustness testing, and exit feasibility.

INTRODUCTION

Today, Security Operations Centers (SOCs) sit at the operational center of cyber defense. A SOC is generally defined as a centralized function that brings together people, processes, and technologies to monitor digital activity in order to identify potential threats, investigate alerts, and coordinate incident response across an organization's enterprise environment. Credible practice guidance acknowledges that there is no single "standard" SOC model; rather, design is shaped by threat profile, sector, and maturity. What remains constant is the requirement for ongoing monitoring, disciplined escalation pathways, and evidence-driven decision-making. In government and critical-infrastructure settings, these decisions are unusually high stakes: a missed intrusion can compromise public services, while over-aggressive containment can create disruptive downtime and cascading operational impacts (Alahmadi et al., 2022; Banstola et al., 2026).

Large language models (LLMs) are increasingly positioned as "cybersecurity copilots" to relieve precisely these SOC pressures. In this chapter, an LLM is a neural language model trained on extremely large corpora to generate and interpret natural language, enabling instruction following, summarization, and interactive question answering at scale. A cybersecurity copilot is an LLM-enabled assistant embedded in security tooling or workflows that supports tasks such as alert triage, log and ticket summarization, phishing email interpretation, incident timeline drafting, procedure retrieval from internal knowledge bases, and rapid translation of technical artifacts into natural-language explanations. Such functionality aligns closely with the SOC's constant need to convert heterogeneous data—telemetry, threat intelligence, and investigative notes—into coherent operational judgments (Kramer et al., 2025; Banstola et al., 2026).

The operational motivation for copilots is therefore credible. SOC analysts deal with extremely high alert volumes, constant pressure to correlate indicators, the need to contextualize signals, and the challenge of communicating incident narratives internally to leadership and externally to third parties. Updated incident response guidance frames response as a risk-management activity integrated with governance, stressing preparedness, coordination, documentation, and continuous learning to reduce incident impact and recurrence. This is precisely the terrain where LLMs can serve as a "copilot": not by replacing forensic reasoning, but by accelerating information retrieval, standardizing reporting outputs, and reducing repetitive cognitive work (Alahmadi et al., 2022; Kramer et al., 2025).

However, incorporating copilots into SOC workflows changes more than productivity. It also shifts the governance boundary of cyber defense. SOC prompts and contextual inputs can contain sovereignty-sensitive information: indicators of compromise, investigative hypotheses, network topology clues, privileged configuration details, vulnerability notes, and response playbooks. When such inputs are processed by externally hosted AI services, the adopting institution may lose effective control over where data reside, how long they are retained, and under which jurisdiction they can be accessed or compelled. This concern is not a generalized "privacy" issue alone; it is a question of operational control over security-critical data and defensive decision support (Pohle & Thiel, 2020; Couture & Toupin, 2019; Office of Management and Budget, 2025b).

To frame that question, the chapter uses "digital sovereignty" in a functional, governance-oriented sense: the capacity of a state or institution to exercise meaningful authority over digital infrastructures, data, and the rules that govern their use while remaining connected to global networks rather than pursuing isolation. This framing is particularly relevant to SOC copilots because cybersecurity data differs qualitatively from most enterprise datasets: SOC telemetry reveals defensive posture, investigative priorities, and sometimes live weaknesses. If sovereignty is expressed partly through effective control over strategically valuable digital functions, routing sensitive SOC workflows through opaque, externally governed AI services undermines that control even when the stated aim is to strengthen cyber resilience (Pohle & Thiel, 2020; Couture & Toupin, 2019).

Thus, the chapter identifies three deployment models that correspond to various levels of control and risk. Fully Sovereign deployment only applies to copilots hosted on sovereign infrastructure under the effective control of the adopting state or institution (e.g., on-premises, a trusted national cloud) with locally governed access controls, logging and retention. Hybrid Sovereign deployment refers to architectures that combine external model components with domestic hosting and enforceable contractual and technical constraints (e.g., dedicated tenancy, restricted subprocessors, locally auditable prompt/response logs, and clear data-handling commitments). Foreign Dependent deployment refers to reliance on a third-party LLM API or cloud service where critical components of inference, logging, model updates, and operational governance remain under foreign corporate and legal control. The chapter's argument is balanced—each model carries trade-offs in cost, performance, and operational convenience—but it emphasizes that governance risk is structurally higher where effective control is weakest (Pohle & Thiel, 2020; Opara-Martins et al., 2016; Office of Management and Budget, 2025b).

A central risk vector for foreign-dependent deployment is jurisdictional exposure. In the U.S. context, for example, providers may be required to preserve and disclose certain communications and related records within their "possession, custody, or control" regardless of where the data are stored. This legal architecture does not, in itself, make functionality dependent on foreign security tooling ipso facto unacceptable; rather it establishes a controlling persistence of governance that non-U.S. governments and regulated operators must treat as an element of cyber risk management moving forward. Similar cross-border conflicts can emerge when domestic requirements, such as those related to confidentiality and incident reporting, together with essential-infrastructure resilience—intersect with the legal environments of third-party providers and sub-processors (U.S. Congress, 2018; Office of Management and Budget [OMB], 2025b).

These sovereignty concerns are compounded by technical security dynamics. Empirical security research has shown that large language models can leak sensitive information: under certain conditions, adversaries can extract memorized training examples by querying a model, underscoring the need for rigorous data-handling and lifecycle controls whenever sensitive text may reach a model or persist in its logs. Furthermore, LLM-integrated applications are susceptible to prompt-injection and instruction-manipulation attacks, whereby untrusted content such as attacker-crafted text in emails, tickets, or web artifacts can influence model behavior and counteract intended safeguards. This is particularly relevant in SOC contexts because analysts routinely consume content controlled by the adversary, including phishing emails, lure documents, and descriptions of attacker infrastructure, as part of their normal work. The governance implication is that procurement and deployment decisions should consider not only model performance but also how models behave under adversarial conditions and whether those behaviors can be audited (Carlini et al., 2021; Liu et al., 2024; Xu et al., 2024). Against this background, the chapter addresses five research questions: (1) What sovereignty-relevant risks arise when LLM copilots are integrated into government and critical-infrastructure SOC workflows? (2) How do these risks relate to established frameworks for AI governance and risk management, including accountability, auditability, and cybersecurity by design? (3) How do the comparative governance regimes of the EU, US, UK, Singapore, and India address these risks, and where do important gaps remain? (4) How do the three deployment models allocate control, accountability, and exposure between institutions and vendors? and (5) What governance controls should be in place before copilots are permitted to support sensitive SOC tasks? The chapter's principal contribution is the SOC-LLM Governance Framework (SLGF), which translates these sovereignty risks into actionable controls across six areas: (a) data sensitivity and prompt hygiene; (b) hosting and jurisdiction; (c) human oversight and decision authority; (d) auditability and explainability of outputs; (e) adversarial robustness testing; and (f) vendor governance, including exit feasibility and lock-in mitigation. Methodologically, the chapter adopts a qualitative, policy-analytic approach that combines structured synthesis of peer-reviewed research on digital sovereignty and LLM security with comparative analysis of primary policy instruments from the five jurisdictions and a design-science-inspired process for mapping risk vectors to governance controls and implementation guidance.

The chapter proceeds as follows. The literature review consolidates key debates on digital sovereignty and platform dependence, SOC operations, and LLM security risks. The methodology part provides an overview of the comparative set used, and also of the framework construction methodology. The findings and analysis will construct the sovereignty risk vectors and deployment typology, and juxtapose with how existing instruments (e.g., EU AI Act; NIST AI RMF; national AI governance frameworks; cybersecurity statutes) approach or overlook SOC-specific realities. The discussion section translates the analysis into policy and procurement recommendations for government and critical-infrastructure SOCs. The conclusion summarizes governance priorities and identifies future research directions for sovereignty-conscious security automation. Figure 1 summarizes these three deployment tiers and their relative sovereignty risk gradient.

Figure 1. Deployment tiers for SOC LLM copilots and their sovereignty risk gradient.

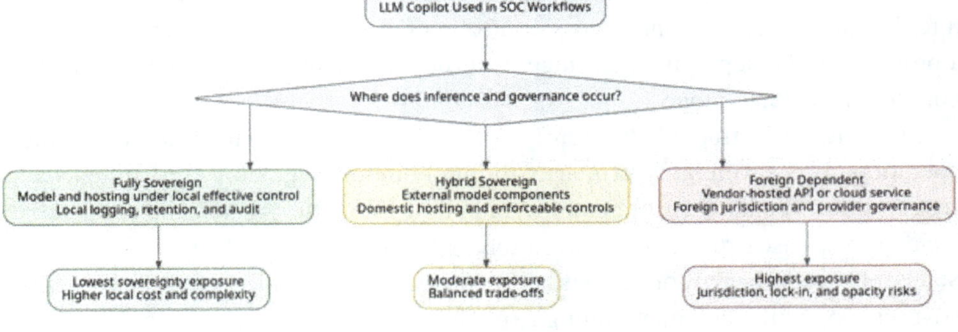

LITERATURE REVIEW

LLM-enabled "copilots" are emerging as productivity tools for Security Operations Centers (SOCs), but this shift also relocates parts of cyber defense into AI and cloud-governance regimes that may be external to the adopting state or critical-infrastructure operator. The literature has advanced debates on digital sovereignty and AI accountability, as well as a rapidly expanding security literature on LLM vulnerabilities, yet limited work integrates these strands for SOC-grade operations in which jurisdiction, secrecy, and adversarial pressure are unusually high (Pohle & Thiel, 2020; Raji et al., 2020; Liu et al., 2024; Kramer et al., 2025).

Digital sovereignty and infrastructure sovereignty in the context of cyber defense

Digital sovereignty has emerged as an often contested but increasingly powerful way of talking about the claims to control and autonomy over digital infrastructures, data flows and technological dependencies (Pohle & Thiel, 2020; Couture & Toupin, 2019). The sovereignty literature underscores how "control" is not simply a matter of law (e.g., jurisdiction with respect to data) but also of material and operational conditions (e.g., dependence on foreign cloud and platform ecosystems), which take on especially prominent salience in security-critical contexts where telemetry and defensive playbooks are strategic intelligence rather than ordinary enterprise data.

A parallel stream focuses on "cloud/data sovereignty" and Europe's pursuit of strategic autonomy via federated governance architectures (e.g., GAIA-X), while recognizing persistent concentration in hyperscale cloud services and the practical difficulty of "sovereign" alternatives at scale (Autolitano & Pawlowska, 2021). In the SOC-LLM context, these themes matter because an LLM copilot (especially API-based) embeds SOC investigation workflows into the provider's infrastructure, logging, retention, and access-control model; sovereignty therefore becomes a property of the deployment arrangement (hosting, control plane, audit surfaces), not the "AI feature" alone.

Sovereignty is framed differently across jurisdictions. The European Union operationalizes sovereignty primarily through binding regulatory instruments and cross-sector cybersecurity obligations, including NIS2, the AI Act, and cooperative incident-response structures such as national CSIRTs and EU-CyCLONe. The United States relies more heavily on standards, executive guidance, and procurement-oriented governance, while also maintaining explicit carve-outs for some national security systems. The United Kingdom adopts a pro-innovation, context-based approach to AI governance while separately maintaining cyber strategies and public-sector cyber-assurance initiatives, producing a relatively loose coupling between AI governance and operational cyber defense. Singapore combines pragmatic, implementable AI-governance frameworks with statutory critical-infrastructure cybersecurity legislation, creating a mixed hard-law and soft-law environment relevant to SOCs serving essential services. India has strengthened digital personal data protection and incident-reporting obligations through the DPDP Act and CERT-In Directions, while its AI governance remains more strategy- and principles-driven, leaving SOC-LLM governance comparatively emergent rather than codified (European Union, 2022;

European Parliament, 2024; Office of Management and Budget, 2025a, 2025b; U.S. Government Accountability Office, 2025; UK Government, 2022, 2023; Infocomm Media Development Authority & Personal Data Protection Commission, 2020; AI Verify Foundation & Infocomm Media Development Authority, 2024; Government of India, Ministry of Electronics and Information Technology, 2023; CERT-In, 2022).

AI governance and accountability frameworks

AI governance scholarship theorizes AI as increasingly socio-technical, with accountability across the lifecycle and transparency and auditable controls superseding abstract ethics (Raji et al., 2020; Oduro et al., 2022). Such an orientation is consistent with risk management frameworks (that emphasize documentation, traceability and organizational controls) that are rationally adjacent to SOC copilots given that incident response decisions entail after-action justification and playback of evidence trails.

Policy instruments diverge on binding force and scope. In the EU, the European Parliament's official AI Act summary describes a risk-based model with prohibited practices, high-risk obligations, general-purpose AI transparency duties, and governance bodies for enforcement—while also noting exemptions such as military/defense use. Importantly for SOC-grade deployments, the summary explicitly lists "management and operation of critical digital infrastructure" among high-risk system contexts, indicating that AI embedded in critical operational processes faces heightened obligations.

NIST's AI RMF 1.0 in the United States offers flexible, sector-agnostic recommendations organized around governing, mapping, measuring, and managing AI risks. Federal procurement and operational requirements have also evolved: a 2025 executive order rescinded EO 14110 and directed the review of actions taken under it, while the Office of Management and Budget issued M-25-21 on AI use and M-25-22 on AI acquisition. GAO reporting notes that M-25-21 requires agencies to establish acceptable-use policies for generative AI and defines "high-impact" AI in ways that encompass effects on critical infrastructure and public safety, concerns closely aligned with SOC contexts, even if some national-security SOCs fall within separate or excluded regimes (National Institute of Standards and Technology, 2023; Office of Management and Budget, 2025a, 2025b; U.S. Government Accountability Office, 2025).

Rather than adopting a single horizontal AI law, the UK's 2023 white paper routes governance through existing regulators and favors a context-based approach intended to support innovation while managing risk. UK policy has also expanded state capacity for understanding advanced AI risk through the AI Safety Institute and has introduced transparency tools for public-sector algorithm use, such as the

Algorithmic Transparency Recording Standard. These efforts, however, do not specifically address SOC workflows as a distinct high-sensitivity operational domain.

Singapore's Model AI Governance Framework (2nd edition) translates principles into operational recommendations such as governance structures, risk management, and transparency, while its Model AI Governance Framework for Generative AI extends these ideas to GenAI-specific risks and deployment controls. AI Verify further positions governance as testable and reportable, including updated considerations for generative AI. India's DPDP Act provides a rights- and obligations-based framework for digital personal data processing, while India's AI strategy documents emphasize national capability building and responsible AI principles without creating a dedicated SOC-specific governance layer.

International standards reinforce "governance as management systems." ISO/IEC 42001 sets out the requirements for establishing, implementing, maintaining and continually improving an AI management system while ISO/IEC 23894 provides guidance on the integration of AI-specific risk management. In the context of SOC copilots, this translates to "trustworthy AI" as one that can be audited (having policies, roles, logging and incident management), although these standards remain high level and do not address jurisdictional sovereignty risks established through inference from external hosts.

Table 1 compares the principal AI and cybersecurity governance instruments across the five selected jurisdictions and highlights their implications for SOC-LLM deployment.

Table 1. Policy instrument comparison across the selected jurisdictions.

Instrument name	Scope	Relevance to SOC-LLM	Key provisions	Limitations
European Parliament AI Act summary (Regulation (EU) 2024/1689)	EU-wide AI regulation summary of risk-based obligations	High: frames high-risk contexts including critical digital infrastructure; includes GPAI transparency and governance	Prohibited practices; high-risk obligations; transparency for GPAI/deepfakes; governance bodies; phased application dates	Summary-level (not operational SOC guidance); exemptions (e.g., military/ defense) can exclude key SOC environments; limited SOC-specific security controls
NIS2 Directive policy overview	EU cybersecurity framework across 18 critical sectors	High: establishes incident reporting, risk management, governance accountability relevant to SOC operations	Risk management and reporting requirements; national strategies; CSIRT cooperation; supervision/enforcement; supply-chain security mentioned as strategy element	Not AI/LLM-specific; does not specify controls for LLM prompts, model auditing, or LLM adversarial robustness
NIST AI RMF 1.0	Voluntary AI risk management framework	Medium-High: provides governance vocabulary for SOC-LLM risk, accountability, measurement	Govern/Map/Measure/Manage functions; trustworthiness characteristics; lifecycle framing	Voluntary; sector-agnostic; does not directly address cross-border sovereignty and jurisdictional exposure
OMB M-25-21 and M-25-22	Federal agency AI use and AI acquisition guidance	Medium-High for civilian federal SOCs: defines high-impact AI (incl. critical infrastructure/public safety) and requires acceptable-use policies for GenAI	AI governance roles; AI inventories; minimum practices for high-impact AI; acquisition documentation expectations	Scope may exclude national security systems; still not SOC-LLM specific; focuses on public-sector governance rather than adversarial LLM threats
UK "Pro-innovation" AI regulation white paper	UK AI governance via sector regulators, context-based	Medium: provides governance principles but not SOC operationalization	Contextual regulation; risk identification and mitigation; avoids single rigid law	No SOC/critical-infrastructure LLM controls; reliance on regulator coordination may leave gaps for cross-cutting SOC-LLM issues

continued on following page

Table 1. Continued

Instrument name	Scope	Relevance to SOC-LLM	Key provisions	Limitations
UK National Cyber Strategy 2022	National cybersecurity strategy and capability development	Medium: shapes SOC modernization priorities and national cyber governance	Strategic cyber resilience objectives; capability development; public/private partnership	Not AI-specific; does not address governance of externally hosted LLM copilots or model manipulation risks
Singapore Model AI Governance Framework (2nd ed.)	Voluntary, implementable AI governance guidance	Medium: supports organizational governance controls that can extend to SOC copilots	Internal governance measures; risk management; transparency/explainability; human involvement	Not tailored to SOC threat environments; limited treatment of cross-border jurisdiction or vendor lock-in as security risks
Singapore Model AI Governance Framework for Generative AI and AI Verify	GenAI governance guidance + testable governance toolkit	High for GenAI copilots: introduces GenAI-specific governance considerations and evaluation	GenAI-oriented governance controls; testing/assessment approach; transparency reporting logic	Not cyber-operations-specific; does not fully specify prompt-level data classification for SOC telemetry or adversarial robustness requirements for security contexts
Singapore Cybersecurity Act	Statutory framework for oversight of critical information infrastructure	High for CII SOCs: anchors SOC governance for essential services and incident powers	Legal obligations for CII protection; regulatory oversight; amendments noted; statutory basis for CI protections	Not AI-specific; does not address LLM vendor governance, inference hosting, or prompt data leakage
India DPDP Act 2023 and CERT-In Directions (2022)	Data protection + incident reporting/logging directions	Medium: constrains personal data handling and forces timely incident reporting	DPDP rights/obligations for digital personal data; CERT-In directions on incident reporting and operational requirements	Not AI-specific; limited guidance on LLM prompt governance, model auditability, or cross-border vendor control in cyber operations

LLM-specific risks in SOC workflows

Cybersecurity and HCI research on SOCs describe longstanding challenges: high alert volumes, false positives, and workflow complexity increase analyst cognitive load and error risk. For instance, the qualitative USENIX Security study notes that SOC practitioners are burdened with persistent false positives and describes operational impacts on decision-making and trust in tools (Alahmadi et al., 2022). This operational backdrop explains why LLM copilots are attractive: they promise translation of complex telemetry into natural language, summarization, query assistance, and documentation support.

However, LLM-integration changes the security model because SOC data is high sensitivity and frequently contains implicit "secrets" (network topology hints, vulnerable asset identifiers, incident timestamps, investigative hypotheses). Even if a copilot is used only for "assistive" tasks, prompts and outputs can become durable records (through logging, caching, or training feedback loops), increasing intelligence exposure risks in foreign-dependent deployments. Evidence from LLM privacy/ security literature shows that models can leak or enable inference of training data or sensitive content under certain conditions (Carlini et al., 2021; Mattern et al., 2023). While these studies do not focus on SOC prompts specifically, they establish that "text data + LLM interface" is a recognized leakage surface—suggesting that SOC prompt streams require explicit classification and handling rules rather than ad hoc analyst judgment.

A second category is integrity and reliability. SOC workflows demand high precision under time pressure; yet LLMs can produce plausible but incorrect outputs ("hallucinations"), and their failure modes can be subtle (e.g., confident misinterpretation of an indicator or playbook step). Governance documents increasingly emphasize risk-based testing and monitoring, but they rarely translate into SOC-specific requirements such as "no automated containment based solely on LLM output" or "mandatory trace logs for every copilot-assisted decision." This is a key gap: general AI governance prescribes accountability, but SOC operations require forensic-grade accountability.

Dependency, vendor lock-in, and infrastructural concentration

Cloud studies have long identified vendor lock-in as a structural barrier to switching, often driven by proprietary APIs, data gravity, and operational retraining costs (Armbrust et al., 2010; Opara-Martins et al., 2016). The sovereignty implication is that "dependency" can become durable even when legal compliance is satisfied: once SOC playbooks, integrations, and analyst habits are built around a specific copilot ecosystem (e.g., SIEM/XDR-native copilots), exit becomes expensive and risky—especially for critical infrastructure where downtime is unacceptable.

Regulatory responses to dependency are uneven. The EU's broader digital policy ecosystem increasingly treats resilience as including portability and reduced switching barriers (e.g., Data Act "fairness" logic and focus on access and usable data), while NIS2 also elevates supply-chain security in national strategy requirements and reporting regimes. In the US, procurement guidance (OMB M-25-22) encourages documentation and responsible acquisition but does not necessarily mandate portability outcomes for AI services; it also may exclude national security systems, leaving critical SOC environments governed elsewhere. The UK's approach similarly emphasizes principles and sector regulators rather than a unified portability rule, potentially leaving copilot lock-in to procurement practice rather than policy constraint.

Singapore's mixed model creates a different dynamic: strong statutory cyber obligations for critical information infrastructure exist alongside voluntary AI governance frameworks (including GenAI governance and testing), but none directly resolve market concentration or the practical exit problem for LLM copilots. India's DPDP/CERT-In regime raises baseline obligations for data processing and incident reporting, but does not yet provide a portability/exit governance layer for foreign AI dependencies in SOC tooling.

For SOC-LLM governance, the literature therefore suggests that "lock-in" should be treated as both (a) a procurement/architecture issue and (b) a continuity-of-operations risk: sovereign/hybrid deployments may reduce dependency externalities, while foreign-dependent deployments heighten them due to opaque service evolution, pricing changes, and policy shifts outside the adopter's control.

Jurisdictional and legal exposure in cross-border AI services

Jurisdictional exposure is a sovereignty hinge: even when data is "hosted locally," legal authority may still reach it through provider-control doctrines. In the US, 18 U.S.C. § 2713 requires covered service providers to disclose data within their possession, custody, or control regardless of whether the data is located inside or outside the United States—a core concern in cross-border cloud/AI dependence debates. This matters for SOC copilots because SOC prompts and context windows may contain incident intelligence; foreign-dependent copilots thus create a pathway where sensitive defensive data can become subject to non-local legal processes, undermining the adopting state/operator's exclusive control.

The EU's legal approach seeks to combine cybersecurity obligations (NIS2) with AI governance (AI Act) to shape both security posture and trustworthy AI deployment, but the policy materials do not specifically resolve cross-border compelled access for non-EU-controlled providers. The UK's regulatory posture similarly emphasizes context and innovation, leaving many jurisdictional issues to procurement, contractual clauses, and sectoral compliance rather than an SOC-specific sovereignty doctrine.

Singapore and India provide a useful contrast: both have strong cyber incident governance levers (Cybersecurity Act for Singapore; CERT-In Directions for India) and increasing data governance constraints (DPDP in India), yet neither offers an explicit "LLM copilot in SOC" cross-border governance framework. This suggests that, in practice, sovereignty protection may depend on deployment tiering (on-prem / sovereign cloud / foreign API), data-classification constraints on prompts, and auditable contractual controls (subprocessors, retention, logging access, and lawful access transparency reporting) rather than on AI governance rules alone.

Adversarial manipulation and robustness for LLM-enabled security tooling

Security research increasingly demonstrates that LLM-integrated applications add new attack surfaces. Prompt injection—attacker-supplied text that causes an LLM-integrated system to deviate from intended instructions—has been formalized and benchmarked in top security venues, showing that LLM apps require explicit defenses rather than generic "policy prompts" (Liu et al., 2024; Chen et al., 2025). In SOCs, this becomes concrete: phishing emails, ticket text, and threat-intel feeds can contain adversarial strings designed to manipulate a copilot that is asked to summarize or recommend investigative steps.

Beyond prompt injection, model integrity can be attacked upstream. Research on instruction tuning shows that backdoors can be introduced through poisoned instruction data with relatively small malicious payloads, enabling triggered behaviors later (Xu et al., 2024). This relates directly to the chapter's "adversarial manipulation risk": if a SOC depends on a foreign-controlled model supply chain, the operator may be unable to independently verify training/fine-tuning provenance, evaluate backdoor exposure, or detect subtle output shaping before harm occurs.

Industry and standards-oriented threat taxonomies consolidate these risks into actionable categories such as prompt injection, training data poisoning, and supply chain vulnerabilities—categories that map well onto SOC copilot deployments that ingest untrusted text at scale (Liu et al., 2024; Xu et al., 2024). Complementing this, NIST has issued generative-AI secure development guidance for dual-use and foundation-model settings, indicating that U.S. standards bodies increasingly view foundation models as security-relevant components requiring secure development and risk control (National Institute of Standards and Technology, 2024).

Cross-jurisdictional comparison highlights an asymmetry: while EU and US governance ecosystems are producing AI-specific governance and security guidance, these documents still do not provide SOC-specific operational rules (e.g., required red-teaming patterns for SOC prompts, minimum adversarial testing before use in incident triage, or mandatory "human-in-the-loop" gating for containment). Singapore's GenAI governance materials emphasize implementability and testing, but they are not tailored to adversarial SOC ingestion pathways (phishing text, attacker-controlled artifacts). India's AI policy documents focus more on national capability and responsible principles than on the security engineering of deployed copilot systems in critical operations. (European Parliament, 2024; European Union, 2022; National Institute of Standards and Technology, 2023; Office of Management and Budget, 2025a, 2025b; AI Verify Foundation & Infocomm Media Development Authority, 2024; Government of India, Ministry of Electronics and Information Technology, 2023; CERT-In, 2022).

Synthesis of gaps motivating this chapter

Taken together, the literature reveals three persistent gaps that justify an SOC-LLM governance chapter focused on digital sovereignty.

First, conceptual sovereignty research richly theorizes state and collective control over the infrastructures and data that organize contemporary digital life, but it rarely treats SOC operations as a sovereignty-critical domain in which telemetry and incident narratives function as strategic assets and in which outsourcing analytical functions to foreign AI services can shift the locus of operational control. Second, AI governance frameworks, including the EU AI Act, the NIST AI RMF, ISO standards, and national strategies, articulate high-level accountability principles but do not translate them into SOC-grade controls for prompt data classification, auditable decision provenance, or pre-deployment adversarial robustness requirements. Third, LLM security research identifies concrete adversarial and privacy failure modes, such as prompt injection, backdoors, and data extraction, but usually frames them as application-security problems rather than as sovereignty and governance risks intensified by offshore supply chains and vendor lock-in in government and critical-infrastructure SOCs.

These gaps become sharper in cross-jurisdictional comparison. The EU provides the strongest binding AI-governance signal and complements it with NIS2 cyber obligations, yet SOC-LLM deployment still sits at the intersection of two regimes that were not designed specifically for one another. The United States offers deep standards and evolving federal guidance, including generative-AI acceptable-use requirements, but governance remains dynamic and may exclude national security systems, precisely where SOC sensitivity is often highest. The UK's pro-innovation approach and transparency instruments improve disclosure and governance capacity but do not yet provide a SOC-specific rulebook for LLM copilots. Singapore offers a distinctive mix of rigorous critical-infrastructure cyber law and highly practical AI-governance tooling, including GenAI-specific guidance, yet still lacks SOC-LLM-specific sovereignty controls on jurisdiction, exit feasibility, and tamper-resistance testing calibrated to SOC threat models. India's legal baseline in data protection and incident reporting is becoming stronger and clearer, but AI governance remains less prescriptive for SOC contexts, making foreign-dependent LLM adoption a governance gray zone for critical sectors.

As a bridge to the Methodology section, this chapter therefore treats SOC co-pilots as "sovereignty-bearing" socio-technical systems and adopts a qualitative comparative policy analysis anchored in the five jurisdictions' primary AI/cyber instruments, while using design-science logic to translate gaps into implementable governance controls.

Figure 2 presents a cross-jurisdictional policy timeline of major AI and cyber-security governance milestones relevant to SOC-LLM deployment.

Figure 2. Major AI and cyber governance milestones relevant to SOC-LLM deployment across the selected jurisdictions.

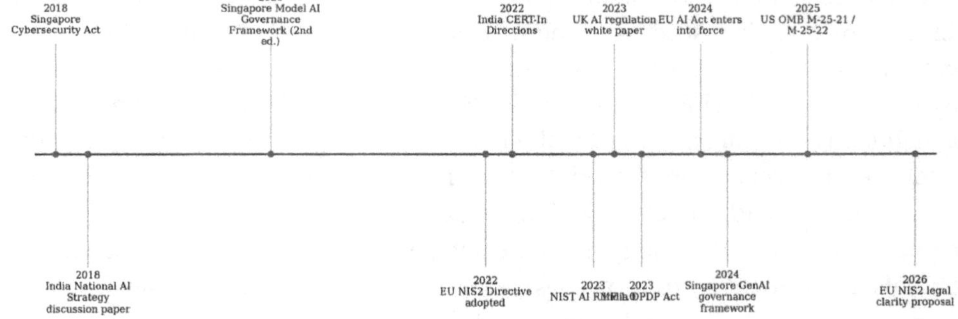

METHODOLOGY

This chapter combines qualitative comparative policy analysis across five jurisdictions with design science research to produce an implementable governance artifact—the SOC-LLM Governance Framework (SLGF)—for sovereignty-conscious use of LLM copilots in government and critical-infrastructure SOCs (Hevner et al., 2004; Peffers et al., 2007).

Research design and rationale

The study is qualitative and document-based, integrating two logics. First, comparative policy analysis is used because sovereignty exposure from SOC LLM copilots is primarily shaped by governance conditions—jurisdictional reach, accountability and audit expectations, data-governance constraints, and procurement/supply-chain structures—rather than by technical performance alone. Second, design science research (DSR) is used because the chapter's central contribution is prescriptive: SLGF is treated as a governance artifact (tiered deployment model plus operational controls) intended to guide real deployment choices. The DSRM sequence (problem identification → objectives → design/development → demonstration → evaluation → communication) structures how policy and security evidence are translated into SLGF elements, while keeping the chapter's argument balanced (LLM copilots can improve SOC effectiveness, but foreign-dependent deployment increases governance risk materially).

Data sources and selection criteria

Evidence is limited to citable, publicly available materials. The main policy corpus, however, is restricted to the official instruments that also qualify as the relevant public policies: EU AI Act (final-act summary) and overview of NIS2 in the EU; U.S. NIST AI RMF 1.0 and OMB M-25-21/M-25-22; UK's white paper on regulating AI; Singapore's Model AI Governance Framework (2nd ed.) and the Model AI Governance Framework for Generative AI; and India's Digital Personal Data Protection (DPDP) Act + CERT-In Directions. Secondary evidence is restricted to peer-reviewed methodology literature and peer-reviewed security research (top journals and leading security venues). Inclusion rules: (1) official issuer or peer-reviewed venue; (2) direct relevance to AI governance, cybersecurity governance, or LLM security; (3) sufficiently specific content to code obligations/controls. Exclusion rules: vendor marketing, unverifiable summaries, and sources without stable provenance. Some publisher versions of methodology papers are paywalled (e.g., MIS Quarterly; JMIS), so open-access copies are used where available and paywall constraints are noted.

Case selection logic

The unit of comparison is the governance regime, not named SOC deployments (which are often proprietary, undisclosed, or security-sensitive). Case selection follows purposive "most-different systems" logic to surface governance variation while holding the operational setting constant: government SOCs and SOCs supporting regulated critical infrastructure. This enables comparison of how different governance styles address (or fail to address) sovereignty-relevant issues such as cross-border legal exposure, auditability requirements, and exit feasibility. The EU is included for binding horizontal AI governance plus expanded cyber obligations; the US for standards-led risk governance plus federal use/acquisition directives; the UK for a context-based, regulator-led approach; Singapore for highly operational, implementable AI governance instruments; and India for a fast-evolving data protection and incident-governance baseline with AI governance still consolidating in practice. Where "major public-sector SOC examples" are not documented in official sources, the analysis does not assume them and remains at the regime/instrument level.

Analytical methods

Documents are analyzed using systematic document analysis—collection, appraisal, coding, and synthesis—treating policy texts and standards as qualitative evidence of governance commitments (Bowen, 2009). Coding combines directed qualitative content analysis and thematic synthesis. A theory-informed codebook is developed around two top-level families (Hsieh & Shannon, 2005): (1) sovereignty risk types, namely intelligence leakage, jurisdictional exposure, adversarial manipulation, and dependency or lock-in; and (2) SLGF control dimensions, namely data classification, hosting and jurisdiction, auditability, adversarial robustness, and exit feasibility. Themes are then integrated in line with good practice in thematic analysis to produce coherent findings that move beyond simple description of the source material (Braun & Clarke, 2006). Cross-jurisdictional comparison is performed through a matrix that records, for each instrument and jurisdiction, the presence, absence, and relative strength of provisions relevant to each SLGF dimension. SLGF is then demonstrated by applying the risk-control mapping to three deployment tiers—Fully Sovereign, Hybrid Sovereign, and Foreign Dependent—and evaluated for coverage and internal consistency against the coded obligations in the selected instruments, including governance and accountability expectations reflected in the AI RMF.

Validity and reliability of the data and limitations

Credibility is enhanced through triangulation across document types (binding/official policy instruments, standards and peer-reviewed research) as well as by an explicit audit trail (search terms, selection decisions, coding memos) in accordance with good practice for document analysis (Bowen, 2009). Reliability is supported through stable code definitions, versioned codebooks, and a recoding check of a subset of documents after a time gap to detect drift (Elo & Kyngäs, 2008). Limitations are material: (1) no primary interviews with SOC practitioners, procurement staff, or vendors; (2) policy texts may lag "as-implemented" practice and may not capture informal controls; (3) some relevant scholarship is paywalled, which can constrain coverage; and (4) policy regimes evolve over time, so findings are scoped to the versions of documents accessed for this chapter (up to 27 March 2026). The next section presents the coded findings and cross-jurisdictional comparisons that directly feed the SLGF risk mapping and deployment-tier analysis.

Findings and Analysis

Across government and critical-infrastructure SOC contexts, the coded corpus shows a consistent pattern: LLM copilots are governance-amplifying technologies that shift incident response work into the operational domain of model providers, hosting jurisdictions, and procurement constraints. The benefits—reduced analyst burden and faster production of readable incident artifacts—are real, but the sovereignty risk profile rises sharply when copilots are foreign-dependent (API-based, provider-controlled inference and logging), because controls over sensitive telemetry, audit trails, and tamper-resistance become partially externalized.

Overview of the coded corpus and analytic approach

Core findings are derived from the chapter's cross-qualitative coding of: (1) primary class-based governance instruments from across AI and cybersecurity (EU AI Act summary; NIS2 directive text and EU-level overview; US AI risk management and federal AI use/acquisition requirements; UK AI principles-based governance texts; Singapore's baseline and generative AI governance frameworks; India's DPDP Act and CERT-In cyber directions); and (2) peer-reviewed security research on SOC work realities and LLM failure/attack modes—including prompt injection, training-data leakage and model backdoors.

Coding was filtered through two connected lenses: manifestations of sovereignty risk (intelligence leakage, jurisdictional exposure, adversarial manipulation, dependency/lock-in) and SLGF dimensions (data classification & prompt handling; hosting/jurisdiction controls; auditability & logging; adversarial robustness/testing; exit feasibility/portability). The analysis below presents repeat patterns in the documents and indicates where provisions exist or do not extend to SOC-LLM specifics (e.g., rules on prompt content, model integrity assurance, or plans for exit under crisis conditions).

Sovereignty risk manifestations in SOC workflows

LLM copilots typically sit on top of SOC workflows that are already overloaded: SOC analysts face high alert volumes and tool fragmentation, which motivates automation and natural-language summarization. Empirical SOC research reports persistent false positives and significant manual validation burdens, reinforcing why copilots are attractive for triage, enrichment, and documentation.

Intelligence leakage risk

How the risk manifests in SOC work. Copilots are often used for log summaries, detection explanations, incident narrative drafts and representative language translation of heterogeneous telemetry for analysts. The leakage risk stems from the case where analysts copy-paste even raw indicators into a model, ticket narratives, hostnames, IP ranges or investigation hypotheses. These inputs can constitute operational intelligence (network topology hints, defensive coverage gaps, incident timelines). The SOUPS incident-response study shows that "summarization" tasks inherently ingest incident facts, remediation steps, and impacted-system details—exactly the data SOC operators would typically treat as sensitive.

Why this is a sovereignty issue (not just privacy). Even without deliberate retention, the exposure surface expands: SOC prompt streams become an additional channel through which sensitive state or critical-infrastructure information is processed outside the SOC's primary security boundary, especially in foreign-dependent deployments. Security research demonstrates that language models can under some conditions output memorized training sequences (including sensitive tokens), illustrating that LLM ecosystems can have real exfiltration pathways—an important analogue for why SOC prompt governance must be strict.

Policy signal from the corpus. The strongest governance texts tend to address "data governance" in general but rarely specify prompt handling as an operational control. For example, Singapore's baseline framework emphasizes data accountability practices such as documenting provenance and enabling algorithm audits, but does not prescribe SOC-grade "do-not-paste" rules for incident telemetry.

Jurisdictional exposure risk

How the risk manifests in SOC work. Jurisdictional exposure is most acute when copilot inference and telemetry processing occur under a foreign provider's legal/control domain. In SOC terms, this is not abstract: audit logs, prompts, and model interaction traces are often exactly what would be relevant in regulatory inquiries, breach investigations, and national incident response cooperation. If these artifacts sit in a foreign-controlled environment, custody and disclosure pathways may diverge from the adopting state's priorities.

High-constraint examples in the corpus. India is the clearest case in the selected documents: CERT-In's directions require organizations to enable logs of ICT systems and maintain them securely for a rolling period (180 days) within Indian jurisdiction, and provide them to CERT-In when reporting incidents or upon direction. This is directly relevant to SOC copilots because copilot interaction logs and AI-in-the-loop decision artifacts become part of "ICT system logs" in practical governance.

Similarly, India's DPDP Act explicitly empowers the central government to restrict cross-border transfers of personal data and treats "potential impact on the sovereignty and integrity of India" as a factor in identifying significant data fiduciaries, reinforcing sovereignty as a recognized governance consideration in data processing.

EU and regulatory jurisdiction linkage. While NIS2 is not an AI law, it contains governance constructs that matter for service-provider relationships: it sets risk-management and reporting obligations across critical sectors and includes provisions that operationalize jurisdiction for certain service providers (e.g., main establishment and requirement for non-EU providers to designate a representative). This is relevant because foreign-dependent copilots are often bundled into cloud/ platform ecosystems that may fall into these regulatory categories, but it still does not translate into "SOC prompt jurisdiction" controls by itself.

Adversarial manipulation risk

How the risk manifests in SOC work. SOC copilots do ingest attacker-controlled text at scale (phishing emails, threat-intel snippets, vulnerability descriptions, ticket comments, etc.). This creates two integrity threats: (1) prompt injection, i.e., input-layer manipulation; and (2) poisoning/backdoors, or a compromised supply chain — model-layer manipulation.

Evidence base. Prompt injection has been formalized and benchmarked in top-tier security research, showing that attacker-controlled inputs can cause LLM-integrated applications to deviate from intended behavior and that defenses remain imperfect. In SOC contexts, this risk maps to routine analyst actions (e.g., asking the copilot to summarize a suspicious email or a pasted log line) where the copilot becomes a reasoning intermediary.

At the model layer, instruction-tuning backdoor research shows that relatively small amounts of malicious instruction content can embed triggered behaviors, which is directly relevant to foreign-dependent deployments where the SOC cannot independently validate the model supply chain, tuning provenance, or hidden behaviors.

Policy signal from the corpus. Several governance instruments gesture toward testing and robustness, but the depth varies. The US federal memo requires pre-deployment testing for high-impact AI uses and explicitly acknowledges that agencies may have to test black-box AI services through querying and output observation when they lack access to underlying models or data—an important admission that governance often occurs under transparency constraints.

Singapore's generative AI governance framework explicitly frames red teaming and benchmarking as common evaluation approaches and emphasizes that natural-language inputs expand security challenges, motivating new safeguards and incident reporting practices.

The EU AI Act summary indicates that powerful general-purpose models that pose systemic risks face additional requirements including model evaluations, systemic risk mitigation, and incident reporting—useful as a governance anchor, but not automatically SOC-specific.

Dependency and lock-in risk

How the risk manifests in SOC work. Dependency is operational: once copilots become embedded in SOC playbooks (triage templates, automated enrichment, report generation, and "recommended action" workflows), switching costs rise quickly. In a crisis, dependency becomes a resilience risk: pricing changes, service outages, policy shifts, or provider deprecation can degrade SOC capacity. The NDSS workshop-based SOC study illustrates how LLM "agents" can unify disjoint SOC tools and automate routine triage—useful, but also structurally increasing coupling between ops workflows and the AI layer (Banstola et al., 2026).

Policy signal from the corpus. The strongest explicit anti-lock-in language appears in the US acquisition memo, which directs agencies to scope IP rights to avoid vendor lock-in and recommends contractual measures such as knowledge transfer, data and model portability practices, and licensing/pricing transparency. This maps directly to SLGF's "exit feasibility" dimension.

NIST's AI RMF also explicitly includes inventorying AI systems and safe decommissioning as governance outcomes (e.g., planning for phasing out AI systems safely), providing a risk-management rationale for "exit plans" beyond procurement.

By contrast, principle-forward approaches (e.g., UK) support accountability and transparency in general, but do not by themselves force portability or enforceability of exit controls in SOC procurement.

Cross-jurisdictional comparison mapped to SLGF dimensions

Table 2 summarizes the net effect of the selected instruments across jurisdictions, focusing on what they enable (strengths) and what they leave unresolved (limitations) for SOC copilots.

Table 2. SLGF readiness comparison across jurisdictions.

Jurisdiction	Data classification & prompt handling	Hosting/jurisdiction controls	Auditability & logging	Adversarial robustness/ testing	Exit/portability measures	Overall SLGF readiness
EU	Strength: AI Act transparency framing and high-risk treatment of critical digital infrastructure contexts gives a governance "hook." Gap: No SOC prompt-specific classification rules in the cited summary.	Strength: NIS2 governance applies across critical sectors; includes jurisdiction constructs (e.g., establishment/representative logic). Gap: Limited direct guidance on cross-border copilot inference and lawful-access pathways in the selected texts.	Strength: AI Act requires registration/impact considerations for some public deployments; NIS2 centers governance and documentation around risk management. Gap: Copilot interaction logs and reasoning provenance not explicitly operationalized as mandatory in SOC settings.	Strength: AI Act summary signals evaluations and incident reporting for systemic GPAI; NIS2 includes vulnerability handling and effectiveness assessment of security measures. Gap: No SOC-specific testing baseline for prompt injection or model backdoors.	Strength: Supply-chain security emphasis implies vendor risk scrutiny. Gap: No explicit portability/exit requirements in the cited EU instruments for AI services in SOCs.	Medium–High (strong legal anchors; weaker SOC-LLM operationalization)

continued on following page

Table 2. Continued

Jurisdiction	Data classification & prompt handling	Hosting/jurisdiction controls	Auditability & logging	Adversarial robustness/ testing	Exit/portability measures	Overall SLGF readiness
US	Strength: M-25-21 requires agencies to create acceptable-use policies for generative AI; high-impact framing supports prompt governance integration. Gap: Specific SOC prompt “do not disclose” rules remain agency-defined.	Strength: Acquisition guidance ties to privacy and lawful use of government data; testing can be required even for black-box services. Gap: Cross-border hosting is not the primary organizing principle in the cited federal texts; national security systems may be exempt in scope areas.	Strength: Inventories, documentation, AI impact assessments, and accountability structures are explicit; NIST emphasizes transparency and traceable measurement. Gap: SOC evidentiary standards (forensic-grade copilot provenance) are not spelled out.	Strength: Pre-deployment testing for high-impact AI is mandatory in M-25-21; NIST explicitly recognizes ML attacks and complex AI attack surfaces. Gap: Specific mandates for prompt injection testing are not explicit.	Strength: M-25-22 directly calls for vendor lock-in protections (portability, knowledge transfer, licensing clarity) and sunset criteria; NIST includes decommissioning governance outcomes.	High (civilian agencies) (strong governance + acquisition controls; sovereignty still depends on hosting choices)

continued on following page

Table 2. Continued

Jurisdiction	Data classification & prompt handling	Hosting/jurisdiction controls	Auditability & logging	Adversarial robustness/ testing	Exit/portability measures	Overall SLGF readiness
UK	Strength: Principles include transparency and accountability; regulators can tailor guidance by sector. Gap: Non-statutory nature limits enforceability; SOC prompt handling remains organizational.	Strength: Context-based approach can accommodate sectoral requirements. Gap: No explicit hosting/ jurisdiction controls in the cited AI governance texts.	Strength: Transparency/ explainability principle supports documentation. Gap: No standardized requirement for copilot audit trails in SOC operations in the cited documents.	Strength: Safety/security/ robustness principle supports testing norms. Gap: No mandatory pre-deployment testing baseline comparable to M-25-21 for SOC usage in the cited texts.	Strength: Governance acknowledges lifecycle and accountability challenges. Gap: No explicit portability/ exit obligations in the cited AI governance texts.	Medium–Low (good principles; weaker enforceable SOC-LLM controls)

continued on following page

Table 2. Continued

Jurisdiction	Data classification & prompt handling	Hosting/jurisdiction controls	Auditability & logging	Adversarial robustness/ testing	Exit/portability measures	Overall SLGF readiness
Singapore	Strength: Baseline governance emphasizes data accountability (provenance, audits) and governance structures; GenAI framework adds user data protection expectations. Gap: SOC prompt classification remains an internal policy decision.	Strength: Frameworks emphasize compliance with existing laws; adaptable to sectoral governance. Gap: No explicit sovereignty/ jurisdiction constraints in the cited AI governance frameworks themselves.	Strength: Baseline framework explicitly discusses algorithm audits and data provenance documentation; GenAI framework elevates disclosure and evaluation transparency. Gap: SOC evidentiary requirements for incident response (legal-grade) are not standardized in the cited texts.	Strength: GenAI framework explicitly discusses red teaming and benchmarking, and security-by-design with attention to natural-language input risks. Gap: Not tailored to SOC adversary models (prompt injection in phishing streams).	Strength: Governance encourages internal risk management. Gap: No explicit exit/portability controls comparable to US acquisition memo.	Medium (high implementability; sovereignty controls depend on deployment architecture/procurement)

continued on following page

Table 2. Continued

Jurisdiction	Data classification & prompt handling	Hosting/jurisdiction controls	Auditability & logging	Adversarial robustness/ testing	Exit/portability measures	Overall SLGF readiness
India	Strength: DPDP risk-based obligations (including audits/ DPIAs for significant data fiduciaries) and cross-border transfer restriction power create a governance basis for prompt data discipline. Gap: No AI/ SOC-copilot-specific prompt rules in the cited texts.	Strength: CERT-In requires logs be maintained within Indian jurisdiction; DPDP Section 16 enables cross-border restrictions—both directly relevant to foreign-dependent copilots. Gap: Scope/application to copilot provider telemetry needs operational clarification in implementation.	Strength: CERT-In logging mandate strengthens auditability; DPDP introduces audit and DPIA expectations for significant data fiduciaries. Gap: AI decision provenance and model governance are not specified.	Strength: CERT-In directions reinforce incident response/ reporting posture. Gap: No AI-specific robustness/red-teaming baseline analogous to Singapore GenAI framework or US high-impact testing requirements.	Strength: Jurisdictional control reduces some dependence risks. Gap: No explicit portability/exit provisions for AI services in the cited texts.	Medium (strong jurisdiction/logging; weaker AI-copilot robustness/portability governance)

Deployment-tier analysis applying SLGF

This section applies SLGF's deployment tiers—Fully Sovereign, Hybrid Sovereign, and Foreign Dependent—to SOC realities, using the coded policy constraints and security failure modes above.

Fully Sovereign deployment

Definition and operational profile. In Fully Sovereign deployments, the SOC operator controls inference infrastructure (on-prem or sovereign-operated environment), model updates, logs, retention, and access pathways. This is the only tier that structurally minimizes both intelligence leakage and jurisdictional exposure because prompt data does not need to cross into provider-controlled environments.

Governance fit. Fully Sovereign best aligns with the strictest jurisdictional expectations in the corpus, especially where audit logs must remain in-country (India's CERT-In requirement is a strong example of "hard" jurisdictional assurance).

Trade-offs. Fully Sovereign raises feasibility constraints: compute capacity, staffing, secure model lifecycle management, and the ability to perform continuous adversarial evaluations. NIST's framing that AI systems have complex attack surfaces and require structured risk management underscores that sovereign hosting does not erase security risk; it changes who owns it.

Hybrid Sovereign deployment

Definition and operational profile. Hybrid Sovereign deployment typically retains local control over sensitive telemetry (e.g., prompts are processed within an onshore environment or within a provider's dedicated/onshore instance) while still leveraging external models or tooling ecosystems. In practice, Hybrid Sovereign is often the "most feasible" sovereignty-conscious compromise for government and CII SOCs, but it requires enforceable contractual and technical controls.

Governance fit. Hybrid aligns well with: (a) testing and assurance expectations (US pre-deployment testing requirements for high-impact AI; Singapore's emphasis on evaluation and red teaming); and (b) supply-chain and vendor governance expectations (NIS2 supply chain security; US procurement lock-in protections).

Key control implication (from findings). The hard point is auditability: SOCs must be able to produce defensible decision trails. Since LLMs can omit critical details and inject factual inaccuracies when used autonomously, SOC copilots in Hybrid models should be constrained to "assistive" roles unless audit-grade verification exists. The SOUPS study quantifies this risk: autonomous summaries omitted critical details in a substantial share of cases and injected inaccuracies in many cases, while collaborative use improved outcomes—supporting an SLGF stance that hybrid deployments should enforce human-in-the-loop gates for high-stakes actions.

Foreign-dependent deployment

Definition and operational profile. Foreign-dependent deployment refers to copilot use via external APIs or vendor-controlled platforms where inference, logging, and model updates occur under the provider's operational governance. This tier is attractive for speed and convenience—but it is consistently the highest sovereignty-risk tier in the coded evidence.

Why the risk is materially higher (finding). Foreign-dependent use combines all four sovereignty risks: (1) intelligence leakage via prompt/case data; (2) jurisdictional exposure via provider-control domains; (3) adversarial manipulation via opaque model updates and supply chain; and (4) lock-in via workflow coupling and proprietary integration. The corpus shows that general AI governance principles do not automatically mitigate these issues; they require deployment-tier-aware controls.

What "safe enough" tends to mean in practice. Under SLGF logic—and consistent with policy requirements that emphasize testing, documentation, and incident preparedness—foreign-dependent copilots should be limited to tasks that can be performed with sanitized inputs (e.g., generic policy drafting, non-sensitive knowledge lookup), and should be prohibited (or heavily constrained) for raw telemetry summarization in government/CII SOCs unless the operator can demonstrate prompt redaction, retention controls, and auditable trace capture.

Figure 3 sets out the decision logic for selecting an appropriate deployment tier under the SLGF.

Figure 3. Decision logic for selecting a deployment tier under the SLGF.

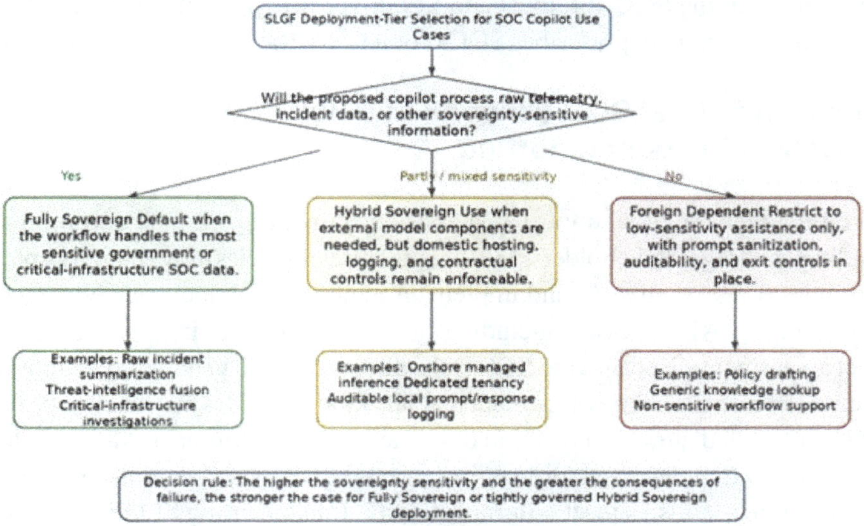

This decision structure reflects the governance levers that appear most concretely in the corpus: high-impact risk practices and testing expectations (US); evaluation and incident reporting norms (Singapore); high-risk/systemic risk governance hooks (EU); and hard jurisdictional logging mandates (India).

Illustrative vignettes

These vignettes are illustrative scenarios (not claims about specific national SOC deployments) grounded in documented policy constraints and empirically observed LLM failure/attack modes in security operations.

EU critical infrastructure SOC adopting an LLM for triage narratives

A water-utility SOC proposes a copilot to summarize alerts and generate incident narratives. Under the EU AI Act summary, AI used as safety components in the management and operation of critical digital infrastructure is framed as a high-risk area, and systemic GPAI models face evaluation and incident-reporting expectations. The SOC's governance response is to adopt a Hybrid Sovereign configuration: on-shore inference (or EU-controlled environment), strict prompt minimization, and formalized audit trails. Simultaneously, NIS2's focus on supply chain security and incident handling motivates structured vendor risk assessment and incident-response integration—but the SOC still must add SLGF-specific prompt handling rules because neither instrument prescribes SOC prompt classification in operational terms.

US civilian federal SOC using an LLM for high-stakes incident reporting

A civilian federal SOC wants LLM assistance to draft post-incident summaries for auditors and legal stakeholders. M-25-21 requires agencies to develop acceptable-use policies for generative AI and implement minimum risk management practices for high-impact AI use cases, including pre-deployment testing and documented impact assessments. Because the SOC lacks direct access to vendor model internals, it follows the memo's acknowledgment that black-box services may need to be tested through controlled queries and output observation. In procurement, M-25-22 drives contract terms to reduce vendor lock-in (portability, knowledge transfer, licensing clarity) and to establish sunset criteria—directly implementing SLGF exit feasibility controls. The SOC's operational decision is to keep the copilot "collaborative" (human-in-the-loop), aligning with empirical evidence that autonomous LLM summarization can omit critical details and inject inaccuracies at nontrivial rates.

India government/CII SOC confronting jurisdictional logging constraints

A CII SOC in India considers a foreign API-based copilot for rapid enrichment and incident documentation. CERT-In's directions require ICT logs to be enabled and retained securely for a rolling period, and that these logs be maintained within Indian jurisdiction. The SOC interprets copilot interaction logs and AI-assisted investigative artifacts as falling within the scope of operational logging expectations, particularly if they affect incident reporting workflows. In parallel, India's DPDP Act authorizes restrictions on cross-border transfers and treats sovereignty/integrity impacts as relevant to significant data fiduciary classification, reinforcing a sovereignty-conscious posture for handling personal data that may appear in incident tickets (e.g., user identifiers, email artifacts). The governance response is to avoid foreign-dependent deployment for telemetry-heavy tasks and either (a) adopt Fully Sovereign inference for sensitive workflows or (b) use Hybrid Sovereign deployment with in-country hosting and explicit retention controls, while keeping any foreign-dependent use restricted to low-sensitivity tasks with sanitized prompts.

Synthesis: how findings justify SLGF controls and policy recommendations

The findings support three sovereignty-relevant conclusions that justify SLGF's control set and the chapter's policy recommendations.

First, prompt handling is the missing operational control across most governance regimes: AI governance texts emphasize accountability and transparency, but SOC copilots require explicit "prompt classification" rules because SOC prompts routinely contain incident intelligence. This gap is especially risky in foreign-dependent deployments, where the governance boundary is partly externalized.

Second, auditability must be treated as forensic-grade in SOCs, not merely "transparency." NIST's emphasis on traceable measurement and governance structures, US requirements for inventories/impact assessments, and Singapore's discussion of algorithm audit and data provenance all point toward auditable controls—but the SOUPS incident-response evidence shows why auditability is not optional: LLM outputs can be plausible yet wrong, so SOCs must preserve the full chain of "what was asked, what was answered, what was relied upon, and what was verified."

Third, robustness and tamper-resistance are governance issues, not just technical ones. Findings of prompt injection and instruction-tuning backdoor indicate adversaries can exploit the AI layer by either tainting its inputs or compromising its supply chain. Policy regimes increasingly call for evaluation and testing (US pre-deployment testing; Singapore red teaming; EU systemic-risk evaluation duties), but none provide SOC-specific test baselines. This reinforces SLGF's position that SOC copilots—especially foreign-dependent ones—should undergo adversarial evaluation calibrated to SOC ingestion surfaces (phishing text, ticket content, threat intel) before operational reliance.

Finally, dependency findings show that exit feasibility is a security requirement. The US acquisition memo operationalizes portability and lock-in controls most directly; NIST adds governance framing for decommissioning; other regimes provide weaker leverage. This supports an SLGF requirement that government/CII SOC procurement includes portability, knowledge transfer, and sunset criteria—because "switchability under stress" is part of sovereignty.

The next Discussion section interprets these findings for policy design and SOC governance practice, including how SLGF can be adopted without over-constraining operational innovation.

DISCUSSION

The findings imply that LLM copilots should be treated not as simple productivity software, but as sovereignty-bearing operational infrastructure within government and critical-infrastructure SOCs. Although copilots can reduce analyst burden and accelerate reporting, sovereignty risks concentrate in foreign-dependent deployments because prompt streams, interaction logs, and model updates are partially governed by external infrastructures and legal jurisdictions (Pohle & Thiel, 2020).

Interpretation of key findings

A central interpretive implication is that "digital sovereignty" is less about symbolic autonomy than tractable control points—who controls infrastructure, data flows, and decision mechanisms in practice (Pohle & Thiel, 2020; Couture & Toupin, 2019). The coded findings show that SOC copilots shift these control points in three ways.

First, copilots convert SOC work into a continuous data-disclosure interface (prompts, context windows, and outputs). For SOCs, these artifacts are often operationally sensitive (network identifiers, investigation hypotheses, incident timelines). This aligns with evidence that SOC operations are already high-pressure and error-prone due to alert overload and validation burdens—precisely the environment where analysts are likely to paste "too much context" into an assistant (Alahmadi et al., 2022).

Second, copilots introduce new security failure modes that are governance-relevant. The security literature shows concrete attack classes against LLM-integrated systems (prompt injection) and upstream compromise paths (instruction-tuning backdoors), implying that "robustness" cannot be left to generic vendor assurances (Liu et al., 2024; Xu et al., 2024). This is operationally supported by incident-response evidence: LLMs used autonomously for IR summarization can omit key details or introduce inaccuracies, while collaborative use can improve quality (Kramer et al., 2025). The governance takeaway is that SOC copilots demand human-in-the-loop and audit-grade traceability if they influence action.

Third, the "deployment tier" is the sovereignty lever. Fully Sovereign and Hybrid Sovereign deployments preserve more control over logging, retention, and model change management; foreign-dependent deployments structurally externalize them. This aligns with risk-management doctrine in NIST's AI RMF, which emphasizes governance as cross-cutting and calls for explicit go/no-go commissioning processes and continuous measurement/management across lifecycle stages (NIST, 2023).

Policy implications for each jurisdiction

This subsection translates findings into jurisdiction-tailored, prioritized recommendations mapped to SLGF dimensions. It does not assume undisclosed national SOC architectures; recommendations operate at the level of governance instruments and deployment choices.

EU. The EU's strongest leverage is the coupling of cyber governance under European Commission's NIS2 policy framework with AI governance under European Parliament's AI Act final-act summary. NIS2 emphasizes risk-management measures, reporting requirements, supply-chain security policy, and top-management accountability in covered critical sectors. The AI Act summary explicitly identifies "safety components" in the management and operation of critical digital infrastructure (including utilities such as water and electricity) as high-risk contexts and calls for fundamental-rights assessments before some public deployments; it also imposes additional evaluation and incident-reporting expectations on systemic-risk general-purpose AI.

Recommendations: (1) Issue sectoral guidance (or NIS2-aligned supervisory expectations) that treats SOC copilots used in critical sectors as requiring prompt classification and minimization controls (data classification dimension). (2) Align NIS2 supply-chain governance with explicit onshore hosting, logging custody, and audit access requirements for SOC copilots supporting essential services (hosting/jurisdiction + auditability). (3) For high-risk contexts, require predeployment evaluation and change-control for model updates and retrieval pipelines consistent with the AI Act's evaluation logic for systemic-risk models—without assuming full model transparency (robustness/testing).

US. The US's principal governance levers in the selected corpus are the Office of Management and Budget memos and the NIST AI RMF. M-25-21 directs agencies to maintain safeguards for civil rights, civil liberties and privacy; implement minimum risk-management practices for "high-impact AI"; and develop generative-AI acceptable-use policies with safeguards and oversight. M-25-22 operationalizes procurement levers: scoping IP rights to avoid lock-in; requiring protections such as knowledge transfer, data/model portability practices, licensing clarity, and pricing transparency; and mandating ongoing testing/monitoring provisions in contracts.

Recommendations: (1) Classify SOC copilots used for incident response decisions, critical-infrastructure protection, or enforcement-supporting workflows as "high-impact" unless demonstrably low-risk; apply M-25-21's minimum practices and insist on collaborative modes for high-stakes actions (auditability + human oversight). (2) Use M-25-22 to make portability, logging access, model/version disclosure, and incident notification standard procurement clauses for SOC copilots (exit feasibility + auditability). (3) Use NIST AI RMF to structure continuous evaluation and risk acceptance for SOC copilots, including explicit go/no-go commissioning gates and periodic reassessment.

UK. The UK AI white paper frames a context-based, proportionate, pro-innovation approach that initially avoids new legislation, relies on regulator expertise, and stresses central monitoring and cross-sectoral risk assessment functions to avoid regulatory gaps.

Recommendations: (1) Use the white paper's "central risk" and monitoring functions to publish SOC-specific guidance for public-sector and critical-infrastructure operators—especially prompt handling rules and audit expectations for LLM copilots (data classification + auditability). (2) Establish a procurement baseline for government/CII SOC copilots that mirrors the strongest available acquisition practices (e.g., US-style lock-in protections), given the white paper's acknowledgment that AI risks can include national security and public-service trust impacts (exit feasibility + hosting/jurisdiction).

Singapore. Singapore's approach is characterized by implementable guidance: the baseline Model AI Governance Framework is explicit that it is sector-agnostic and intended as a practical tool for internal governance structures, human involvement, operations management, and stakeholder communication. The Generative AI framework adopts a "systematic and balanced approach" to address genAI concerns while facilitating innovation and identifies new risks such as hallucination and value alignment.

Recommendations: (1) Extend the existing "sector-agnostic baseline" approach by issuing a SOC-specific module or annex that codifies prompt minimization and "do-not-disclose" constraints for incident telemetry (data classification). (2) Require SOC copilots to follow governance-by-testing principles (evaluation evidence, red-team-informed controls) and align them with incident response governance (robustness/testing + auditability). (3) In procurement, adopt explicit exit feasibility requirements (portability and knowledge transfer) to prevent operational fragility under vendor disruption (exit feasibility).

India. India's corpus provides unusually direct sovereignty anchors. CERT-In directions mandate enabling logs for ICT systems, secure retention for a rolling 180 days, and that logs be maintained within Indian jurisdiction; they also list "attacks or suspicious activities affecting AI/ML systems" among reportable incident types. The DPDP Act provides cross-border transfer restriction authority (Section 16), applies extraterritorially for processing tied to goods/services offered in India, and explicitly references "sovereignty and integrity of India" in exemption contexts.

Recommendations: (1) Treat SOC copilot interaction logs, prompt streams, and AI-assisted incident artifacts as potentially in-scope "ICT logs" for compliance planning; avoid foreign-dependent copilots for telemetry-heavy workflows unless the operator can demonstrate in-country logging, controllable retention, and auditable access (hosting/jurisdiction + auditability). (2) Use DPDP Section 16 authority as a governance basis for restricting cross-border processing of personal data embedded in incident tickets and investigations, strengthening the case for Fully Sovereign/Hybrid Sovereign tiers in government/CII SOCs (hosting/jurisdiction + data classification).

Operational guidance for SOCs and procurement teams

Operationalization is where sovereignty succeeds or fails. The discussion highlights five "controls clusters," each mapped to SLGF dimensions and grounded in the corpus.

Prompt governance and data minimization. SOCs should implement a prompt data-classification regime: define what cannot be entered into copilots (e.g., sensitive network identifiers, privileged details, investigation hypotheses), require sanitization/redaction for needed context, and provide approved prompt templates to reduce improvisation under pressure. This recommendation is consistent with M-25-21's requirement for agency generative-AI acceptable-use policies and safeguards, and with the practical reality that SOC overload increases error likelihood (OMB, 2025a; Alahmadi et al., 2022).

Auditability as forensic capability. SOC copilots should produce audit-grade traces: user identity, timestamp, prompt (or hashed prompt with secure storage), retrieval sources, output, model/version, and downstream actions taken. NIST's RMF emphasizes governance across lifecycle and the need for explicit processes and documentation; CERT-In establishes strict logging expectations and jurisdictional custody.

Robustness testing and change control. Before operational use, copilots should undergo adversarial evaluation calibrated to SOC ingestion surfaces (attacker-controlled email text, web content, ticket narratives). Prompt injection research shows that indirect attacker-controlled inputs can manipulate LLM-integrated applications; instruction-tuning research shows upstream poisoning/backdoors can embed triggered behaviors. After deployment, any model update should trigger reassessment (including regression testing on a protected evaluation set). This aligns with M-25-21's minimum practices for high-impact uses and with the EU AI Act's emphasis on model evaluation and incident reporting for systemic-risk GPAI.

Human-in-the-loop gating for high-stakes actions. In fact, the SOUPS incident response study suggests that while autonomous LLM summarization can miss key facts or insert inaccuracies out of context, collaborative approaches may be a great complement to an analyst. Therefore, SOCs should prohibit automated containment or escalation decisions based solely on copilot outputs and require analyst corroboration and the capture of evidence for significant response action.

Procurement and contracting as sovereignty instruments. M-25-22 provides unusually concrete levers, and its logic is transferable more broadly: contract provisions should cover (a) limits on data use and retention; (b) access to and documentation of audit results; (c) rights to testing and monitoring during service use; (d) protections against vendor lock-in, including knowledge transfer, portability, and licensing or pricing transparency; and (e) sunset criteria and executable exit plans. For non-US jurisdictions, these clauses can still be adopted as best practice even where they are not mandated, because they directly reduce the fragility associated with foreign-dependent deployment.

Research and evaluation agenda

The findings point to a research agenda that is both empirical and operational.

First, field evidence is needed on how SOCs actually use copilots under pressure: what analysts paste, how often copilots influence response decisions, and how "prompt minimization policies" affect productivity and risk. Workload stresses are suggested, in SOC false-positive literature; specific copilot failure modes and collaborative gains can be evidenced by incident-response studies; thus it supports a real-world SOC deployment measurement need versus more lab benchmark only (Alahmadi et al., 2022; Kramer et al., 2025).

Second, evaluation protocols must become SOC-specific. LLM robustness research has established prompt injection benchmarks, but SOC copilots require scenario-driven test suites built around threat intel ingestion, phishing triage, and incident ticket summarization (Liu et al., 2024). A priority deliverable is a public, non-sensitive "SOC-copilot evaluation harness" that tests (a) injection resilience, (b) hallucination impact in reporting, and (c) trace completeness.

Third, SLGF requires governance artifact evaluation: it should be a decision framework tested in real procurement cases and their outcomes (reduced sensitive prompt exposure, audit readiness, exit feasibility). This reflects an accountability scholarship emphasizing documentation and evaluation as regulatory trends and auditing frameworks encasing accountability in lifecycle processes (Oduro et al., 2022; Raji et al., 2020).

Ethical and legal considerations

Ethically, SOC copilots are a cross-section of public safety, privacy and state capacity. Three issues dominate.

Privacy and confidentiality: SOC artifacts often contain private information, including user identifiers, email headers, and access logs. India's DPDP Act establishes notice, consent, and cross-border restriction powers under Section 16, meaning that prompt streams containing personal data should be governed in ways that can demonstrate lawful processing and justified transfers (Government of India, 2023). Even where the AI tool is assistive, the ethical duty remains to avoid unnecessary disclosure and to support retention and deletion practices consistent with applicable law.

Transparency, accountability, and contestability: The EU AI Act summary emphasizes safeguarding of fundamental rights and demands an impact assessment on fundamental rights for some high-risk deployments; M-25-21 underlines the need to assess civil and civil liberties safeguards as well as innovation alongside it. In SOC settings, this means: documented reasoning provenance, explicit scope limits (what copilots can/can't recommend), error reporting/learning loops.

Due process and "automation creep." Even if copilots begin as "reporting assistants," there is a predictable drift toward operational reliance (summarize → recommend → decide). Governance should therefore enforce escalation rules and ensure that consequential actions remain attributable to accountable officials, consistent with NIST's framing of accountability and with OMB's insistence on oversight for acceptable generative AI use.

Implementation roadmap and prioritization

Table 3 prioritizes the recommended actions and indicates where each jurisdiction should place the greatest implementation emphasis.

Table 3. Prioritized actions for SLGF implementation across the selected jurisdictions.

Action	SLGF dimension	Jurisdictional priority (EU/US/UK/SG/IN)	Timeframe	Implementation complexity
Establish SOC prompt classification rules, templates, and DLP/redaction workflow	Data classification & prompt handling	EU:H US:H UK:H SG:H IN:H	Short	Medium
Adopt SLGF tier decision gate for every copilot use case; restrict foreign-dependent use to low-sensitivity tasks	Hosting/jurisdiction controls	EU:H US:H UK:H SG:H IN:H	Short	Low
Implement audit-grade copilot interaction logging (prompt/output/version/user/time) integrated with SOC case management	Auditability & logging	EU:H US:H UK:M SG:H IN:H	Short–Medium	High
Require predeployment adversarial testing (prompt injection + untrusted input) and regression after model updates	Adversarial robustness/testing	EU:H US:H UK:M SG:H IN:M	Medium	High

continued on following page

Table 3. Continued

Action	SLGF dimension	Jurisdictional priority (EU/US/ UK/SG/IN)	Timeframe	Implementation complexity
Standardize procurement clauses: retention limits, documentation, audit rights, incident notification, model version disclosure	Hosting/jurisdiction + auditability	EU:H US:H UK:H SG:H IN:H	Short	Medium–High
Implement lock-in controls: portability, knowledge transfer, escrow/sunset criteria, and parallel-run exit exercises	Exit feasibility/ portability	EU:M US:H UK:M SG:M IN:M	Medium	Medium–High
Enforce human-in-the-loop gating for containment/escalation decisions; prohibit action solely on copilot output	Auditability + safety	EU:H US:H UK:H SG:H IN:H	Short	Low
Create governance ownership: named SOC AI owner, risk acceptance log, periodic review board	Auditability + governance	EU:H US:H UK:M SG:H IN:H	Short	Medium
Deliver analyst training on prompt hygiene, failure modes, and adversarial awareness	Data classification + robustness	EU:H US:H UK:H SG:H IN:H	Short	Low
Update incident response playbooks to include "copilot failure/compromise" scenarios and reporting pathways	Auditability + resilience	EU:H US:H UK:M SG:H IN:H	Medium	Medium

Legend for "jurisdictional priority": H = high priority, M = medium priority.

Figure 4 presents an implementation roadmap for phased SLGF adoption in government and critical-infrastructure SOCs.

Figure 4. Implementation roadmap for phased SLGF adoption in government and critical-infrastructure SOCs.

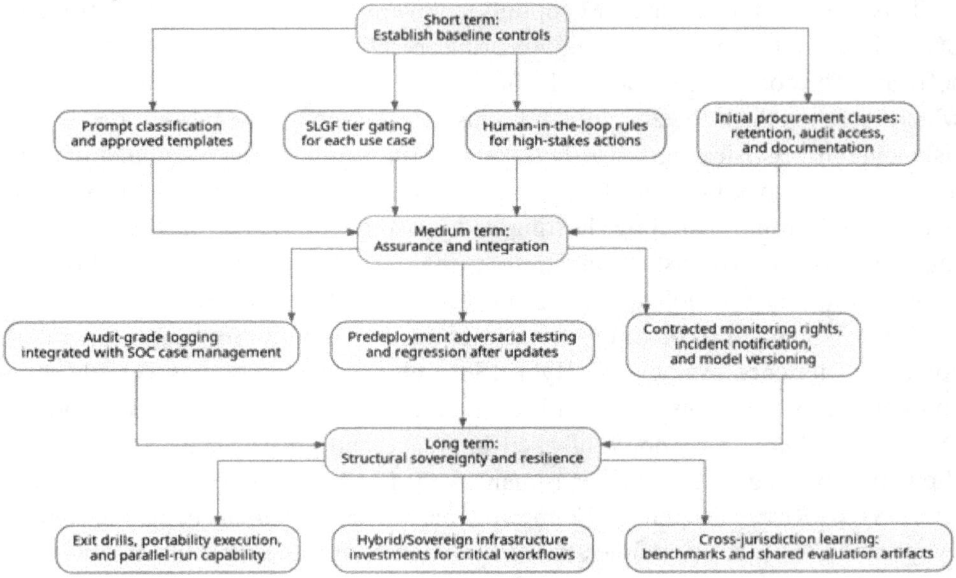

The prioritization logic follows the findings: quick wins center on prompt discipline, tier gating, and human oversight; medium-term work builds auditable records and test regimes; long-term reforms reduce dependency and enable credible exit and sovereign capabilities—especially for critical infrastructure where continuity and jurisdictional control are core operational requirements (CERT-In, 2022; OMB, 2025b).

CONCLUSION

LLM copilots can materially improve SOC productivity and reporting quality, but they also relocate parts of cyber defense into the governance domain of AI infrastructure, contracts, and cross-border control. Across the five jurisdictions studied, the chapter's core finding is consistent: foreign-dependent SOC copilots carry materially higher sovereignty risk than Hybrid Sovereign or Fully Sovereign deployments because sensitive prompts, interaction logs, and model updates are partially governed outside the operator's control (European Union, 2022; NIST, 2023).

Central argument and contributions

This chapter argued that LLM copilots in government and critical-infrastructure SOCs should be treated as sovereignty-bearing operational infrastructure, not ordinary software. The core contribution is the SOC-LLM Governance Framework (SLGF), which operationalizes sovereignty-conscious adoption by correlating four sovereignty risks—intelligence leakage, jurisdictional exposure, adversarial manipulation, and dependency or lock-in—with five implementable control dimensions: data classification and prompt handling; hosting and jurisdiction controls; auditability and logging; adversarial robustness and testing; and exit or portability (National Institute of Standards and Technology, 2023; Liu et al., 2024; Xu et al., 2024).

SLGF is applied through three deployment tiers—Fully Sovereign (operator-controlled inference and logging), Hybrid Sovereign (sovereignty-preserving hosting and enforceable controls while still leveraging third-party models), and Foreign Dependent (API- or vendor-controlled inference and governance). The analysis shows that existing governance instruments—the EU AI Act, the NIS2 Directive, the US NIST AI Risk Management Framework and Office of Management and Budget memoranda, the UK's principles-based approach, Singapore's implementable governance frameworks, and India's DPDP and CERT-In obligations—close important gaps, but do not yet fully articulate SOC-grade prompt governance, adversarial evaluation baselines, or exit-feasibility requirements (European Parliament, 2024; Office of Management and Budget, 2025a, 2025b; CERT-In, 2022).

Prioritized recommendations across jurisdictions

The chapter's actionable suggestions can be distilled into a sovereignty baseline that all five jurisdictions can adopt and then calibrate locally.

Data classification & prompt handling (highest priority): Mandate SOC-specific prompt governance: clear "do-not-paste" categories for sensitive telemetry, approved templates for allowable queries, and redaction/DLP workflows for incident narratives. This operationalizes responsibilities already implied by government guidance on acceptable generative-AI use and by AI governance frameworks emphasizing accountability (OMB, 2025a; Infocomm Media Development Authority [IMDA] & PDPC, 2020).

Hosting/jurisdiction controls: For government and critical-infrastructure SOCs, Hybrid Sovereign deployment should be the default for most operational copilot workflows, while Foreign Dependent use should be reserved for low-sensitivity tasks with demonstrably sanitized prompts. This is especially important in settings shaped by in-country log-custody requirements and cross-border transfer powers (CERT-In, 2022; Government of India, 2023).

Auditability & logging: Require forensic-grade copilot traceability (who asked, what was asked, what sources were retrieved, model/version, output, and what actions followed). This extends NIS2's governance logic for critical entities and aligns with risk-management expectations in NIST AI RMF (European Union, 2022; NIST, 2023).

Adversarial robustness/testing: Make predeployment adversarial evaluation a condition of operational use, prioritizing prompt-injection testing for SOC ingestion surfaces (e.g., phishing text, ticketing comments) and regression testing after model updates, reflecting the empirically documented attack surface of LLM-integrated applications (Liu et al., 2024; Xu et al., 2024).

Exit/portability: Treat "switchability under stress" as a sovereignty requirement. Procurement should standardize portability, knowledge transfer, logging access, incident notification, and sunset/exit criteria—controls explicitly encouraged in US acquisition guidance and transferable as best practice elsewhere (OMB, 2025b).

Operational implications for SOC practice and procurement

Operationally, SLGF signals a transition from experimental pilot adoption to governed operationalization. Evidence that LLMs can miss critical facts or introduce inaccuracies, but perform better in collaborative workflows, should lead SOCs to formalize restrictions preventing copilots from independently assuming full responsibility for high-stakes tasks (Kramer et al., 2025). Relatedly, the well-documented alert burden in SOCs increases the risk of premature oversharing unless clear rules and training are in place, which further emphasizes the importance of prompt hygiene and workflow-integrated guardrails (Alahmadi et al., 2022).

The central implication for procurement teams is that sovereignty protections do not reside in principle statements alone; they are embedded in contracts and technical architectures. Procurement arrangements should therefore require vendors to provide audit artifacts, disclose model or version changes that could affect behavior, facilitate secure access to relevant logs, and support portable off-boarding without jeopardizing SOC continuity—especially where legal obligations require rapid, demonstrable incident reporting and accountability (CERT-In, 2022; Office of Management and Budget, 2025b).

Research and evaluation agenda

Four near-term research priorities follow from the findings. First, empirical studies should examine how SOC analysts prompt copilots under workload pressure and whether governance interventions reduce risky disclosure (Alahmadi et al., 2022). Second, SOC-specific red-teaming protocols should target prompt injection and other untrusted-input pathways (Liu et al., 2024). Third, a shared "SOC-copilot evaluation harness" should benchmark error modes in incident narratives, audit-trace completeness, and resilience to adversarial manipulation (Kramer et al., 2025). Fourth, governance pilots should apply SLGF to real procurement and deployment decisions and measure changes over time in sensitive-prompt exposure, audit readiness, and exit feasibility (National Institute of Standards and Technology, 2023).

Ethical and legal restrictions and boundaries

Ethically, SOC copilots exist at the nexus of public safety, privacy, and state capacity. The data governance requirements of the EU AI Act and India's DPDP emphasize that transparency, accountability and lawfulness cannot be afterthoughts when AI has a role in significant operations (European Parliament, 2024; Government of India, 2023). Practically, governance must also consider confidentiality: LLM ecosystems have demonstrated data-extraction and memorization risks in prior work, reinforcing why SOC prompt governance is essential even when copilots are marketed as "secure" (Carlini et al., 2021).

This chapter has three important limitations. First, the analysis is document-based and includes no primary interviews with SOC operators or vendors; it therefore does not purport to describe undisclosed national SOC architectures. Second, policy regimes are dynamic, including evolving guidance and implementation timetables, so the findings are limited to the versions of instruments accessed for this chapter (European Union, 2022; Office of Management and Budget, 2025a). Third, some relevant scholarship remains behind paywalls, which may have constrained full-text coverage even where the core arguments and metadata could still be verified.

Forward look

The immediate next step for policy and practice is to treat SLGF as a "minimum viable sovereignty framework" for SOC copilots: enforce prompt discipline, residency/jurisdiction gating, audit-grade traces, adversarial testing, and credible exits—then iterate using empirical evidence and cross-jurisdiction learning. With these controls in place, governments and critical infrastructure operators can capture LLM productivity gains without silently transferring operational control and defensive intelligence into external governance domains.

REFERENCES

AI Verify Foundation, & Infocomm Media Development Authority. (2024). Model AI Governance Framework for Generative AI: Fostering a trusted AI ecosystem. https://aiverifyfoundation.sg/wp-content/uploads/2024/06/Model-AI-Governance-Framework-for-Generative-AI-19-June-2024.pdf

Alahmadi, B. A., Axon, L., & Martinovic, I. (2022). *99% false positives: A qualitative study of SOC analysts' perspectives on security alarms. In 31st USENIX Security Symposium (USENIX Security 22).* USENIX Association. https://www.usenix.org/system/files/sec22-alahmadi.pdf

Armbrust, M., Fox, A., Griffith, R., Joseph, A. D., Katz, R. H., Konwinski, A., Lee, G., Patterson, D. A., Rabkin, A., Stoica, I., & Zaharia, M. (2010). A view of cloud computing. *Communications of the ACM*, *53*(4), 50–58. DOI: 10.1145/1721654.1721672

Autolitano, S., & Pawlowska, A. (2021). Europe's quest for digital sovereignty: GAIA-X as a case study (IAI Papers 21|14). Istituto Affari Internazionali. https://www.iai.it/en/pubblicazioni/europes-quest-digital-sovereignty-gaia-x-case-study

Banstola, K., Al Faisal, F., & Ou, X. (2026). Experiences of using agentic AI to fill tooling gaps in a security operations center. In Proceedings of the Workshop on SOC Operations and Construction (WOSOC 2026). NDSS Symposium. https://www.ndss-symposium.org/wp-content/uploads/wosoc26-02.pdf

Bowen, G. A. (2009). Document analysis as a qualitative research method. *Qualitative Research Journal*, *9*(2), 27–40. DOI: 10.3316/QRJ0902027

Braun, V., & Clarke, V. (2006). Using thematic analysis in psychology. *Qualitative Research in Psychology*, *3*(2), 77–101. DOI: 10.1191/1478088706qp063oa

Carlini, N., Tramèr, F., Wallace, E., Jagielski, M., Herbert-Voss, A., Lee, K., Roberts, A., Brown, T., Song, D., Erlingsson, Ú., Oprea, A., & Raffel, C. (2021). *Extracting training data from large language models. In 30th USENIX Security Symposium (USENIX Security 21).* USENIX Association., https://www.usenix.org/system/files/sec21-carlini-extracting.pdf

CERT-In. (2022). Directions under sub-section (6) of section 70B of the Information Technology Act, 2000 relating to information security practices, procedure, prevention, response and reporting of cyber incidents. https://www.cert-in.org.in/PDF/CERT-In_Directions_70B_28.04.2022.pdf

Chen, S., Piet, J., Sitawarin, C., & Wagner, D. (2025). *StruQ: Defending against prompt injection with structured queries. In 34th USENIX Security Symposium (USENIX Security 25)*. USENIX Association., https://www.usenix.org/system/files/usenixsecurity25-chen-sizhe.pdf

Couture, S., & Toupin, S. (2019). What does the notion of "sovereignty" mean when referring to the digital? *New Media & Society*, *21*(10), 2305–2322. DOI: 10.1177/1461444819865984

Elo, S., & Kyngäs, H. (2008). The qualitative content analysis process. *Journal of Advanced Nursing*, *62*(1), 107–115. DOI: 10.1111/j.1365-2648.2007.04569.x PMID: 18352969

European Parliament. (2024). Artificial Intelligence Act (2021/0106(COD))—Procedure document summary (final act) (Regulation (EU) 2024/1689). https://oeil.europarl.europa.eu/oeil/en/procedure-document-summary/pdf?id=1786308

European Union. (2022). Directive (EU) 2022/2555 of the European Parliament and of the Council of 14 December 2022 on measures for a high common level of cybersecurity across the Union (NIS2). EUR-Lex. https://eur-lex.europa.eu/legal-content/EN/TXT/?uri=CELEX:32022L2555

Government of India, Ministry of Electronics and Information Technology. (2023). The Digital Personal Data Protection Act, 2023. https://www.meity.gov.in/static/uploads/2024/06/2bf1f0e9f04e6fb4f8fef35e82c42aa5.pdf

Hevner, A. R., March, S. T., Park, J., & Ram, S. (2004). Design science in information systems research. *Management Information Systems Quarterly*, *28*(1), 75–105. DOI: 10.2307/25148625

Hsieh, H.-F., & Shannon, S. E. (2005). Three approaches to qualitative content analysis. *Qualitative Health Research*, *15*(9), 1277–1288. DOI: 10.1177/1049732305276687 PMID: 16204405

Infocomm Media Development Authority, & Personal Data Protection Commission. (2020). Model Artificial Intelligence Governance Framework (2nd ed.). https://www.imda.gov.sg/-/media/imda/files/infocomm-media-landscape/sg-digital/tech-pillars/artificial-intelligence/second-edition-of-the-model-ai-governance-framework.pdf

International Organization for Standardization. (2023a). ISO/IEC 23894:2023, Information technology—Artificial intelligence—Guidance on risk management. https://www.iso.org/standard/77304.html

International Organization for Standardization. (2023b). ISO/IEC 42001:2023, Information technology—Artificial intelligence—Management system. https://www.iso.org/standard/81230.html

Kramer, D., Rosique, L., Narotam, A., Bursztein, E., Kelley, P. G., Thomas, K., & Woodruff, A. (2025). Integrating large language models into security incident response. In 21st Symposium on Usable Privacy and Security (SOUPS 2025). USENIX Association. https://www.usenix.org/system/files/soups2025-kramer.pdf

Liu, Y., Jia, Y., Geng, R., Jia, J., & Gong, N. Z. (2024). Formalizing and benchmarking prompt injection attacks and defenses. In 33rd USENIX Security Symposium (USENIX Security 24). USENIX Association. https://www.usenix.org/system/files/usenixsecurity24-liu-yupei.pdf

Mattern, J., Mireshghallah, F., Jin, Z., Schölkopf, B., Sachan, M., & Berg-Kirkpatrick, T. (2023). Membership inference attacks against language models via neighbourhood comparison. In Findings of the Association for Computational Linguistics: ACL 2023 (pp. 11330–11343). Association for Computational Linguistics. DOI: 10.18653/v1/2023.findings-acl.719

National Institute of Standards and Technology. (2023). Artificial Intelligence Risk Management Framework (AI RMF 1.0) (NIST AI 100-1). https://nvlpubs.nist.gov/nistpubs/ai/nist.ai.100-1.pdf

National Institute of Standards and Technology. (2024). Secure software development practices for generative AI and dual-use foundation models: An SSDF community profile (NIST Special Publication 800-218A). DOI: 10.6028/NIST.SP.800-218A

Oduro, S., Moss, E., Metcalf, J., & Narayanan, A. (2022). Obligations to assess: Recent trends in AI accountability regulations. *Patterns (New York, N.Y.)*, *3*(11), 100608. Advance online publication. DOI: 10.1016/j.patter.2022.100608 PMID: 36419454

Office of Management and Budget. (2025a, April 3). M-25-21: Accelerating federal use of AI through innovation, governance, and public trust. The White House. https://www.whitehouse.gov/wp-content/uploads/2025/02/M-25-21-Accelerating-Federal-Use-of-AI-through-Innovation-Governance-and-Public-Trust.pdf

Office of Management and Budget. (2025b, April 3). M-25-22: Driving efficient acquisition of artificial intelligence in government. The White House. https://www.whitehouse.gov/wp-content/uploads/2025/02/M-25-22-Driving-Efficient-Acquisition-of-Artificial-Intelligence-in-Government.pdf

Opara-Martins, J., Sahandi, R., & Tian, F. (2016). Critical analysis of vendor lock-in and its impact on cloud computing migration: A business perspective. *Journal of Cloud Computing (Heidelberg, Germany)*, *5*(1), 4. Advance online publication. DOI: 10.1186/s13677-016-0054-z

Peffers, K., Tuunanen, T., Rothenberger, M. A., & Chatterjee, S. (2007). A design science research methodology for information systems research. *Journal of Management Information Systems*, *24*(3), 45–77. DOI: 10.2753/MIS0742-1222240302

Pohle, J., & Thiel, T. (2020). Digital sovereignty. *Internet Policy Review*, *9*(4). Advance online publication. DOI: 10.14763/2020.4.1532

Raji, I. D., Smart, A., White, R. N., Mitchell, M., Gebru, T., Hutchinson, B., Smith-Loud, J., Theron, D., & Barnes, P. (2020). Closing the AI accountability gap: Defining an end-to-end framework for internal algorithmic auditing. In *Proceedings of the 2020 Conference on Fairness, Accountability, and Transparency* (pp. 33–44). Association for Computing Machinery. DOI: 10.1145/3351095.3372873

UK Government. (2022). National Cyber Strategy 2022. https://www.gov.uk/government/publications/national-cyber-strategy-2022

UK Government. (2023). AI regulation: A pro-innovation approach. https://www.gov.uk/government/publications/ai-regulation-a-pro-innovation-approach/white-paper

U.S. Congress. (2018). Clarifying Lawful Overseas Use of Data Act, Pub. L. No. 115-141, div. V, 132 Stat. 1213. https://www.law.cornell.edu/topn/clarifying_lawful_overseas_use_of_data_act

U.S. Government Accountability Office. (2025). Artificial intelligence: Generative AI use and management at federal agencies (GAO-25-107653). https://www.gao.gov/products/gao-25-107653

Xu, J., Ma, M., Wang, F., Xiao, C., & Chen, M. (2024). Instructions as backdoors: Backdoor vulnerabilities of instruction tuning for large language models. In *Proceedings of the 2024 Conference of the North American Chapter of the Association for Computational Linguistics: Human Language Technologies* (Volume 1: Long Papers) (pp. 3421–3438). Association for Computational Linguistics. DOI: 10.18653/v1/2024.naacl-long.171

KEY TERMS AND DEFINITIONS

Adversarial Manipulation: Efforts to influence, subvert, or misdirect an AI system through malicious inputs, compromised training processes, or other intentional interference with model behavior.

Auditability: The extent to which an AI-supported workflow produces records, evidence trails, and documentation that allow decisions, outputs, and responsibilities to be examined after the fact.

Cybersecurity Copilot: An AI assistant used to support cyber defense tasks such as alert triage, investigation support, incident summarization, and analyst decision-making.

Digital Sovereignty: The practical ability of a state or institution to exercise meaningful control over digital infrastructure, data flows, governance rules, and technology dependencies.

Foreign Dependent Deployment: A deployment model in which the organization relies primarily on externally hosted AI services governed by a foreign provider's infrastructure, contracts, and legal environment.

Fully Sovereign Deployment: A deployment model in which inference infrastructure, logging, retention, access control, and governance remain under the effective control of the adopting organization or domestic authority.

Hybrid Sovereign Deployment: A deployment model that combines external AI components with locally governed hosting, data handling, or contractual controls intended to preserve critical aspects of sovereignty.

Jurisdictional Exposure: The risk that sensitive data, logs, or AI-assisted decisions may become subject to foreign legal authority, disclosure obligations, or regulatory reach.

Prompt Governance: The policies, restrictions, and operational controls that determine what information may be entered into an AI system and how that information is sanitized, logged, and reviewed.

Security Operations Center (SOC): A centralized organizational capability that monitors, investigates, and responds to cybersecurity events using coordinated people, processes, and technologies.

Vendor Lock-In: A condition in which dependence on a specific provider's tools, formats, or integrations makes switching costly, disruptive, or operationally risky.

Chapter 4
Corporate Digital Sovereignty Strategies and Geopolitical Positioning

Amit Verma
http://orcid.org/0000-0002-9283-7873
Kalicharan PG College, Lucknow, India

Jikku Susan Kurian
http://orcid.org/0000-0003-3334-0055
Symbiosis Institute of Business Management, Symbiosis International (Deemed to be) University, Pune, India

N. Bindu Madhavi
http://orcid.org/0000-0002-5457-6748
KLEF (Deemed to be) University, India

Nimmy Saira Zachariah
O.P Jindal Global University, Sonipat, India

ABSTRACT

This chapter examines the evolving concept of corporate digital sovereignty within the context of global geopolitical dynamics and technological transformation. It highlights how organizations increasingly navigate complex regulatory environments, data localization policies, and geopolitical tensions while maintaining operational efficiency and strategic autonomy. The discussion integrates key dimensions such as digital infrastructure control, data governance, AI sovereignty, and cybersecurity frameworks to explain how firms adapt to fragmented digital ecosystems. Furthermore,

DOI: 10.4018/979-8-2600-0288-9.ch004

the chapter explores the role of sovereign cloud strategies, digital supply chain resilience, and cross-border governance in shaping corporate competitiveness. By linking geopolitical forces with corporate digital capabilities, the study provides a comprehensive framework for understanding how businesses achieve sustainable advantage in a multipolar digital economy.

1. INTRODUCTION

Nowadays, technology is moving into a key stage of its development, and aside from other considerations, the term "digital sovereignty" is gradually starting to get a foothold. As completely new industries begin to emerge in the digital economy era, our old notions of what constitutes sovereignty have to change. Artificial intelligence, cloud computing, global data networks and the web are all products of this technological Mold whose operations have already spread worldwide. Each recalled today that financial security, technological sovereignty and geopolitical dominance increasingly depend on government agencies being able to directly address such issues as digital infrastructure governance, data flows and techno systems. Regarding digital sovereignty, what is generally understood is that governments, institutions and social organizations should maintain supervision over their digital assets, techno systems and data infrastructure-as a matter of their own affairs when problems threaten to arise when they are in charge of them. Originally this term, from the beginning with its connotation that eminent reflectors put on events of significance to authority and country, was kept within the purview of governmental policy discourse. But since a few years ago, it has become popular also in corporate circles (Jansen et al., 2023). Now, digital infrastructures in today's world, where transnational corporations play an overriding role, cut deeply into both the global system of norms and institutions and the geopolitical domain. The European Union's General Data Protection Regulation (GDPR), China's Cybersecurity Law and the gradual promulgation of national data protection laws in many countries are examples of government authorities establishing rules for their digital ecosystems. To corporations, these systems of regulation influence heavily how they organize the storage of data, how data is treated during processing and what they must do in operation to supply digital infrastructure (Gorwa, 2019).

In the twenty-first century, a nation 's digital structure also sometimes referred to as its infrastructure for nought dollars-- has become one of the most important factors determining whether it will rise or fall technologically and economically in the contemporary digital economy, infrastructure constitutes the backbone. It includes semiconductor production plants and data centres the cloud. These infrastructures are the place where digital services of all kinds and levels are born offering processing power, data exchange communication over computer networks or digital satellite links among IPv6-ready networked devices on land line points for buses or subways that collect flight information in record time– and also determine by algorithms decisions made by people who inhabit them hospitals built according to futuristic plans on former coal mines where ponds breed fish for sale with the work of our robots. Digital communication blows across all places and limited by none; indeed, if you put your tent up in minus-three-degree temperatures waiting for good weather to come by helicopter from far off regions then you can be camouflaged by the internet (Wicki, 2020).

Governments all over the world are investing heavily into 'sovereign digital instructions', creating larger and more durable targets of economic competitiveness that also lock in technological self-sufficiency with these new structures. The increase in investment made pertains both to general fears about internationalized digital supply chains offer too many points where adversaries could intervene (with unknown results) and to reliance upon foreign suppliers of information technology products. Nor is it merely for software and hardware that dependency is increasing like this. This trend can be exemplified well by the establishment of national or regional cloud systems. Examples include Hi Cloud project equip with full legal protection its own government, where data produced in France is subject to French law and is well defended Marionette cloud infrastructure project a cloud computing system which follows strict national data protection regulations. Large US multinational companies which rely on global cloud services face substantial changes as a result of these moves (Cath et al., 2018).

For digital ecological planning and investment decision-making in this background, such an outcome has gone up as if meeting express ticket prices. As a result, now enterprises have to take into consideration where their data canters are located; what type of organization structure they should adopt in their Digital supply chains and partner technology is to finally just which current regulations national digital sovereignty policies may entail. As a result of the scenario, businesses had to balance establishing complaint systems in their own nations and creating regulations which are global. In other words, this would be a little sense. When a digital platform is managed from a single geographic place across hundreds of markets, they can extract large efficiency benefits from economies of scale and global integration. National governments, on the other hand, had a demand for more regulatory control and compliance with local data storage regulations as well as better protection against cyber assaults. Twelve: Geopolitical tension and a multipolar world make it far more difficult for businesses to take decisions (Belli et al., 2024).

You can prevent, with trade resting, export controls and technical sanctions foreign comrades who push the envelope to go as far as they want in this or that dimension of spreading a particular type of information from achieving their own aims.

Stability and competition are therefore essential for trade between two continents in sectors like semiconductors, telecoms and artificial intelligence, which have their own state-run export laws, corporations must be extremely cautious about coping with such geoeconomic dangers. From this perspective, corporations are increasingly becoming the arbiters and practitioners of geotechnology crosses national borders. The strategic course of action they chart in areas like infrastructure investment, Messrs Edgar Mitte co-operation and digital platform governance holds potential to present what global geophysical standards frameworks under which different kinds of attacks can operate. Tais would be very bad for us. At the beginnings of digital life, when corporate digital strategies were being represented afresh all over again in China. I Jinping took the lead in laying out the five guiding principles behind this neighbourhood-building endeavour. One principle is that digitization is a significant road to strengthening humanity. Companies engage the purpose of this chapter is to provide an all-round analysis of the way companies juggle with and cope in light change corporate discretion to a changing face-- changes that in turn speak cautious statements about. The central idea behind this explanation is corporate digital capability and how it interacts with the law on a global basis. 12 Faced with a world where geopolitics shapes each side of the digital economy, what choices can be made by major corporations which will help them succeed (Hoofnagle et al., 2019).

The meaning of corporate digital sovereignty is the first order of business. And in this quest, it's more or less essential to take up the question of how this notion has changed from something primarily concerned with State politics into a concern of strategic business instead. Yes indeed, that is corporate digital sovereignty. The second objective is what geopolitical factors are relevant for corporate digital strategy. Aside from these four aspects, still more critical elements arrived--digital infrastructure and its geographic underpinnings in technology: as a universal category becomes the international standard for data governance, cybersecurity issues can be effectively learned through competition among major powers at sea or in space. These four key variables break down the world into six critical aspects. They make clearer structural issues affecting decision-making in digital economy companies. This third objective is to study how different policies affect enterprises. We may have to establish collaboration with other technology providers, shift digital infrastructure toward home, or eliminate certain national data governance frameworks in order to combat the numerous and complex rules that prevail across various countries. These problems do not just come unsought so far because international codes such as market integration Of course, do not handle them. Instead, they show that each of these firms is now dominant in finding its own way through a more separated world font. In this chapter, we will unravel the mystery by putting forward a theoretical framework that traces a company's digital capability back to its geopolitical location. Actually, every one of them is just one more button which we smear together into a vocabulary. From a commercial point of view, we should consider what kind of fresh ideas we want from it in terms of technology, Following the law and how soundly this organization has a digital backbone being Together, these things affect the company's ability to do business in many different political areas. On the basis of cyber governance, international political economics and business strategy, it constructs a theoretical model explaining corporate digital sovereignty in the modern global economy. This chapter marks an intervention in the amplifying of the opening literature on digital sovereignty within the context of geopolitics, business strategy and contemporary global joins. The specific issue society discusses is that digital sovereignty emerges in today 's geopolitical Information Environment as a vital consideration (Floridi, 2020).

2. CONCEPTUAL FOUNDATIONS OF DIGITAL SOVEREIGNTY

With the rise of digital technologies, business strategy and control has a new area. At the same time, as digital technologies have shaped human life and work in more and more aspects over time, traditional definitions have lost some relevance. Sovereignty was no longer anchored in national territories. In the digital-platform era, cloud computing infrastructure, and AI system first setting foot on economic and social systems. Governments on many levels including international organizations along with enterprises take for granted what compact is even influxes reliance (Zuboff, 2015).

2.1 Evolution of Sovereignty in the Digital Age

The classical politico-theological concept of sovereignty as it has been largely defined in most texts past 150 years is that covering the entire population and territory an independent State is unique superpower. The main issue in the definition was this one ability--control over those National boundaries both economic activity and political procedures at home separated by an external interference from abroad. It's this state-centric idea of sovereignty that created the foundation for modern international relations and governance forms (von Scherenberg et al., 2024).

This has led to an expansion of the idea of sovereignty due to digitization with regard to digital infrastructure management, governance in cyberspace and mandates for preventing improper data use. Indeed, protecting digital infrastructure has now turned into a national security matter for every government. Failure of a data breach can lead to severe economic and social troubles.

2.2 Corporate Digital Sovereignty

The easiest way to steal it is by emptying the original essence out of the term both online and in information systems, which will be colonized by companies privatizing strategies on top of dissolved states. Multinational companies engage in different countries and regions around the world with their own legal systems, differing requirements on cyber security needs and regimes established regulating data protection (Kotsios et al., 2019). Net Result: as organizations traverse risk across data sovereign worlds, they need to fulfil the requirements of operations centric capabilities that safeguard strategic control within execution systems while operating holistically atop disjointed digital regulatory environment of today through free and managed services.

2.3 Data Sovereignty and Corporate Strategy

As a result, the regulations for data sovereignty are impacting how multi-national companies design and develop their technology. Companies need to adhere to the applicable laws of every country they operate in when data is involved. These regulations govern how data is stored, processed, and shared. There is also the data sovereignty law, which has resulted in local data centres. This is partially because many countries want to keep certain types of data, such as bank statements, medical records and government information, within their borders. Companies will either have to build their own data storage in the country or partner with a local cloud vendor that can attest to meeting all of the criteria. The data governance and reporting rules in organizations also change and become aligned with the rules of that country which enacted a data sovereignty law. This may motivate companies to further enhance their privacy and security. To protect their private data and comply with the law, businesses now need to implement full encryption, identity and access control, as well as auditing systems (van Hoboken & Ó Fathaigh, 2021).

2.4 Technological Sovereignty

Digital sovereignty also has something to do with technology. It means the extent to which a government or entity controls the basic technical capabilities and supply lines for digitally enabled infrastructure and advanced ideas. Especially in recent years the force of actions for other countries and supply chain issues that have emerged, show that it is very necessary to be technically self-sufficient to a much greater extent. "Beginning-maker" story might be an example of technical sovereignty. It made today's digital economy all the more central. The products of "beginning makers" technology range from cables transmitting information, networks, AI technologies to tracking chips recording how you use your computer. But only small clusters of these things appear in the world production pattern. That means they are open to trade restrictions and others come to cause problems for other countries. But are at such times called for? Then, after that, governments and corporations all over the world put a whole lot more than money into semiconductor manufacturing facilities. That helped them diversify their supply chains. Artificial Intelligence Ecosystems based on a single national technology is another example of technical sovereignty. Already, AI research and development requires potent computers, skilled artisans, and a great stockpile of data, just as any large corporation would need. The person owning these things may determine global technological standards and therefore have great say in where development go next.

In addition, software platforms are key for the realization of technological independence. The ICT ecosystem is courtesy of the software platforms — cloud infrastructure as a service, app development environments as a service, and digital markets. Enterprises can reduce their dependence on these platforms and better understand their technology stack by building their own software. As for communication networks, that field of strategic technology is another matter entirely. Telco networks, from 5G and beyond into nascent 6G networks, provide the connective tissue and enablement for all manner of digital service s of various kinds; but control over those communication networks is a universally required property both of keeping security in digital infrastructure where it belongs and also about whether there will be any technological innovation at all these days (Misra et al., 2025).

For businesses, technological sovereignty means dissolving the technological dependencies and having fewer sole suppliers. Unlike most corporations, these companies today are acting on both corporate documents and discussions: They do not adopt a headers-of-hare approach by adopting the piecemeal technological system but rather enhancing internal R&D capability and Participants in Innovation network projects.

Figure 1. Architecture of Corporate Digital Sovereignty

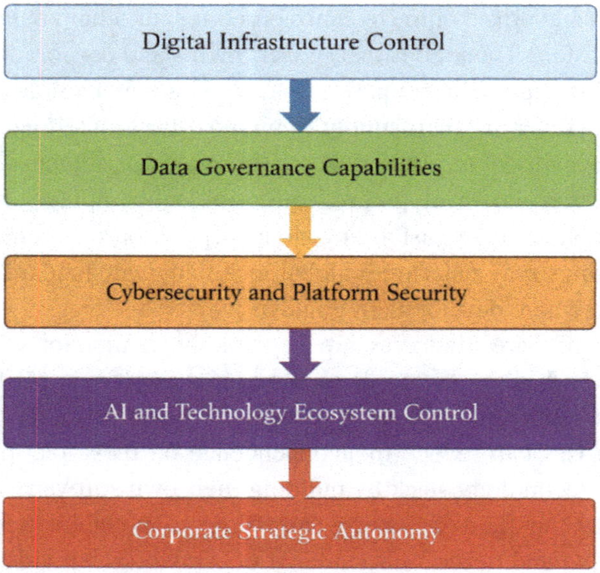

3. GEOPOLITICAL DRIVERS OF DIGITAL SOVEREIGNTY

3.1 Technology Nationalism

Technology nationalism is the rising conviction that a country's technological capabilities are core to national sovereignty and security. But unlike previous phases of globalisation, where the key piece was introducing technology across national borders, we are now living in a world shaped by strategic protectionism and competitive tech progress. Semiconductors, artificial intelligence (AI), quantum computing and telecommunications are all new pillars of a competitive economy that no government can afford not to possess. This is the beginning of actions that invoke independence and are meant to make us less dependent on others abroad (Helmond, 2015).

To achieve this goal, the US has imposed export restrictions on parts related to artificial intelligence (AI) and advanced semiconductor technologies. To be honest, the society we belong to now is not that special. Unless, that is, you get up every day to have a friend only during special traffic light events and where the tension in the air is always at an adolescent level.

3.2 Data Localization Policies

Another key element of digital sovereignty is data localization. These rules state that this type of information, which covers almost all personal, financial and proprietary national information must be held and processed in his country for security of everyone. Based on where we take our assets a kind of asset that needs to be kept there. From ensuring national secrets are not lost or misused, to protecting privacy, from preventing covered firms collapsing. Governments have justified this in several ways, including national security, regulation and industry oversight and individual privacy. None was more substantive than the European Union's General Data Protection Regulation (GDPR). The rule does not say that data has to be stored in the same place, but it certainly makes it extremely difficult to share information across borders and therefore promotes keeping data in the same place. India has also proposed special rules for governing data that prioritize the security of sensitive national data inside its borders, particularly in industries including banking and telecommunications. The Cybersecurity Law indicates that it is serious about data localization. It forces information infrastructure managers to take all personal and important data out of the United States. That is a more comprehensive approach to ensure that the country can follow how digital information crosses its borders (Roberts et al., 2023).

This does not only refer to resources that are being consumed, but military assets that are under national control as well. These policies force governments to opt for either political primacy, economic efficiency or both. Opportunity: As a result, navigating these assets is an exercise in rule-following, efficiency and innovation. Table 1: Current Regime in Regions of Importance; The Main Strategic/Ideational Focus Areas for Particular Regimes (EU Will this include Data Protection or the US Technology Competitiveness, likely a monopolistic perception/overstate attack on market information-based approaches laid out, and for China data-localization internet services/data commitment to Asia was clearly secure etc.; where it is especially principally around India having clarity of preservation aimed at gainful exchange for Indians, they have no consideration with domestic/political development argument.

Table 1. Major Global Digital Sovereignty Policies

Region	Policy Framework	Strategic Focus
European Union	GDPR, Digital Markets Act	Data protection and regulatory oversight
United States	Cloud Act, AI regulation frameworks	Technological competitiveness and security
China	Cybersecurity Law	Data localization and state control
India	Digital Personal Data Protection Act	Data governance and privacy protection
Russia	Sovereign Internet Law	Internet control and national network sovereignty

3.3 Global Technology Decoupling

Sovereignty cloud initiatives designed to ensure that data is only stored and processed in national or regional boundaries, are also accelerating fragmentation of cloud infrastructure. This trend is quite contrary to a more commonly adopted notion of the cloud whereby these global, law-abiding, and regionally localized/ infrastructural services are offered. Decoupling from the technology particularly presents businesses with significant strategic challenges. Conflicting marketplaces can cause systems to clash, causing both system breakdowns and the potential for an entire area or country's corporate activities to cease. That would mean devising a system very adaptable and compatible with the full spectrum of local control systems, technology needs. So, if, say, a business is unprofitable it will lose money through the texturing payment. Companies will build distinct supply chains for various markets if there are any geopolitical shocks, he said. This will make things more expensive and less efficient. This is doing the need for a risk reduction plan (Blancato, 2024).

4. CORPORATE STRATEGIES FOR DIGITAL SOVEREIGNTY

4.1 Sovereign Cloud Strategies

The emergence of national cloud strategies is one indication of the increasing importance of jurisdiction-specific data management rules. By a variety of governments in a diverse range of markets, from Europe & Asia to newer economies like India. As a result, enterprises are rethinking a network of global data centre principles for distributed cloud ecosystem transition at home and internationally (Micheli et al., 2020).

The implementation of data centres in proximity, cloud service providers which are locally owned state-owned Cloud Storage framework is an integral aspect of every national cloud strategy of nations such as India. All such methods allow an enterprise to follow its home nation's rules while remaining capable of operating flexibly. For example, national data centres initiatives are about the rights of residency for data and control over which state law applies — until full domestic independence from foreign surveillance frameworks is achieved. In turn, the level of data protection now required by India's evolving laws is spurring businesses to establish local infrastructures for data storage and processing. Regional data centres – A few of the first tactical steps is implementing regional data centres and helping organisations to either store their information in a certain national boundary or region, or such (Tallberg et al., 2023).

This ensures the adherence to data localization requirements, besides enhancing quality of service by resolving latency opting for a local player rather than going with global players. You can imagine that it adds a lot of complexity to operate them, and in turn, capital expenditure.

Global cloud providers oftentimes build a "trusted cloud" by partnering with local organization which fulfil the adherence to country specific compliance laws A fireproof architecture rate or multicolour path is needed by leaders. Organizations can further bolster resilience to a potential system failure that could occur if any one of a cloud provider s data centre were to be put out of action by distributing applications across multiple cloud providers. And lowering their risk from geopolitical confrontation or over reliance on any individual provider. Multi-cloud strategies also enable companies to adapt quickly when regulations change in different jurisdictions (Karjalainen, 2022).

Table 2 discusses the three main types of sovereign cloud strategies increasingly adopted by corporations as they adjust their digital operations to adapt to jurisdictional-specific regulatory structures whilst balancing flexibility, resilience and control over critical digital assets.

Table 2. Corporate Sovereign Cloud Strategies

Strategy	Description	Strategic Benefit
Regional Data Centers	Deployment of localized cloud infrastructure	Ensures regulatory compliance
Hybrid Cloud Systems	Integration of private and public cloud systems	Enhances data control
Sovereign Cloud Partnerships	Collaboration with local/cloud providers	Facilitates market access
Multi-Cloud Architectures	Use of multiple cloud service providers	Reduces geopolitical risk

4.2 Data Governance Architectures

Digital sovereignty can only materialise with a more holistic picture of data governance architecture, in addition to just infrastructure. And the development of such an architecture has already been taking place, as the emergence of a data governance program addressing everything between legal compliance and cybersecurity through company decision-making shows. Encryption also helps you stay up to date on new issues. Enables the organization to fulfil specific regulatory requirements for data protection and privacy. Due to the increasing need for accountability, businesses are performing (more precisely) data sovereignty audits. Agencies conduct self-examinations, or use external assessments to confirm compliance with data legislation and identify potential security vulnerabilities. Most often, they have deployed automated systems that monitor data flows in real time and identify irregularities. Overall, digital governance is the cornerstone on which organizations establish their digital sovereignty (Janssen et al., 2020).

4.3 AI Sovereignty and Algorithm Governance

Policies that effectively promote AI sovereignty number among the most critical given that artificial intelligence and machine learning will have such impact across all areas of innovation—and increasing relevance to competitive disadvantage. AI sovereignty means that an organization is capable of developing, operating and deploying AI systems and technologies in-house, to an extent where they do not need to rely on third-party suppliers or platforms.

Instead of starting from a blank slate, many companies are investing heavily in building proprietary AI models to reduce their dependency on third-party platforms (Su & Tang, 2023).

That might ease things with a regulator, in terms of establishing trust with all constituencies and on behalf of the corporation. The emergence of standards-based AI architectures has also been supported by an increased focus on AI systems — and regulators' initiatives to establish applicable standards. That page is useful because it ensures that AI agents benefit from compliance by applying the rules and regulations of a company within its legal framework.

Miles Rhizomes of Corporate Digital Sovereignty, a Model with Varied Levels of Capability (Figure 2) Demonstrating at least one-way businesses are building sovereign systems in (hopefully) the direction of Building AI capability independence through infrastructure and data management. That also aids regulatory compliance and, coupled with nailing the details of flexibility and control down to a tee, provides businesses with freedom that's strategic to winning a long-term competitive advantage in an increasingly fragmented world of global digital commerce (Carrapico & Farrand, 2025).

Figure 2. Corporate Digital Sovereignty Capability Model

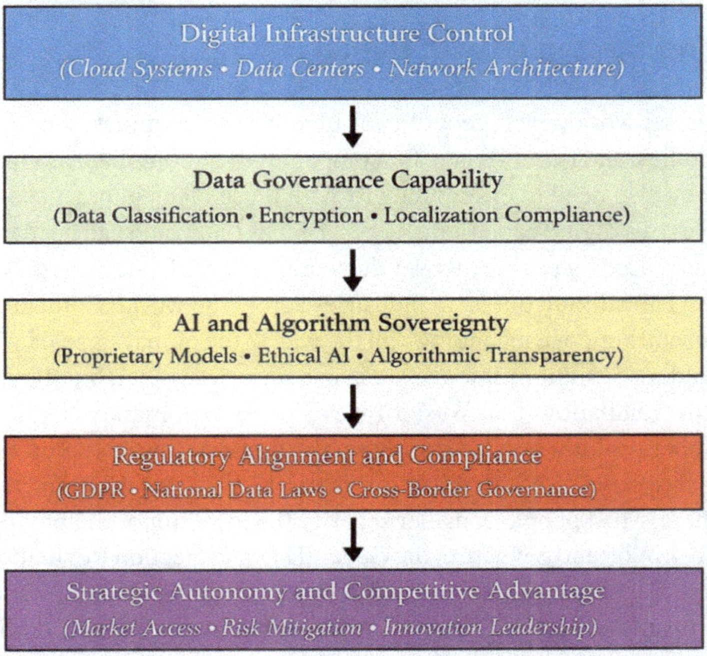

4.4 Strategic Integration and Organizational Implications

It will then fall on the companies to make sure that the obstacles they face in their own quest for digital sovereignty are aligned with and thus conducive to the long-term value creation of every business. It's little wonder that a significant part of the challenge there is striking some kind of balance between forces toward globalization and localization." Local variation is the name of the game in standardization and deviation but once it comes to global business, you need consistent processes and oneness of action. SQL server 2014 must have both generic and decorated designs.

Step 2: Cross-Functional Collaboration is the Key Among the innumerable functional departments within a company that partake of digital sovereignty plans are IT, legal and compliance and strategic management. (They all need to be working together for these tactics to prove effective (Falkner et al., 2024).

5. CORPORATE GEOPOLITICAL POSITIONING

5.1 Aligning Strategies with Digital Blocs

In the digital world, each geopolitical bloc has its own technical architecture, governing bodies, and rules. Hence, for companies to be compliant, competitive and enduring, they also need to ensure they fit with these blocs in practice. Americans wish to be part of a digital ecosystem based on ideas but which can be market driven. One that can be used by people all over the world. The U.S. is a great player in cloud computing, AI and digital platform industries across the world. Companies run this system, from cutting-edge technology all the way to the global stage. However, such benefits could also entail problems, such as data privacy Reich policy or bowing to the antitrust regulations and Western views on foreign markets (Rone, 2024).

The European digital regulatory system, by contrast, rests on moral principles, user rights and privacy of personal information. It's very different from what's happening here. Most people consider security the most important part of this ethic system. More importantly, whereas the General Data Protection Regulation (GDPR) establishes global standards for protecting privacy, it puts stringent regulations in place for companies based in the European Economic Area (EEA) or doing business with European clients. This usually entails backing ethical AI implementation in practice and principled ways of getting data correct.

Unlike the US and Europe, Chinese digital platforms are far more state-led. The data infrastructure space for the end-to-end logic of process controls is integrated into the platform on which it is produced. This may cover everything from data (such as laws and rules) to a little cyber security, including how long you can keep your (zero-sum) data under storage or at rest through new legal doctrines; it will also include flow management that is excellent for any small deposit per decentralized platform. However, this also shows the boundaries of operational independence and emphasis on tech integration and data flow while much is in commercial potential (Ganz et al., 2024).

Companies who aspire to leverage these broken digital spaces should prepare or revise their regionally focused business strategies in a holistic/integrated manner. Maintaining sustainable adaptability between both directions would be crucial since adopting either one group will ultimately lead to slumber energy in other groups.

Table 3. Geopolitical Technology Blocs

Bloc	Key Technologies	Corporate Implications
United States	Cloud, AI platforms	Global digital dominance
European Union	Data governance	Compliance requirements
China	Digital platforms	Market access restrictions

Table 3 shows the central technological capabilities and strategic significance of each geopolitical bloc. The USA boasts technologically advanced and highly scalable systems; EU provides regulatory structures that ensure compliance, governance, and ethical considerations at the core of its policies, while China possesses a large controlled ecosystem with exceptional opportunities to grow. Corporate considerations for these dimensions will need to be considered when developing geopolitical positioning strategies (DeNardis & Hackl, 2015).

5.2 Digital Diplomacy by Corporations

As we saw earlier in this era of digital sovereignty, many responsibilities that were once exclusively reserved for nation-states are now shared with commercial firms. Digital diplomacy refers to smart government-business relationships to influence regulatory architecture, gain market access and establish standards technology. There are a number of points in digital diplomacy, one of them is regulatory environment. Organizations are always in high demand and intellectual debates, promoting the rules require for innovation on time without being a heavy burden of compliance cost and also can be a partner in terms of providing know - how. Examples of such involvement include participation in cybersecurity standards and black-letter AI / data governance. Equally, the technology co-partnerships across borders. Companies are working with local firms, governments and research institutions to help them build local relationships as well as stronger tech capabilities. Through these friendships, they share local resources, tailor their products to local conditions and access new markets. For example, in emerging markets the extent of sophisticated joint venture arrangements often ensures that expertise gets transferred but at home cash is king services and products will require localisation (Mantelero, 2017).

5.3 Strategic Market Segmentation

In light of this accelerating and aggravated issues of technological displacement, and widening gaps caused by standards/diversity in laws and regulations in an era of increased geopolitical fragmentation, there is reflection happening within enterprises towards strategic market segmentation as a cure. Data architecture varies by region. To comply with sovereignty data laws, companies would construct local data canters to house any sensitive information inside a nation's borders. That will require redesigning the operation to ensure it complies with regulations, which will make it more expensive and complex to implement (Santaniello, 2025).

Regional platform governance frameworks are foundational in order to conduct public policy. Companies tweak their platform rules, content moderation operations and user-to-user interactions from one venue to the next so that they comply with local laws or cultural customs." Because the legal and social conventions that these rules are built on diverge by location, we should expect a great deal of variation in content rules depending on where you are. Geographical mapping of national enterprises Figure. 3 illustrates the synergy between pressure for regulatory sovereignty and technical autonomy.

The firms fit into one of four strategic categories that reflect the nature of the tension: globalized platforms, regionally conforming corporates, sovereign technological champions and fragmented digital players.

Figure 3. Corporate Geopolitical Positioning Matrix

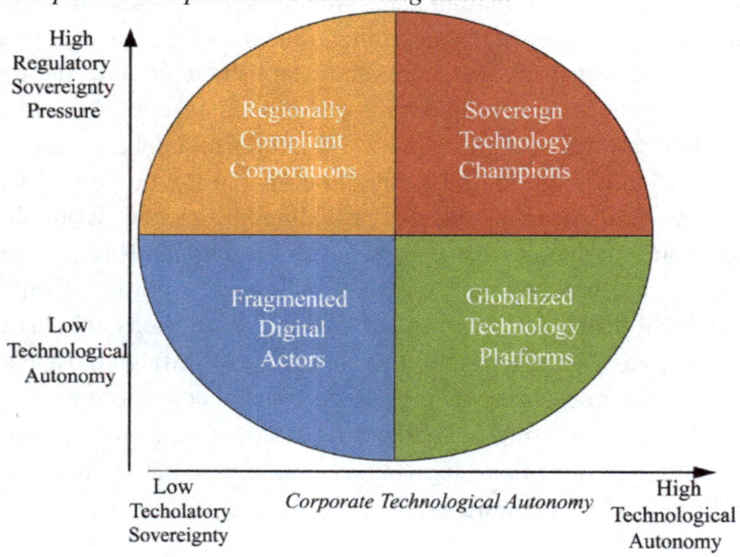

6. SOVEREIGNTY OF THE DIGITAL SUPPLY CHAIN

In the global landscape of the fractured digital age, supply chain sovereignty is not an option-it is strategy. Digital supply chain sovereignty is simply about managing dependencies that exist across multiple layers of technology infrastructure. These include layers for semiconductor manufacturing, cloud computing systems, software platforms and telecommunications networks and hardware chains. While all of these elements play a critical role in enabling certain digital operations, they are at the same time tightly interlinked and exposed to geopolitical threats (Horneber & Laumer, 2023).

Table 4 shows a more holistic view of the interdependencies & strategic importance of critical elements of digital supplies chain infrastructure for corporate digital sovereignty, thus getting further insights about these dependencies.

Table 4. Critical Digital Supply Chain Components

Component	Strategic Importance
Semiconductors	Hardware foundation
Cloud infrastructure	Data processing capability
Software platforms	Digital ecosystem control
Telecommunications networks	Connectivity backbone

6.1 The Global Geopolitics of Semiconductors

The riskiest and more difficult part of our digital supply chains is semiconductor manufacturing. If they're in limited quantities, no sum of money will obtain them — as an example, SoC prices have been rising across the world since late 2018 when faced with a chip shortage for new iPhone models. Often called the "new oil" of the digital economy, semiconductors are fundamental to all manner of digital technologies. They are at the centre of AI machines, cloud computing, telecommunications and consumer electronics — all with their own rules for charging by marginal revenue product (MRP). It is for this reason that control of the production of semiconductor chips has become such a flashpoint on the geopolitical stage. This is especially true in light of the U.S. action against ZTE earlier this year (Vaile, 2014).

The architecture of the global semiconductor supply chain is a geographical contiguous and highly concentrated social network. Because the production stages of valuable chips–for example design engineering manufacture and final assembly are integrated into certain region's economy, selling models for high-value chips is conditioned by specialist areas. By way of example, the monopoly over sophisticated chips or advanced technology is that of a small number firms condensed in certain regions –this generates strategic dependencies and impediments. This is no secret to their governments in the West (Zukis, 2022).

6.2 Platform Dependence Risk

The absence of platform dependence is one of the principal upsides of our platform dependency, yet one weight off our minds. The key is that firms may find themselves hopelessly caught up in process, and subject to all sorts of advice about how they should be stewarding data, building systems and setting policy if they lean too heavily on external platforms. And this will have their hands tied behind them in adjusting future regulatory requirements or commercial needs, making it even harder for you to pivot. A second key issue is data sovereignty. With the trans-national reach of externalised platforms, issues of data custody are often cited in relation to both where a secret key is generated and encrypted/decrypted, as well as when data is transported across international boundaries. When countries have clear policies on where their data can be domiciled, such as we see with data localisation or privacy-shri legislation, so corporates can only manage it within their regions. And you end up with so many atomized state laws for individuals that they emerge as zoning codes in municipalities (Braun & Hummel, 2025).

Furthermore, some governance regimes should be established and developed to suit for platform dependency. This includes setting clear policies on how to choose a vendor, how to handle data and what security measures will be taken. Ongoing monitoring and risk analyses verify adherence to related frameworks & the capability to identify possible vulnerabilities.

Figure 4. Digital Supply Chain Sovereignty Framework

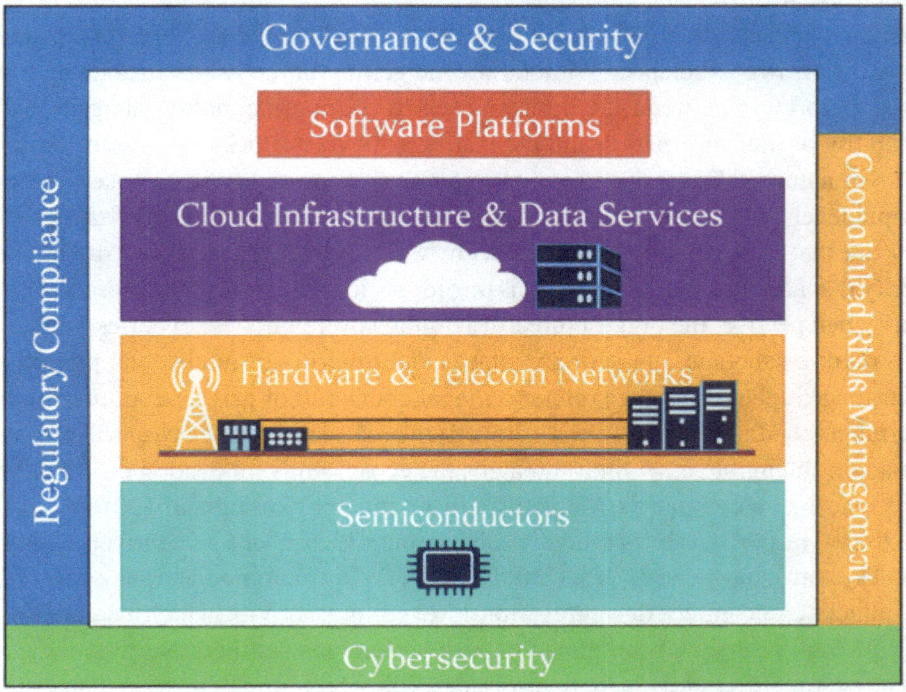

Applications of The Digital supply chain sovereignty layered architecture as shown in Figure 4, semiconductors are the basic units for all electronic systems. That means they can power any kind of computer gear. The second is the transmission media that carry these electric impulses across telecommunication networks and computer hardware (such as a modem) to transfer information between protocols. Cloud Infrastructure allows you to process and store data on the next level at the top of this stack are the software platforms that govern user experiences within digital spaces. Most of these levels have their own governance systems around it; think regulations compliance, cyber, geopolitical risk management (Lawo et al., 2023).

7. CYBERSECURITY AND DIGITAL SOVEREIGNTY

Stability within cyberspace sovereignty has become so interdependent on the world order that cyber security itself is now considered the Order of Cyberspace. As such, these groups still will not be permitted access to the properties. As part of the protection mechanism, they will remain in charge of the digital corporation (Gordon, 2024).

When it comes to cyber, digital sovereignty means being able to log, protect and manage your own cyberspace without anyone getting in the way. This demands a careful calibration between the threats posed to the confidentiality, integrity and availability of this information and the reality that cyber-attacks can also be cross-border in nature. "The threats have evolved away from those being tokenized at multiple levels, and state-sponsored action represents a far larger part of the threat landscape that companies must contend with." So, they need to transition to proactive security that aligns with their ambitions of geopolitical independence. From a cyber security perspective, the biggest threats to digital sovereignty are cyber-espionage, infrastructure sabotage, ransomware attacks and pilfering of intellectual property. For instance, cyber espionage refers to illegal collection of private commercial or governmental information, as well as the activities of a nation-state or a quasi-nation-state actor. Intangible asset theft threatens the ecosystem's innovation co-efficient and jeopardizes a company's competitive differentiator (Rosenbaum, 2010).

A third type of risk is infrastructure subversion, which means perceptively roiling critical systems, like power grids, banking networks and communications networks. Such attacks could induce disaggregation-level sectoral activity, which we saw from the 2003 power outage phenomenon in northeastern and southern North America: each ko seems sufficiently large to have a cascading failure within the industry that makes up each ko. Conversely, Ransomware assaults have transformed into an organized cybercrime enterprise in the form of encrypting corporate data and asking for monetary payment at the release ('Ransomware assaults'). Also, these phases are growing in numbers and a large scale so that we should also embed cybersecurity into some traditional sovereignty models (Janssen et al., 2012).

Therefore, companies need to move from reactive security thought processes and regimentation to proactive. That means imbuing the organization with security as part of its very DNA -- from its design, to its strategic planning process, and into its end-to-end operations. The core of this sovereignty-based cyber security strategy is internal capability generation, external dependency reduction and key infrastructure control.

Table 5. Corporate Cybersecurity Sovereignty Strategies

Strategy	Purpose
Zero-trust security	Infrastructure protection
Encryption systems	Data confidentiality
Security audits	Compliance assurance
Threat intelligence	Risk detection

The strategies in Table 5 represent the multidimensionality of cybersecurity sovereignty. Zero-trust security models, for instance, work on the premise of "never trust, always verify," meaning that to get into systems all users and devices are continuously authenticated. This method minimizes the risk of insider threats and unauthorized access significantly.

7.1 Governance of Cybersecurity

This attached the fact that cyber is no longer seen or understood as a technical problem because it encapsulates issues of such state business secrets, governance from its corporations and to prevent organizations. Cyber security does appear in the context of good governance work, via an enterprise risk management framework (ERM) underpinned by generally accepted board practices. However, the is also responsible for ensuring that strategy regarding cybersecurity is well-designed and adequately meets in all respects all organizational rules, industry regulations and market expectations. Cyber risk has finally gone mainstream, and it's entering into the cycle of Enterprise Risk Management framework setters (ERM). We drag part of cyber activity industry into the wider basket of financial, operational and reputational risks by taking a holistic approach to risk management. That regimen also translates into a more efficient allocation of resources that allows companies to double down on investment re-establishing security they already had in place and prove less susceptible under cyber-attack. Furthermore, cybersecurity governance faces regulatory compliance issue. Across all over the globe, extremely stringent data protection and conferencing competitions cybersecurity guidelines have been put in place that require organizations to exhibit enforce a strong security ease of transcription while alongside reporting incidents transparently. These are some of the rules that need to be followed through for gaining trust from all stakeholders, avoiding penalties by the law and for the continuity solution (Monesees & Lambach, 2022).

Fourth but most definitely not the least factor that affects cybersecurity governance is corporate culture. Likewise, employees, at any level of the process need to be fully aware and will have to remain cautious about cyber risks during their business-as-usual routines. And this is why all companies should be committed to an environment of security through skills training, information campaigns and behavioural intervention programmes (Popa, 2025).

Figure 5 Cybersecurity Sovereignty Framework showing the conversion of cyber awareness to structured governance and strategic execution within organizations They systematically attempt to identify those there, from the rise of cyber threats. They also put into place specific cybersecurity measures like zero-trust architectures or encrypted systems. Within organizations, these strategies are maintained at-board level, through an understanding of enterprise risk management formalized into the compliance machinery.

Figure 5. Cybersecurity Sovereignty Framework

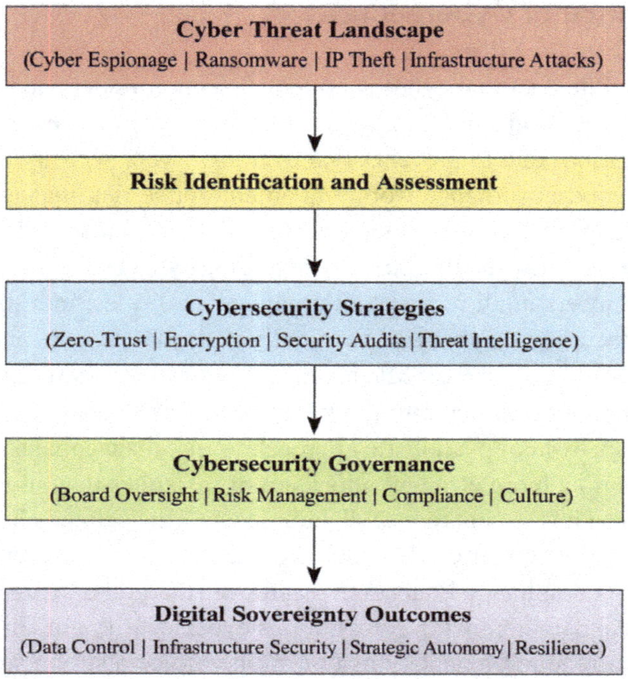

8. FUTURE TRENDS AND STRATEGIC FRAMEWORK FOR CORPORATE DIGITAL SOVEREIGNTY

8.1 Evolution of Digital Sovereignty in the Next Decade

Corporate digital sovereignty is now at the stage where a second wave of change has caught fire as geopolitical competition spikes and technology accelerates. It will draw more fully on a diversity of new strategic incentives, legislative prescriptions and next generation technology that will recalibrate the power dynamic that businesses have over their digital sovereignty (Kuner et al., 2020).

Digital sovereignty thus occupies a much larger kekune, not just as regulation and data localization but also as a new vocabulary of organisations aligning themselves with specific mega internet geopolitical blocs, tech autonomy and governance over digital ecosystems. Businesses wishing to remain strong, flexible and relevant over time must be prepared for all potential threats to their business model and actively work to mitigate them (Zygmuntowski, 2023).

8.2 Sovereign AI Systems and Algorithmic Independence

Sovereign AI systems can substantially reduce the degree of external technical risk to enterprises, and implicitly tie them to their local regulatory environments, simply by negotiating about who has rights over what data flows in an end-to-end sense (potentially back up through that very cloud) whilst ensuring privacy if executed. They can also write their own algorithms. This is especially important for regulated sectors like finance, health and defence that are at risk of geopolitical exposure or data security breaches or both by relying on foreign AI platforms. Others are also partnering with domestic companies and focusing on their own AI development to give the country a better grip over its technological system. Simultaneously, this transformation allows a national AI ecosystem of company and government collaborations with research institutions and technology providers to create integrated innovation networks. And thus, ecosystems of this kind in a progressively more fragmented word digital world creates resources not only for domestic intellectual, innovation and strategic resilience as well as long-run competitive advantage. They also verify specific business needs (Irion, 2012).

8.3 Digital Currency Infrastructures and Financial Sovereignty

Welcome to this new digital age of nationalism — today's enterprises now find themselves in a state of digital nationalism, as the emergence of digital currencies have quickly become a centrepiece of national strategy. These so-called superficialities bestow upon enterprises the key strategic advantages of being able to control their own financial data flows, transparency and accountability through transactions, as well as doing business with fewer ingoing- and outgoing-links to traditional banking institutions (Mindel et al., 2018).

8.4 Quantum Computing and Cybersecurity Transformation

Quantum computing constitutes both a threat to cyber security and an enabler of digital sovereignty. It may do so, if while also providing computational capabilities beyond anything conceivable allow unforeseen changes in problems solved (and even systems broken) by designing around the computing power; whereas modern cyber security merely confines such attacks. Such newly evolved methods enable attackers to pierce through cipher layers that are not yet hardened enough, heralding the beginning of an entirely different type of elegant encryption. That has accelerated the emergence of quantum safe cyber islands, focusing on the construction of yet more secure institutions like post-quantum encryption calculators. An example is Quantum Key Distribution, one of the themes of this chapter. Now quantum cybersecurity has gone from being a choice to necessity for enterprises. Ensuring cyber security through recovery of digital infrastructure, protection of sensitive data and rebuilding confidence with stakeholders as well as decreasing chance for future attack has become more critical than ever. The results of a security breach may include anything from disruptions in day-to-day operations, damage to reputation and legal consequences. As society has become so interconnected, data-driven, any sort of digital delay is intolerable. This generally means that businesses must start adopting post-quantum cryptography immediately (Mitchell & Samlidis, 2022).

Which means they need to devise solid secure architectures for the future. Having half a foot in the future and wishing that some generation of technologies passes by to make you feel full as far as threat model in those two domains is the very recipe for making vulnerabilities at scale, once that environment happens. Early adopters, for instance, are adept at managing new risks as they arise and can make sure to be addressing them beforehand.

8.5 Cross-Border Digital Trade and Governance Agreements

There are many opportunities in digital economies, and trade agreements increasingly center on the rules that determine what happens with electronic commerce and data flow across borders. They form a critical mass within the global trading system thanks to these agreements. Governments certainly are very busy at the moment of trying to get bilateral or international discussions off the ground in terms of how knowledge crosses borders or how you provide digital services. The future of corporate digital sovereignty can be summarized through key strategic trends, as presented in Table 6.

Table 6. Emerging Digital Sovereignty Trends

Trend	Strategic Implication
Sovereign AI ecosystems	Technological independence
Quantum cybersecurity	Secure digital infrastructure
Digital currency platforms	Financial sovereignty
Cross-border data agreements	Global digital trade

8.6 Integrated Future Digital Sovereignty Ecosystem

The future digital sovereignty ecosystem can be conceptualized as a layered architecture integrating multiple technological and governance components.

Figure 6. Integrated Future Digital Sovereignty Ecosystem

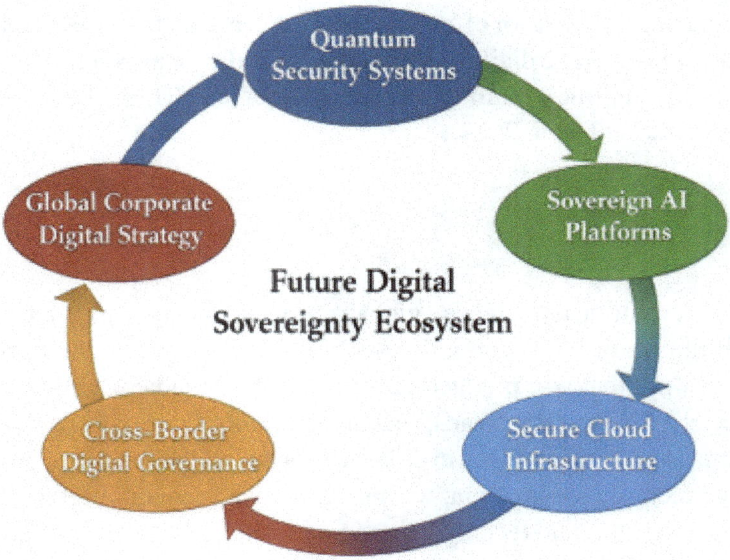

An example of digital sovereignty. Complementary governance mechanisms and novel technology contribute to enhancing digital sovereignty (Figure6). The unfortunate reality is that it's no easier to defend digital infrastructure from these kinds of assaults. These technologies will underlie sovereign AI platforms, enabling businesses to control data analytics and algorithmic processes (Roberts, 2024). These are compliant, agile and secure cloud infrastructures that run behind the scenes of how digital systems actually work. By adapting them into the category of cross-border digital governance, you can tell a different story. This story would include not only watching how people connect across borders but also the mechanisms we need to negotiate it and "make sure that data flows under certain conditions. At the top, all of them are corporate global - digital strategy telling machines that decide where is politically unstable world to place client-corporates.

8.7 Strategic Integration, Managerial Implications, and Future Outlook

On the contrary Strategic integration viably align organizations into not being threatened with demise but ensures that structures are embedded to keep up resilience to operations to ensure continuity even in the wake of collapse of regulation. It also reduces dependence on outside vendors while automating its own internal computer systems to conform to laws in various jurisdictions, thereby improving compliance. This is how companies achieve a better competitive position; sovereignty specifically becomes an asset of offense, not only defense. A few organizations look at their capacity to leverage digital sovereignty capabilities, as potentially enabling a transformation opportunity through regulatory pressure. This is how can they go far in global markets (Topor, 2024).

9. CONCLUSION

The most revolutionary change: globalization to the system we're working with now. It illustrates how geopolitics, technical infrastructure and business are converging in ways that will produce benefits that will fundamentally change our notion of society. Sovereignty means, first and foremost, that a country is in charge of its economy and territory. However, sovereignty isn't just concerned with the real world anymore. In a digital era, we must also take account of Internet culture, data ecological systems and technological frameworks. Also, there are no laws for any of these lands. These areas are entirely under the private control of businesses. The more control a company has over major digital assets (like data, infrastructure, algorithms and platforms), the prevailing more corporate digital sovereignty it enjoys. Between the lines It can't be reduced just any longer to a purely computer problem! The issue also involves the activities of governments, national interests and global balance of power. In this way, organizations become entities that live, move, watch, guard, and ensure correct behaviours. At least in outline, one finding of these talks was very significant – that there is no possible separation of or, at least a difference in thinking about, digital sovereignty. To go from somebody running the system for technical benefits, learning as you go about boos to the entire company being run by someone who thinks consistently and strategically, this is what they need read Those methods will change according to different regions, with some being entirely technical and others considering broader management questions; however, they all need to draw on this knowledge. This could include things like geopolitical awareness, avoiding being hacked by enemies, legal issues and other such things in a larger pattern of things that fit together. At first, a critical part of digital sovereignty is that the company is compliant. Since the rules in different places about digital services, data security and governance frameworks are all different. Businesses need to learn to follow the strict rules laid down by. Not only that, but we need data storage frameworks that are geofenced but not confined to any specific area; rules, patterns, models and checks based on needs and scenarios at every level of things. But not breaking the rules is not enough. Businesses which continue to regard regulation as a means of fulfilling its obligations afterwards in a world getting more complex all the time because of digitalization run a risk.

At least in the early stages, this means there must always be a constant stream of new technology tipsters which make a difference. Then competitors paying for specialized expertise emerges. For instance, how to solve AI-problem, stem the cloud computing flood and combine private/public clouds; or how to face largest threat today in cyber security. There is also greater strategic agility and independence in this reduced interweaving of technologies and platforms. in other words, the more that a technology can be native to applications and run with infrastructure and enterprise AI models (let's not forget multi-cloud situations), the better. However, on the basis that achieving such goals by creative means is the goal, the only path that beckons us forward is creativity. But what you should do before anything else is to brush up on modern political knowledge all over the world. The global digital ecosystem is gradually breaking up into regional hubs that battle each other and have their own tech ecosystem goals, standards and laws to pursue. Multinationals need to know new ideas likes of digital collaborations, exporting goods on a tech basis, and "Trade Flight" in these markets. In certain instances, organizations have to implement their business models over an entire nation while at the same time making sure that the right extent of international and local compliance is clearly conveyed so as to meet these requirements. These position tactics that change the businesses into "quasi-geopolitical actors" can shift about as world power rebalances. A strong cyber coverage posture enhances national digital sovereignty.

Digital infrastructures are becoming ever more central components of the social and economic structures, but also appear increasingly vulnerable to attack e.g. infrastructure breaches, ransomware and cyber espionage. That is one means that organisations need to be fitted with relatively decent security frameworks, which produce the needed defences against the brand-new threat environment — such items as real-time threat assessment of data feeds encryption techniques and zero trust architectures. Security has also become an issue when there are attempts at only defence, where all of which one does attracts attention from a power-relating and we do not see initiatives in the continuity or people need to use methods to achieve digital sovereignty Security can no longer be a simply a exercise about defence, but rather is now a strategic capability providing the bedrock of trust; an initiative for continuity and means used to achieve this.

These are the four dimensions in which the synergy manifests itself--regulation, invention, geopolitics and cyber security. It also uses them as in the following sentence: Regulatory constraints can be strategic opportunities for organisations with these -- often redundant -- capabilities. In addition to technical advances, blockchain, advanced analytics, AI and quantum processing are all strategic tools. In order to remain competitive in the long run, companies must disrupt things — which is why they are a key part of the future of digital sovereignty. Companies must rethink how they think about their strategic goals." This is not only about doing what you need to do in order to meet your basic needs, and also the end goal of being able to help you learn new skills. Companies must simultaneously work with other states and manage political risk responsibly, not merely put together legal infrastructure and do hire IT folks. The threat is likely to be a windfall for some companies, particularly those that see digital sovereignty as the strategic opportunity of our time. There will be the opportunity, as nothing can be solved and prosperity can be a true, permanent thing or a flexible target. Which means that we are always left having to adapt to new tech, shifts in the law, and changes in the world. Nevertheless, digital-first strategic leadership is nearly all about conceptualizing and executing corporate policy on digital sovereignty and streamlining operations.

REFERENCES

Belli, L., Gaspar, W. B., & Jaswant, S. S. (2024). Data sovereignty and data transfers as fundamental elements of digital transformation: Lessons from the BRICS countries. *Computer Law & Security Review*, *54*, 106017. DOI: 10.1016/j.clsr.2024.106017

Blancato, F. G. (2024). The cloud sovereignty nexus: How the European Union seeks to reverse strategic dependencies in its digital ecosystem. *Policy and Internet*, *16*(1), 12–32. DOI: 10.1002/poi3.358

Braun, M., & Hummel, P. (2025). Is digital sovereignty normatively desirable? *Information Communication and Society*, *28*(10), 1721–1734. DOI: 10.1080/1369118X.2024.2332624

Carrapico, H., & Farrand, B. (2025). EU data sovereignty: An autonomy–interdependence governance gap? *Politics and Governance*, *13*, 10331. Advance online publication. DOI: 10.17645/pag.10331

Cath, C., Wachter, S., Mittelstadt, B., Taddeo, M., & Floridi, L. (2018). Artificial intelligence and the "good society": The US, EU, and UK approach. *Science and Engineering Ethics*, *24*(2), 505–528. DOI: 10.1007/s11948-017-9901-7 PMID: 28353045

DeNardis, L., & Hackl, A. M. (2015). Internet governance by social media platforms. *Telecommunications Policy*, *39*(9), 761–770. DOI: 10.1016/j.telpol.2015.04.003

Falkner, G., Heidebrecht, S., Obendiek, A., & Seidl, T. (2024). Digital sovereignty: Rhetoric and reality. *Journal of European Public Policy*, *31*(8), 2099–2120. DOI: 10.1080/13501763.2024.2358984

Floridi, L. (2020). The fight for digital sovereignty: What it is, and why it matters, especially for the EU. *Philosophy & Technology*, *33*(3), 369–378. DOI: 10.1007/s13347-020-00423-6 PMID: 35194548

Ganz, A., Camellini, M., Hine, E., Novelli, C., Roberts, H., & Floridi, L. (2024). Submarine cables and the risks to digital sovereignty. *Minds and Machines*, *34*(3), 1–23. DOI: 10.1007/s11023-024-09683-z

Gordon, G. (2024). Digital sovereignty, digital infrastructures, and quantum horizons. *AI & Society*, *39*(1), 125–137. DOI: 10.1007/s00146-023-01729-7

Gorwa, R. (2019). What is platform governance? *Information Communication and Society*, *22*(6), 854–871. DOI: 10.1080/1369118X.2019.1573914

Helmond, A. (2015). The platformization of the web: Making web data platform ready. *Social Media + Society*, *1*(2), 1–11. DOI: 10.1177/2056305115603080

Hoofnagle, C. J., van der Sloot, B., & Borgesius, F. Z. (2019). The European Union general data protection regulation: What it is and what it means. *Information & Communications Technology Law*, *28*(1), 65–98. DOI: 10.1080/13600834.2019.1573501

Horneber, D., & Laumer, S. (2023). Algorithmic accountability. *Business & Information Systems Engineering*, *65*(6), 723–730. DOI: 10.1007/s12599-023-00817-8

Irion, K. (2012). Government cloud computing and national data sovereignty. *Policy and Internet*, *4*(3–4), 40–71. DOI: 10.1002/poi3.10

Jansen, B., Kadenko, N., Broeders, D., van Eeten, M., Borgolte, K., & Fiebig, T. (2023). Pushing boundaries: An empirical view on the digital sovereignty of six governments in the midst of geopolitical tensions. *Government Information Quarterly*, *40*(4), 101862. Advance online publication. DOI: 10.1016/j.giq.2023.101862

Janssen, M., Brous, P., Estevez, E., Barbosa, L. S., & Janowski, T. (2020). Data governance: Organizing data for trustworthy artificial intelligence. *Government Information Quarterly*, *37*(3), 101493. Advance online publication. DOI: 10.1016/j.giq.2020.101493

Janssen, M., Charalabidis, Y., & Zuiderwijk, A. (2012). Benefits, adoption barriers and myths of open data and open government. *Information Systems Management*, *29*(4), 258–268. DOI: 10.1080/10580530.2012.716740

Joris van Hoboken, R. Ó. (2021, July). Fathaigh, Smartphone platforms as privacy regulators. *Computer Law & Security Review*, *41*, 105557. Advance online publication. DOI: 10.1016/j.clsr.2021.105557

Karjalainen, T. (2022). The battle of power: Enforcing data protection law against companies holding data power. *Computer Law & Security Review*, *47*, 105742. DOI: 10.1016/j.clsr.2022.105742

Kotsios, A., Magnani, M., Rossi, L., Shklovski, I., & Vega, D. (2019). An analysis of the consequences of the general data protection regulation (GDPR) on social network research. *ACM Transactions on Social Computing*, *2*(3), 12. Advance online publication. DOI: 10.1145/3365524

Kuner, C., Bygrave, L. A., & Docksey, C. (Eds.). (2020). *The EU General Data Protection Regulation (GDPR): A commentary*. Oxford University Press., DOI: 10.1093/oso/9780198826491.001.0001

Lawo, D., Neifer, T., Esau, M., & Stevens, G. (2023). Digital sovereignty: What it is and why it matters for HCI. In *Extended Abstracts of the 2023 CHI Conference on Human Factors in Computing Systems* (Article 317). ACM. DOI: 10.1145/3544549.3585834

Mantelero, A. (2017). From group privacy to collective privacy: Towards a new dimension of privacy and data protection in the big data era. In Taylor, L., Floridi, L., & van der Sloot, B. (Eds.), *Group privacy: New challenges of data technologies* (pp. 139–158). Springer., DOI: 10.1007/978-3-319-46608-8_8

Micheli, M., Ponti, M., Craglia, M., & Berti Suman, A. (2020). Emerging models of data governance in the age of datafication. *Big Data & Society*, *7*(2), 1–15. DOI: 10.1177/2053951720948087

Mindel, V., Mathiassen, L., & Rai, A. (2018). The sustainability of polycentric information commons. *Management Information Systems Quarterly*, *42*(2), 607–631. DOI: 10.25300/MISQ/2018/14015

Misra, S., Barik, K., & Kvalvik, P. (2025). Trust in digital sovereignty: A review of security, privacy, and governance challenges. *Public Organization Review*. Advance online publication. DOI: 10.1007/s11115-025-00968-0

Mitchell, A. D., & Samlidis, T. (2022). Cloud services and government digital sovereignty in Australia and beyond. *International Journal of Law and Information Technology*, *29*(4), 364–394. DOI: 10.1093/ijlit/eaac003

Popa, D. M. (2025). Frontrunner model for responsible AI governance in the public sector: The Dutch perspective. *AI and Ethics*, *5*(3), 2789–2799. DOI: 10.1007/s43681-024-00596-2

Roberts, H. (2024). Digital sovereignty and artificial intelligence: A normative approach. *Ethics and Information Technology*, *26*(4), 1–10. DOI: 10.1007/s10676-024-09810-5

Roberts, H., Hine, E., & Floridi, L. (2023). Digital sovereignty, digital expansionism, and the prospects for global AI governance. In Timoteo, M., Verri, B., & Nanni, R. (Eds.), *Quo vadis, sovereignty? New conceptual and regulatory boundaries in the age of digital China* (pp. 51–75). Springer., DOI: 10.1007/978-3-031-41566-1_4

Rone, J. (2024). The sovereign cloud in Europe: Diverging nation state preferences and disputed institutional competences in the context of limited technological capabilities. *Journal of European Public Policy*, *31*(8), 2343–2369. DOI: 10.1080/13501763.2024.2348618

Rosenbaum, S. (2010). Data governance and stewardship: Designing data stewardship entities and advancing data access. *Health Services Research*, *45*(5 Pt 2), 1442–1455. DOI: 10.1111/j.1475-6773.2010.01140.x PMID: 21054365

Santaniello, M. (2025). Attributes of digital sovereignty: A conceptual framework. *Geopolitics*, *31*(2), 1–22. DOI: 10.1080/14650045.2025.2521548

Su, C., & Tang, W. (2023). Data sovereignty and platform neutrality: A comparative study on TikTok's data policy. *Global Media and China*, *8*(1), 57–71. DOI: 10.1177/20594364231154340

Tallberg, J., Erman, E., Furendal, M., Geith, J., Klamberg, M., & Lundgren, M. (2023). The global governance of artificial intelligence: Next steps for empirical and normative research. *International Studies Review*, *25*(3), viad040. Advance online publication. DOI: 10.1093/isr/viad040

Topor, L. (2024). *Cyber sovereignty: International security, mass communication, and the future of the internet*. Springer., DOI: 10.1007/978-3-031-58199-1

Vaile, D. (2014). The Cloud and data sovereignty after Snowden. *Journal of Telecommunications and the Digital Economy.*, *2*(1), 60. DOI: 10.18080/jtde.v2n1.317

von Scherenberg, F., Hellmeier, M., & Otto, B. (2024). Data sovereignty in information systems. *Electronic Markets*, *34*(1), 15. Advance online publication. DOI: 10.1007/s12525-024-00693-4

Wicki, D. (2020). The Budapest Convention and the General Data Protection Regulation: Acting in concert to curb cybercrime? *International Cybersecurity Law Review*, *1*(1-2), 63–72. DOI: 10.1365/s43439-020-00012-5

Zuboff, S. (2015). Big other: Surveillance capitalism and the prospects of an information civilization. *Journal of Information Technology*, *30*(1), 75–89. DOI: 10.1057/jit.2015.5

Zukis, B. (2022). Digital and cybersecurity governance around the world. *Annals of Corporate Governance*, *7*(1), 1–92. DOI: 10.1561/109.00000032

Zygmuntowski, J. O. (2023). Data governance in a trilemma: A qualitative analysis of rights, values, and goals in building data commons. *Digital Society : Ethics, Socio-Legal and Governance of Digital Technology*, *2*(2), 30. Advance online publication. DOI: 10.1007/s44206-023-00058-y

Chapter 5
New Sovereigns States, Corporations, and the Struggle Over Data

Sarbjit Kaur
University of Delhi, India

Radha Meena
http://orcid.org/0009-0007-4596-8145
University of Delhi, India

ABSTRACT

This chapter examines transformation of sovereignty in the digtial age by a comparative analysis of major data governance regimes existing in the world. Comparison among European Union, United States, China, India, Brazil and Africa is analysed. The chapter develops upon the different types of sovereignty models among the states. It also demonstrates about the demonstrates about the digital sovereignty and its dependency on several factors. With the rise of technology corporations have become a quasi-sovereign actors which exercises functional authority over data and digital markets and its challenge to the traditional state dominance. The reassertion and role of the states through several mediums such as legislative framework, infrastructure development is also discussed.

INTRODUCTION

Big Tech Corporations such as Apple, Amazon, Google/Alphabet, Facebook/Meta, and Microsoft, emerging as new forms of sovereignty apart from states, are referred to as 'new sovereigns' in recent literature, as their data-driven authority

DOI: 10.4018/979-8-2600-0288-9.ch005

competes with that of governments. The companies, though, have no control over the territory; own and operate critical digital infrastructure. This infrastructure includes cloud platforms, data centres, satellite networks, and identity systems, which are essential to communications, the economy, and even security. The power is handed to these companies through infrastructural control and data dominance, previously coming under the domain of the states only. On the other hand, many states are reasserting digital sovereignty through regulation or development of their own data infrastructure. China has activated the "Great Firewall," also known as the "Golden Shield Project," which controls internet traffic and the flow of information in the country (Clayton et al., 2006). The EU has declared the General Data Protection Regulation, 2016 (GDPR), as a tool for controlling data flows and reclaiming regulatory authority. Definitely, the new sovereigns have challenged traditional notions of authority, and this conceptual framework will allow us to examine how each actor uses its levers of power.

To understand how governments and tech firms claim authority over data, this Chapter examines scholarship and policy since 2019. The abovementioned tussle between the state and big tech can be realised with the evolution of law-making across jurisdictions. In 2018, the European Union's GDPR was enforced, and the United States Clarifying Lawful Overseas Use of Data (CLOUD) Act was enacted. In 2020, Brazil's data protection law *Lei Geral de Proteção de Dados* (LGPD) became effective. China's Personal Information Protection Law (PIPL), the Data Security Law (DSL), and the Cybersecurity Law (CSL) are the three main legislations for data protection in the country, enacted in 2016, 2021, and 2022, respectively. The European Union's Digital Services Act (DSA) and Digital Markets Act (DMA) were adopted in 2022, and India's Digital Personal Data Protection Act was enacted in 2023. To highlight the diverse legal and economic strategies, a comparative study of the European Union, the United States, China, India, Brazil, and Africa is conducted.

Key technological drivers, such as cloud computing, Artificial Intelligence (AI), Internet of Things (IoT), blockchain, and quantum, are reshaping the authority of power. Platform governance, private standards, ownership of infrastructure, and aggressive lobbying are some of the corporate tactics contrasted with states' countermeasures. The role of civil society is another domain that interferes with the actions of the state and big tech, serving as a countervailing force. Throughout, tensions emerge between values such as security vis-à-vis privacy, innovation vis-à-vis rights, and growth vis-à-vis accountability, which will be further elaborated upon.

The Focus of the Chapter is to understand the essential concept of new sovereigns in the digital realm by conducting a comparative study of the six jurisdictions mentioned above. The discussion is further broadened through the analysis of approximately 9 statutes and policies in these jurisdictions to identify the issues and challenges faced by them due to the emergence of Big Tech Corporations as new sovereigns. The Chapter concludes with an analysis of trends likely to occur.

CONCEPTUAL FORMULATION: 'NEW SOVEREIGNS' IN THE DIGITAL REALM

The dictionary meaning of sovereign in contemporary times is "having the highest power or being completely independent" (Hinsley, 1986) or "one possessing or held to possess supreme political power or sovereignty" (Besson, 2011) or "having unlimited power or authority" (Besson, 2011). When the historical trace is conducted, the origin of the word dates back to circa 1300; however, it had a different meaning than it does today. Moreover, as far as this chapter is concerned, the legal scholars referred to 'sovereignty' for the authority that creates the law. Richard Falk (Krieger, 1993) suggests that the historical concept of the term is of 'conceptual migration' (Besson, 2011). Though claimed to have existed since the time of Aristotle, in a different sense, the modern meaning of the term is said to have emerged with the Treaty of Westphalia in 1648. However, the credit for originally conceptualising the term goes to Jean Bodin, who in the 16th century defined sovereignty as "the absolute and perpetual power of the Republic" (Bodin, 1530-1596). In the late 18th century, the concept of sovereignty began to apply in the 'domestic' arena, as Thomas Hobbes argued in his work 'Leviathan', and the same can be traced through the writing of later scholars such as John Locke, Jean-Jacques Rousseau, Hugo Grotius, Alberico Gentili, and Francisco Suarez. The transition from internal to external sovereignty emerged in the 19th century, during which the application of sovereignty to international law was debated. Modern international law was developed in the 20th century following three world wars. The modern concept included the normative concept of sovereignty, where domestic sovereignty remains the supreme authority and ultimate power within that territory. The concept of sovereignty, as it developed historically, occurred in pairs: political and legal, domestic and international, absolute and limited, and unitary and fragmented (Besson, 2011). The international and domestic development of the concept resulted in a means of territorial boundaries. In the late 20th and early 21st century, globalisation, liberalisation, and privatisation emerged. These reforms enhanced the interaction of international and domestic actors through technological innovations and global institutions such as the United Nations (UN), the World Health Organisation (WHO), and the World Trade Organisation (WTO). The world is further integrated and interconnected as a result of technological innovations, which are enhanced due to globalisation.

Transnational platforms, data economies, and algorithmic governance are among the features of transnational digital platforms. The development of non-territorial constructions such as data, engineered algorithmic/automated decision-making, the internet, and digitalisation creates another domain of sovereignty that cannot be found in historical literature. At present, the legal and constitutional constraints/ limitations and the democratic mandate are absent, despite attempts by domestic governments to control the authority of transnational and digital data platforms. Sovereignty, in the context of such platforms, is often referred to as 'digital sovereignty' and encompasses dimensions such as data, technology, and cyber sovereignty. In contrast to the state's assertion of digital sovereignty through regulation, localisation requirements, and cybersecurity laws, the technology corporations exercise a parallel form of sovereignty through platform governance, creating a duality. Duality refers to the fragmentation of power across the policy framework, the nature of algorithms and digital codes associated with them, and much more. This duality thus results in a fragmented sovereignty landscape, distributing authority across multiple actors.

COMPARATIVE CASE STUDIES: REGIONAL STRATEGIES UNDERTAKEN TO MINIMISE DUALITY IN POWER

The duality with the parallel form of sovereignty leading to fragmentation of sovereignty among different actors is sought to be minimised by the state through law-making and policies, which will be elaborated upon in this section.

This section discusses: what steps do traditional sovereigns take to address the duality of power? And, why is there a need to minimise duality? By answering these questions, the lessons learned from studying jurisdictions worldwide are analysed. The jurisdictions referred to are the European Union, the United States, China, India, Brazil, and Africa.

European Union (EU)

The European Union is an international organisation established by the Maastricht Treaty (1993) and comprising 27 European countries, governing common economic, social, and security policies (Gabel, 2026). With the enactment of the General Data Protection Regulation (GDPR), the EU became one of the earliest and most influential models of digital governance. Exercising the legitimate and authoritative source and power in law is considered to be an example of 'normative sovereign' (Lindahl, 2001). In other words, it means a power that shapes global standards through law, either through territorial control or technological dominance (Green, n.d.). The EU exemplifies the emergence of 'new sovereigns' in the digital domain. Questions that arise: whether the EU's approach to digital governance can compete with both state-centric and corporate-driven paradigms? Can the EU be a central actor in redefining sovereignty in the digital age?

It is important to reiterate that the concept of 'normative power Europe', i.e., the EU's influence on global governance through the export of legal norms and standards, remains its key strategy (Wunderlich, 2025). Three interrelated dimensions- regulatory sovereignty, data sovereignty and strategic autonomy remain key to digital sovereignty in the EU (Czerniawski, 2025). To elaborate further, regulatory sovereignty refers to the state's capacity to create, implement, and enforce rules that shape behaviour within and beyond its jurisdiction. The EU's operation through market-access conditionality, rather than territorial coercion, allows such a dimension to exist. In contrast to classical sovereignty, which involves enforcement through borders and state apparatus, EU rules must be complied with for access to the internal market; therefore, transforming regulation into a powerful extraterritorial tool (Tamim, 2024). Now, recognizing data as more than an economic asset and treating it as a strategic and political resource introduces the concept of data sovereignty. The digital economy defines power in terms of control over data, which is equivalent to control over knowledge and behaviour, ultimately leading to power. The EU's conceptualisation of data sovereignty is dual: individual data sovereignty empowers individuals with rights over their personal data, and collective/institutional data sovereignty ensures that the EU's norms govern data generated within the EU. Therefore, the EU model is distinguished by this dual approach from both laissez-faire (i.e., market-driven) and authoritarian frameworks. Recognising that regulation in isolation is insufficient for sovereignty, therefore, strategic autonomy is also enunciated. As true digital sovereignty requires the capacity to design, produce, and control the technological infrastructure, this marks a shift from normative power to material capability in the EU. To summarise, the EU's digital strategy reflects an effort to reclaim control from both foreign technological corporations and fragmented national regimes, and thereby, consolidating sovereignty at the supranational level, i.e. beyond its territorial reach.

The General Data Protection Regulation (GDPR)

Enforcement of GDPR dates back to 2018, and it is considered a regulatory instrument and widely considered as the most comprehensive and influential data protection framework across the globe (Regulation (EU) 2016/679). Here, we ponder whether it has developed a constitutional moment in digital governance. What are the core elements of sovereignty in the digital age according to this Regulation?

This section discusses the answers to these questions and the philosophical and constitutional foundations.

The Regulation is grounded in the recognition of data protection as a fundamental right. Article 8 of the EU Charter of Fundamental Rights reflects this position of data protection (2000/c 364/01), ensuring that "everyone has the right to the protection of personal data concerning him or her", "such data must be processed fairly for specified purposes" and "compliance with the rules shall be subject to control by an independent authority" (2000/c 364/01). The EU frames the right to privacy as an intrinsic human right tied to dignity, autonomy and identity. Thereby, it can be stated that the rights-based approach distinguishes the GDPR from market-driven regulatory models in a digital society. The philosophy reinforces the concept of "informational self-determination", which stems from the German Constitutional Court's 1983 ruling, that is enshrining the individuals' autonomy to decide how their personal information is shared (Elliot et al., 2024). The GDPR, however, has transformed this abstract principle into an enforceable legal right by reconceptualising individuals as active agents in the data ecosystem, leading to the empowerment of passive data subjects.

Additionally, the Regulation embodies a shift, through Article 3, from traditional sovereignty, which was bound by geographic boundaries, to a transnational approach, as data is transnational, thereby challenging nation-states' regulatory capacity. Article 3, titled "territorial scope", applies the regulation/GDPR to the processing of personal data, whether it takes place in the EU or not (Regulation (EU) 2016/679). Therefore, introducing the extraterritorial characteristic to the regulation and making it transnational in operation. The extension of regulatory reach beyond its physical territory resulted in the "Brussels effect" (Bradford, 2019). Therefore, the EU acts as a normative sovereign, setting global data protection standards that multinational corporations must comply with regardless of their home jurisdiction (Bradford, 2019). Thus, the regulation is an instance of how sovereignty in the digital age is no longer monopolised by the nation-state but instead exercised through regulatory frameworks that influence global market behaviour.

Apart from the protection of personal data and extraterritorial scope, what is the position of corporations? The regulation strengthens the state and also reveals the enduring power of corporations as quasi-sovereign actors. What kind of companies/corporations remain under consideration? Companies such as Google, Meta Platforms, and Amazon operate across jurisdictions and therefore have the ability to control vast amounts of their users' data, infrastructure, and algorithmic systems. However, the regulation imposes penalties and accountability mechanisms, which include heavy administrative fines, consent requirements, and transparency obligations. However, the question remains whether it is practical to enforce the regulation's penalties? Enforcement is definitely hindered by several challenges, including uneven enforcement, constrained by jurisdictional complexities and resource asymmetries between regulators and corporations. This dynamic underscores a central tension in the new sovereign's framework: while states seek to regulate their subjects, corporations retain significant *de facto* sovereignty through their control over digital architectures they have created.

Cross-border data transfers involving subjects in different jurisdictions reflect broader concerns about the strategic and technological autonomy of states, and the regulations enacted by traditional sovereigns/states take this into consideration. It is done by restricting the transfer of personal data outside the EU unless the receiving country ensures an "adequate" level of protection in their own jurisdiction. This, therefore, led to significant legal and geopolitical developments across jurisdictions. The legal and geopolitical developments include the invalidation of transatlantic data transfer frameworks in cases such as *Maximillian Schrems* v *Data Protection Commissioner,* 2015 *(Schrems I)* and *Data Protection Commissioner* v *Facebook Ireland Ltd., 2020 (Schrems II).* Both decisions highlighted the EU's insistence on maintaining sovereignty over its citizens' data, even in the face of the USA, a powerful ally. The cases also demonstrated the courts' key role in the governance of digital sovereignty, particularly regarding transatlantic data transfers. If it is seen from a comparative perspective, the EU's approach differs from China's data localisation regime, which prioritises state security and control over data transfer and from India's evolving data protection framework, which balances its sovereignty concerns with economic interests (Mishra & Agarwal, 2026), which will be discussed in detail in a later section. The GDPR not only reflects a model of regulated openness that allows data flows while tightly controlling them by the state, but also reflects a model of regulated openness that allows data flows while tightly controlling them by the state.

The global influence of the regulation has been significant since its enforcement, not only in its implemented jurisdiction but also across the globe. Countries around the world have adopted legislation inspired by the GDPR. These include Brazil's LGPD and certain aspects of India's Digital Personal Data Protection Act, 2023, resulting in the Brussels effect, demonstrating how regulatory power can translate the same into normative sovereignty. The EU has effectively compelled global corporations to adopt its rules universally, even when compliance standards are high and are framed from the mindset of a developed state. Therefore, through such provisions, it can avoid the fragmentation of corporate operations and ensure universal applicability of the regulation. Here, the questions that emerge for our consideration are: whether GDPR represents a new form of regulatory imperialism? Or, does it provide a rights-based global public good? The answer lies in how laws are adapted across different jurisdictions and in the reinterpretation of GDPR principles within their domestic contexts.

The limitations of this regulation are several, including compliance burden, enforcement gaps, substantive consent issues, and technological lag, which have also led to reduced data (Yaraghi, 2018). Small and medium enterprises remain the most affected, as they often struggle to meet compliance costs, raising concerns about market concentration and entry barriers. Across the EU, national data protection capacities vary across different state authorities, leading to inconsistent enforcement. Further, the critics may argue that the consent mechanisms are often reduced to a "click-through" formalities, which undermine the regulation's normative goals. Another criticism revolves around the technological aspect. Rapid advancements in artificial intelligence, big data analytics, and surveillance technologies often challenge the effectiveness and relevance of regulations by superseding the conditions under which they were enacted.

GDPR exemplifies the emergence of multi-layered sovereignty in the digital age, where the authority is distributed among states, individuals, corporations, and courts (Spalević & Vićentijević, 2022). It demonstrated that states can assert control through regulatory innovation, that individuals can be empowered as rights-bearing actors, that corporations remain powerful quasi-sovereigns, and that global governance emerges through norm diffusion and legal contestation. In the broader struggle over data, the regulation does not resolve tensions between these actors; rather, it institutionalises them within a complex legal framework. It is, however, possible to understand sovereignty reimagination in an invisible territorial context where data over territory remains the primary site of power.

Digital Services Act 2022 (DSA)

The EU's Digital Services Act, enacted in 2022, aims to reclaim public authority over private digital orders (Regulation (EU) 2022/2065). The private digital orders include the roles assumed by the private regulators of digital space, ranging from media to online marketplaces. The roles include rule-making, adjudication, and enforcement across platforms ranging from social media to online marketplaces. These platforms mediate communication, commerce, and information flows. Unlike earlier regulatory frameworks, which were focused primarily on data protection, this Act addresses the systemic governance of online intermediaries, including content moderation, algorithmic transparency, and platform accountability (Regulation (EU) 2022/2065). Therefore, this section examines whether DSA 2022 exemplifies a normative and regulatory model of digital sovereignty. A model where the state seeks to assert control over corporate actors while simultaneously empowering users as rights-bearing participants in a platform ecosystem enunciated by new sovereigns.

Digital platforms were originally conceptualised as neutral transmitters, but their evolution into centralised gatekeepers of information and interaction has fundamentally altered their role in shaping that information. Now, the platforms determine what content is visible or suppressed. They establish community standards and rules and enforce sanctions, including account suspension and content removal (Gillespie, 2018). The functions of these digital platforms mirror core attributes of sovereignty, leading scholars to characterise them as "quasi-sovereign" entities (Gillespie, 2018), as they exercise regulatory authority over vast amounts of demographic data. Whereas the Act operates within a framework of functional sovereignty, which involves a defined authority controlling specific territorial domains. Digital platforms, including Meta and Google, exercise authority through algorithmic systems that shape user behaviour, public discourse and economic transactions, an algorithmic governance, which is often opaque and without any territorial restrictions. Concerns, such as accountability bias and democratic legitimacy, have been raised about these platforms. Therefore, this Act directly targets the opacity of algorithmic governance and seeks to promote transparency by subjecting algorithmic systems to public oversight.

A differentiated regulatory response to intermediaries is required due to their uneven distribution of power. The Act seeks to achieve such a response through its core objectives, which are interrelated and consist of enhancing user safety and fundamental rights, ensuring platform accountability, and maintaining a transparent and trustworthy digital environment, as mentioned under its Recital, which is numbered 12 (Regulation (EU) 2022/2065). These objectives situate the Act within a broader project of digital constitutionalism, meaning that legal norms govern the exercise of power in digital spaces. Further, the Act establishes standardised procedures for the removal of illegal content, which aims to balance freedom of expression with the need to combat harmful content under Article 9, para 1-6 (Regulation (EU) 2022/2065). This is done when platforms implement the mechanisms that enable users to report illegal content. Thus, this can help achieve timely, reasoned removal decisions and safeguard against arbitrary or excessive censorship. The law introduces, under Article 22, the concept of "trusted flaggers," under which reports will be prioritised for entities with expertise in identifying illegal content (Regulation (EU) 2022/2065). A hybrid governance model is created by introducing such provisions that involve both public and private actors as trusted flaggers. The Act further allows for coordinated responses at the EU level in situations of systemic risk involving disinformation during elections or public health crises. Therefore, a need for oversight is reflected in an emerging understanding of platforms as critical infrastructure that requires oversight, similar to that of traditional public utilities. By mandating that the platforms explain the main parameters of their algorithms and provide users with alternative, non-profiling-based options, the Act allows content curation and its presentation. It also indicates that a significant intervention, such as the "monitoring action" mentioned under Article 72, targets the informational power of algorithms, which, for a long time, operated as opaque "black boxes".

It also imposes strict transparency requirements on online advertising, including: identification of the advertiser, disclosure of targeting data, and a prohibition on certain forms of sensitive data-based targeting. The concerns regarding manipulation, surveillance, and political influence, particularly involving micro-targeted advertising, are addressed. Additionally, the Very Large Online Platforms (VLOPs) and very large online search engines explicitly mentioned under Article 33 are required to conduct annual risk assessments; however, under Article 29, a leeway is provided to micro and small enterprises in certain circumstances (Regulation (EU) 2022/2065). It addresses the dissemination of illegal content, the impact on fundamental rights and the risks to public security and democratic processes. They must also implement mitigation measures, which are subject to independent audits. Furthermore, building on the rights-based approach of the EU law, it also strengthens the position of users within platform ecosystems. The procedural rights granted by the Act to users are several, including the right to receive reasons for content moderation decisions, access to internal systems for handling complaints, and the ability to seek redress outside the court. It further provides protection against the consent mechanisms which are deceptive by explicitly prohibiting manipulative interface designs under Article 25 (Regulation (EU) 2022/2065). Also, as the number of users increases, individuals have emerged as 'micro sovereigns' who can demand the enforcement of their rights in digital spaces, which are privately governed by corporations with the help of this Act (Helberger et al., 2017). With regard to enforcement and institutional design, the Act establishes multi-level governance that includes National Digital Services Coordinators (NDSCs) under Chapter IV, Section 1, and the European Commission for VLOPs (Regulation (EU) 2022/2065; European Commission, 2022). The sanctions under the Act for non-compliance include significant fines and corrective measures to ensure that platforms internalise the costs of regulatory violations (Regulation (EU) 2022/2065).

As a result of this regulatory framework by the EU, it can be said to be an attempt by the state authority to regain power over corporate governance in digital spaces (Kaye, 2019) and to regulate it accordingly. The legal obligations on platforms that challenge their autonomy as private regulators are a clear sign of the reassertion of the state's power (Bradford, 2019). However, the effectiveness of the Act depends on the State's enforcement capacity, corporate compliance, and technological adaptability. It can be said that significant structural power lies in the hands of corporations, particularly when they control infrastructure and innovation. It represents a pivotal moment in the evolution of digital governance. As the platforms can no longer operate as unchecked private sovereigns, states can reclaim authority through innovative frameworks, and users can be empowered as active participants in digital ecosystems.

Digital Markets Act, 2022 (DMA)

The Digital Markets Act was adopted in 2022 and took effect in 2023. Contrary to DSA (2022), it represents a decisive regulatory intervention aimed at rebalancing power asymmetries in the global economy through digitisation (Regulation (EU) 2022/1925). Asymmetry of power arises when a small number of technology firms control key digital infrastructure. Search engines, app stores, social networks, and cloud services enable the exchange of vast amounts of data and economic activity. Therefore, unlike traditional competition law, which addresses anti-competitive conduct ex post, this law introduces an ex ante regulatory framework designed to prevent abuses before they occur (Regulation (EU) 2022/1925). Therefore, in this section, the question for discussion is whether the Act exemplifies a form of economic digital sovereignty? What is the role of the regulatory authority which is deployed? Is it to discipline the corporate "sovereigns" and restore contestability in digital markets? Further, it will highlight how control over data and infrastructure has become central to sovereignty in the digital age.

Digital platforms have evolved into multi-sided markets that connect users, advertisers, developers, and businesses. This ecosystem enables them to set rules for market participation, prioritise their own services (i.e., self-preferencing), and aggregate and exploit vast datasets (Bradford, 2019). The VLOPs further exemplify the platform-based dominance. Therefore, such corporations are allowed to govern economic activity within their ecosystems that exist without any external restrictions. Further, the data is concentrated with VLOPs and other corporations, which leads to the dominance of such corporations in the market, providing ultimate power to those possessing 'control over data'. Such network effects, economies of scale, and data-driven personalisation create barriers to entry that competitors find difficult to overcome.

The platforms designated as "gatekeepers" are those that have a significant impact on the internal market, control a core platform service, and have a large and stable user base, as defined under Article 2 and the designation set out in Article 3 of the Act. Their services include online search engines, social networking services, app stores, operating systems and online marketplaces (Regulation (EU) 2022/1925). The Act distinguishes itself from GDPR in terms of applicability and recognises that not all platforms pose equal risks (Crémer et al., 2019). Therefore, the framers/legislators of the Act considered that regulatory intervention should focus on those with systemic influence (Crémer et al., 2019). Nonetheless, a departure from traditional competition law is evident in the adoption of a preventive regulatory approach that imposes predefined obligations and prohibitions on gatekeepers (Khan, 2017). This shift marks a move toward rule-based governance, enhancing predictability and enforcement efficiency (Crémer et al., 2019). The methods used for the enhancement include prohibitions such as self-referencing, data-use restrictions, and interoperability, as well as the imposition of fair conditions for the access and portability of data (Regulation (EU) 2022/1925). The Act prohibits gatekeepers from favouring their own services over competitors, and these practices include ranking proprietary services higher in search results and pre-installing and privileging default applications on devices. Through such practices, competition is distorted, and market dominance is entrenched. The Act also limits the ability of gatekeepers to combine personal data across services without consent and to use data of business users to compete (Regulation (EU) 2022/1925) against them to curtail the unfair use of the data. Therefore, recognising that data asymmetries underpin competitive advantage (Crémer et al., 2019). Additionally, gatekeepers must ensure interoperability with third-party services, as defined under Article 2, and the portability of user data across platforms, as mentioned under Article 6 (Regulation (EU) 2022/1925). Through such provisions, the Act aims to reduce lock-in effects and enhance user choice, thereby promoting market contestability/competition. Other provisions of the law require gatekeepers to provide fair and non-discriminatory access to their platforms and to offer transparent terms for business users. This is because such obligations seek to dismantle structural barriers to entry. These provisions challenge corporate autonomy on dominant platforms, reassert public authority over private economic governance, restore market pluralism and redefine the capacity to maintain open and competitive markets (Crémer et al., 2019). Primarily, the European Commission enforces the law through sanctions, including fines, as well as structural remedies such as divestitures under Article 31 of the Act. Gatekeepers are continuously monitored through reporting obligations and compliance audits mandated by the Act under Articles 15, 23, and 35 (Regulation (EU) 2022/1925). The corporations have adapted to the law but also resisted it due to reservations. The adaptations in Act involve modifications to app store policies, adjustments to data-sharing practices, and increased transparency. However, these changes are often incremental and strategically calibrated by the corporations. Both legal and political resistance from the gatekeepers is also present. Legal challenges to designations and obligations under the Act, and lobbying efforts by corporations to influence its implementation, continue to hinder its implementation. Ultimately, these dynamics between traditional and new sovereigns highlight the digital sovereignty negotiated, in which regulation is contested and reshaped by powerful actors.

The Act is criticised, and it is argued that strict regulations may deter innovation when firms are limited in their ability to leverage scale and data (Crémer et al., 2019). The Act imposes detailed obligations that may create compliance challenges, particularly in a rapidly evolving technological environment (Crémer et al., 2019). The global platforms may adapt their operations to exploit differences in compliance across jurisdictions, thereby undermining the effectiveness of the regulation. Like

GDPR, this Act has the potential to extend the Brussels effect into competition policy when companies align their practices with EU requirements, leading to global standards for platform governance.

To conclude, this Act represents a transformative moment in the governance of digital economies and demonstrates that market power in the digital age is inseparable from data control and platform infrastructure. Thus, it may cause the corporations to function as economic sovereigns (Peitz & Motta, 2020). In contrast, it can be said that the states can still persist in reasserting their authority over the new sovereign, and this can be achieved through innovative and preventive laws and regulations (Varian, 2018). In the economic domain, this Act is an example that highlights the ongoing contest between state public regulation and corporate power. It can be concluded that sovereignty is not merely about territory, but about the entities that control the rules of digital markets and manage the data that sustains them.

United States of America (USA)

In contrast to the EU model, the USA model focuses on a market-oriented, sectoral, and fragmented approach to the governance of data. A deeper constitutional, economic, and ideological commitment, in particular to free markets, innovation, and limited state intervention, is reflected in this model. In the USA, corporations play a dominant role because sovereignty over data is not centralised within the state but is distributed across multiple actors. This section analyses the Clarifying Lawful Overseas Use of Data Act 2018 (CLOUD Act) to answer the question: what kind of model for digital sovereignty is represented in the USA? In what manner does the enforcement of the USA model take place? Do private actors play a key role in this model?

Economic liberalism remains the basis of the USA's approach, in which markets are considered the primary mechanism for regulating behaviour. The state intervention is selective and present to correct market failures or prevent harm. This results in the emergence of "market sovereignty", where private corporations rather than public institutions largely exercise authority over data and digital infrastructure. Here, corporations are the dominant sovereigns due to their control over data collection and processing, platform infrastructures and algorithmic decision-making systems. This is additionally enhanced by the network effects, economies of scale, and data accumulation, enabling them to function as quasi-sovereign actors within digital ecosystems.

Clarifying Lawful Overseas Use of Data Act 2018 (CLOUD Act)

In the USA, the defining feature is the absence of a unified federal data protection law. Instead, regulation is organised around a sectoral model where different statutes govern different data types. For instance, the health data under the Health Insurance Portability and Accountability Act (HIPAA) 1966, the financial data under the Gram-Leach-Bliley Act (GLBA) 1999, children's data under the Children's Online Privacy Protection Act (COPPA) 1998, and educational records under the Family Educational Rights and Privacy Act (FERPA) 1974 (Rothmann, 2024). In contrast to the EU's 2016 omnibus GDPR, protections are dependent on data categorisation rather than on a universal right to privacy (Swindle, 2002).

With the rise of globalisation, the storage of data in the cloud has posed a profound challenge to traditional legal frameworks governing jurisdiction, surveillance, and law enforcement access (Landesberg, 1998). The data stored is relevant to criminal investigations and is stored across multiple jurisdictions in an interconnected world which is being outside the territorial boundaries of the investigating state (Anix, 2026). This existing fact has made the conventional mechanisms inadequate for instance Mutual Legal Assistance Treaties (MLATs), which are crticised on being slow and procedurally cumbersome (National Privacy Authority, 2024). To tackle the disavantages of conventional mechanisms the USA enacted the CLOUD Act in 2018 as an amendment to the Stored Communications Act. The Act, therefore, representing a significant proclamation by state authority over transnational data flows (Anix, 2026). The Act enables the law enforcement agencies to disclose data from domestic service providers, regardless of its jurisdiction. Therefore, in this section, the role of the Act is examined which prioritises law enforcement and national security objectives over territorial limitations. Therefore, the question to ponder is - can this kind of legislation lead to superseding the sovereignty claims of other legitimate states?

As discussed previously, traditional legal frameworks are centred on the principle that jurisdiction is territorially bounded; however, cloud computing disrupts this paradigm by decoupling data from physical location. When a single dataset is distributed across servers in multiple countries, it is difficult to determine which state has legitimate authority over these datasets. The Act addresses these challenges by refining jurisdiction in a personal rather than territorial sense and focusing on the location and control of the service provider rather than the data itself. In this framework, sovereignty is understood as the ability to compel service providers to grant access to data, rather than control over territory. The reconceptualisation by the Act therefore aligns with broader trends in digital governance, in which authority is increasingly exercised through control over information flows and the enhancement of the power in the hands of new sovereigns over state sovereigns. To reassert the control of the State, there are specific provisions under the Act.

The provisions on extraterritorial reach, executive agreements, and comity analysis are considered the core of the legislation and are mentioned in Section 102. The Act authorises law enforcement agencies to require service providers under US jurisdiction to produce data stored abroad whenever they require it. The result of this provision is that it extends US legal authority into foreign jurisdictions and creates a framework for bilateral executive agreements as provided under Section 105 of the Act. Such agreements allow foreign governments to request the data directly from US companies (Abraha, 2019). Thus, it reflects a shift toward a networked sovereignty in which states cooperate to manage cross-border data access as needed. The Act includes provisions that allow companies to challenge data requests that are in conflict with foreign laws, and in such circumstances, courts play a key role (Abraha, 2019). They may conduct a comity analysis by balancing US interests against those of the foreign jurisdiction; however, this is considered to be a limited mechanism for managing conflicts over sovereignty (Abraha, 2019). Here, critics may argue that it remains heavily in favour of US interests (Abraha, 2019) due to the tilt toward national interests by corporations, courts, and legislators of the same nationality.

This law is centred on technology companies, which remain the primary focus of cross-border data governance. Under the Act, the intermediaries between the state authority and individuals' data are technology firms such as Microsoft, Google, and Amazon. Various ways in which corporate intermediation is carried out include delegated sovereignty, corporate resistance, and negotiations. Private actors are responsible for following up on government orders; they are mandated to assess the legality of requests made to them, navigate conflicts arising across jurisdictions, and implement technical systems to ensure data access. This results in a hybrid model where the state has delegated its power to private actors, thus producing a shared or co-produced sovereignty by states and corporations.

The *United States* v *Microsoft Corporation* (2018) can be cited as the origin of the Act. In this case, Microsoft challenges US government warrants seeking data stored outside its jurisdiction. Thus, forcing Microsoft to provide the data of an individual located outside the US. Microsoft argued that the government lacked sufficient grounds to seek such data and that the customer's privacy could not be breached. The Court accepted the argument. and it was also upheld by court. The relevance of this case is also important because the court's intervention was sought for a law which was enacted before the interconnected world that exists as of yet (Daskal, 2018). In the same year, i.e., 2018, the Act was enacted, requiring the service provider to comply with its obligations and to provide data stored by it within or outside the United States (*United States* v *Microsoft Corp.*, 2018). Now, it can be said that the Act is a negotiated settlement between state and corporate power, in which corporations influence legislative frameworks. The Act not only remains a ground of legal disputes but also remains a point of tension among foreign regimes, as it supersedes their sovereign authority. For instance, the European Union data protection framework upheld the rights-based approach and emphasised the privacy and territorial integrity. If the data requests under the Act are to be followed, obligations under the EU regulations will be in conflict. Therefore, legal uncertainty will arise for companies operating in both jurisdictions, potentially leading to "overlapping claims" over the same data. Overstepping the sovereignty of other jurisdictions and leaving it unresolved under the Act can create a gap for negotiation and legal balancing, potentially necessitating an institutional framework in the future.

National security, criminal investigation, and intelligence gathering are prioritised under the Act, which conflicts with the EU's rights-based approach (Daskal, 2018). Therefore, critics argue that the Act may undermine the privacy protections by facilitating cross-border surveillance without specifying any adequate safeguards (Daskal, 2018). The concerns under the Act are its opacity, limited judicial oversight of foreign requests, and the potential for partner governments to abuse the Act. It can therefore be emphasised that state power and security, which legitimately spark global debates over cross-border data access, can also encourage other states to develop similar frameworks. Another trend that could emerge from this Act is a broader shift towards bilateral and multilateral cooperation in digital governance.

Extraterritorial overreach, corporate burden, and insufficient safeguards are some of the disadvantages of the Act (Swire & Hemmings, 2016). An assertion of US legal imperialism is explicit in the Act, which allows the US to enter foreign territories without their consent (Swire & Hemmings, 2016), further creating difficulties for corporations when legal obligations conflict across jurisdictions. It lacks protections for privacy and due process, particularly in the context of foreign government requests, and this remains hard to digest.

Definitely, the Act represents a critical development in the evolution of digital sovereignty towards networked and negotiated digital sovereignty (Swire & Hemmings, 2016). Through this Act, it can be seen that sovereignty in the digital age is defined by access to data rather than control over territory, the extraterritorial extension of states' authority to achieve their security objectives, and the assignment of corporations as intermediaries in the exercise of sovereign power (Swire & Hemmings, 2016). This Act highlights state authority, corporate control, and global legal conflict by underscoring that the struggle over data is not only about governance and markets but also about security, surveillance, and the limitations faced by state power in a digital world without territorial limits (Woods, 2016).

China

The most distinctive and assertive model of digital governance in the contemporary world is seen in China. Unlike the rights-based or market-oriented approaches of the above jurisdictions, China has developed a state-centric framework for digital sovereignty, in which digital platforms are controlled and integrated with national security, political authority, and economic strategy. The Cybersecurity Law of the People's Republic of China, the Data Security Law of the People's Republic of China (DSL), and the Personal Information Protection Law, 2021 (PIPL) are three comprehensive Laws that are institutionalised by China's state-centric model. All these laws create a regulatory ecosystem that governs data collection, processing, storage, and transfer across jurisdictions.

This section analyses China's model of digital governance and the roles of state, corporates, and the individual rights in achieving political and security objectives, by examining China's legislative framework regarding digital infrastructure.

Cybersecurity Law, 2016 (CSL)

The Cybersecurity Law, though enacted in 2016, was enforced in 2017, becoming one of the earliest legal frameworks and a foundational pillar of China's digital governance architecture. It has also been amended in 2025, which mainly strengthened the penalty regime. The unamended CSL is also considered to be an attempt by a major state to institutionalise its control over cyberspace through a unified legal framework. While subsequent laws such as DSL (2021) and PIPL (2021) have refined and expanded the framework, Cybersecurity Law remains the central pillar to understand China's approach to digital sovereignty. In this section, the role of this Law is analysed, along with China's adopted model.

This Law is enshrined in China's doctrine of cyber sovereignty, which emphasises upon State's power and authority to regulate and control the internet within its territorial boundaries. This doctrine rejects idea of a borderless internet by reaffirming territorial sovereignty over digital infrastructure which can be interpreted through the provisions under Chapter 3 Section 2, consisting of operations security for critical information infrastructure, state authority over information flows and the legitimacy of national regulatory frameworks mentioned under Chapter 5 (Articles 51-58) of the law, legal responsibilities on the network operator under Chapter 6 (Articles 59-75). Cybersecurity law extends the traditional concepts of sovereignty into the digital domain by emphasising control over data rather than openness of data. Furthermore, infrastructure governance under Article 2 is another defining feature. Here, it can be emphasised that sovereignty is not merely exercised through laws or rights, but it can also be exercised through control of networks, servers, and technical systems. This suggests a shift from a legal to techno-legal sovereignty, an approach in which state authority is embedded in both the regulation and infrastructure. Such regulation applies to network operators, which consist virtually of entities operating networks and Critical Information Infrastructure (CII) operators. This expansive scope, therefore, ensures that the law under discussion covers nearly all digital activity in China. Further, the law pursues multiple objectives such as safeguarding national security, protecting critical infrastructure, maintaining social order and promoting secure digital development. Its objectives, therefore, reflect the integration of security, governance and economic policy.

To obtain localisation of data and territorial sovereignty, there are certain significant provisions, e.g., Article 37 of the CSL, which mandates data localization by CII operators regarding personal and sensitive data. A security assessment is required under Article 38, and regulatory approval by national authorities is required if the data is to be used outside China for any business purpose. The data localisation reinforces territorial sovereignty over digital assets and this is presumed to ensure that data generated in the country remains accessible to domestic authorities so that reliance on foreign infrastructure can be reduced and strategic autonomy can be enhanced. Apart from the state access, the network operators which are mentioned under Article 39, are obligated to provide the technical support to security agencies to assist in investigations and retain logs and data for specified periods so that it can accessed whenever required. Therefore, these obligations lead to institutionalisation of state access to data and embed surveillance capabilities within the legislative/legal framework. The Law includes provisions that protect personal information and the lawful rights of citizens, which are mentioned in Articles 1, 12, 14, and 43, but the rights remain secondary to state security objectives. It can be interpreted that the balance between privacy and security is tilted in favour of the state. This is also because the Law imposes obligations on platforms to monitor and remove prohibited content, prevent the dissemination of information that threatens social stability and enforce real-name registration systems. Similar to the US legislation, in the CSL the system of co-regulation emerges in which private actors are provided with the responsibility for implementing state policies. Apart from this, the Companies such as Tencent and Alibaba Group play a key role in content governance, and they are acting as intermediaries who enforce state rules as obligated by the CSL. A model of delegated sovereignty is created by this Law in which corporate actors function as an extension of the state authority rather than independent regulators without any interference. This has resemblance with the United States legislative framework which provides similar positioning to corporations.

CII includes sectors such as energy, finance, telecommunications, transportation, and public services and the operators in these sectors are subject to enhanced regulatory obligations. They are mandated to conduct regular security assessments, implement robust cybersecurity measures, and ensure supply chain security, as mentioned under Articles 31-39 of the CSL. These provisions recognise digital infrastructure as an essential element to national security and sovereignty but from corporate perspective, their positioning remains subordinate to the state authority. This is due to mandates including data localisation requirements, government access requests, and content regulation requirements under the CSL which needs to be complied with. It is unlike the US, where corporations often act as independent sovereigns but in China relationship between the state and corporations can be described as embedded governance, in which corporations drive economic activity while the state retains the ultimate control. Therefore, in China's model, the corporate capabilities are integrated into a broader framework of state sovereignty but they remain subordinate and under control and surveillance of state authority.

The challenges that are tied to Cybersecurity Law are human rights, economic and global fragmentation. The Law enables extensive surveillance, restrictions on freedom of expression and limited judicial oversight, thus violating human rights of an individual. The economic implications of the Law include increased compliance costs, limited cross-border innovation, and the barriers to foreign companies. China's approach has contributed to the emergence of a "splinternet" which involves fragmentation of internet and controlled network by restricting it across national territory for their national interest. Despite criticism, the model of China has influenced across the globe and the elements that influenced other countries are data localisation and infrastructure regulation, which are increasingly adopted worldwide. The China's model advocates for a competing model of the digital sovereignty over a single global standard.

The above discussion suggests that the Cybersecurity Law of China is a powerful example of how sovereignty can be reasserted through control over digital infrastructure and data flows. It demonstrates that sovereignty in the digital age is deeply connected to technical systems and infrastructure. Also, the state can maintain dominance through integration of legal and technological control. From a corporate perspective, it will bring them under a hierarchy framework of governance which can result in bureaucratic hurdles and complications in regulations (Khanal, Zhang, & Taeihagh, 2026). This Law is an instance of the state's persistence in sustaining state-centric authority even when digital technologies have transformed the nature of power through digital platforms. This model provides that it is important to understand that the control of the system which sustains the digital world is given primary value over the markets or rights. Here, the state authority remains the controller of this system.

Data Security Law, 2021 (DSL)

The Data Security Law was enacted in 2021 and this marks a critical evolution in China's digital regulatory architecture. While the above discussion suggests that Cybersecurity Law's focus is primarily on network and infrastructure security, the discussion on the DSL expands the scope of governance to data as a strategic resource. A framework for regulating the collection, processing, classification, and cross-border transfer of data is set out in Article 1 of the Law. The DSL reflects a shift in the concepts, and therefore, it is important to understand this shift by studying this statute. The elements of the Law and its exemplification is discussed in this section.

With the evolution of data and its growing importance, China is approaching the view that data generated within a state's jurisdiction is a national resource, subject to sovereign control. It is different from liberal models as found in the US, which treat data as a commodity and its governance is through market forces; this model, rather, integrates the data into state planning and security frameworks, as seen in China. A shift from territorial sovereignty to functional sovereignty has occurred in this model where authority is exercised through data classification, control over processing activities and regulation of cross-border flows is done. The DSL controls the information systems, which is similar to other jurisdictions rather than control over physical territory alone. It is evident from Article 2 applying the statute to all entities and individuals who are engaged in data activities within or outside China which threaten its national security or public interest. This extraterritorial jurisdiction creates a concept of sovereignty which seems to be expansive in nature. But, this Law takes into account multiple goals, such as, safeguarding national security, promoting data development and utilisation of this data, protecting lawful rights and interests, and establishing a comprehensive governance system, comprehended from Articles 2, 4, 5, 6, 8, 21, 24, 25, 35, and 48 which integrate security, economic policy and governance.

This categorisation of data by the importance it holds to the national security, economic and social significance, and potential risk, is mentioned in Article 21. Data, as per this law, is broadly divided into ordinary data, important data and core state data; however, the definition of such terms is not explicitly mentioned anywhere in this legislation, though such classification is considered to be significant. Such a classification system also enables the state to exercise differentiated control in prioritising the protection of critical data. It transforms data governance into a system of sovereign control, divided into tiers, with the level of regulation determined by the perceived importance of the data. It also provides for a governance framework in which the central government leads, and regulatory authorities coordinate. Such a transformation of sovereign authorities in line with the need for data governance underscores its importance and makes it a core function of the state.

Data activities affecting state interests are inspected under the ‘National Security Review Procedure’, which includes risk assessment and approval required for sensitive activities. The existing mechanism in the CSL is preventive and strict. Preventive mechanisms controls data-related risks, whereas strict mechanisms restricts cross-border data transfers by critical infrastructure operators. Such transfers may require security assessment and government approval. It also applies to foreign entities expanding into multiple jurisdictions that engage in data activities in China, thereby ensuring territorial and strategic control over critical data. Corporations are obligated to establish data security management systems, conduct risk assessments, report incidents, and comply with classification requirements. Take the examples of Alibaba Group and Tencent, which operate within an embedded governance framework, as seen earlier, distinct from the US model, where corporations often act as independent regulators. The Law under Chapter VI (Articles 45-52) provides for significant fines, suspension of operations and revocation of licenses. There are serious violations that may result in criminal penalties, reinforcing the coercive power of the Law. There are strong enforcement mechanisms which underscore the capacity of the state to enforce compliance and maintain control over data ecosystems, highlighting the manner in which this Law integrates security, sovereignty, and economic policy, by distinguishing it from both the EU and US models.

The criticism of the Law is surrounded in its ambiguous and its inability to provide clear definitions of some important terms. There are ambiguities in definitions, such as “important data” and “core data”, which are not clearly defined. It creates uncertainty for businesses when it imposes significant obligations on companies under Chapter IV, in particular to those operating internationally. The state has the control over individual privacy and freedom despite this it is influential among countries who want to maintain greater control over data. The concepts widely discussed as a result of this Law are Law is data localisation, security reviews and state authority, which has shaped the concept of digital sovereignty since its enactment.

This Law can be considered a significant step in the evolution of the digital governance model in China and around the world. Three important things are demonstrated through the Law (Ding, 2018). One, the data can be treated as a strategic national resource. Second, sovereignty can be exercised by classifying and controlling how the data is transferred or transmitted. Third, the state authority can be maintained by integrating legal, technical, and economic tools. These three concluding remarks illustrate how state power can be reasserted in the digital age: when data is prioritised over territorial restrictions, it becomes the central object of sovereignty.

Personal Information Protection Law, 2021 (PIPL)

The Personal Information Protection Law was enacted in 2021 and is considered China's first comprehensive data protection statute, often compared to the EU's GDPR. It establishes a framework for regulating and processing personal information, and also introduces concepts such as consent, purpose limitation, and data subject rights. It operates within a broader legal ecosystem shaped by the Cybersecurity Law and the Data Security Law, both of which prioritise security and state authority, as elaborated in an earlier section (Creemers, 2022). Therefore, in this section, it is necessary to examine the model this Law represents, how individual rights are recognised, and its positioning in contrast to collective and state interests (Borgogno & Zangrandi, 2024).

It provides a framework which is rights-based for protection of personal information, however, it is subject to broad restrictions such as national security, achievement of public interest objectives, and state discretion (Rafaelof, 2020). It has a contrasting feature over European Union law which advocates privacy as a fundamental right where data subjects are provided with certain entitlements under Chapter IV (Articles 44-50), including the rights of access, correction, and deletion but operation of these rights subject to state's ultimate authority when the data is to be governed. It also provides segregation of information into 'personal information' under Chapter II (Section 1, Articles 13-27) and 'sensitive personal information' under Chapter II (Section 2, Articles 28-32). The personal information is defined broadly as any data which is relating to an identified or identifiable natural person as enumerated in Article 4 of the statute. Article 28 defines sensitive personal information that includes biometric data, health information, financial data, and location tracking. The categorisation of the personal information data and sensitive personal information has enabled enhanced regulatory control over sensitive data specific to health, finances and biometric information. There are key principles that govern data processing, namely, lawfulness, legitimacy and necessity, purpose limitation, data minimisation, transparency, and accountability and which are in consonance with global data protection norms but has and have been implemented within China's governance framework which is unique in itself. There are several rights of data subjects which are provided in Chapter IV of the Law. The individual rights include the right to know and decide (Article 44), the right to access and copy data (Article 45), the right to correct (Article 46) and delete data (Article 47) and the right to restrict or refuse processing (Article 50). These rights are subject to exceptions, particularly where national security and public authorities require access of the data. It provides similarity to the CSL (2016) and DSL (2021), in the sense that the individuals, though are recognised participants in data governance can be constrained by state if there need be. Moving on to the obligation of the corporate/

data processors that are enumerated under Chapter V (Articles 51-59), the Law includes obtaining informed consent, implementing security measures, conducting impact assessments (Article 55-56) for high-risk processing and appointing data protection officers (Article 52). However, the large platforms are subject to additional obligations which include establishing independent oversight bodies and also ensuring fairness and transparency in algorithms, thus reflecting the integration of corporate activity into an ecosystem which is regulated by the state.

As provided under Article 3, the application of the statute is extraterritorial and cross-border data transfers are another aspect where the Law imposes strict conditions on the transfer of personal data. The conditions consist of going through government security assessments, certification needs to be obtained, and entering into standard contracts. There are certain entities such as, critical infrastructure operators, who are mandated to store personal data within China, or in other words emphasising upon data localisation, thus establishing territorial control on data. Through data localisation and established territorial control personal information remains within the reach of Chinese regulatory authorities and public authorities may access the data regarding regulatory and security purposes, thus establishing cooperation from the corporations. The state on the other hand is provided with a leeway and thus the restriction are imposed mostly against the private actors. By referring the statute it can be formulated that violations of the law, administrative and individual liability is provided under Chapter VII (Articles 66-71). The violations under Article 66 may result in fines up to 5% of the annual revenue, suspension of operations, and revocation of business licenses. Personal sanctions are provided under Article 68 in cases against personnel, therefore, reinforcing accountability not on the state but on concerned public servants.

The challenges that are faced by the Law are ambiguity and discretion, state surveillance and compliance burden (Borgogno & Zangrandi, 2024). The ambiguity arises when the key provisions do not have any precise definitions thus granting regulators significant discretion over the interpretation and application. The provisions of the Law do a little to limit state surveillance raising speculations and concerns about civil liberties and individual's rights (Borgogno & Zangrandi, 2024). The regulatory framework which is provided by the Law is complex and it poses challenges for domestic and foreign companies which operates in multiple jurisdictions.

It is to be noted that this Law must not be taken in silos but it must be understood alongside CSL (2016) and DSL (2021). Therefore, these laws together form a holistic model of digital sovereignty that integrates security, governance, and rights. Through this Law it can be understood that the sovereignty is layered in three ways (Borgogno & Zangrandi, 2024). One, individuals have limited control over their personal data. Second, the corporations can manage the data within regulatory constraints mentioned under the Law. Third, the state has authority that supersedes over the rights individuals and corporations. A significant development in global data governance is represented by the Personal Information Protection Law, 2021 which demonstrates three things. One, privacy protections can coexist with strong state control. Two, individual rights can be incorporated into a state-centric sovereignty model. Third, data governance can serve both economic and political objectives. Thus, it represents a state-mediated privacy sovereignty model where individuals are recognised but remain subordinate to collective interests and state power. Therefore, it reflects a hybrid approach which blends elements of rights-based governance with a fundamentally state-centric conception of sovereignty.

India

The aim of Indian data protection law is to recognise the rights of citizens and the need for data processing. GDPR has influenced the existing data protection law, DPDP Act, 2023; however, prior to this, the Information Technology Act, 2000, remains a reference for addressing emerging technological issues in data protection. However, the earlier laws and policies remained insufficient; hence, the present law was enacted.

The key question to be discussed in this section is: What led to the enactment of the data protection law in the context of India? What are the features of this law that provide protection to the citizens' right to the data and also the right to use the data by corporations? Does India's approach play a significant role in the management of new sovereigns and the development of digital rights?

Digital Personal Data Protection Act, 2023 (DPDP Act 2023)

In India, the Digital Personal Data Protection Act 2023 provides a pivotal moment in the country's digital governance trajectory (Digital Personal Data Protection Act, 2023). It was enacted after years of debate following the landmark judgment in *Justice K.S. Puttaswamy* v *Union of India* (2017), which recognised privacy as a fundamental right. The Act establishes a statutory framework for the regulation of personal data. Therefore, in this section, it is necessary to discuss how Indian law differs from other laws and the model it reflects.

The Act draws normative legitimacy from the *Puttaswamy* judgment. The Act operationalises the right to privacy in a limited and structured manner by emphasising consent-based data processing, state exemptions, and regulatory flexibility. It can be said to reflect a shift from constitutional idealism to pragmatic governance (Greenleaf, 2025). India's approach through the law conceptualises data as a driver of digital economic growth and state service delivery, and as a resource requiring regulated openness. Thus, in the Indian scenario, sovereignty is exercised not by strict control as illustrated by the Chinese, US and EU models but is managed in a flexible sense (Basu, 2021).

This Act as per Section 3 is applicable to the digital personal data processing within the country and outside if it is to offer goods or services to Indian citizens. The extraterritoriality provision aligns with other global laws discussed before. Some key definitions under Section 2 of the Act include data principal, data fiduciary, and significant data fiduciary. The data principal is an individual to whom the data relates. A data fiduciary defined under Section 2(i) is an entity determining the purpose and means of processing data. A significant data fiduciary under Section 2(z) of the Act is an entity that is subject to enhanced obligations. A fiduciary model of data governance is reflected through this terminology, which emphasises trust and responsibility. The core principles of data governance include consent and lawful processing, purpose limitation, data minimisation, accuracy and security standards, and the accountability of data fiduciaries. Though similar to global standards, these principles are less prescriptive than those in the GDPR (2016). The provisions include a consent-centric framework and data principals' rights. Consent is the primary legal basis for processing personal data. It must be free, specific, informed and unambiguous as provided under Section 6. The EU Law grants individual rights such as the right to access information, correction and erasure, grievance redressal and nomination. In contrast, the Indian Law does not provide a broad right to data portability and does not regulate automated decision-making (Mishra & Agarwal, 2026). It also curtails rights in the name of administrative ease and economic growth. Moving forward, state authorities are exempt from data processing for national security, public order, or the prevention of offences. Such exemptions highlight the primacy of state sovereignty over individual privacy, a distinction that distinguishes India's model from the EU's. Apart from the exemption, the state has significant discretion to use data for welfare delivery, governance and law enforcement. Thereby, reflecting a model where data is a tool of developmental governance. Apart from stating that the role of data fiduciaries is to ensure data security, notify breaches, obtain consent and delete data when no longer necessary. A condition under Section 10 requires significant data fiduciaries to appoint Data Protection Officers (DPOs), conduct impact assessments, and implement additional compliance measures. Corporations retain relative autonomy but are subject to clear statutory obligations reflecting a balanced regulatory approach.

The Act allows cross-border data transfers (Sections 16-17) to countries notified by the government, marking a departure from the proposed strict data localisation. It also reflects openness to global data flows and retention of state control through selective restrictions. The Indian model can be considered as "regulated openness", which allows balancing of sovereignty with economic integration. Additionally, the regulation is implemented through the establishment of the Data Protection Board

(Chapter V, Section 18), which serves as the primary enforcement authority. The authority is responsible for adjudicating complaints, imposing penalties and ensuring compliance with the Act. There are significant monetary penalties that create incentives for compliance under Chapter VIII, Section 33. It reflects a system that is centralised yet flexible, aligned with India's administrative structure.

The Act faces several challenges and criticisms. The state has broad powers, a limited rights framework, enforcement concerns and regulatory ambiguity. Critics argue that extensive government exemptions undermine privacy protections (Sinha, 2017). The absence of certain rights, such as portability and strong profiling safeguards, may weaken individual autonomy, and the independence and capacity of the Data Protection Board remain uncertain (Greenleaf, 2025). The key provisions of the Act rely on future rules, thereby creating regulatory uncertainty. It illustrates an Indian approach which is distinctive and is characterised by pragmatism over ideology. A balance between growth, regulation, and flexibility in governance positions Indian law alongside global models.

The Act constructs a hybrid framework and represents a negotiated model of sovereignty that distributes power, but ultimate authority remains in the hands of the state. The Indian position reflects a hybrid model of digital sovereignty that balances individual rights, state interests, and economic and innovation priorities. This model provides a form of digital sovereignty in which data governance aligns with broader goals of economic growth, digital inclusion, and state capacity building.

Brazil

The right to privacy and personal data protection in Brazil are within the ambit of fundamental rights after the 2021 constitutional reform in Brazil's Constitution. In addition, Brazil's Supreme Federal Court (STF) has upheld data protection rights protected by the Constitution. The strict privacy requirements and state scrutiny of the big tech firms brings transparency between corporate practice and public oversight. Therefore, Brazil treats data protection as the right of individuals and as an instrument of state authority that can lead to reduce the impact and dominance of the new sovereigns. However, the laws and their implementation under Brazil's jurisdiction is to be discussed in this section.

Lei Geral de Proteção de Dados 2020 (LGPD)

Lei Geral de Proteção de Dados, enacted in 2018 and enforced from 2020, initiated a transformative moment in Latin America's digital governance landscape by positioning Brazil within the global shift toward stronger data regulation (Law No. 13.709, 2018). It establishes a comprehensive legal framework for the protection of personal data which can be considered to be influenced by GDPR. It reflects Brazil's constitutional traditions and socio-economic priorities. The data is regulated as a fundamental right adapted to local constitutional realities. In this section, the discussion is focused on the kind of sovereignty illustrated and adopted by Brazil through the LGPD.

Privacy, human dignity, and the free development of personality have deep roots in the constitutional principles of Brazil (Doneda & Zanatta, 2022). In 2022 a constitutional amendment was made to recognise data protection as a fundamental right strengthening the Law's normative foundation (Doneda & Zanatta, 2022). Brazil's sovereignty is expressed by aligning with the international standards, participation in global data flows, and the adoption of interoperable legal frameworks. A strategy of "harmonised sovereignty", in which legitimacy is derived from compatibility with global norms, is reflected here.

It applies to data processing carried out in Brazil, to the processing of data of individuals located in Brazil, and to data collected within Brazilian territory (Law No. 13.709, 2018). However, similar to GDPR (2016), it also has extraterritorial reach provided under Article 3 of the Law (Law No. 13.709, 2018). It also has provisions that distinguish between personal data and sensitive personal data, and their processing, which are explicitly set out in Sections I and II of Chapter II (Law No. 13.709, 2018). Article 5 defines sensitive personal data that includes health information, biometric data, religion, and political opinions (Law No. 13.709, 2018). This categorisation provides enhanced protection for high-risk data. The principles provided in Article 6 of the Law are purpose limitation, adequacy and necessity, transparency, security and prevention, non-discrimination, and accountability (Law No. 13.709, 2018) which closely resembles GDPR and establishes its alignment with global standards. Apart from the principles, the rights provided to the individuals are extensive including confirmation of data processing, access to personal data, correction of inaccurate data, anonymisation or deletion, data portability and information about data sharing. While the rights framework is considered to be strong, enforcement is dependent on institutional capacity, which underscores the challenges of implementing sovereignty which is based on rights in a developing context. The rights of individuals is dependent on the corporate obligations and their compliance therefore, they are mandated to implement security measures, maintain records of processing activities, report data breaches, and appoint a Data Protection Officer, as defined under Article 5 and further elaborated under Article 41 (Law No. 13.709, 2018). For compliance, enforcement, guidance, and regulatory oversight, the Autoridade Nacional de Proteção de Dados (ANPD) is responsible as highlighted in Article 55-A of the Law (Law No. 13.709, 2018). A regulated market approach where corporations are obligated to operate under clear legal obligations but are not subordinate to the state as suggested by the findings in China.

Cross-border data transfers are allowed in the LGPD when certain conditions are followed and they include adequacy decisions, standard contractual clauses, and consent of data subjects (Law No. 13.709, 2018). Brazil's participation in the global digital economy is facilitated by these mechanisms while regulatory safeguards are maintained (Doneda & Zanatta, 2022). The model of open but regulated data flows, which balances sovereignty with international economic integration is adopted. For violations, penalties which are included in the Law consists of fines up to 2% of a company's revenue in Brazil, suspension of data processing activities, and disclosure of violations to public (Law No. 13.709, 2018). The enforcement effectiveness is dependent on the ANPD's capacity and independence (Doneda & Zanatta, 2022) because ANPD has constrains regarding resource and structure (Doneda & Zanatta, 2022). Overall, the challenges of the Law are enforcement limitations, economic pressures, and regulatory maturity. Institutional incapacity may weaken the execution especially in a developing country which is maintaining its economic growth, data protection regimes might be difficult (Doneda & Zanatta, 2022). Lastly, Brazil's Law is still evolving through regulatory guidance and judicial interpretation.

Brazil's approach showcases characteristics of a "harmonised rights-based sovereignty" which means alignment of national regulation with global standards while maintaining domestic constitutional grounding. There is a strong emphasis on establishing individuals' rights, openness to international data flows, and institutional reliance on regulatory authorities, all of which can be considered to be the key features in the country. Brazil holds an important position in the ecosystem of global data governance. This study establishes three things. One, when developing economies adopt a comprehensive data protection framework. Second, exercising sovereignty through legal harmonisation rather than isolation. Third, a rights-based approach to governance that coexists with the goals of economic development. Therefore, Brazil reflects a rights-based sovereignty that is development sensitive; however, it also seeks to balance privacy, economic growth, and regulatory capacity. By representing a bridging model which connects global standards with local realities, it highlights the struggle over data, which is not only between the states and corporations, but, it is also about how emerging economies assert their place in the evolving digital order.

Africa

Africa is an example of a unique, complex, and evolving landscape of digital governance, distinct from the jurisdictions discussed above. It has characteristics, including plurality, fragmentation, and experimentation, found across more than 50 jurisdictions. Though this diversity is a concern however, it reflects a multi-layered approach to digital sovereignty, shaped by postcolonial state-building, developmental priorities, and global regulatory influence. At the continental level, there are two frameworks: the African Union Convention on Cyber Security and Personal Data Protection (Malabo Convention, 2014) and the African Union's Digital Transformation Strategy (2020-2030), which provide a normative framework for action. At the national level, there are countries like South Africa, Nigeria, Kenya and Rwanda who have adopted data protection laws with different degrees of sophistication (Data Protection Africa, 2026). Therefore, in this section, the type of model adopted/ represented by Africa, and its distribution across governance levels, are discussed.

The history of colonialism and economic dependency has deeply influenced the African approach to digital sovereignty which also results in believing that digital governance should be framed as a tool to reclaim autonomy and a mechanism by digital dependency can be avoided. It can be considered to be a strategy for participating in the global digital economy. A dual imperative arises in this case where sovereignty is asserted while integration to world is maintained. Similar to Indian approach, many African states have also adopted an approach which is development-oriented in which data governance is linked to digital infrastructure development, financial inclusion, e-governance, and service delivery. However, the limited institutional capacity leads to slow implementation.

On the one hand, the Malabo Convention (2014) is Africa's primary continental instrument which governs cybersecurity, personal data protection and electronic transactions. The Convention consists of three key features. First, the recognition of privacy and data protection principles. Two, the emphasis of handling cybersecurity on the state. Third, encouragement to form national legal frameworks. The constraints that are surrounding this convention are limited ratification and implementation, and weak enforcement mechanisms and it reflects an attempt to construct collective digital sovereignty, however, the impact remains uneven across the continent. On the other hand, regional and national data protection regimes also exist in few regions that includes South Africa, Nigeria, Kenya and Rwanda that can be discussed here. South Africa has enacted the Protection of Personal Information Act (POPIA), 2013, which is strongly influenced by the EU's GDPR. The emphasis is on the consent, accountability and data subject rights, which represent a model which is "rights-based sovereignty" within Africa. Nigerian data protection regime is named as the Nigeria Data Protection Act (NDPA) 2023. It establishes a national data protection authority and focuses on the economic development and the digital economy reflecting a "developmental and regulatory hybrid model". Another instance is Kenya's data protection regime which is named as the Data Protection Act 2019, it establishes a Data Protection Commissioner and incorporates GDPR like principles demonstrating a model which can be termed as "institutional sovereignty through regulatory bodies". The data protection regime in Rwanda is named as the Protection of Personal Data and Privacy Law, 2021, which focuses on the governance which is driven by data, initiatives including smart city developments and digital infrastructure representing a state-led developmental model which is similar to China in ambition.

The African digital ecosystems are heavily influenced by global technology companies and they control the jurisdictions cloud infrastructure, digital platforms and data flows. It results in a form of external corporate sovereignty when data is usually stored outside Africa, local regulatory capacity is limited, and states lack the capacity and power to assert control. Data localisation requirements are lacking and are not strict in most of the African countries however, interest is growing in development of regional data centres and sovereign cloud initiatives. To achieve such a goal, limited digital infrastructure, dependency on foreign cloud providers, and uneven connectivity are among the infrastructure constraints that African nations are constantly struggling. Therefore, digital sovereignty in Africa is tackling factors such as technology and economic advancement and not just by legal frameworks (Greenleaf, 2025). Initiatives such as the African Continental Free Trade Area (AfCFTA), which have the aim to facilitate digital trade, harmonise regulations and promote cross-border data flows, because different national laws create fragmentation, compliance challenges and barriers to integration. Some African states have expanded their surveillance capabilities, which are often justified by national security, counterterrorism, and public order, though it raises concerns about civil liberties, democratic accountability, and the abuse of power, which can lead to tension between security sovereignty and rights-based governance. Apart from the challenges such as institutional capacity and legal fragmentation already discussed, digital dependency and global power asymmetries are additional ones. The reliance on foreign infrastructure and platforms constrains their sovereignty and forces them to operate within a global system dominated by powerful states and corporations, creating power asymmetries.

Africa represents a layered, emergent digital sovereignty in which authority is distributed across multiple levels and is shaped by both internal and external factors. Continental/national norm-setting, national legal experimentation, external corporate influence, and developmental priorities under the Malabo Convention are some of the key features that elucidate the emerging layered digital sovereignty (African Union Convention on Cyber Security and Personal Data Protection 2014). Africa's digital governance landscape illustrates that sovereignty is not static and it is constructed over time through legal, institutional and technological development. It demonstrates that sovereignty is multi-level and negotiable, legal frameworks alone are insufficient without infrastructure and capacity, and the struggle over data is deeply intertwined with global inequalities and development challenges. Thus, the African model has "emergent and layered" digital sovereignty in which authority is distributed across continental, regional, and national levels and is also shaped by external regulatory influences.

SUMMARY

This section summarises the comparative case studies of six regions. The EU, by enacting the GDPR (2016), sought to enact a comprehensive regulation that would serve as a role model for values in digital data protection beyond its borders. The legislation establishes strict privacy rules for corporations to access and process the personal data of EU citizens, thereby extending EU authority globally. Corporations are further constrained by the DSA (2022) and DMA (2022) enactments. Therefore, the EU uses legal and technical standards to assert its sovereignty and curb corporate dominance. In the United States, it seeks to favour its open data flows for the benefit of its tech industry. Under the CLOUD Act 2018, the accessibility of data from US companies worldwide is ensured for security purposes. Though the US lacks a comprehensive federal digital data protection laws but, it relies on sector-specific regulations such as the Health Insurance Portability and Accountability Act 1966 (HIPAA), Children's Online Privacy Protection Act 1998 (COPPA), Gram-Leach-Bliley Act 1999 (GLBA), trade agreements such as United States-Mexico-Canada Agreement 2020 (USMCA), also known as "North American Free Trade Agreement (NAFTA 2.0)" privacy chapter (i.e. Chapter 19), and legal judgments. In China, digital sovereignty is a matter of state control. The cybersecurity law and, subsequently, PIPL (2021) and DSL (2021) create one of the world's strictest regimes for data localisation and security. The companies are required to store Chinese users' data in China and share the encryption keys with the authorities. The country also advances in its technology and internet to depend minimally on foreign aid. Through laws and investment, China serves as a case study to justify state security and social control as the main reasons for regulating data in this manner. In India, evolution of data strategy is rapid in the present context and it signals a move toward stronger privacy protections but it also provides for broad government powers. Before the enactment the proposals considered enforcement of data localisation for "critical" data, but the final enacted legislation relaxes the strict localisation requirements, which is reflecting trade-offs. The approach is to safeguard data of citizens but it also promote local digital businesses simultaneously. Data trusts and local cloud initiatives are discussed in the legislation to help state control over key data, though a formal compliance considering certain rules lags due to enforcement date in future (Digital Personal Data Protection Rules, 2025) however, it is pertinent that India is demonstrating a middle path. Moving forward, Brazil's LGPD and the 2021 constitutional amendment have developed a model which can be termed as "digital constitutionalism" resulting into the active intervention of Supreme Court in the country in platform governance. Therefore, by combining legal rights, judicial enforcement, and pressure on platforms to align with public policy, Brazil is ensuring that digital governance is integral to democracy rather than merely private or market-driven. Lastly, the African emphasises digital equity rather than outright lockdowns and the benefits of data sharing, the need to enhance participation in global data infrastructure, and the importance of crafting open data governance models have also been emphasised by African leaders. However, without broader reforms, sovereignty through capacity-building would not be enough and collectively, it shows that states use laws, courts, and infrastructure projects to wield data power, but the strategies may vary.

The data-power balance is shifted by the ones who contain advanced technological systems. Cloud computing and massive data centres are concentrated on technical advancement of state and it is pertinent to note that AI and online services run on a few hyperscale platforms which are controlled by US and Chinese firms. Thus, allowing the corporations *de facto* control over the "nervous system" of the digital economy through concentration of technical advancement in few jurisdictions. AI and machine learning has the power to influence unilaterally because companies with the largest datasets and the most powerful computers can shape global applications. However, edge computing and federated/decentralised AI may distribute this power, this is because these two run smaller models at local level or on regional servers. This is because sensitive data remains with the owner, reducing reliance on distant cloud providers. Therefore, the question remains can AI's next phase align the competitiveness with sovereignty?

CONCLUSION

Looking ahead, there are several trends that are likely to take place in future. One, increased regulatory convergence in theory but divergence in implementation. Second, increase in data localisation and policies of strategic autonomy. Third, greater scrutiny of Big Tech and platform power. Fourth, the emergence of regional digital blocs. Fourth, tension between globalisation and sovereignty remain prevalent. The digital age, therefore, does not signal the decline of sovereignty but its reconfiguration. The States have not disappeared due to emergence of digital platforms but they have adapted, though at times aggressively, to the new forms of power. At the same time, the corporations can be considered as parallel centres of authority, and individuals evolved as subjects and stakeholders in data governance. Therefore, within this evolving landscape, sovereignty is plural, layered and contested. It is plural because multiple actors can exercise authority. It is layered because global, national, regional and local levels are contested due to the ongoing struggle over control and legitimacy. Conclusively, the study reveals that data governance is not only about regulation or technology but it is also about power in its most fundamental sense i.e. who governs, who benefits, and who decides the future of the digital world.

REFERENCES

Abraha, H. H. (2019). How compatible is the US 'CLOUD Act' with cloud computing? A brief analysis. *International Data Privacy Law*, *9*(3), 207–215. DOI: 10.1093/idpl/ipz009

African Union Convention on Cyber Security and Personal Data Protection. (2014).

Anix. (2026). *U.S. Regulators and Big Tech Compliance Issues.* SIIT. https://siit.co/blog/u-s-regulators-and-big-tech-compliance-issues/50399

Basu, A. (2021, October 18). *Sovereignty in a datafied world* (Issue Brief No. 501). Observer Research Foundation. https://www.orfonline.org/research/sovereignty-in-a-datafied-world

Besson, S. (2011). *Sovereignty.* https://www.merriam-webster.com/dictionary/sovereign

Borgogno, O., & Zangrandi, M. S. (2024). *Chinese Data Governance and Trade Policy: From Cyber Sovereignty to the Quest for Digital Hegemony?* Taylor and Francis., DOI: 10.1080/10670564.2023.2299961

Bradford, A. (2019). *The Brussels Effect: How the European Union Rules the World.* Oxford University Press.

Brazil. (2018). Law No. 13/709, of August 14, 2018 (General Data Protection Law-LGPD). https://www.lgpdbrasil.com.br/wp-content/uploads/2019/06/LGPD-english-version.pdf

Charter of Fundamental Rights of the European Union. (2000/C 364/01). (2000). *Official Journal of the European Communities*, C 364, 1–22. https://www.europarl.europa.eu/charter/pdf/text_en.pdf

Clarifying Lawful Overseas Use of Data Act, Pub. L. No. 115–141, § 103, 132 Stat. 348, 1213 (2018).

Clayton, R., Murdoch, S. J., & Watson, R. N. M. (2006). Ignoring the great firewall of China. In *Proceedings of the 6th International Workshop on Privacy Enhancing Technologies* (pp. 1–13). PET., https://www.cl.cam.ac.uk/~rnc1/ignoring.pdf DOI: 10.1007/11957454_2

Court of Justice of the European Union. (2015, October 6). *Maximillian Schrems v. Data Protection Commissioner* (Case C-362/14), [2015] ECLI:EU:C:2015:650.

Court of Justice of the European Union. (2020, July 16). *Data Protection Commissioner v. Facebook Ireland Ltd and Maximillian Schrems* (Case C-311/18), [2020] ECLI:EU:C:2020:559.

Creemers, R. (2022). China's Emerging Data Protection Framework. *Journal of Cybersecurity*, *8*(1), tyac011. Advance online publication. DOI: 10.1093/cybsec/tyac011

Crémer, J., De Montjoye, Y. A., & Schweitzer, H. (2019). *Competition policy for the digital era*. Publications Office of the European Union.

Cybersecurity Law of the People's Republic of China (promulgated by the Standing Comm. Nat'l People's Cong., Nov. 7, 2016, effective June 1, 2017). http://www.npc.gov.cn/englishnpc/c23934/202012/1abd8829788946ecab270e469e13c39c.shtml

Czerniawski, M. (2025). *EU's Digital Sovereignty and the Rights-Based Imperative: Linking Enforcement, Competences and Fundamental Rights*. VerfBlog., DOI: 10.59704/221c82ced6d670b6

Daskal, J. (2018). *Microsoft Ireland, the CLOUD Act, and International Lawmaking 2.0.* SLR. https://www.stanfordlawreview.org/online/microsoft-ireland-cloud-act-international-lawmaking-2-0/

Data Protection Africa. (2026). *Which African Countries Have a Data Protection Law?* *https://dataprotection.africa/which-african-countries-have-a-data-protection-law*

Data Security Law of the People's Republic of China (promulgated by the Standing Comm. Nat'l People's Cong., June 10, 2021, effective Sept. 1, 2021). http://www.npc.gov.cn/englishnpc/c23934/202112/31728d29836940388796593a86377771.shtml

Ding, J. (2018). *Deciphering China's AI Dream.* Future of Humanity Institute, University of Oxford. http://advancedinvestor.com/resources/Research-Materials/China/China_AI_Dream.pdf

Doneda, D., & Zanatta, R. A. F. (2022). *Personality Rights in Brazilian Data Protection Law: A Historical Perspective.* Springer Nature Link. https://link.springer.com/chapter/10.1007/978-3-030-90331-2_3

Elliot, M., Mandalari, A. M., Mourby, M., & O'Hara, K. (2024). *Dictionary of privacy, data protection and information security*. Edward Elgar Publishing.

European Commission. (2022). *Digital Services Package.* Brussels. https://ec.europa.eu/commission/presscorner/api/files/document/print/en/ip_22_4313/IP_22_4313_EN.pdf

Gabel, J. M. (2026). *European Union.* https://www.britannica.com/topic/European-Union

Gillespie, T. (2018). *Custodians of the Internet.* Yale University.

Green, Leslie. (nd). The *Normativity of Law: What is the Problem?* University of Victoria, Canada. https://www.uvic.ca/victoria-colloquium/assets/docs/Green_Normativity.pdf#

Greenleaf, G. (2025). *Global Data Privacy Laws 2025: 172 Countries, Twelve New in 2023/24.* Macquarie Law School. https://papers.ssrn.com/sol3/papers.cfm?abstract_id=5275559

Helberger, N., Pierson, J., & Poell, T. (2018). Governing online platforms: From contested to cooperative responsibility. *The Information Society*, *34*(1), 1–14.

Hinsley, F. H. (1986). *Sovereign.* Cambridge University Press.

Justice K.S. Puttaswamy (Retd.) v. *Union of India* (2017) 10 SCC 1

Kaye, D. (2019). *Speech Police: The Global Struggle to Govern the Internet.* Columbia Global Reports. https://globalreports.columbia.edu/books/speech-police

Khan, L. M. (2017). Amazon's Antitrust Paradox. *The Yale Law Journal.*

Khanal, S., Zhang, H., & Taeihagh, A. (2026). The rise of Big Tech as super policy entrepreneurs. *Policy and Society*, puag005. Advance online publication. DOI: 10.1093/polsoc/puag005

Krieger, J. (1993). *The Oxford Companion to Politics of the World.* Oxford University Press.

Landesberg, M. K., Levin, T. M., & Curtin, C. G. Lev, Ori., (1998). *Privacy Online: A Report To Congress.* Federal Trade Commission.

Lei Geral de Proteção de Dados Pessoais [General Personal Data Protection Law], Lei No. 13.709, de 14 de agosto de 2018 (Braz.). https://www.lgpdbrasil.com.br/wp-content/uploads/2019/06/LGPD-english-version.pdf

Lindahl, H. (2001). Sovereignty and the Institutionalisation of Normative Order. *Oxford Journal of Legal Studies*, *21*(1), 165–180. Advance online publication. DOI: 10.1093/ojls/21.1.165

Ministry of Electronics and Information Technology. (2025). *Digital Personal Data Protection Rules, 2025.* Government of India. https://pib.gov.in/PressReleasePage.aspx?PRID=2090271

Mishra, N., & Agarwal, B. (2026). The emerging framework for non-personal data protection in India: Perils, promises, and lessons for the developing world. *International Journal of Law and Information Technology*, *34*(1), eaaf025. Advance online publication. DOI: 10.1093/ijlit/eaaf025

National Privacy Authority. (2024). *Federal Privacy Framework Overview.*

Peitz, M., & Motta, M. (2020). Big Tech Mergers. *Information Economics and Policy*.

Personal Information Protection Law of the People's Republic of China (promulgated by the Standing Comm. Nat'l People's Cong., Aug. 20, 2021, effective Nov. 1, 2021). http://www.npc.gov.cn/englishnpc/c23934/202112/1bed4cd1443340a2aabc94e391bd35e0.shtml

Rafaelof, E., Webster, G., Tai, K., Neville, K., Creemers, R., & Sacks, S. (2020). *Translation: China's 'Data Security Law (Draft)'*. New America. https://www.newamerica.org/insights/translation-chinas-data-security-law-draft/

Regulation (EU) 2016/679 of the European Parliament and of the Council 27 April 2016.

Regulation (EU) 2022/1925 of the European Parliament and of the Council of 14 September 2022.

Regulation (EU) 2022/2065 of the European Parliament and of the Council of 19th October 2022.

Rothmann, C. C. (2024). *Modernizing U.S. Commercial Privacy Standards for a Digital Economy.* https://www.csis.org/analysis/modernizing-us-commercial-privacy-standards-digital-economy

Sinha, A. (2017). *India's Data Protection Framework Will Need to Treat Privacy as a Social And Not Just an Individual Good.* EPW. https://www.epw.in/engage/article/for-indias-data-protection-regime-to-be-efficient-policymakers-should-treat-privacy-as-a-social-good

Spalević, Ž., & Vićentijević, K. (2022). Spalević, žaklina and Vićentijević, Kosana. (2022). *GDPR And Challenges of Personal Data Protection. The European Journal of Applied Economics*, *19*(1), 55–65. Advance online publication. DOI: 10.5937/EJAE19-36596

Swindle, O. (2002). The Effectiveness of Privacy Protection in Economic Systems. The Italian Garantì©'s International Conference. https://www.ftc.gov/news-events/news/speeches/effectiveness-privacy-protection-economic-systems

Swire, P., & Hemmings, J. D. (2016). *Mutual Legal Assistance in An Era of Globalised Communications: The Analogy to the Visa Waiver Program.* NYU Annual Survey of American Law. https://annualsurveyofamericanlaw.org/wp-content/uploads/2017/04/71-4_swirehemmings.pdf

United States v. Microsoft Corp., 584 U.S. _ 2018 https://supreme.justia.com/cases/federal/us/584/17-2/

Varian, H. (2018). *Artificial Intelligence, Economics, And Industrial Organisation.* NBER Working Paper Series. https://www.nber.org/system/files/working_papers/w24839/w24839.pdf

Webster, M. (March 2026). *Sovereign.* https://www.merriam-webster.com/dictionary/sovereign

Woods, A. K. (2016). *Against Data Exceptionalism.* Stanford Law Review. https://www.stanfordlawreview.org/wp-content/uploads/sites/3/2016/04/68_Stan_L._Rev._729_-_Woods.pdf

Wunderlich, U. (2025). *Can the EU become a Strategic-normative Power in a Fractured World?* London School of Economics. https://blogs.lse.ac.uk/europpblog/2025/07/03/can-the-eu-become-a-strategic-normative-power-in-a-fractured-world/

Yaraghi, N. (2018). *A Case against the General Data Protection Regulation.* Brookings. https://www.brookings.edu/articles/a-case-against-the-general-data-protection-regulation/

KEY TERMS AND DEFINITIONS

Artificial Intelligence: It is the capacity of the human-made computer and machine to stimulate the speed and time for the tasks conducted by humans such as mathematics, decisions-making, reasoning etc.

Big Tech Corporations: Commonly referred as the companies that are dominating the market through investment in Artificial intelligence and technology. It consists of Alphabet/Google, Amazon, Apple, Meta/Facebook, and Microsoft.

Brussels Effect: Coined by Anu Bradford and named after Brussels a *de facto* capital of EU. It can be defined as the process through which European Union regulations are adopted by jurisdictions outside EU's territory. Due to different reasons the corporations adopt EU's laws outside its territorial border.

Digital Data: Information, facts, statistics and figures regarding different entities that can be processed, programmed and transferred.

Information Self-Determination: Decision and control of the individuals on the collection, storage, usage and processing of their information.

New Sovereigns: Quasi-sovereign entities that has control over data, digital infrastructure, customer/user behavior, algorithm-creation, framing rules on their own and setting compliance and enforcement standards. They often have rivalling authority with the nation-states.

Traditional Sovereignty: also known as Westphalian sovereignty, considered to be a principle in which the state has the supreme authority over its territorial boundaries and the internal matters, which remain immune to outside interference.

Chapter 6
Digital Evolution and the Web 2.5 Economy: Neither a Bridge nor a Destination

Nikos Astroulakis
http://orcid.org/0000-0002-0819-2145
Hellenic Mediterranean University and Business College of Athens, Greece

ABSTRACT

This chapter examines the evolution of the digital economy by focusing on the emergence of Web 2.5 economy. The Web 2.5 economy is defined here as the eclectic embeddedness of blockchain-based decentralized technologies into the prevailing platform economy. Although the term "Web 2.5" is widely used in informatics and technology-oriented media, explicit references to "Web 2.5 economy" are absent from the economics and business literature. The chapter investigates the Web 2.5 economy as a necessary analytical category for studying emerging techno-economic and institutional formations within the digital economy. It conceptualizes the Web 2.5 economy as an organic component of platform capitalism and as a system of technological and institutional relations that constitutes a distinct state of play in the evolution of the digital economy. By providing conceptual grounding alongside empirical illustration, the chapter lays the foundation for future scholarly inquiry and offers a framework for more effective strategies, policies and governance.

1. INTRODUCTION AND OBJECTIVES

The evolution of World Wide Web technologies is reshaping the global economy and giving rise to new formations within the digital economy. One such formation is the Web 2.5 economy: an emerging hybrid form characterized by the integration of

DOI: 10.4018/979-8-2600-0288-9.ch006

the blockchain economy into the platform economy. Despite the increasing presence of the term "Web 2.5" in informatics and technology-oriented media discourse, its reflection in the digital economy and in economy broadly remains absent from the economics and business literature.

The analysis pursues two objectives. The first is to lay the groundwork for introducing a new analytical category into economics and business scholarship. The second is to inform the broader discussion on the evolution of the digital economy by incorporating this new category. In addressing these objectives, the study

a) introduces the concept of the "Web 2.5 economy" as a hybrid configuration and a distinct *state of play* in the evolution of the digital economy;
b) situates this configuration within the technological, institutional, and economic trajectories of the Web 1.0, Web 2.0, and Web 3.0 technological stages;
c) examines the rise of the blockchain economy and its integration into the platform economy;
d) and provides empirical evidence demonstrating that the Web 2.5 economy is already materializing across both financial and non-financial sectors.

The analysis is relevant not only to scholars in economics and business, but also to business executives and policy makers. The former will find fertile ground for further scholarly inquiry, while the latter may gain a clearer understanding of contemporary techno-economic and institutional formations within the digital economy, thereby supporting more effective strategy, policy, and governance.

Regarding the structure of the chapter, Section 2 develops the necessary analytical considerations and reveals the research gap in economics and business scholarship. Section 3 highlights the importance of the digital economy to global affairs and the emergence of Web 2.5 economy. Section 4 traces the evolution of the digital economy based on its technological and institutional configurations. Section 5 focuses on the rise of the blockchain economy. Section 6 presents empirical evidence on the Web 2.5 economy. Section 7 concludes with the key remarks.

2. CONSIDERATIONS AND THE RESEARCH GAP

The digital economy is fundamentally shaped by technological developments, and as such, it is profoundly transformed. Despite partial transformations, the prevailing technological stage of the digital economy remains the Web 2.0 technological environment (e.g., Müller, 2024). Its economic formation is characterized by the global dominance of centralized platform corporations, particularly U.S. and Chinese conglomerates such as GAFAM (Google, Apple, Facebook [META],

Amazon, Microsoft) and BAT (Baidu, Alibaba, Tencent). This economic formation is referred to as the platform economy[1] (Kenney & Zysman, 2016;Srnicek, 2017; Boyer, 2022; Zander et al., 2025). Since the mid-2010s, the development of Web 3.0 technologies (e.g. blockchain, smart contracts, tokenization) has introduced new forms of digital interaction and economic coordination, thereby facilitating what is increasingly termed the blockchain economy (Davidson et al., 2018; Xiangjuan et al., 2025).

The notion of "Web 2.5" appears primarily in informatics and technology-oriented media as a term used to denote the passage from Web 2.0 to Web 3.0 technologies. Gaweł (2022, p. 6) describes Web 2.5 as "a transitional stage in the development of the computer web, consisting of the implementation of new principles of information and digital resource management, allowing a smooth transition to the third generation of the digital environment (Web 3)." The cybersecurity platform HACKEN (2025) approaches Web 2.5 as a hybrid architecture that merges centralized user interfaces, databases, and authentication with blockchain-based elements such as decentralized storage, wallet sign-ins, and smart contracts. In the domain of Web marketing, Brähler (2023) questions whether Web 2.5 is a mere buzzword or a useful strategic framework for firms transitioning toward Web 3.0. LCX (2023), a crypto-fintech platform, characterizes Web 2.5 as the next evolution of the internet—bridging the gap between Web 2.0 and Web 3.0 through selective adoption of blockchain technologies. (Titanium Ventures n.d.), a venture capital firm, presents Web 2.5 as a foundational layer for the future of business-to-consumer (B2C) digital interactions. Despite differences in terminology, these perspectives converge in conceptualizing Web 2.5 primarily as a technological transition toward decentralized architectures within the digital economy.

This chapter aligns partially with such accounts but departs in a crucial analytical respect. The study conceptualizes the Web 2.5 economy not merely as a technological bridge but as a system of relations in a Polanyian sense. In Polanyi (1944 [2001]) broad view, the economy is not an autonomous sphere but a socially embedded system of relations, institutions, and practices that structure how economic activity is organized and governed. This chapter suggests that the Web 2.5 economy should be analyzed not as a mere transitional technology but as a distinct *state of play*; a hybrid formation combining decentralized technological affordances with the organizational logic of platform capitalism. Whether this hybrid formation evolves into a new economic model or stabilizes as an enduring economic system remains open. As Knight (1977, p. 35) observed, "[a]n economic system is in a state of constant flux, and even the most basic relationships change, so that we can never be certain that results explaining the past will apply in the present or the future". No empirical evidence suggests that Web 3.0 or the blockchain economy currently constitutes a dominant technological paradigm or an established economic regime.

Clusters of information-related innovations may destabilize existing forms without forming a new socio-economic regime; to do so, they must become embedded in coherent and socially accepted practices (Boyer 2022). Within this context, the Web 2.5 economy can be better understood as a hybrid state emerging inside the Web 2.0 environment—an institutional and techno-economic configuration in which blockchain capabilities are selectively absorbed by centralized Web 2.0 platforms in the political economy framework of platform capitalism.

Methodologically, the study adopts a conceptual–empirical approach aimed at introducing a new analytical category in economics and business. Blaug (1992) suggests that methodology in economics concerns the examination of the logical and empirical foundations of economic inquiry, with the aim of understanding how economists construct explanations of economic phenomena rather than merely describing them. In turn, economic phenomena must be historically specific requiring concepts that acknowledge the social and institutional embeddedness, while the emergence of new socio-economic phenomena may necessitate the development of new analytical categories if they are to be adequately understood (Hodgson, 2013; 2001). Lawson (1997) maintains that theoretical categories must correspond to the nature of social reality. Within the philosophy of science, the introduction of new conceptual categories is commonly associated with the early stages of paradigm formation (Kuhn 1970) or with the development of a research program structured around a core set of assumptions and analytical commitments (Lakatos 1978). The present study does not claim to establish a definite paradigm or a fully articulated theoretical model. Rather, within the constraints of article length, it outlines the conceptual foundations of the Web 2.5 economy, which future research may develop into a more fully specified theoretical model or paradigm. In any case, Hausman (1992) argues that theories and models necessarily rely on abstraction and idealization, functioning as simplified representations rather than direct descriptions of complex social reality. While, Lawson (2003) similarly emphasizes that models function as abstractions that isolate mechanisms within open and complex social systems. In this sense, the present analysis should be methodologically understood as groundwork for future paradigm-building, methodological refinement, and model construction, recognizing that conceptualizations necessarily constitute selective abstractions from complex and evolving empirical reality.

The significance of this study derives from the absence of a conceptual treatment of the Web 2.5 economy in economics and business scholarship, despite clear techno-economic and institutional developments that demand theoretical attention. Existing categorization—such as *information economy*, *platform economy* and *blockchain economy*—are insufficient to capture how centralized platforms selectively integrate blockchain components, altering economic coordination, governance, and value creation. In turn, blockchain is no longer a niche innovation; it has developed into a functioning ecosystem intersecting with finance, capital markets, governance, and institutional design. As Davidson et al. (2018, p. 640) note, blockchains constitute a foundational institutional technology of market capitalism, underscoring the analytical importance of studying how such institutional technology is incorporated into platform architectures.

Brynjolfsson & McAfee (2014) argue that the rapid pace of digital innovation is transforming economic structures more quickly than economic theories and analytical frameworks are able to adapt, leaving many traditional models increasingly inadequate for explaining economic dynamics in the digital era. Hodgson (2001, p. 9) clearly mentions that "there are many cases in the history of science where facts have first emerged without a theory that explains them. Science may subsequently triumph by supplying a theoretical explanation". Also, evolving institutional configurations may escape inherited analytical frameworks (Boyer 2022).

To date, no scholarly literature in economics or business has examined the Web 2.5 economy in the manner advanced here. A systematic Scopus literature review[2] confirms the absence of the term "Web 2.5 economy" in economics and business journals, and even the term "Web 2.5" appears only in adjacent fields. In informatics, Bernal (2010) refers to a "Symbiotic Web"; Gaweł (2022) and Pileggi et al. (2012) use the term in a technological context; Schrepel (2023) examines the interface between Web 2.0 and Web 3.0 without naming Web 2.5; and Agrawal (2023) discusses related concepts in digital banking.

Taken together, these considerations reveal a clear research gap. While "Web 2.5" is increasingly used as a technological notion, its economic, institutional, and organizational significance remains untheorized. Addressing this gap is central to understanding the ongoing evolution of the digital economy and the hybrid configurations emerging within it. The Web 2.5 economy now observable across financial and non-financial sectors requires analytical clarity.

3. DIGITAL ECONOMY AND THE EMERGENCE OF WEB 2.5 ECONOMY

This section situates the digital economy within the global economy and develops the analytical framework by clarifying how both the digital economy and the Web 2.5 economy are perceived in this study.

3.1. Digital Economy

Even a brief disruption in the functioning of the Internet can paralyze entire sectors of economic and social activity such as airport operations, banking systems, global communications, and supply chains. In terms of scale and growth of the digital economy, the Organisation for Economic Co-operation and Development (OECD 2024b)reports that the Information and Communication Technology (ICT) sector expanded at an average annual rate of 6.3% between 2013 and 2023, nearly three times faster than the overall economy in OECD countries. The U.S. Interactive Advertising Bureau report (Deighton and Kornfeld 2025) estimates that the digital economy accounted for 18% of U.S. GDP in 2024, or approximately USD 4.9 trillion, up from 11% in 2020. At the international level, United Nations Conference on Trade and Development (UNCTAD, 2024) emphasizes that cross-border digital communications form the backbone of global e-commerce, noting a thirty-fold increase in international data traffic between 2010 and 2022. Scholarly estimates suggest that by 2024, the digital economy contributes approximately 24% of global GDP (Oloyede et al., 2023, p. 9). Despite variations across sources and methodologies, there is a strong consensus that the digital economy constitutes a significant and rapidly expanding economy that shapes not only commerce and finance, but also communication, social networks, logistics, and innovation systems, worldwide. Based on the rapid growth and the extension of digital interactions and transactions, the view is increasingly strengthened that the digital economy is not merely a part of the global economy, but is increasingly becoming the global economy itself (e.g., OECD, 2024b; 2024a). In words of Bukht & Heeks (2017, p. 11) "as more and more services, manufacturing and even primary production activities rely on ICTs, the digital economy … increasingly becomes just 'the economy'."

As defined by the OECD (2020, p. 5), "the digital economy incorporates all economic activity reliant on, or significantly enhanced by the use of digital inputs, including digital technologies, digital infrastructure, digital services and data, it refers to all producers and consumers, including government, that are utilizing these digital inputs in their economic activities." In this study, the digital economy refers to what is often termed the Internet economy, as it has evolved since the advent of the World Wide Web (WWW) technological protocols. The digital economy can be understood as an umbrella concept encompassing the ways in which traditional and novel human activities are globally organized and executed through WWW-based technologies. Although the Internet existed before the introduction and widespread adoption of WWW in the early 1990s, the "pre-Web Internet"[3] did not constitute an economy in the contemporary sense in terms of widespread global adoption, transactional capabilities, and economic outcomes. The decisive role of WWW technologies in enabling the rapid, planetary-scale expansion of Internet-based activity and the digital economy.

The WWW, invented by Tim Berners-Lee in the late 1980s, provided a transformative suite of protocols that allowed for the creation and navigation of interlinked documents over the Internet. These included the Hypertext Transfer Protocol (HTTP),

Hypertext Markup Language (HTML), and the use of Uniform Resource Locators (URLs) (Tim Berners-Lee et al.1992). Together, these protocols offered users an intuitive, standardized interface for accessing and sharing information across distributed computer networks. The introduction of WWW marked a decisive turning point, transforming the Internet from a specialized, expert-driven system into a massively accessible global medium enabling information exchange, communication, social networking, and commerce, among other activities. This foundational shift not only supported the exponential growth of online content and services but also laid the technical groundwork for subsequent stages of the Web technology evolution: Web 1.0, Web 2.0, and Web 3.0. Each of these technological stages builds on the core principles of connectivity, interactivity, and information flow that were first institutionalized through the architecture of the WWW protocols.

3.2. The Emergence of Web 2.5 Economy

This analysis does not advocate that the Web 2.5 economy constitutes a distinct technological stage in its own right; nor can it be conclusively categorized as a bridge toward Web 3.0 technology dominance. Instead, it should be interpreted as a *state of play*; a configuration in which elements of blockchain infrastructure are selectively embedded into established Web 2.0 platform environments. In this hybrid form of economy, users continue to operate within familiar platform interfaces, while back-end operations increasingly rely on decentralized technologies. Thus, the Web 2.5 economy describes applied cases where Web 3.0 decentralized technologies are integrated—partially or fully—into Web 2.0 platforms, without altering the user's experience (UX).

The platform economy, grounded in Web 2.0 technological infrastructure, continues to be dominated by global technology giants, while Web 3.0 technologies remain largely emergent. For instance, Schrepel (2023) makes a categorical distinction between Web 2.0 giants platform corporations—such as GAFAM and BAT—and Web 3.0 projects, which are decentralized, and experimental in nature. Platform corporations are centralized in nature. Srnicek (2017) argues that although platforms connect distributed users, control of the infrastructure and governance remains centralized in the platform owner, leading to strong concentration of power. While, Web 3.0 blockchain-based projects enable electronic transactions through protocolized mechanisms that reduce reliance on trusted intermediaries (Werbach 2018). This distinction reflects profound differences in organizational form, scale, and governance logic.

In turn, the Web 2.5 economy is not best understood as a revolutionary triumph of the blockchain economy over platform economy, but rather as a strategic absorption of blockchain technologies into dominant platform structures. In this sense, Web 2.5

economy represents a technological and institutional hybridization. It signals not the end of platform capitalism, but a state in which the platform economy co-opts the innovations of the blockchain economy within its operational models. Whether this ongoing integration will eventually transform the digital economy into a decentralized, blockchain project-based economy remains an open empirical and theoretical question. For now, this study advocates for approaching the Web 2.5 economy not as a transitional stage, but as an organic part of the platform economy that reflects the adaptive capacity of platform capitalism and the co-evolution of centralization and decentralization.

4. THE EVOLUTION OF THE DIGITAL ECONOMY

The Web 2.5 economy can be better understood within the broader evolutionary trajectory of the digital economy. This study examines the evolution of the digital economy as comprising three main technological stages—Web 1.0, Web 2.0, and Web 3.0—and their corresponding economic formations, while introducing a fourth analytical configuration: the Web 2.5 economy. Each configuration represents a distinct socio-technical and institutional arrangement of digital interaction, business models, and governance logics over time. The evolution of the digital economy is analyzed across seven analytical dimensions (Table 1), selected to provide a concise yet comprehensive overview of its historical, technological, economic, and social transformation.

Table 1. Analytical Dimensions

Dimension	Description
Period:	Situates the historical timeframes
Type of Economy:	Clarifies the reflection to the economy
Status of Acceptance:	Denotes the level of adoption
Web Architecture:	Highlights the technical and information technology structures and infrastructures
Governance and Business Model:	Reveals how control and value distribution are organized
User Experience (UX):	Captures how users interact with technology and how their role evolves.
Significance:	Indicates why each categorization matters in broader economic and social terms

4.1. Web 1.0: The Information Economy

The technological stage of Web 1.0 (early 1990s–early 2000s) marked the rise of the information economy. It was defined by static content provision and one-way communication, often described as the "Read-Only, Web" (Tapscott 2014). Its status of acceptance was dominant, with rapid adoption reflected in data showing an increase number of internet users from 44 million in 1995 to 413 million in the year 2000 (Murphy and Roser 2019). The Web 1.0 architecture consisted of static websites hosted on centralized servers. The governance and business model were top-down, controlled by firms and webmasters who provided content and experimented with early e-commerce and banner advertising. The user experience was characterized by passive consumption with limited interactivity (Berners-Lee and Cailliau 1990). The significance of Web 1.0 lies in its foundational role: it enabled global information dissemination and laid the technical and economic groundwork for subsequent stages of the digital economy.

4.2. Web 2.0: The Platform Economy

Web 2.0 technology (early 2000s–present) introduced the platform economy as the dominant type of economy. Its status of acceptance remains dominant to this day. The Web 2.0 architecture expanded through giant platforms' corporations, extensive application programming interfaces (APIs), cloud computing, and large-scale big data infrastructures. In the "Read–Write, Web" (JinCheng and Chuen 2024), interactivity and user-generated content became central. However, governance and business models shifted to powerful platform corporations, such as GAFAM and BAT, which institutionalized platform capitalism and monetized user data through targeted advertising and network effects (van Dijck, Poell, and de Waal 2018; Fuchs et al. 2010). The user experience involved high interactivity and participation, but without ownership of data or content. The significance of Web 2.0 lies in its institutionalization of the platform economy, reshaping commerce, communication, and social networking at a global level.

4.3. Web 3.0: The Blockchain Economy

Web 3.0 technology (mid-2010s–present) represents the emergence of the decentralization. Its reflection on the economy here is defined by the vision of decentralization and the blockchain economy (Tapscott and Tapscott 2016). Its status of acceptance is emerging, as blockchain applications and adoption are still developing. The web architecture is built on blockchain infrastructure, smart contracts, decentralized storage, decentralized applications (dApps) and tokenization (Calzada

2024; Ray 2023). In terms of governance and business model, this stage introduces disintermediation, community-based decentralized coordination, decentralized autonomous organizations (DAOs), and peer-to-peer blockchain transactions. The user experience is described as the "Read–Write–Own, Web" (Lin et al. 2022; Tapscott 2023), giving users sovereignty over data, identities, and digital assets. The significance of Web 3.0 lies in its vision, redefining ownership, finance, and governance models and moving beyond the centralized logic of Web 2.0.

4.4. Web 2.5 Economy: The Blockchain Economy Integration to Platform Economy

Web 2.5 economy (mid-2010s–present) refers to a hybrid type of digital economy. It constitutes a condition of cohabitation and techno-economic experimentation within the platform economy. Its status of acceptance is emerging, reflecting the ongoing integration of the blockchain economy to platform economy. The Web 2.5 architecture blends familiar Web 2.0 interfaces with blockchain-based components, including wallet authentication, token-based access, smart contracts, and partial decentralization (Gaweł 2022). The governance and business models are mixed: centralized platforms strategically incorporate decentralized features and tokenized assets. The user experience can be defined as a "Read–Write–Partially Own, Web," where users maintain the usability of Web 2.0 while gaining partial ownership through blockchain integration. Blockchain technology enables distributed trust and new forms of economic participation that shift control from centralized platforms to network participants (Tapscott and Tapscott 2016). The significance of Web 2.5 economy lies in the adaptive capacity of platform capitalism to encapsulate blockchain economy within the established Web 2.0 platforms operational models.

It is important to note that the boundaries between Web 1.0, Web 2.0, Web 3.0, and Web 2.5 are not rigid. Rather, they serve as heuristic constructs to facilitate conceptual clarity. Technological and economic elements from earlier phases persist in subsequent ones: for example, static content from Web 1.0 still exists, just as Web 2.0 did not entirely displace its predecessor. The emergence of Web 3.0 coexists with, and advances through, the structures and user environments of Web 2.0, rather than displacing them. In practice, these configurations overlap, with multiple layers of technology and business models coexisting. The operational adoption of Web 3.0 technologies within the platform economy does not necessarily imply that the Web 2.5 economy represents a superior or end-state model. Instead, it reflects a contingent and adaptive integration within the platform economy.

Table 2 presents the evolution of the digital economy based on the above analysis.

Table 2. The Evolution of the Digital Economy

	Period	Type of Economy	Status of Acceptance	Web Architecture	Governance / Business Model	User Experience (UX)	Significance
Web 1.0 Technological Stage	Early1990s – early 2000s	Information Economy	Dominant	Static websites, centralized servers	Controlled by webmasters, firms as content providers. Early e-commerce, banner ads, top-down content provision	"Read-Only, Web" Passive consumption of information, low interactivity	Foundation of the WWW technology-based economy, global access to information, first wave of online commerce and groundwork for the Web evolution
Web 2.0 Technological Stage	Early 2000s – present	Platform Economy	Dominant	Platforms, APIs, cloud & big data infrastructures	Controlled by corporations, platform-based ecosystems, targeted advertising, app economies, network effects	"Read–Write, Web" Interactive and participatory; user-generated content under platform's control	Institutionalized the platform economy, reshaping commerce, social networking, and innovation
Web 3.0 Technological Stage	Mid-2010s – present	Blockchain Economy	Emerging	Blockchain, smart contracts, decentralized storage, dApps	Community-driven decentralized governance, DAOs, tokenization, peer-to-peer blockchain transactions	"Read–Write–Own, Web" Peer-to-peer, user sovereignty, full digital ownership, decentralized identity	Vision of a decentralized digital economy, redefining ownership, finance, governance, and innovation.

continued on following page

Table 2. Continued

	Period	Type of Economy	Status of Acceptance	Web Architecture	Governance / Business Model	User Experience (UX)	Significance
Web 2.5 Economy ***State of play***	Mid-2010s – present	Hybrid Economy: Blockchain economy integration to platform economy	Emerging	Web 2.0 environment with Web 3.0 projects (wallet sign-in, smart contracts, partial decentralization)	Mixed: centralized platforms incorporating projects of decentralized governance. Platforms embedding blockchain tokenization and digital ownership	"Read–Write–Partially Own, Web" Familiar Web 2.0 UX enriched with Web 3.0 blockchain-enabled features	Gradual integration of blockchain economy within platform economy

5. FROM DOT-COM BUBBLE TO BLOCKCHAIN ECONOMY

As noted, the early 1990s marked the establishment of World Wide Web technology on the Internet. The subsequent years witnessed the rapid expansion of the digital economy in the form of information economy under the Web 1.0 technology, laying the foundations for its global growth while simultaneously generating the speculative dynamics of the digital market that ultimately culminated in the "dot-com bubble"[4] of the early 2000s and its market collapse.

Nevertheless, the digital economy did not die. Instead, it was transformed and expanded. The years following the collapse of the dot-com bubble were marked by both consolidation and transformation. Many speculative ventures disappeared, but the infrastructure investments of the 1990s—fiber-optic networks, server capacity, and widespread internet adoption—remained in place, providing the foundation for renewed growth. Surviving firms such as Amazon and eBay refined their business models, while new entrants like Google (founded in 1998 with an initial public offering in 2004) and Facebook (launched in 2004) came to dominate the digital economy a couple of years later. The post-bubble era gave rise to Web 2.0 technology characterized by user-generated content, social networks effect, and platform-based ecosystems. Also, this shift represented a maturation of the digital economy; from speculative excess toward sustainable, data-driven, and network-based models that redefined global commerce, communication, and culture.

In many respects, the evolution of the digital economy does not occur in a vacuum but is closely intertwined with broader economic/financial, sociopolitical, and technological configurations. Here, two major global financial events are stated. As mentioned, the collapse of the dot-com bubble in the early 2000s paved the way for the rise of Web 2.0 technologies and the dominance of the platform economy. The global financial crisis of 2007–2008 triggered the foundation of Bitcoin and, subsequently, the emergence of the blockchain economy.

The global financial crisis of 2008 exposed systemic vulnerabilities in the global financial system, including excessive reliance on centralized intermediaries, opacity in financial instruments, and moral hazard in financial practices. In this context of declining trust in traditional financial institutions, Bitcoin was introduced in 2008 by the pseudonymous figure Satoshi Nakamoto, who explicitly framed it as a peer-to-peer electronic cash system designed to bypass centralized authorities (Nakamoto 2008)[5]. The timestamp of Bitcoin's genesis block (Block 0) famously embedded a headline from The Times, (2009, January 3), "Chancellor on brink of second bailout for banks" underscoring its symbolic connection to the financial crisis and its positioning as an alternative to the incumbent monetary and banking order. Thus, Bitcoin's creation can be seen not only as a technological innovation but also as a response to the failures of the financial system, laying the foundation for the blockchain economy. The blockchain economy originated directly after the 2008 global financial crisis, emerging as a response to the limitations of centralized digital infrastructures that defined the Web 2.0 technology era by the encapsulation of the Web 3.0 technology and particularly the emergence of smart contracts technology with the birth and the expansion of Ethereum since 2015. Bitcoin is the most well-known cryptocurrency, and it signaled the emergence of Web 3.0 decentralized technology in the field of transactions. Nevertheless, what is understood today as the blockchain economy extends far beyond Bitcoin alone.

In the subsequent years, the blockchain economy has evolved into a broad ecosystem with growing institutional acceptance (Davidson et al. 2018). In a business-oriented article, Astroulakis (2024) outlines the milestones underlying the rise of the blockchain economy within the field of the crypto economy up to 2024. A synopsis of this article is presented in the Table 3.

Table 3. The Rise of Blockchain Economy

Time / Period	Milestone	Description/Significance
2009	Global Financial Crisis (GFC) & Bitcoin	Bitcoin launched after GFC: Bitcoin emerged in response to the 2008 crisis, driven by distrust of central financial institutions and the desire for decentralized alternatives.
2010	First Real-Economy Bitcoin Transaction	Purchase utility established: The first documented use of Bitcoin to purchase goods occurred when 10,000 BTC bought two pizzas, giving Bitcoin purchase utility.
2015	Launch of Ethereum 1.0 blockchain	Smart contracts, programmable blockchain: Ethereum introduced programmable smart contract functionality, enabling decentralized applications beyond mere peer-to-peer transfers.
2015	Introduction of first stablecoin	Fiat-pegged value for transactions: Tether stablecoin was created to peg value to the US dollar, supporting transactions within crypto ecosystems.
2015-present	Rise of Altcoins & Crypto Exchanges	Rise of DeFi, NFTs, exchanges: The ecosystem diversified with alternative cryptocurrencies (altcoins), decentralized finance (DeFi), Non-Fungible Tokens (NFTs), and the expansion of crypto exchanges.
2020 - present	Integration with Global Payment Networks	Major payment firms (Visa, Mastercard, PayPal) began integrating crypto and blockchain technology, allowing conversions and directly supporting certain tokens.
2021	Bitcoin as Legal Tender	First nation-state adoption: El Salvador adopted Bitcoin as legal tender in 2021; the Central African Republic followed in 2022.
2022	Ethereum 2.0 ("The Merge")	Ethereum blockchain transitioned from Proof of Work to Proof of Stake consensus mechanism, reducing energy consumption and reshaping its protocol.

continued on following page

Table 3. Continued

Time / Period	Milestone	Description/Significance
2024	U.S. Capital Markets Institutional Recognition	Institutional legitimization: The U.S. Securities and Exchange Commission approved Bitcoin and Ethereum spot ETFs, opening crypto assets to institutional investment.
Ongoing	Active Addresses & Price Relationship	The article also highlights the correlation between active addresses in BTC and ETH (as indicators of user adoption) and price trajectories, arguing that on chain metrics of active addresses adoption is a key driver of long-term valuations.

Source: Astroulakis (2024)

Recent developments in financial technology (fintech) are increasingly converging with Web 3.0 technology. Fintech services such as digital banking as well as regulatory technology solutions provide the institutional and operational scaffolding through which blockchain applications scale into mainstream finance (Kou and Lu 2025). Web 3.0 technology projects and blockchain infrastructure adoption within fintech platforms are expanding across multiple domains: smart contracts, crowdfunding, decentralized banking, digital identity, trade finance, regulatory compliance, and lending (Tanchangya et al. 2025). The development of smart contracts[6] has enabled programmable transactions, laying the foundation for decentralized finance (DeFi) applications such as lending, borrowing, decentralized exchanges, and yield farming, all of which replicate and expand upon traditional financial services without centralized intermediaries (Schär 2021). Furthermore, tokenization[7] has transformed the way value is represented, giving rise to digital assets that underpin Initial Coin Offerings and token-based funding models, while more recently Security Token Offerings and even blockchain-enabled Initial Public Offerings illustrate the growing institutionalization of blockchain within global capital markets (Davidson et al. 2018). Alongside these developments, the rapid growth of the field of stablecoins[8] further demonstrates the increasing expansion of the blockchain economy. Serving as a bridge between traditional finance and decentralized ecosystems, stablecoins provide price stability and transactional efficiency that support the expansion of both DeFi applications and institutional adoption (e.g., PWC, 2025). In 2025, the stablecoins' market capitalization exceeds USD 250 billion[9]. While, according to the International Monetary Fund (IMF 2025), the total crypto-asset market capitalization surpassed USD 3.5 trillion during the 2nd Quarter of 2025. The global blockchain technology market was valued at USD 31.28 billion in 2024 and is projected to reach USD 1,431.54 billion by 2030, expanding at a compound annual growth rate (CAGR) of 90.1% during the forecast period (Grand View Research 2025).

To sum up, the abovementioned highlights that blockchain is not a single innovation but a multi-layered economic and technological ecosystem driving profound transformations across finance, governance, and ownership. As Davidson et al., (2018, p. 640) argue, blockchains function as a "new institutional technology", creating new forms of governance and economic coordination that expand the institutional boundaries of market capitalism.

Here, it is useful to note that the term "blockchain economy" is often used interchangeably with related concepts such as "decentralized economy" and "token economy", particularly within discussions of the emerging Web 3.0 technologies. In this paper, the term blockchain economy is employed to describe the broader field of economic, organizational, and societal transformations enabled by blockchain infrastructures and Web 3.0 technology. The notion of a decentralized economy is more closely aligned with the technological dimension of Web 3.0, emphasizing distributed ledger technologies, peer-to-peer interactions, and novel governance structures (Hsieh and Vergne 2023; Tapscott and Tapscott 2016). By contrast, the term token economy is best understood in relation to the processes of tokenization and the creation of digital assets that function as units of value, exchange, or governance, which are central mechanisms of blockchain economy business models (Catalini and Gans 2020). In the present analysis, the blockchain economy includes the whole preview discussion.

6. EMPIRICAL EVIDENCE ON THE WEB 2.5 ECONOMY

This section presents empirical evidence supporting the emergence of the Web 2.5 economy. It distinguishes between direct empirical cases — where blockchain is explicitly integrated into Web 2.0 platforms — and indirect evidence drawn from on-chain analytics. This emergence primarily takes the form of blockchain tokenization of real-world assets. To support this, in his 2025 annual letter, BlackRock's CEO Larry Fink describes tokenization of real-world assets as the process of "turning real-world assets—stocks, bonds, real estate—into digital tokens tradable online," with each token certifying ownership of the corresponding underlying asset (BlackRock 2025). Also, since March 2024, BlackRock has launched the BlackRock USD Institutional Digital Liquidity Fund (BUIDL), which integrates traditional finance with Web 3.0 technologies through public blockchains (Huang 2024). What follows outlines indicative empirical cases (examples and data) on the Web 2.5 economy.

6.1. Direct empirical evidence

6.1.1. Financial sector

Worldwide financial sector - banks, financial corporations, and FinTech's Web 2.0 platforms - has adopted blockchain infrastructures and projects. The international banking and financial company Santander (www.santander.com) integrates blockchain for cross-border payments. The Japanese holding company SBI Group (www.sbigroup.co.jp) leverages blockchain through its joint venture in Asia. The payments platform PayPal (www.paypal.com) supports blockchain payments and has issued its own stablecoin – PYUSD- by the Paxos Trust Company in the blockchain of Ethereum. Visa (www.visa.com) and Mastercard (www.mastercard.com) explore blockchain for payments and settlements and are providers of crypto backed cards for real world transactions. The fintech bank Revolut (www.revolut.com) offers crypto trading and wallet services within its Web 2.0 platform. The fintech and trading company Robinhood (www.robinhood.com) has introduced blockchain tokenization of real-world assets in the stock market (stocks, ETFs, options) and also offers the Robinhood digital wallet, which gives users direct access to the blockchain economy for holding and transferring cryptocurrencies and tokens. AZA Finance (www .azafinance.com) utilizes blockchain rails and stablecoin liquidity to provide efficient cross-border payments and currency exchange across African and emerging markets, advancing financial inclusion where traditional banking infrastructure is limited.

6.1.2. Other sectors

Beyond financial sector, Web 3.0 technologies are increasingly incorporated by Web 2.0 platforms across diverse fields such as real estate, commerce, luxury goods, sports industry, digital identity, insurance, crowdfunding, governance, and others. In real estate, Web 2.0 platforms are adopting blockchain via tokenization. For example, platform corporations such as RealT (https://realt.co) and Lofty (https://www.lofty.ai) tokenize rental properties at scale, enabling fractional ownership, while Propy (https://propy.com) supports blockchain-based property sales and title transfers. In luxury goods, artwork and commerce, LVMH (https://www .lvmh.com) uses blockchain to authenticate products, and Christie's (https://www .christies.com) auctions digital artwork via NFTs. Similarly, Gucci (https://www .gucci.com) and Nike (https://www.nike.com) have launched Web 3.0 initiatives around digital fashion and on-chain ownership. In the sports industry, clubs such as FC Barcelona (https://www.fcbarcelona.com) and Paris Saint-Germain (PSG) (https://en.psg.fr) issue blockchain-based fan tokens; comparable initiatives include Juventus (https://www.juventus.com) and Manchester City (https://www.mancity

.com). For digital identity, Estonia's e-ID[10] ecosystem (https://e-estonia.com) and Microsoft's ION (Decentralized Identifier project: https://identity.foundation/ion/) exemplify large-scale blockchain-enabled identity frameworks. In insurance, ACRE Africa (https://acreafrica.com) collaborates with Etherisc (https://etherisc.com), an open-source, Web 3.0 decentralized insurance protocol using smart contracts for automated, parametric products. Lemonade (www.lemonade.com), a New York Stock Exchange-listed insurtech company, integrates blockchain technologies through initiatives such as the Lemonade Crypto Climate Coalition, combining traditional insurance operations with decentralized infrastructure. In crowdfunding, Kickstarter (https://www.kickstarter.com) is transitioning core infrastructure toward public-blockchain-based rails, while Gitcoin (https://gitcoin.co) and Mirror (https://mirror.xyz) use Web 3.0 primitives for open-source and creator funding. In web browsers field, the Brave browser (https://brave.com) integrates its token BAT on the blockchain of the Ethereum to reward users and creators. I will conclude the examples references to Web 2.0 platforms that integrate Web 3.0 technologies with a case from the attention economy, specifically in the field of SocialFi. The recently launched platform X.me (https://x.me/home) directly connects Web 3.0 token rewards to content creators and users of the platform.

6.2. Indirect empirical evidence

In the case of the Web 2.5 economy, indirect empirical sources drawn from on-chain analytics. They provide observable and verifiable indicators of blockchain adoption in contexts where direct data from Web 2.0 platforms are not publicly available. On-chain indicators —such as verified smart contract deployments, total value locked in real - world asset protocols, stablecoins supply, and transaction volumes - function as reliable proxies. These proxies may not measure the absolute scale of the incorporation of the blockchain economy into the platform economy, but they offer evidence of the underlying tensions and dynamics.

The total verified smart contracts on the Ethereum blockchain were 848,055[11] in the 28 February 2026. Verified contracts are especially relevant because they represent publicly auditable, production-grade deployments where developers have disclosed source code for transparency. In the context of the Web 2.5 economy, this metric functions as an indirect indicator of the extent to which blockchain infrastructures are being embedded into platform economies. Unlike the broader pool of undeployed or unverified contracts, verified contracts are more likely to underpin applications that interact with mainstream users—ranging from tokenized finance and real-world assets to SocialFi and loyalty systems piloted by Web 2.0 platforms. Thus, the number of verified contracts reflects not only the technical maturity of the

Ethereum blockchain but also the growing convergence between Web 2.0 platforms and Web 3.0 infrastructures.

The total value locked in Real-World Assets protocols across blockchains is $21.161 billion (DeFiLlama 2026) This offers an empirical lens on the Web 2.5 economy because it signals the scale at which blockchain infrastructures have gone beyond purely cryptographic or speculative uses and are being harnessed to tokenize physical, financial, and real-estate assets. In a Web 2.5 paradigm, traditional Web 2.0 platform actors—banks, asset managers, marketplaces—can leverage these deployed smart contracts to create new lines of business, liquidity, and value capture. Thus, the $17.2 billion locked in real world assets contracts constitutes a tangible measure of how deeply Web 2.0 platforms are integrating with blockchain, enabling a shift from mere technical experiments toward productive, cross-domain assetization.

Stablecoins statistics can also be interpreted as empirical indicators of the Web 2.5 economy. Figure 1 illustrates the average supply of stablecoins in circulation across all major stablecoins from January 2019. The data shows a pronounced increase in stablecoin supply beginning in early 2020, coinciding with the acceleration of decentralized finance (DeFi) markets. The average supply resumed its upward trajectory, reaching a peak of nearly $260 billion by September 2025. This trend highlights the growing role of stablecoins as a core transactional and settlement layer in blockchain ecosystems. In the context of the Web 2.5 economy, the expansion of stablecoin supply can be interpreted as an empirical indicator of adoption, reflecting how conventional platforms and financial intermediaries are embedding tokenized, on-chain infrastructures into their operations.

Figure 1. Average Stablecoins Supply, since 2019

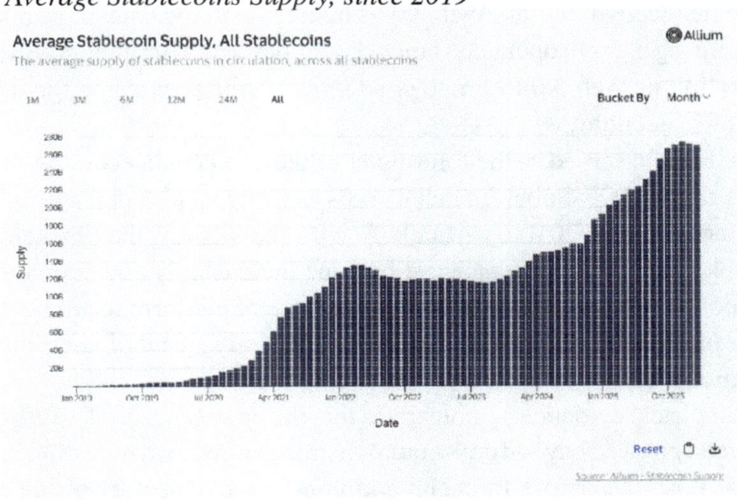

Source: Visa (2026)

Overall, the evidence underscores that the blockchain economy is no longer developing in isolation but is increasingly embedded within the infrastructures of Web 2.0 platforms, giving rise to the hybrid dynamics of the Web 2.5 economy. Blockchain smart contracts, tokenized real-world assets, and the rapid growth of stablecoins illustrate how blockchain economy is being translated into practical mechanism that platform capitalism can adopt and scale. The Web 2.5 economy operates as both a testing ground and an applied form of the blockchain economy, enabling mainly financial but also non-financial sectors to integrate tokenization, decentralized rails, and on-chain value creation into familiar centralized models. What emerges is a hybrid economy in which Web 2.0 platforms and users encounter blockchain economy.

7. INSTEAD OF A CONCLUSION

This chapter fills a gap in the economics literature by introducing the Web 2.5 economy as a distinct analytical category. In the current evolutionary trajectory of the digital economy, it is observed the emergence of a hybrid socio-technical, institutional and economic configuration in which in its present formation the platform economy integrates elements of the blockchain economy. The Web 2.5 economy represents a system of relations that captures how Web 3.0 technologies and blockchain infrastructures are being gradually embedded into existing centralized web models. The key remarks from this analysis can be summarized along three interrelated axes.

First, the Web 2.5 economy is better conceptualized as a *state of play* rather than a technological bridge between Web 2.0 and Web 3.0. In this state, Web 2.0 platforms eclectically integrate Web 3.0 technology and blockchain infrastructures without requiring users to operate as "blockchain-native." This integration interprets the acceleration of Web 3.0 technology adoption while preserving the dominance of the platform economy.

Second, Bitcoin served as the forerunner of the blockchain economy, conceived in the wake of the 2008 global financial crisis as a radical alternative to centralized finance. Since the mid-2010s, particularly with the birth of the blockchain smart contracts, blockchain ecosystems have become increasingly embedded within the platform economy. This reflects both the resilience of platform incumbents and the capacity of platform capitalism to appropriate disruptive technologies into existing dominant models.

Third, empirical evidence demonstrates that the emergence of the Web 2.5 economy has already moved beyond conceptual abstraction and is manifesting in concrete institutional practices across financial and non-financial sectors of the economy. However, a robust conceptual foundation for the Web 2.5 economy remains absent within the scholarship of economics and business. Thus, instead of presenting a definitive conclusion, this study aims to initiate a scholarly dialogue.

REFERENCES

Agrawal, A. (2023). Web 2.5: The Vision of the Future Needs a Plan for the Now. *Journal of Digital Banking*, *7*(4), 290–300. DOI: 10.69554/ZIGH6972

Astroulakis, N. 2024. "Nine (+ 1) Milestones in the Adoption of Cryptocurrencies." https://medium.com/@n.astroulakis/nine-1-milestones-in-the-adoption-of-cryptocurrencies-a492bdbfff21

Bernal, P. A. (2010). Web 2.5: The Symbiotic Web. *International Review of Law Computers & Technology*, *24*(1), 25–37. DOI: 10.1080/13600860903570145

Berners-Lee, T. J., & Cailliau, R. (1990). WorldWideWeb: Proposal for a HyperText project.

BlackRock. (2025). *Larry Fink's 2025 Annual Chairman's Letter to Investors -The Democratization of Investing: Expanding Prosperity in More Places, for More People*. MKTGM0425U/M-4377239.

Blaug, M. (1992). *The Methodology of Economics: Or How Economists Explain* (2nd ed.). Cambridge University Press. DOI: 10.1017/CBO9780511528224

Boyer, R. (2022). Platform Capitalism: A Socio-Economic Analysis. *Socio-economic Review*, *20*(4), 1857–1879. DOI: 10.1093/ser/mwaa055

Brähler, N. 2023. "Web2.5: A Clever Term or a Useful Step for Brands Entering Web3?" https://www.brandingmag.com/nathalie-brahler/web2-5-a-clever-term-or-a-useful-step-for-brands-entering-web3/

Brynjolfsson, E., & McAfee, A. (2014). The second machine age: Work progress and prosperity in a time of brilliant technologies. WW Norton & company.

Bukht, R., & Heeks, R. (2017). *Defining, Conceptualising and Measuring the Digital*. https://diode.network/wp-content/uploads/2017/08/diwkppr68-diode.pdf.

Bullmann, D., Klemm, J., & Pinna, A. (2019). "In Search for Stability in Crypto-Assets: Are Stablecoins the Solution?" *ECB Occasional Paper Series No 230* 1–55.

Calzada, I. (2024). Decentralized Web3 Reshaping Internet Governance: Towards the Emergence of New Forms of Nation-Statehood? *Future Internet*, *16*(10), 361. Advance online publication. DOI: 10.3390/fi16100361

Catalini, C., & Gans, J. S. (2020). Some Simple Economics of the Blockchain. *Communications of the ACM*, *63*(7), 80–90. DOI: 10.1145/3359552

Davidson, S., De Filippi, P., & Potts, J. (2018). Blockchains and the Economic Institutions of Capitalism. *Journal of Institutional Economics*, *14*(4), 639–658. DOI: 10.1017/S1744137417000200

DeFiLlama. (2026). "RWA Protocols." *DeFiLlama*.

Deighton, J., & Kornfeld, L. (2025). Measuring the Digital Economy. Interactive Advertising Bureau (IAB), 1-179.

Fuchs, C., Hofkirchner, W., Schafranek, M., Raffl, C., Sandoval, M., & Bichler, R. (2010). Theoretical Foundations of the Web: Cognition, Communication, and Co-Operation. towards an Understanding of Web 1.0, 2.0, 3.0. *Future Internet*, *2*(1), 41–59. DOI: 10.3390/fi2010041

Gaweł, H. (2022). "Web 2.5 as a Safe Shift from Web 2.0 to Web 3.0: A Definition of Web 2.5 in Informatological Approach." *Cambridge Open Engage* 1–15. DOI: 10.33774/coe-2022-sj2w3

Grand View Research. (2025). *Blockchain Technology Market Size & Outlook, 2030. Horizon Databook*. https://www.grandviewresearch.com/industry-analysis/blockchain-technology-market/dashboard

HACKEN. (2025). "What Is Web2.5? A Builder's Guide to the Web2–Web3 Bridge." https://hacken.io/discover/web2-web3-bridge/

Hausman, D. M. (1992). *The Inexact and Separate Science of Economics*. Cambridge University Press. DOI: 10.1017/CBO9780511752032

Hodgson, G. M. (2001). *How Economics Forgot History:The Problem of Historical Specificity in Social Science Economics As Social Theory*. Taylor & Francis Routledge. DOI: 10.4324/9780203519813

Hodgson, G. M. (2013). *From Pleasure Machines to Moral Communities: An Evolutionary Economics without Homo Economicus*. The University of Chicago Press.

Hsieh, Y. Y., & Vergne, J. P. (2023). The Future of the Web? The Coordination and Early-Stage Growth of Decentralized Platforms. *Strategic Management Journal*, *44*(3), 829–857. DOI: 10.1002/smj.3455

Huang, V. G. (2024). "BlackRock Launches First Tokenized Fund on Ethereum Blockchain." *The Wall Street Journal*, March 21.

IMF. (2025). "CRYPTO-ASSET MONITOR: 2Q25." *International Monetary Fund* 1–11.

JinCheng. Z., & Chuen, D. L. K. (2024). Understanding the Evolution of the Internet: Web 1.0 to Web3. 0, Web3, and Web 3+. In Handbook of Digital Currency (pp. 553-581). Academic Press.

Kenney, M., & Zysman, J. (2016). The Rise of the Platform Economy. *Issues in Science and Technology, 32*(3). https://issues.org/rise-platform-economy-big-data-work/

Knight, J. B. (1977). "Economics: The State of Play." *Social Dynamics. Social Dynamics, 3*(2), 34–40. DOI: 10.1080/02533957708458201

Kou, G., & Lu, Y. (2025). FinTech: A Literature Review of Emerging Financial Technologies and Applications. *Financial Innovation, 11*(1), 1. Advance online publication. DOI: 10.1186/s40854-024-00668-6

Kuhn, T. S. (1970). *The Structure of Scientific Revolutions* (2nd ed.). University of Chicago Press.

Lakatos, I. (1978). *The Methodology of Scientific Research Programmes. Philosophical Papers* (Worrall, J., & Currie, G., Eds.). Vol. 1). Cambridge University Press. DOI: 10.1017/CBO9780511621123

Lawson, T. (1997). *Economics and Reality*. Routledge. DOI: 10.4324/9780203195390

Lawson, T. (2003). *Reorienting Economics*. Routledge.

LCX. (2023). "Introduction to Web 2.5." https://lcx.com/en/introduction-to-web-2-5

Leiner, B. M., Kahn, R. E., Postel, J., Cerf, V. G., Kleinrock, L., Roberts, L. G., Clark, D. D., Lynch, D., & Wolff, S. (2009). A Brief History of the Internet. *Computer Communication Review, 39*(5), 22–31. http://www.acm.org. DOI: 10.1145/1629607.1629613

Lin, Y., Gao, Z., Tu, Y., Du, H., Niyato, D., Kang, J., & Yang, H. (2022). A blockchain-based semantic exchange framework for web 3.0 toward participatory economy. arXiv preprint arXiv:2211.16662.

Müller, J. (2024). *Turning Point: How IT Is Changing Our World*. Springer. DOI: 10.1007/978-3-658-46079-2

Murphy, J., & Roser, M. (2019). "Internet." https://ourworldindata.org/internet

Nakamoto, S. (2008). Bitcoin: A peer-to-peer electronic cash system.

OECD. (2020). *The Tokenisation of Assets and Potential Implications for Financial Markets*. https://www.oecd.org/content/dam/oecd/en/publications/reports/2020/03/the-tokenisation-of-assets-and-potential-implications-for-financial-markets_370f9853/83493d34-en.pdf

OECD. (2024a). *OECD Digital Economy Outlook 2024 (Volume 2):Strengthening Connectivity, Innovation and Trust*. OECD Digital Economy Outlook. OECD Publishing, Paris.

OECD. (2024b). *OECD Digital Economy 2024 (Volume 1): Embracing the Technology Frontier*. OECD Digital Economy Outlook. OECD Publishing, Paris.

Oloyede, A. A., Faruk, N., Noma, N., Tebepah, E., & Nwaulune, A. K. (2023). Measuring the Impact of the Digital Economy in Developing Countries: A Systematic Review and Meta- Analysis. *Heliyon*, *9*(7), 1. DOI: 10.1016/j.heliyon.2023.e17654 PMID: 37501966

Pileggi, S. F., Fernandez-Llatas, C., & Traver, V. (2012). When the Social Meets the Semantic: Social Semantic Web or Web 2.5. *Future Internet*, *4*(4), 852–864. DOI: 10.3390/fi4030852

Polanyi, K. (2001). *1944. The Great Transformation The Political and Economic Origins of Our Time*. Beacon Press.

PWC. (2025). *PwC Global Crypto Report 2025: Navigating the Global Landscape*. https://legal.pwc.de/content/services/global-crypto-regulation-report/pwc-global-crypto-regulation-report-2025.pdf

Ray, P. P. (2023). Web3: A Comprehensive Review on Background, Technologies, Applications, Zero-Trust Architectures, Challenges and Future Directions. *Internet of Things and Cyber-Physical Systems*, *3*, 213–248. DOI: 10.1016/j.iotcps.2023.05.003

Schär, F. (2021). Decentralized Finance: On Blockchain-and Smart Contract-Based Financial Markets. *Review - Federal Reserve Bank of St. Louis*, *103*(2), 153–174. DOI: 10.20955/r.103.153-74

Schrepel, T. (2023). The Complex Relationship between Web2 Giants and Web3 Projects. *Computer Law & Security Review*, *50*, 1–11. DOI: 10.1016/j.clsr.2023.105845

Srnicek, N. (2017). *Platform Capitalism*. Polity Press.

Szabo, N. 1997. "The Idea of Smart Contracts." https://www.fon.hum.uva.nl/rob/Courses/InformationInSpeech/CDROM/Literature/LOTwinterschool2006/szabo.best.vwh.net/smart_contracts_idea.html

Tanchangya, T., Sarker, T., Rahman, J., Islam, M. S., Islam, N., & Siddiqi, K. O. (2025). Mapping Blockchain Applications in FinTech: A Systematic Review of Eleven Key Domains. *Information (Basel)*, *16*(9), 1–33. DOI: 10.3390/info16090769

Tapscott, A. (2023). *Web3: Charting the Internet's Next Economic and Cultural Frontier*. Harper Business.

Tapscott, D. (2014). *The Digital Economy: Rethinking Promise and Peril in the Age of Networked Intelligence*. McGraw-Hill Education.

Topscott, A., & Topscott, D. (2016). Blockchain revolution: How the technology behind bitcoin and other cryptocurrencies is changing the world.

The Times. (2009). "Chancellor on Brink of Second Bailout for Banks." *The Times*, January 3.

United Nations Conference on Trade and Development (UNCTAD). (2024). *Digital Economy Report 2024: Shaping an Environmentally Sustainable and Inclusive Digital Future*. https://unctad.org/system/files/official-document/der2024_en.pdf?utm_source=chatgpt.com

van Dijck, J., Poell, T., & de Waal, M. (2018). *The Platform Society*. Oxford University Press. DOI: 10.1093/oso/9780190889760.001.0001

Titanium Ventures. (n.d). "Web 2.5 Is a Bridge to a New Digital Era."

Visa. (2026). "Average Stablecoin Supply, All Stablecoins." https://visaonchainanalytics.com/

Werbach, K. (2018). *The Blockchain and the New Architecture of Trust*. The MIT Press. DOI: 10.7551/mitpress/11449.001.0001

Xiangjuan, J., Fang, X., Zhang, Y., Heng, Y., Chen, X., Ge, W., Liu, W., & Huang, F. (2025). Integration and Innovation of Blockchain in Web3.0: Current Status and Standardization Prospects. *World Wide Web (Bussum)*, *28*(1), 7. Advance online publication. DOI: 10.1007/s11280-024-01319-7

Zander, U., Lu, L., & Chimenti, G. (2025). The Platform Economy and Futures of Market Societies: Salient Tensions in Ecosystem Evolution. *Journal of Business Research*, *189*, 115037. Advance online publication. DOI: 10.1016/j.jbusres.2024.115037

ENDNOTES

1 The terms "platform capitalism" and "digital capitalism" are also used to describe the regime of capital accumulation driven by web-based platforms. In this study, the term "platform economy" is more appropriate, as it aligns with an analysis that approaches the economy as a system of relations. The aforementioned terms are often overlapping or used interchangeably.

2 The search using the Scopus database showed that across all journal publications within the subject areas of *Business, Management and Accounting* and *Economics and Econometrics and Finance* from 2009 to 2024 - maximum available time frame for searching within the Scopus database -, the term "Web 2.5 economy" does not appear in the Abstracts and the Keywords. Even the term "Web 2.5" on its own—without the qualifier "economy"—is absent from this body of literature.

3 In 1969, Advanced Research Projects Agency Network (ARPANET) established the first successful message transmission between computers at UCLA and Stanford Research Institute. Later, the development of the TCP/IP protocol by Vinton Cerf and Robert Kahn (published in 1974 and adopted by ARPANET in 1983) created the standard for internetworking (e.g., Leiner et al., 2009).

4 The dot-com bubble refers to the speculative investment frenzy of the early 2000s, during which stock valuations of Internet-based companies surged and subsequently collapsed.

5 Satoshi Nakamoto's 2008 paper, "Bitcoin: A Peer-to-Peer Electronic Cash System," has accumulated over 37,000 citations (up to October 2025) according to its listing on ResearchGate.

6 A smart contract is a self-executing digital agreement encoded on a blockchain, in which the terms of the contract are directly written into code and automatically enforced without the need for intermediaries (e.g., Schär, 2021; Szabo, 1997).

7 Tokenization is the process of converting rights to a real or digital asset into a digital token recorded on a blockchain, enabling fractional ownership, transferability, and programmability of value, (Catalini and Gans 2020; OECD 2020).

8. A stablecoin is a type of crypto-asset designed to maintain a stable value by pegging its price to a reserve asset, such as a fiat currency, or a commodity (e.g., Bullmann et al., 2019)

9 https://coinmarketcap.com/

10 https://e-estonia.com/solutions/estonian-e-identity/id-card/

11 https://etherscan.io/contractsVerified

Chapter 7
Data Localization, AI Governance, and Digital Sovereignty in Emerging Economies:
A Comparative Governance Framework

Abdelraouf Ishtaiwi
http://orcid.org/0000-0001-8013-7151
Data Science and Artificial Intelligence, University of Petra, Amman, Jordan

Feda AlShahwan
Public Authority for Applied Education and Training, Kuwait

Ahmad Hajyasien
http://orcid.org/0000-0002-2974-7808
Higher College of Technology, UAE

ABSTRACT

This chapter addresses that analytical fragmentation by developing a comparative framework through which localization rules, AI governance instruments, and sovereignty claims are examined as mutually conditioning layers of digital statecraft rather than as isolated legal categories. A structured review of an uploaded Scopus corpus, which contained 139 records, was combined with a comparative analysis of India, Indonesia, Kenya, and Brazil, alongside official instruments issued by the African Union, UNESCO, the OECD, and NIST. The analysis demonstrates that broad territorial restrictions on data do not by themselves produce operational digital

DOI: 10.4018/979-8-2600-0288-9.ch007

sovereignty; durable sovereignty is achieved when selective localization is aligned with data classification, compute and cloud capacity, risk-based AI governance, and interoperable cross-border transfer mechanisms.

I. INTRODUCTION

In this section, the domain context, the specific problem addressed by the chapter, the relevant literature streams, and the chapter contributions are established in a funnel structure that moves from broad transformations in data-driven governance to the unresolved challenge faced by emerging economies. Digital transformation is now organized around data-intensive infrastructures, platform intermediation, and machine learning systems whose value depends on continuous data access, scalable computing capacity, and legally reliable cross-border exchange arrangements. At the same time, regulatory authority over those infrastructures remains territorially anchored, which means that states seeking developmental autonomy must govern resources that are globally networked but institutionally unevenly distributed (Burri, 2024; UN Trade and Development (UNCTAD), 2021; Yakovleva, 2024). Consequently, the governance of data and AI is no longer confined to privacy or innovation policy alone; it has become a central mechanism through which states negotiate security, industrial upgrading, public-sector modernization, and geopolitical dependence (Chesterman, 2021; Png, 2022).

Furthermore, data localization has expanded from a narrow concern with privacy-sensitive records into a broader repertoire of legal and administrative instruments through which states require that specific categories of data be stored, mirrored, processed, or made accessible within national jurisdiction. This expansion has been justified by several policy rationales, namely: supervisory access, cyber resilience, protection of critical infrastructure, leverage over digital firms, and support for domestic data-driven industry formation (Han, 2024; Taylor, 2020). However, the policy consequences of localization remain contested because territorial restrictions can strengthen state oversight while simultaneously increasing costs, fragmenting digital markets, and constraining the development of globally competitive AI ecosystems if complementary infrastructures are absent (Aaronson, 2019; Kalin, 2024; Taylor, 2020). Thus, the central question is not whether localization exists, but under what institutional and infrastructural conditions it contributes to meaningful sovereignty rather than symbolic control.

However, the literature and policy debate remain analytically fragmented. Data localization is often treated as a trade or privacy issue; AI governance is often treated as a risk-management or ethics issue; and digital sovereignty is often treated as a strategic or geopolitical discourse whose operational content remains unstable

(Carrapico & Farrand, 2025; Glasze et al., 2023; Nanni et al., 2024). In emerging economies, these separations are analytically unsatisfactory because regulatory choices concerning one domain immediately condition the feasible options in the others; a state that mandates local data retention without cloud capacity, for example, does not secure autonomy but merely relocates dependence. This chapter therefore addresses the following problem: how can data localization, AI governance, and digital sovereignty be conceptualized together in a way that explains variation across emerging economies and supports the design of coherent, development-oriented regulatory frameworks?

A. Background Review

This subsection reviews the principal literature streams that inform the chapter and identifies the unresolved integrative gap that motivates the comparative framework. The review is organized by theme rather than chronology because the relevant scholarship proceeds through partially overlapping debates on localization, sovereignty, trade, AI regulation, and Global South governance. Table I summarizes the representative streams and the specific unresolved gap carried forward into the analytical framework.

The first literature stream conceptualizes data localization as a territorial policy response to the transnational character of data flows. Taylor analyzed localization as part of the tension between information sovereignty and trans-border data flow regimes, and emphasized that the regulatory stakes extend beyond privacy into internet architecture, human rights, and the future of data-intensive innovation (Taylor, 2020). Han subsequently connected localization to economic statecraft by demonstrating that states employ localization to manage network effects and security externalities associated with platforms, while Aaronson examined localization and related controls through the broader language of digital protectionism and demonstrated the difficulty of separating legitimate public policy from protectionist state practice (Aaronson, 2019; Han, 2024). Islam and Khan then provided a developing-country perspective by examining Bangladesh and demonstrating that localization generates tangible compliance and ecosystem trade-offs when institutional readiness and market structure remain constrained (Islam & Khan, 2024). In summary, localization-based approaches clarify motives and instruments, but they remain limited in terms of explaining when localization contributes to developmental sovereignty rather than regulatory fragmentation.

The second literature stream addresses digital sovereignty as a contested political and legal project. Glasze and colleagues analyzed digital sovereignty as a spatial and geopolitical discourse through which borders, jurisdictions, and infrastructures are re-imagined under digital conditions, while Nanni, Bizzaro, and Napolitano demonstrated that sovereignty claims framed around individual autonomy may remain institutionally thin when platform power and infrastructural dependence persist (Glasze et al., 2023; Nanni et al., 2024). Catanzariti further argued that territoriality itself is being reworked by data fragmentation, and Carrapico and Farrand demonstrated that even the European Union, despite its regulatory density, encounters an autonomy–interdependence gap when sovereignty ambitions confront transnational semiconductor and data dependencies (Carrapico & Farrand, 2025; Catanzariti, 2024). In summary, sovereignty-centered approaches clarify the symbolic and jurisdictional dimensions of regulation, but they remain limited in terms of specifying how sovereignty becomes operational under conditions of unequal infrastructural capacity.

The third literature stream examines the governance of AI through ethics, risk management, and institutional design. Chesterman synthesized the legal limits of governing AI and argued that effective regulation depends on calibrated combinations of rules, institutions, and legitimacy-preserving oversight rather than on technological determinism alone (Chesterman, 2021). Global norm-setting instruments issued by UNESCO, the OECD, and NIST then advanced complementary architectures centred on trustworthy AI, risk governance, accountability, transparency, and lifecycle management (National Institute of Standards and Technology, 2023; OECD, 2019; UNESCO, 2021). Parasol, working from the Chinese context, demonstrated that AI development and data law interact through strategic ambiguity, while Gao illustrated that competing conceptions of personal data as trade asset, rights object, or security resource lead to divergent regulatory paradigms for cross-border transfers (Gao, 2023; Parasol, 2021). In summary, AI-governance approaches clarify normative principles and institutional techniques, but they remain limited in terms of connecting AI regulation to the territorial and developmental politics of data control.

The fourth literature stream foregrounds emerging economies, inequality, and Global South perspectives. Png argued that dominant AI-governance discourse has been led by Global North institutions and that Global South actors are often positioned as norm-takers despite bearing disproportionate infrastructural, labour, and extractive burdens (Png, 2022). Burri examined how digital trade regulation reproduces inequality by privileging governance models shaped by powerful actors, while Díaz Vera and Mishra and Agarwal analyzed non-personal data regulation in Latin America and India respectively as attempts to correct asymmetries in market power, data access, and developmental opportunity (Burri, 2024; Díaz Vera, 2023; Mishra & Agarwal, 2026). Osorio and Gojo Cruz further argued, in the Southeast Asian context, that regional competition-law harmonization can support freer flows of data, compute, and models without abandoning public-interest governance objectives, and Zhang, Ong, and Findlay proposed digital self-determination as an alternative paradigm more attentive to the priorities of emerging economies (Osorio & Gojo

Cruz, 2025; Zhang et al., 2023). In summary, emerging-economy approaches clarify developmental asymmetry and institutional inequality, but they remain limited in terms of offering a single comparative framework that jointly evaluates localization, AI governance, and sovereignty outcomes.

Table 1. Representative literature streams and the unresolved integrative gap.

Literature stream	Representative sources	Primary analytical focus	Principal contribution	Remaining limitation
Localization and digital trade	Aaronson (2019); Taylor (2020); Han (2024); Kalin (2024)	Territorial control over data flows	Clarifies motives, transfer restrictions, and trade tensions	Does not explain when localization produces developmental autonomy
Digital sovereignty	Glasze et al. (2023); Nanni et al. (2024); Catanzariti (2024); Carrapico and Farrand (2025)	Jurisdiction, autonomy, and infrastructural dependence	Clarifies sovereignty as a contested legal-political project	Does not specify how sovereignty becomes operational in lower-capacity settings
AI governance	Chesterman (2021); UNESCO (2021); OECD (2019); NIST (2023); Parasol (2021)	Ethics, risk management, and institutional design	Clarifies governance principles and oversight models	Treats territorial data control and development strategy as secondary concerns
Emerging-economy and Global South perspectives	Png (2022); Burri (2024); Díaz Vera (2023); Mishra and Agarwal (2026); Zhang et al. (2023); Osorio and Gojo Cruz (2025)	Inequality, development, and policy space	Clarifies asymmetry, capability gaps, and alternative normative priorities	Lacks an integrated cross-case framework linking localization, AI capacity, and sovereignty

Furthermore, the representative works can be considered individually in order to clarify the gap with greater precision. Aaronson achieved conceptual clarification regarding the language of digital protectionism; however, the analysis remained centred on trade politics and did not provide an operational method for assessing state capacity. In addition, Taylor achieved a historically grounded synthesis of localization arguments; however, the framework did not distinguish adequately between selective localization supported by domestic infrastructure and blanket localization unsupported by local capacity (Aaronson, 2019; Taylor, 2020). Han achieved an important bridge between localization and statecraft; however, the argument remained oriented toward motives rather than toward layered institutional design. In addition, Kalin achieved a careful reconciliation of trade and privacy debates; however, the monographic treatment remained less attentive to the developmental constraints specific to emerging economies (Han, 2024; Kalin, 2024).

Moreover, Png achieved a decisive critique of Global North dominance in AI-governance discourse; however, the article did not convert that critique into a comparative policy architecture. Glasze and colleagues achieved a strong account of sovereignty's contested spatiality; however, the framework remained primarily interpretive and did not specify actionable regulatory sequences. Mishra and Agarwal achieved a nuanced evaluation of India's non-personal-data debates, and Osorio and Gojo Cruz achieved a regional blueprint for freer and fairer AI-related flows in Southeast Asia; however, neither contribution was designed to compare heterogeneous national trajectories through a common analytical lens (Glasze et al., 2023; Mishra & Agarwal, 2026; Osorio & Gojo Cruz, 2025; Png, 2022). One can observe that the reviewed literature remains limited in terms of integrated treatment of territorial control, AI-governance capacity, and interoperable transfer mechanisms, which motivates the comparative framework developed in this chapter.

B. Chapter Contributions

This subsection states the chapter contributions in a form aligned with the analytical problem identified above. The contributions are conceptual, comparative, and framework-oriented because the chapter does not report laboratory experimentation; instead, it develops a structured evidence base and an integrative policy design model.

- **Integrative analytical lens:** This chapter develops a triadic lens through which data localization, AI governance, and digital sovereignty are examined as mutually conditioning layers of digital regulation rather than as separate fields. The lens establishes that sovereignty claims remain incomplete when they are detached either from AI-governance capacity or from infrastructures capable of storing, processing, auditing, and leveraging localized data. Consequently, the chapter replaces binary debates, in which localization is either celebrated or rejected, with a capacity-sensitive account of when territorial controls become substantively effective.
- **Comparative evidence design:** This chapter constructs a transparent evidence base by combining an uploaded Scopus corpus with verified official policy and legal instruments from India, Indonesia, Kenya, Brazil, the African Union, UNESCO, the OECD, and NIST. The resulting design permits scholarly interpretation to be cross-checked against primary legal and strategy documents, thereby reducing the risk that sovereignty rhetoric is mistaken for operational governance capacity. In this way, the analysis maintains evidentiary rigor without fabricating empirical quantities that are not present in the source material.

- **Cross-case synthesis for emerging economies:** This chapter provides a structured comparison of four emerging-economy trajectories that differ in localization intensity, AI-governance maturity, infrastructural capacity, and regional positioning. India, Indonesia, Kenya, and Brazil were selected because together they render visible four distinct pathways: sectorally differentiated localization, moderated localization with strategy-led AI governance, institution-building with limited territorial restriction, and rights-based data governance coupled with industrial AI planning. The synthesis demonstrates that durable sovereignty is not produced by maximal territorial control but by alignment among regulation, compute capacity, and external interoperability.
- **Capacity-aligned governance framework:** This chapter proposes a four-layer governance framework that organizes policy design around strategic data classification, compute and cloud capability, model and application governance, and institutional coordination with external alignment. The framework translates comparative findings into an actionable architecture through which policymakers can determine where localization is justified, where trusted transfer mechanisms are preferable, and which complementary investments are necessary for sovereignty claims to acquire practical effect. As a result, the chapter contributes both an analytical model for scholarship and a design heuristic for public policy.

The rest of this chapter is organized as follows. Section II defines the conceptual relationship among data localization, AI governance, and digital sovereignty. Section III explains the evidence base, case-selection logic, and coding scheme employed for the comparative analysis. Section IV presents the cross-case analysis of India, Indonesia, Kenya, and Brazil. Section V develops the capacity-aligned governance framework and formal analytical propositions. Section VI identifies future research directions. Finally, Section VII concludes this chapter.

II. CONCEPTUAL FOUNDATIONS AND ANALYTICAL LENS

In this section, the core concepts are defined, differentiated, and brought into a single analytical architecture. The section proceeds from definition to instantiation because conceptual ambiguity has been a central obstacle in debates where localization, sovereignty, and AI governance are invoked with high political intensity but inconsistent operational meaning.

A. Data Localization

This subsection defines data localization as a family of territorial governance instruments rather than as a single legal rule. Data localization comprises obligations through which particular categories of data are required to be stored domestically, mirrored within national territory, processed locally, made accessible to domestic authorities, or transferred abroad only under specific safeguards and approvals (Han, 2024; Taylor, 2020; Yakovleva, 2024). Consequently, localization must be distinguished from general data protection law, from cybersecurity obligations, and from transfer-accountability mechanisms because each of those can exist without a strict territorial residency requirement. This distinction is analytically important because many states employ hybrid arrangements in which only high-risk or strategically salient datasets are localized, while other categories remain transferable under regulated conditions.

Furthermore, localization performs several distinct functions whose coexistence often produces conceptual confusion. It can operate as an enforcement device when regulators require supervisory access; it can operate as a security instrument when critical systems are ring-fenced; it can operate as an industrial-policy tool when domestic cloud or analytics ecosystems are to be stimulated; and it can operate as a bargaining device when multinational technology firms are required to negotiate with domestic authorities from within the jurisdiction (Aaronson, 2019; Han, 2024). However, these functions do not produce identical outcomes. If localization is imposed without domestic storage, cloud, audit, and compute capability, then the formal relocation of data does not eliminate dependence because foreign firms may continue to control the relevant technical stack, standards, and model pipelines. Thus, localization is best treated as a conditional instrument whose value depends on institutional and infrastructural complements.

B. AI Governance

This subsection defines AI governance as the set of legal, institutional, organizational, and technical arrangements through which the development, deployment, oversight, and use of AI systems are directed toward public-interest objectives. In the contemporary literature, AI governance includes ethical principles, risk classification, accountability mechanisms, audit procedures, procurement rules, standards, redress pathways, and ecosystem-building measures directed toward talent, research, and infrastructure (Chesterman, 2021; National Institute of Standards and Technology, 2023; OECD, 2019; UNESCO, 2021). Consequently, AI governance is broader than algorithmic ethics and narrower than digital governance as a whole; it concerns the lifecycle of AI systems, but it also concerns the conditions under which those systems become socially legitimate, economically useful, and institutionally governable.

Moreover, AI governance is not exhausted by harm prevention. Developmental contexts require that governance be understood simultaneously as a risk-management architecture and as a capacity-building architecture because states that lack compute, training data access, public-sector procurement capability, or technical regulatory literacy are unable to shape AI markets even when formal rules exist (Burri, 2024; Png, 2022). Parasol demonstrated this duality in a distinct political context by examining how data law and innovation strategy interacted in China, while Chesterman emphasized that governance must preserve legitimacy by combining rules with institutions capable of implementation (Chesterman, 2021; Parasol, 2021). Therefore, AI governance in emerging economies must be evaluated not only by the stringency of norms but also by the degree to which institutional, infrastructural, and economic prerequisites for effective oversight are present.

C. Digital Sovereignty

This subsection defines digital sovereignty as the practical capacity of a political community, acting through public institutions and legally recognized authority, to shape the infrastructures, data flows, standards, and digital markets on which public power and social life depend. This definition intentionally departs from maximalist notions of autarky because complete technological self-sufficiency is neither empirically common nor normatively necessary in deeply networked digital economies (Carrapico & Farrand, 2025; Glasze et al., 2023). Instead, sovereignty is treated as graded and relational: it concerns the degree to which strategic dependence can be governed, the extent to which domestic institutions can set and enforce rules, and the ability to participate in transnational networks without forfeiting regulatory agency (Catanzariti, 2024; Nanni et al., 2024). Thus, digital sovereignty is neither pure territorial closure nor pure openness; it is controlled interdependence.

Furthermore, digital sovereignty in emerging economies is shaped by development constraints that are not adequately captured in many Global North debates. Where domestic cloud markets are shallow, public digital infrastructure is uneven, or foreign platforms mediate large portions of domestic economic life, sovereignty claims become tightly linked to industrial policy, competition governance, and access to cross-border capital and technology (Burri, 2024; Png, 2022; Zhang et al., 2023). Kokas demonstrated how data can become a geopolitical resource in contestation among large powers, while Díaz Vera and Mishra and Agarwal examined how non-personal data debates in Latin America and India reflect concerns over local value capture and market asymmetry rather than privacy alone (Díaz Vera, 2023; Kokas, 2022; Mishra & Agarwal, 2026). Accordingly, sovereignty in emerging economies must be analyzed as a combined problem of territorial authority, developmental capability, and negotiated interoperability.

D. Integrative Analytical Lens

This subsection develops the integrative lens through which the cases are interpreted. As illustrated in Fig. 2, data localization, AI governance, and digital sovereignty form a triadic relationship in which each dimension conditions the efficacy of the others. Localization determines where strategically important data can reside and who can lawfully access them; AI governance determines whether those data are processed within accountable and developmentally useful institutional arrangements; and sovereignty describes the aggregate capacity to convert legal control and technical capability into sustained public authority.

Figure 1. Evidence-construction workflow for the chapter corpus.

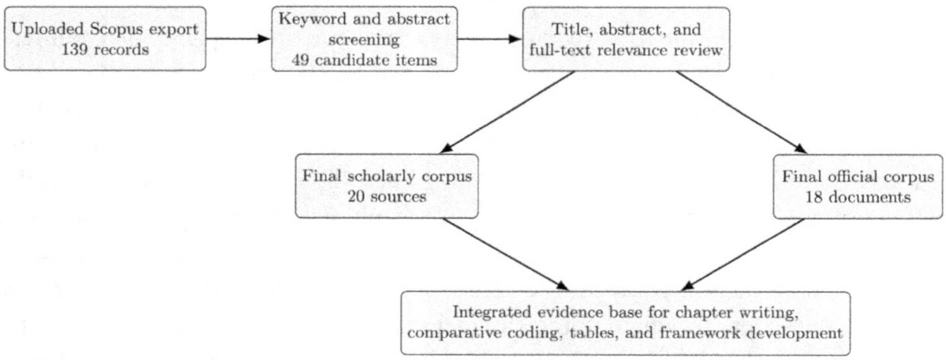

Furthermore, the lens rests on three analytical assumptions. First, localization is meaningful only when data categories are differentiated because personal, non-personal, public-interest, and critical-infrastructure data generate distinct governance risks and policy opportunities (Díaz Vera, 2023; Mishra & Agarwal, 2026). Second, AI governance is meaningful only when the institutions responsible for oversight possess at least minimum audit, procurement, and technical coordination capacity; otherwise, normative frameworks remain aspirational (Chesterman, 2021; National Institute of Standards and Technology, 2023). Third, sovereignty is meaningful only when external interdependence is governed through transfer mechanisms, competition tools, procurement leverage, and regional cooperation rather than denied through rhetorically expansive but operationally thin territorial claims (Carrapico & Farrand, 2025; Osorio & Gojo Cruz, 2025; Yakovleva, 2024).

Moreover, the lens is operationalized through four comparative dimensions that recur throughout the chapter, namely: localization intensity, AI-governance maturity, infrastructural capacity, and external alignment. Localization intensity denotes the breadth and stringency of territorial data requirements; AI-governance maturity denotes the degree to which principles, institutions, and enforcement pathways are articulated; infrastructural capacity denotes the domestic ability to store, compute, audit, and deploy at scale; and external alignment denotes the extent to which a country's framework remains interoperable with regional and international rules. By combining those dimensions, the chapter avoids two common errors: the first is to infer sovereignty from legislation alone, and the second is to infer openness from the absence of localization rules. In this way, the conceptual foundation prepares the comparative analysis developed in the next section.

III. RESEARCH DESIGN AND EVIDENCE BASE

In this section, the evidence base, case-selection logic, and analytical validation procedure are specified. Because the chapter is review-based and conceptual rather than experimental, rigor is provided through transparent corpus construction, conservative coding, and systematic comparison rather than through statistical inference.

A. Corpus Construction

This subsection explains how the chapter evidence base was constructed from the materials supplied for the task and from traceable official policy documents. The uploaded Scopus export, which comprised 139 bibliographic records, was treated as the initial scholarly universe for the topic area. A first-stage screening, based on titles, abstracts, and keywords related to data localization, cross-border data flows, digital sovereignty, AI governance, emerging economies, and adjacent terms, retained 49 candidate items; that intermediate set was preserved in a working file for auditability. A second-stage screening then excluded records that were topically tangential, sectorally unrelated, duplicative in analytical contribution, or insufficiently connected to the chapter's core triad. The final analytical set comprised 20 scholarly items and 18 official policy documents, as illustrated in Fig. 1.

Figure 2. Integrative relationship among data localization, AI governance, and digital sovereignty.

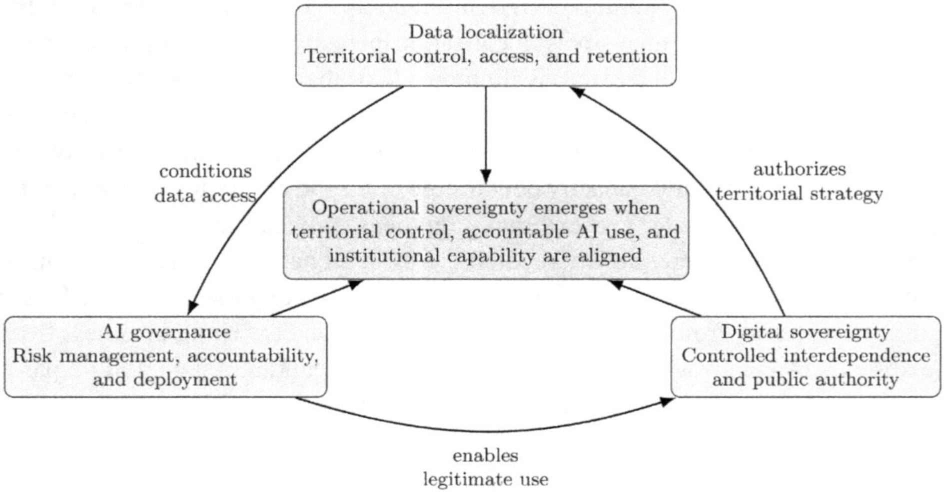

Furthermore, the official corpus was constructed because the chapter addresses rapidly evolving statutes, policy strategies, and standards whose authoritative content cannot be inferred reliably from secondary commentary alone. Official materials were therefore added from India, Indonesia, Kenya, Brazil, the African Union, UNESCO, the OECD, NIST, and UNCTAD in order to verify legislative titles, strategic objectives, and public-policy framing (African Union, 2022, 2024; Government of India, 2023; Government of Indonesia, 2019, 2022; IndiaAI, 2024; KORIKA, 2020; Ministério da Ciência, Tecnologia e Inovação, 2024; Ministério da Ciência, Tecnologia e Inovações, 2021; Ministry of Information, Communications and the Digital Economy, Kenya, 2025; National Institute of Standards and Technology, 2023; NITI Aayog, 2021; OECD, 2019; Presidency of the Republic of Brazil, 2018; Republic of Kenya, 2019; Reserve Bank of India, 2018; UN Trade and Development (UNCTAD), 2021; UNESCO, 2021). Consequently, the chapter does not rely on inferred descriptions of laws or strategies where primary documents are available. This evidentiary structure supports citation integrity and reduces the risk of attributing policy features to sources that do not substantiate them.

B. Case Selection

This subsection explains why India, Indonesia, Kenya, and Brazil were selected as the focal cases. The cases were chosen on the basis of four criteria, namely: documented policy salience in data and AI governance, geographic and regional diversity, variation in localization intensity and institutional design, and the availability of both scholarly interpretation and official documentary evidence. India was selected because it combines strong sovereignty discourse, sectoral localization, large-scale digital public infrastructure, and active non-personal-data debates. Indonesia was selected because it illustrates a moderated localization trajectory in Southeast Asia, where territorial restrictions coexist with strategic openness and developmental ambition. Kenya was selected because it demonstrates an institution-building pathway in which data protection and AI strategy have advanced without an expansive localization model. Brazil was selected because it combines a comprehensive personal-data regime with national AI strategy instruments and an increasingly explicit industrial-policy orientation.

Table 2. Case-selection logic and principal regulatory instruments.

Case	Selection logic	Localization profile	AI-governance profile	Principal official instruments
India	Large digital market; strong sovereignty discourse; public digital infrastructure	Sectorally differentiated and strategically salient	Strategy plus mission-driven capacity building	DPDP Act 2023; RBI payment-data storage; IndiaAI Mission; NITI Responsible AI
Indonesia	Southeast Asian case with moderated localization and staged reform	Narrower than blanket territorialism after regulatory revision	Strategy-led and developmental	PDP Law 2022; Government Regulation 71/2019; STRANAS KA 2020–2045
Kenya	Institution-building pathway with rising continental relevance	Limited explicit localization outside general data governance	Newly formalized national AI strategy	Data Protection Act 2019; Kenya National AI Strategy 2025–2030
Brazil	Rights-based data governance combined with industrial AI planning	General transfer safeguards rather than economy-wide localization	Established strategy framework and new implementation plan	LGPD 2018; EBIA 2021; PBIA 2024

Furthermore, the selected cases are not intended to be statistically representative of all emerging economies. Instead, they are analytically contrasting cases through which the interaction among localization, AI governance, and sovereignty can be observed under different regional and institutional conditions. This logic is appropriate for a review-based chapter because the goal is theory-building and framework development rather than population-level estimation. The resulting comparison therefore emphasizes patterned variation, causal plausibility, and design implications, which are sufficient for the conceptual purpose of the chapter.

C. Coding Scheme and Analytical Validation

This subsection specifies the coding dimensions through which the cases were compared. Each case was coded across four dimensions, namely: territorial data control, AI-governance architecture, infrastructural capability, and external interoperability. Territorial data control captures whether localization obligations are broad, sectoral, or limited; AI-governance architecture captures whether rules exist only as principles, or whether institutions, missions, standards, and implementation pathways have been articulated; infrastructural capability captures the domestic ability to host, compute, secure, and scale data-intensive systems; and external interoperability captures whether the framework remains compatible with trusted transfers, regional standards, and international engagement. Table III summarizes the coding dimensions and interpretive rules.

Table 3. Coding dimensions and interpretive rules.

Dimension	Operational indicator	Primary evidence source	Interpretive rule
Territorial data control	Storage mandates, processing mandates, mirroring, transfer approvals, supervisory-access requirements	Laws, regulations, central-bank directives, policy strategies	Broad mandates indicate high localization intensity; sectoral mandates indicate differentiated localization; accountability-based transfers indicate limited territorial restriction
AI-governance architecture	Ethical principles, risk-management provisions, mission structures, oversight bodies, implementation roadmaps	National AI strategies, responsible-AI documents, standards frameworks	Principles alone indicate low maturity; principles plus institutions indicate medium maturity; principles plus institutions, funding, and implementation pathways indicate higher maturity
Infrastructural capability	Compute initiatives, cloud capacity, public digital infrastructure, state ability to audit and procure	Mission documents, strategy texts, scholarly interpretation	Capability is treated as weak when rules exceed implementation infrastructure, and stronger when investment, procurement, and ecosystem design are aligned
External interoperability	Transfer mechanisms, regional alignment, competition and trade openness, international standards adoption	Laws, regional frameworks, trade-oriented scholarship	High interoperability exists when territorial control is selective and transfer governance remains legible to external actors

Moreover, analytical validation was achieved through source triangulation rather than through quantitative replication. A coding judgment was treated as valid only when it could be grounded in at least one authoritative official instrument and one relevant scholarly interpretation where such interpretation existed; where scholarship remained thin, the coding was stated conservatively and tied closely to the primary document. Contradictions between rhetorical sovereignty claims and operational provisions were resolved in favor of operative legal or programmatic text rather than political branding. This procedure matters because digital policy discourse frequently overstates institutional capability, especially in rapidly evolving AI sectors.

At this point, the chapter possesses a defined corpus, an explicit case logic, and a transparent coding scheme. Consequently, the next section converts these elements into comparative analysis in order to determine how the interaction among localization, AI governance, and sovereignty differs across the selected emerging economies.

IV. COMPARATIVE ANALYSIS OF EMERGING-ECONOMY TRAJECTORIES

In this section, the four cases are analyzed comparatively through the lens developed above. Each subsection follows a claim-then-elaboration pattern in order to identify the dominant governance logic of the case, explain how the logic manifests in law and policy, and interpret the implications for operational digital sovereignty.

A. India

This subsection argues that India represents a model of sectorally differentiated localization combined with ambitious sovereignty and capability-building objectives. India's trajectory has not been defined by a single blanket localization statute; rather, it has been assembled through layered interventions that include sector-specific residency requirements, a general personal-data framework, public digital infrastructure, and explicit investment in AI compute capacity (Government of India, 2023; IndiaAI, 2024; Reserve Bank of India, 2018). The Reserve Bank of India's payment-data storage directive established one of the clearest sectoral localization mandates by requiring payment-system data to be stored only in India, thereby linking territorial control directly to supervisory access and systemic oversight (Reserve Bank of India, 2018). The Digital Personal Data Protection Act, 2023, then established a general framework for digital personal-data processing and cross-border transfer governance without converting all digital regulation into a universal localization mandate (Government of India, 2023). Thus, India's model is best characterized as selective but strategically consequential localization rather than indiscriminate territorial closure.

Furthermore, India's AI-governance posture combines normative guidance with mission-oriented capability building. NITI Aayog's responsible-AI framework articulated a trust-centred governance agenda, while the IndiaAI Mission was approved with explicit emphasis on large-scale computing infrastructure, ecosystem enablement, and national capability development (IndiaAI, 2024; NITI Aayog, 2021). This combination matters because localization rules generate greater sovereign value when domestic actors possess the ability to process, audit, and deploy data within national infrastructures rather than merely to warehouse data locally. Mishra and Agarwal demonstrated a related dynamic in the non-personal-data debate, where data were framed not simply as objects of privacy but as developmental resources whose governance implicated market access, data intermediaries, and domestic economic opportunity (Mishra & Agarwal, 2026). Consequently, India's sovereignty strategy is not reducible to legal control over flows; it is oriented toward the domestication of value creation.

However, India's model also illustrates the coordination burdens created by sovereignty-oriented digital policy. Separate institutions, sectoral regulators, mission structures, and debates over personal and non-personal data have produced a dense but fragmented architecture in which interoperability, rights protection, competition, and industrial policy must be continually reconciled (Han, 2024; Mishra & Agarwal, 2026). If such coordination is weak, then localization can generate compliance complexity without producing fully integrated state capacity. Nevertheless, Table IV and Fig. 4 indicate that India occupies the quadrant where localization intensity and infrastructural ambition are both relatively high, which gives the country greater potential than many peers to convert territorial control into operational sovereignty when institutional coherence is maintained.

B. Indonesia

This subsection argues that Indonesia represents a moderated localization pathway in which earlier territorial controls were recalibrated to accommodate openness, investment, and functional differentiation. Han's comparative analysis identified Indonesia as an important case because the state's localization posture evolved in response to the interaction between statecraft concerns and platform-driven network effects (Han, 2024). Government Regulation No. 71 of 2019 differentiated between public and private electronic-system operators, thereby moving away from interpretations associated with blanket in-country data placement for all operators, while the 2022 Personal Data Protection Law established a more general legal framework for personal-data governance (Government of Indonesia, 2019, 2022). Accordingly, Indonesia's model does not reject territorial control; it narrows and conditions it.

Furthermore, Indonesia's AI-governance architecture remains strategy-led rather than statute-led. The National Strategy for Artificial Intelligence 2020–2045, commonly referred to as STRANAS KA, identifies ethics and policy, talent, infrastructure and data, and research and innovation as core focus areas, thereby embedding

AI governance within a longer developmental horizon rather than within a solely compliance-oriented framework (KORIKA, 2020). This design is analytically significant because it recognizes that data governance without capability building does not generate domestic AI value. At the same time, strategy-led governance can remain institutionally thinner than statute-backed systems if implementation authority, funding discipline, and inter-agency coordination are not continuously reinforced. Thus, Indonesia illustrates both the promise and the fragility of calibrated openness.

Moreover, Indonesia's sovereignty posture appears to be oriented toward managed interdependence. Localization is treated as appropriate for selected functions and sectors, but broader economic ambition requires ongoing participation in regional and global digital ecosystems, especially where cloud services, advanced chips, and model-development tools remain externally concentrated (Han, 2024; Osorio & Gojo Cruz, 2025). In comparative terms, Indonesia therefore occupies a middle position in Table IV and Fig. 4: localization intensity is moderate, AI-governance articulation is present, but infrastructural and institutional consolidation remain incomplete. This position renders the case especially instructive because it demonstrates that moderation in territorial policy does not weaken sovereignty if accompanied by credible ecosystem-building measures.

C. Kenya

This subsection argues that Kenya represents an institution-building strategy in which governance capacity is being developed before expansive localization claims are adopted. Kenya's Data Protection Act of 2019 established a general personal-data governance framework, but it did not create the kind of economy-wide localization regime associated with more restrictive territorial models (Republic of Kenya, 2019). The recently issued Kenya National Artificial Intelligence Strategy 2025–2030 then identified three core pillars, namely: AI digital infrastructure, data ecosystems and governance, and AI research, innovation, and commercialization (Ministry of Information, Communications and the Digital Economy, Kenya, 2025). Consequently, the Kenyan case is defined less by territorial closure and more by the attempt to construct the institutional and infrastructural preconditions of AI-enabled development.

Furthermore, Kenya's trajectory must be read in relation to continental African governance developments. The African Union Data Policy Framework emphasizes common data spaces, harmonized governance, and integrated systems, while the African Union Continental AI Strategy situates AI within a broader agenda of inclusive transformation, ethics, capacity, and shared regional capability (African Union, 2022, 2024). Kenya's national strategy aligns with this continental orientation by linking AI development to data governance and infrastructure without treating localization as the primary or exclusive mechanism of sovereignty. This alignment is important because lower-capacity states often derive greater sovereign benefit from coordinated regional standards and shared market scale than from isolated domestic territorial restrictions. Therefore, Kenya illustrates a sovereignty pathway grounded in institution-building and regional embedding.

However, the Kenyan pathway also reveals the limits of strategy where resource constraints remain binding. If compute infrastructure, skilled regulatory personnel, and implementation financing are not scaled, then data governance principles and AI ambitions remain aspirational. Nevertheless, Kenya's relative restraint on localization avoids a common policy trap in which states adopt data-residency requirements that exceed their domestic ability to host, secure, and leverage the retained data. In Table IV and Fig. 4, Kenya therefore appears as a case of lower localization intensity but increasingly coherent governance design, which suggests that sovereignty can develop through sequencing and coordination rather than through immediate territorial maximalism.

D. Brazil

This subsection argues that Brazil combines rights-based data governance with a gradually more explicit industrial and developmental AI agenda. Brazil's Lei Geral de Proteção de Dados Pessoais, or LGPD, established a comprehensive framework for personal-data processing and protection, but the law did not convert data governance into a general residency mandate for all digital activity (Presidency of the Republic of Brazil, 2018). Instead, cross-border data governance under the LGPD proceeds through legal safeguards and accountability conditions, which means that territorial control is exercised more through governance standards than through blanket domestic storage commands. This design distinguishes Brazil from strongly localization-centered models and aligns it more closely with regulated transfer governance.

Furthermore, Brazil's AI-governance architecture has evolved through the Estratégia Brasileira de Inteligência Artificial, published in 2021, and the more recent Plano Brasileiro de Inteligência Artificial, which articulates implementation pathways and public-interest ambitions in a more operational form (Ministério da Ciência, Tecnologia e Inovação, 2024; Ministério da Ciência, Tecnologia e Inovações, 2021). The strategic combination is significant because it places AI within a national development agenda that includes research, innovation, public services, governance, and ecosystem formation rather than treating AI solely as a private-sector compliance problem. Díaz Vera's analysis of non-personal-data regulation in Latin America is relevant here because it demonstrates how regional debates increasingly connect data governance to questions of local value capture, access, and structural asymmetry (Díaz Vera, 2023). Therefore, Brazil's approach reflects a sovereignty logic that is developmental and standards-based rather than territorially restrictive in a narrow sense.

Moreover, Brazil demonstrates that sovereignty can be pursued through institutionalization rather than residency mandates. The LGPD confers rights and obligations that structure transfer governance; the EBIA and PBIA attempt to align innovation policy, state capacity, and strategic orientation; and the broader policy discourse situates AI within national modernization and public-interest frameworks (Ministério da Ciência, Tecnologia e Inovação, 2024; Ministério da Ciência, Tecnologia e Inovações, 2021; Presidency of the Republic of Brazil, 2018). However, the effectiveness of this model depends on implementation continuity and on the ability to convert strategy into procurement capability, compute access, and industrial depth. In comparative terms, Brazil occupies a position of moderate territorial control, comparatively stronger rights-based governance, and rising developmental ambition, which makes it an important contrast to India's more localization-salient pathway.

E. Cross-Case Synthesis

This subsection synthesizes the principal comparative findings. Table IV indicates that the four cases vary not only in the stringency of territorial data control but also in how localization is embedded within broader capability-building and governance architectures. India achieves supervisory and strategic leverage through sectoral localization and major infrastructure ambition; however, the architecture incurs coordination complexity across multiple policy domains. Indonesia achieves a calibrated rebalancing between territorial control and openness; however, the long-run sovereign value of that model depends on implementation depth and infrastructure scaling. Kenya achieves relative policy coherence through institution-building and regional alignment; however, its strategy remains vulnerable to resource and capability constraints. Brazil achieves a rights-based and developmental model without broad localization mandates; however, the translation of strategy into industrial and computational depth remains decisive.

Table 4. Cross-case comparison of policy design profiles.

Case	Territorial data control	AI-governance maturity	Infrastructural capability	External alignment	Indicative sovereignty outcome
India	High in selected sectors; strategic and differentiated	Medium to high; principles plus mission infrastructure	Rising and explicitly prioritized	Moderate; sovereignty claims coexist with selective transfer governance	Strong potential for operational sovereignty if coordination remains coherent
Indonesia	Moderate; recalibrated after earlier broader controls	Medium; strategy-led and developmental	Intermediate and uneven	Moderate to high; managed interdependence	Sovereignty through calibrated control rather than blanket localization
Kenya	Limited explicit localization beyond general governance	Medium; strategy newly formalized	Lower but improving	High regional orientation	Sovereignty through sequencing, institution-building, and regional harmonization
Brazil	Moderate-low; transfer safeguards over blanket residency	Medium to high; strategy plus implementation plan	Intermediate; strengthened by policy continuity	High; standards-based and outward-facing	Sovereignty through institutional governance and developmental AI planning

Furthermore, the comparison demonstrates that no linear relationship exists between localization intensity and operational digital sovereignty. If localization is high while compute, cloud, audit, and procurement capacity remain weak, then sovereignty remains performative because dependence is merely relocated rather than reduced. If governance principles are strong while territorial and infrastructural strategies are absent, then states remain normatively articulate but strategically dependent. Hence, the most consequential finding is relational: sovereignty emerges when selective territorial control is combined with capability formation and interoperable external engagement. Fig. 4 summarizes this relationship by locating the four cases within a capacity-aligned localization matrix.

Figure 3. Capacity-aligned localization matrix with conceptual positioning of the four cases.

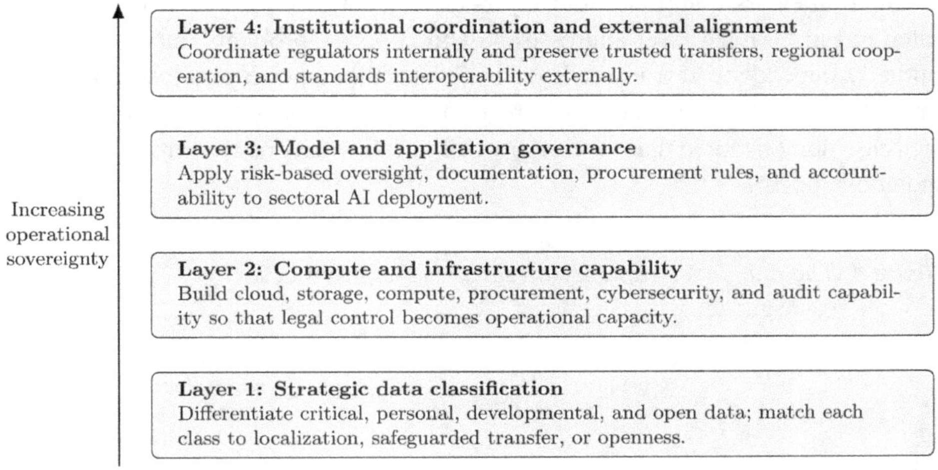

Moreover, the comparison also demonstrates that emerging economies cannot be understood through a simple opposition between protectionism and openness. Burri's analysis of inequality in digital trade regulation is instructive because it explains why unrestricted openness can lock structurally weaker actors into unfavorable governance arrangements (Burri, 2024). At the same time, Aaronson and Taylor demonstrate why expansive localization, if untethered from capability and public-interest calibration, can degrade innovation and digital integration (Aaronson, 2019; Taylor, 2020). The cases therefore point toward a middle proposition: effective sovereignty requires controlled openness supported by selective localization, developmental investment, and trusted transfer governance. This proposition motivates the framework developed in the next section.

At this point, the comparative analysis has identified the central explanatory pattern of the chapter. Consequently, Section V translates that pattern into a capacity-aligned governance framework designed for policymakers and scholars concerned with digital sovereignty in emerging economies.

V. A CAPACITY-ALIGNED GOVERNANCE FRAMEWORK

In this section, the comparative findings are converted into an integrative governance framework. The framework is not presented as a universal legal model; instead, it is presented as a policy design architecture through which emerging economies can align localization choices, AI-governance instruments, and sovereignty objectives with actual institutional and infrastructural conditions.

The framework comprises four layers arranged as a sovereignty stack, as illustrated in Fig. 3. Each layer addresses a distinct policy problem, but the layers are mutually dependent: if a lower layer is absent, the upper layers lose operational force. This architecture is derived directly from the comparative findings because each case demonstrated that sovereignty claims fail when one or more layers remain underdeveloped.

Figure 4. The four-layer capacity-aligned sovereignty stack.

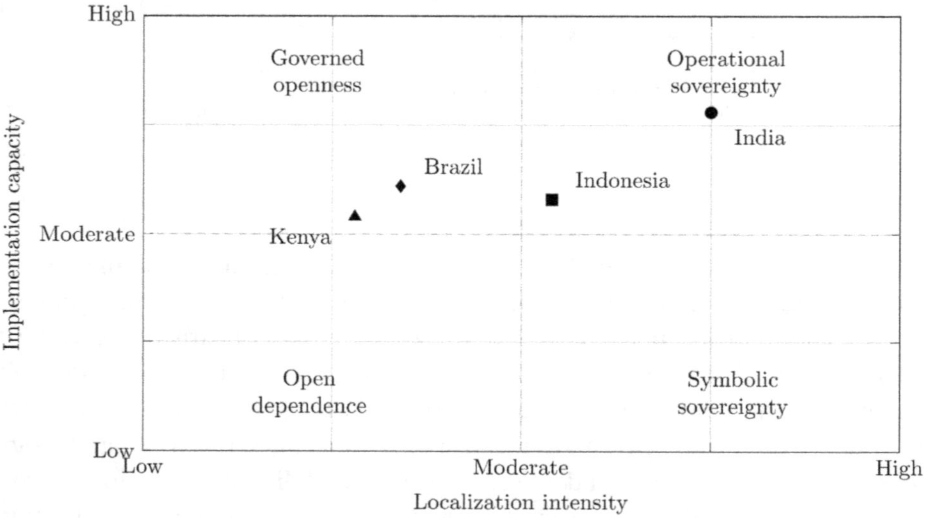

A. Layer 1: Strategic Data Classification

This subsection establishes strategic data classification as the first layer of the framework. Data are not governed effectively when they are treated as a single undifferentiated category because personal data, payment data, public-interest administrative data, critical-infrastructure telemetry, anonymized industrial datasets, and open government data present distinct combinations of rights, security, and developmental concerns (Díaz Vera, 2023; Mishra & Agarwal, 2026). Therefore, the first design task is to classify data according to regulatory purpose and systemic importance, after which localization, controlled transfer, or openness can be assigned proportionately. This classification layer prevents two frequent failures: over-localization, in which low-risk datasets are unnecessarily territorialized, and under-protection, in which strategically sensitive datasets remain exposed to unmanaged external dependence.

Furthermore, classification must be tied to clear transfer pathways. If a dataset is classified as critical or supervisory, then local storage or assured domestic accessibility may be justified; if a dataset is developmental but non-sensitive, then structured sharing and portability may create greater sovereign value than territorial retention alone (Osorio & Gojo Cruz, 2025; Yakovleva, 2024). The purpose of this layer is thus not to maximize domestic retention, but to ensure that each class of data is governed by the instrument most likely to advance public goals while preserving interoperability where appropriate.

Proposition 1. Digital sovereignty is strengthened by data localization only when localization is preceded by strategic data classification and accompanied by explicit transfer pathways for non-critical datasets.

Justification. A regulator confronting the data-governance problem has three flawed approaches: (a) imposing blanket localization on all relevant datasets, (b) allowing unrestricted export of all datasets, or (c) constructing sectoral rules without a common classification logic. Approach (a) increases compliance cost and may trap low-risk data inside institutions that cannot productively employ them; approach (b) forfeits supervisory leverage and weakens domestic value capture over strategically important data; approach (c) generates regulatory inconsistency that impairs both enforcement and investment planning. If classification precedes localization, then critical and high-risk data can be territorialized with defensible precision, while developmental and lower-risk data can circulate under safeguarded transfer mechanisms. This proves that targeted classification is the necessary condition through which localization contributes to sovereignty rather than fragmentation.

B. Layer 2: Compute and Infrastructure Capability

This subsection establishes compute and infrastructure capability as the second layer of the framework. Sovereign control over data remains incomplete when the domestic capacity to store, process, audit, and train on those data is absent. Cloud dependency, limited high-performance computing, weak public-sector procurement, and inadequate cybersecurity capacity can all neutralize the public value of nominally localized data because effective control remains vested in foreign providers or in inaccessible technical systems (Burri, 2024; Png, 2022). Therefore, investments in public digital infrastructure, cloud capacity, secure data environments, technical standards, and procurement capability are not auxiliary to sovereignty; they are constitutive of it.

Moreover, the comparative analysis demonstrates that the absence of this layer explains why many localization measures generate symbolic rather than operational results. India's strategy is comparatively stronger because compute capacity is explicitly prioritized, while Kenya's pathway remains prudently sequenced precisely because aggressive localization without infrastructure would produce limited sovereign gain (IndiaAI, 2024; Ministry of Information, Communications and the Digital Economy, Kenya, 2025). Brazil and Indonesia similarly demonstrate that strategy documents acquire greater credibility when infrastructural capability is treated as an implementation condition rather than as a downstream consequence. Hence, the second layer converts legal control into usable state and societal capacity.

C. Layer 3: Model and Application Governance

This subsection establishes model and application governance as the third layer of the framework. Once data governance and infrastructure are aligned, AI systems must still be governed through risk classification, accountability, evaluation, documentation, public procurement rules, and sector-specific safeguards in order to ensure that domestic AI deployment remains legitimate and developmentally aligned (Chesterman, 2021; National Institute of Standards and Technology, 2023; OECD, 2019; UNESCO, 2021). This layer matters because sovereignty is not exhausted by possessing data and compute; it also requires the ability to decide how AI systems affecting citizens, markets, and public institutions are designed, audited, and contested. Therefore, the governance of models and applications supplies the normative and administrative discipline through which digital capability becomes publicly accountable power.

Furthermore, this layer should be risk-based and context-sensitive rather than uniformly prohibitive. Public-sector decision systems, health applications, financial AI, and infrastructure-control systems require stronger oversight than low-risk productivity tools. At the same time, overly abstract ethical principles are insufficient if they are not translated into procurement criteria, documentation duties, audit practices, and incident-response channels (Chesterman, 2021; National Institute of Standards and Technology, 2023). Consequently, the chapter treats AI governance as an implementation architecture rather than as a declaration of principles alone.

Proposition 2. AI governance enhances digital sovereignty only when risk-based model governance is integrated with domestic implementation capacity and public-sector procurement authority.

Justification. A state seeking to govern AI can pursue three incomplete strategies: (a) adopt ethical principles without implementation machinery, (b) build infrastructure without model-accountability rules, or (c) import foreign governance templates without adapting them to domestic institutions and markets. Strategy (a) yields legitimacy language without enforceable practice; strategy (b) accelerates deployment while leaving harms and institutional distrust unaddressed; strategy

(c) produces formal compliance that remains detached from local administrative capacity and developmental priorities. If risk-based governance is linked to procurement, auditing, and implementation institutions, then domestic authorities can shape how models are developed and deployed across priority sectors. This proves that AI governance becomes sovereignty-enhancing only when institutional capacity and regulatory design co-evolve.

D. Layer 4: Institutional Coordination and External Alignment

This subsection establishes institutional coordination and external alignment as the fourth layer of the framework. Digital sovereignty cannot be sustained through unilateral rulemaking alone because data, models, chips, cloud infrastructure, and standards remain transnationally distributed. Domestic coordination among data-protection authorities, sectoral regulators, competition bodies, trade officials, innovation agencies, and procurement institutions is therefore required in order to prevent sovereignty policy from fragmenting into incompatible mandates (Burri, 2024; Carrapico & Farrand, 2025). At the same time, regional and international alignment is required so that trusted transfers, standards recognition, research collaboration, and market access remain possible (Osorio & Gojo Cruz, 2025; Yakovleva, 2024). Consequently, the fourth layer translates controlled interdependence into governance design.

Furthermore, external alignment should be treated as a sovereignty multiplier rather than as a concession. The African Union Data Policy Framework and Continental AI Strategy illustrate how regional coordination can expand policy space for states that individually possess limited bargaining power or infrastructure scale (African Union, 2022, 2024). Similarly, competition-oriented and interoperability-oriented proposals in Southeast Asia indicate that freer flows of data, compute, and models can be reconciled with public-interest oversight when regional governance is constructed deliberately (Osorio & Gojo Cruz, 2025). Therefore, the final layer ensures that sovereignty is exercised through negotiated architectures of interdependence rather than through isolation.

Table 5. Policy design matrix for the capacity-aligned governance framework.

Framework layer	Design objective	Principal instruments	Failure mode if absent
Strategic data classification	Match data category to proportionate governance instrument	Data taxonomies, critical-data lists, transfer rules, sharing protocols	Blanket localization or uncontrolled export
Compute and infrastructure capability	Convert legal control into usable domestic capacity	Cloud investments, compute missions, public digital infrastructure, cybersecurity and audit capability	Symbolic control without operational autonomy
Model and application governance	Ensure legitimate and accountable AI deployment	Risk classification, procurement rules, audits, documentation, standards, redress mechanisms	Capability without accountability or public trust
Institutional coordination and external alignment	Preserve coherence and interoperable sovereignty	Inter-agency coordination, regional frameworks, trusted transfer mechanisms, competition and trade tools	Fragmented domestic regulation and unmanaged external dependence

Moreover, the framework can be operationalized through a sequential implementation process.

1. **Establish the national data taxonomy:** The first step is to classify datasets by sensitivity, public-interest relevance, and developmental value, while assigning each class to localization, controlled transfer, or openness. This step prevents subsequent legal design from collapsing into indiscriminate territorialism.
2. **Audit domestic technical capability:** The second step is to assess storage, cloud, compute, audit, cybersecurity, procurement, and talent capacity against the obligations implied by the data taxonomy. If the capability gap is large, then localization mandates must be narrowed or staged until implementation infrastructure is strengthened.
3. **Embed AI governance in sectoral deployment:** The third step is to connect AI principles to sector-specific rules, procurement decisions, documentation duties, and accountability procedures. In this way, governance becomes administratively actionable rather than declaratory.
4. **Align domestic design with regional and international interfaces:** The fourth step is to preserve trusted transfers, competition safeguards, standards alignment, and regional cooperation so that domestic sovereignty does not become economically self-defeating. This step ensures that interdependence remains governed rather than uncontrolled.

Furthermore, the framework is designed for practical institutional use. Regulators can employ it to decide where residency mandates are defensible; digital ministries can employ it to prioritize compute and cloud investments; development banks and regional organizations can employ it to identify which sovereignty deficits are primarily legal, infrastructural, or coordination-based. In each application, the central insight remains constant: sovereignty is not obtained through a single statute, a single AI code, or a single cloud investment. It is produced through layered alignment.

At this point, the chapter has moved from comparative diagnosis to actionable design. Consequently, the next section identifies research directions that arise directly from the conceptual and comparative limits identified in the present analysis.

VI. FUTURE RESEARCH DIRECTIONS

In this section, the principal research directions generated by the chapter are identified. Because the present chapter is conceptual and comparative, the next phase of scholarship requires more systematic measurement of the relationships among localization intensity, infrastructural dependence, and AI-governance effectiveness across a broader set of emerging economies.

The first research direction concerns measurement. Existing scholarship still lacks sufficiently precise comparative indicators for compute dependence, cloud concentration, audit capability, public-sector AI procurement capacity, and the practical enforceability of cross-border transfer rules in emerging economies (Burri, 2024; Png, 2022). Without such indicators, sovereignty claims remain difficult to compare across jurisdictions because legal provisions and strategy documents often overstate operational capability. Future studies therefore require datasets and mixed-method designs that connect formal legal instruments to infrastructural and budgetary realities.

The second research direction concerns sectoral variation. Payment systems, public health, agricultural data platforms, smart-city infrastructures, educational technology, and industrial Internet of Things environments do not generate identical governance requirements, although localization debates frequently treat them as if they did (Ministério da Ciência, Tecnologia e Inovação, 2024; Ministry of Information, Communications and the Digital Economy, Kenya, 2025; Reserve Bank of India, 2018). Comparative sectoral studies are therefore needed in order to determine when localization enhances resilience, when trusted transfers enhance innovation, and when hybrid models produce superior outcomes. Such work would refine the data-classification layer of the framework and render policy design more proportionate.

The third research direction concerns regionalism and political economy. The chapter has demonstrated that external alignment is a sovereignty multiplier, yet major questions remain regarding how regional organizations, development financiers, and standard-setting bodies can support compute access, interoperability, and bargaining capacity for lower-capacity states (African Union, 2022, 2024; Osorio & Gojo Cruz, 2025). In addition, future scholarship should examine how competition law, public procurement, digital trade commitments, and industrial policy interact in shaping AI-market concentration. Research along these lines would deepen the framework's fourth layer and clarify how sovereignty can be exercised through coordinated interdependence rather than through national isolation.

VII. CONCLUSION

We described our proposed capacity-aligned governance framework, designed to align data localization, AI governance, and digital sovereignty in emerging economies. We also demonstrated that our proposal can withstand fragmented regulation, symbolic territorialism, infrastructure dependence, and cross-border governance asymmetry. In addition, we demonstrated that our framework supports selective localization, interoperable transfer governance, institutional coordination, and developmental AI capacity. Findings from the comparative evaluation also demonstrated that durable digital sovereignty is achieved when territorial control over data is coupled with compute capability, regulatory coherence, and externally coordinated governance instruments.

REFERENCES

Aaronson, S. A. (2019). What are we talking about when we talk about digital protectionism? *World Trade Review*, *18*(4), 541–577. DOI: 10.1017/S1474745618000198

Aayog, N. I. T. I. (2021). *Responsible AI for all: Approach document for india, part 2—operationalizing principles for responsible AI*. NITI Aayog. https://www.niti.gov.in/sites/default/files/2021-08/Part2-Responsible-AI-12082021.pdf

African Union. (2022). *AU data policy framework: An integrated, prosperous and peaceful africa*. African Union. https://au.int/sites/default/files/documents/42078-doc-DATA-POLICY-FRAMEWORKS-2024-ENG-V2.pdf

African Union. (2024). *Continental artificial intelligence strategy: Harnessing AI for africa's development and prosperity*. African Union. https://au.int/sites/default/files/documents/44004-doc-EN-_Continental_AI_Strategy_July_2024.pdf

Burri, M. (2024). Inequalities in digital trade and digital trade regulation. In Askin, E., & Stoll, H. (Eds.), *Contested equality: International and comparative legal perspectives* (pp. 203–220). Edward Elgar Publishing., DOI: 10.4337/9781035325771.00020

Carrapico, H., & Farrand, B. (2025). EU data sovereignty: An autonomy–interdependence governance gap? *Politics and Governance*, *13*, 10331. Advance online publication. DOI: 10.17645/pag.10331

Catanzariti, M. (2024). *Disconnecting sovereignty: How data fragmentation reshapes the law*. Springer., DOI: 10.1007/978-3-031-60734-9

Chesterman, S. (2021). *We, the robots?: Regulating artificial intelligence and the limits of the law*. Cambridge University Press., DOI: 10.1017/9781009047081

Díaz Vera, L. M. (2023). Non-personal data regulation — A latin american perspective. *GRUR International*, *72*(1), 37–53. DOI: 10.1093/grurint/ikac123

Gao, R. Y. (2023). A battle of the big three? — Competing conceptualizations of personal data shaping transnational data flows. *Chinese Journal of International Law*, *22*(4), 707–787. DOI: 10.1093/chinesejil/jmad040

Glasze, G., Cattaruzza, A., Douzet, F., Dammann, F., Bertran, M.-G., Bômont, C., Braun, M., Danet, D., Desforges, A., Géry, A., Grumbach, S., Hummel, P., Limonier, K., Münßinger, M., Nicolai, F., Pétiniaud, L., Winkler, J., & Zanin, C. (2023). Contested spatialities of digital sovereignty. *Geopolitics*, *28*(2), 919–958. DOI: 10.1080/14650045.2022.2050070

Government of India. (2023). *The digital personal data protection act, 2023*. https://www.meity.gov.in/static/uploads/2024/06/2bf1f0e9f04e6fb4f8fef35e82c42aa5.pdf

Government of Indonesia. (2019). *Government regulation of the republic of indonesia no. 71 of 2019 on the implementation of electronic systems and transactions*. https://peraturan.bpk.go.id/Details/122030/pp-no-71-tahun-2019

Government of Indonesia. (2022). *Law of the republic of indonesia no. 27 of 2022 on personal data protection*. https://peraturan.bpk.go.id/Details/229798/uu-no-27-tahun-2022

Han, S. (2024). Data and statecraft: Why and how states localize data. *Business and Politics*, *26*(2), 263–288. DOI: 10.1017/bap.2023.41

India, A. I. (2024). *Cabinet approves india AI mission at an outlay of rs 10,372 crore*. https://indiaai.gov.in/news/cabinet-approves-india-ai-mission-at-an-outlay-of-rs-10-372-crore

Islam, M. T., & Khan, B. U. (2024). Impacts of data localization policies and lessons for bangladesh. *International Data Privacy Law*, *14*(2), 150–168. DOI: 10.1093/idpl/ipae002

Kalin, R. P. (2024). *Digital trade and data privacy: Cross-border flows of personal data between data protection and data protectionism*. Springer., DOI: 10.1007/978-3-031-73857-9

Kokas, A. (2022). *Trafficking data: How china is winning the battle for digital sovereignty*. Oxford University Press., DOI: 10.1093/oso/9780197620502.001.0001

KORIKA. (2020). *Strategi nasional kecerdasan artifisial indonesia 2020–2045*. Kolaborasi Riset dan Inovasi Industri Kecerdasan Artifisial. https://korika.id/wp-content/uploads/2024/07/stranas-ka-2045.pdf

Ministério da Ciência. Tecnologia e Inovações. (2021). *Estratégia brasileira de inteligência artificial (EBIA)*. MCTI. https://www.gov.br/mcti/pt-br/acompanhe-o-mcti/transformacaodigital/arquivosestrategiadigital/copy_of_RelatoriofinalEBIA_Eixo6V2.4.pdf

Ministério da Ciência. Tecnologia e Inovação. (2024). *Plano brasileiro de inteligência artificial (PBIA)*. MCTI. https://www.gov.br/mcti/pt-br/acompanhe-o-mcti/transformacaodigital/plano-brasileiro-de-inteligencia-artificial-pbia-_vf.pdf

Ministry of Information, Communications and the Digital Economy, Kenya. (2025). *Kenya national artificial intelligence strategy 2025–2030*. Government of Kenya. https://ict.go.ke/sites/default/files/2025-03/Kenya%20AI%20Strategy%202025%20-%202030.pdf

Mishra, N., & Agarwal, B. (2026). The emerging framework for non-personal data protection in india: Perils, promises, and lessons for the developing world. *International Journal of Law and Information Technology*, *34*, eaaf025. Advance online publication. DOI: 10.1093/ijlit/eaaf025

Nanni, R., Bizzaro, P. G., & Napolitano, M. (2024). The false promise of individual digital sovereignty in europe: Comparing artificial intelligence and data regulations in china and the european union. *Policy and Internet*, *16*(4), 711–726. DOI: 10.1002/poi3.424

National Institute of Standards and Technology. (2023). *Artificial intelligence risk management framework (AI RMF 1.0)*. NIST. https://nvlpubs.nist.gov/nistpubs/ai/nist.ai.100-1.pdf

OECD. (2019). *OECD AI principles*. https://www.oecd.org/en/topics/ai-principles.html

Osorio, C. P., & Gojo Cruz, J. I. (2025). Promoting free flows via competition law: An AI industry blueprint for southeast asia. *Telecommunications Policy*, *49*(5), 102953. DOI: 10.1016/j.telpol.2025.102953

Parasol, M. (2021). *AI development and the "fuzzy logic" of chinese cyber security and data laws*. Cambridge University Press., DOI: 10.1017/9781009064804

Png, M.-T. (2022). At the tensions of south and north: Critical roles of global south stakeholders in AI governance. *Proceedings of the 2022 ACM Conference on Fairness, Accountability, and Transparency*, 1434–1445. DOI: 10.1145/3531146.3533200

Presidency of the Republic of Brazil. (2018). *Lei no. 13.709, de 14 de agosto de 2018 (lei geral de proteção de dados pessoais)*. https://www.planalto.gov.br/ccivil_03/_ato2015-2018/2018/lei/l13709.htm

Republic of Kenya. (2019). *Data protection act, 2019*. https://new.kenyalaw.org/akn/ke/act/2019/24/eng@2022-12-31

Reserve Bank of India. (2018). *Storage of payment system data*. https://www.rbi.org.in/Scripts/NotificationUser.aspx?Id=11244&Mode=0

Taylor, R. D. (2020). "Data localization": The internet in the balance. *Telecommunications Policy*, *44*(8), 102003. Advance online publication. DOI: 10.1016/j.telpol.2020.102003

UN Trade and Development (UNCTAD). (2021). *Digital economy report 2021: Cross-border data flows and development—for whom the data flow*. UNCTAD. https://unctad.org/system/files/official-document/der2021_en.pdf

UNESCO. (2021). *Recommendation on the ethics of artificial intelligence*. https://www.unesco.org/en/articles/recommendation-ethics-artificial-intelligence

Yakovleva, S. (2024). *Governing cross-border data flows: Reconciling EU data protection and international trade law*. Oxford University Press., DOI: 10.1093/oso/9780192899248.001.0001

Zhang, W., Ong, L. M., & Findlay, M. (2023). Digital self-determination: An alternative paradigm for emerging economies. In M. Findlay, L. M. Ong, & W. Zhang (Eds.), *Elgar companion to regulating AI and big data in emerging economies* (pp. 158–179). Edward Elgar Publishing. DOI: 10.4337/9781785362408.00016

Chapter 8

Deepfakes and Digital Sovereignty:

Governance Challenges of Synthetic Media in the AI-Driven Data Economy

S. M. Nafiz Rayun
http://orcid.org/0009-0002-2505-6265
University of Science and Technology, Chittagong, Bangladesh

Muhammad Abdus Salam
http://orcid.org/0000-0001-9599-632X
Universiti Brunei Darussalam, Brunei

Vai Shiem Leong
Universiti Brunei Darussalam, Brunei

Waziha Islam
http://orcid.org/0009-0004-6016-1778
Noakhali Science and Technology University, Bangladesh

Mohammad Sahabuddin
University of Science and Technology, Chittagong, Bangladesh

Maruf Ahmed
http://orcid.org/0009-0006-2149-7433
University of Science and Technology, Chittagong, Bangladesh

Md. Sarour Hosen
University of Science and Technology, Chittagong, Bangladesh

Chandra Das
University of Science and Technology, Chittagong, Bangladesh

ABSTRACT

The rapid rise of deepfake technologies has fundamentally challenged the reliability of digital information, raising urgent questions about who controls data, identity, and truth in the global data economy. This chapter analyzes deepfakes as a governance problem that reshapes power across digital systems. Using the Data Technology Platform Governance model, it explains how synthetic media operates through

DOI: 10.4018/979-8-2600-0288-9.ch008

interconnected layers of data, artificial intelligence, platforms, and governance structures. The chapter argues that existing regulatory approaches remain fragmented and reactive, struggling to address the transnational and scalable nature of synthetic media. It highlights key risks, including violations of privacy, manipulation of digital identity, and erosion of trust in democratic processes. The chapter also examines emerging forms of resistance and concludes by emphasizing the need for coordinated and adaptive governance strategies that balance innovation with the protection of rights and public trust.

1. INTRODUCTION

1.1 Background and Rise of Synthetic Media

Artificial intelligence (AI) has evolved at a very high rate, changing the processes of production, manipulation, and distribution of digital content and introducing, as a characteristic phenomenon of modern digital space, synthetic media (Wang, 2023). Synthetic media Digital content, - such as images, audio, video, and text is created through machine learning methodology and not through more conventional human-intensive methods (Kumar et al., 2024; Rostomyan, 2026). Deepfakes are among the most eminent and controversial instances of synthetic media, and they are built upon deep learning models such as generative adversarial networks (GANs) to generate the most realistic simulations of human faces, voices, and actions (Goodfellow et al., 2014; Westerlund, 2019). Originally used in research laboratories and experimental applications, deepfake technologies have quickly spread to the domain of everyday use owing to the rise of computational power, the presence of large datasets, and the spread of readily accessible software applications that can be used even by a nonexpert to create synthetic content (Karnouskos, 2020). This availability has significantly changed the dynamics of production in digital content, creating opportunities to establish new forms of creativity and customization in areas such as entertainment, education, marketing, and virtual communication (George & George, 2023). However, the increasing realism and scalability of synthetic media have also led to deep problems related to the integrity of digital information ecosystems (He & Fang, 2024). With the evolution of synthetic content into one that cannot be separated from genuine media, conventional methods of verification are undermined, which questions the potential of fake news, influence, and loss of trust in society (Farid, 2022). Such issues are especially important in political or social terms, as deepfakes have been applied to create speeches, change social history, and alter the opinion-making process (Mansoor, 2024). Moreover, the creation of synthetic media is also entrenched in the greater process of the global data economy, where large volumes of user-generated content and biometric data are gathered, analyzed, and used to train AI systems (He & Fang, 2024; Natarajan et al., 2025; Omogiate & Legal, 2022). This dependency on massive data infrastructures underscores the relationship between technological advancement and data mining practices, casting essential concerns on the ownership, consent and ethical use of data (Usman, 2025a). Moreover, the central role of digital platforms is to increase the use of synthetic media through global networks, swiftly increasing their influence on society and regulatory complexity (Westerlund, 2019). In this context, synthetic media is not just a technological innovation but a structural change in digital information production, dissemination, and regulation, and a more critical exploration of its implications in the changing digital environment is needed.

1.2 Deepfakes as a Governance and Policy Challenge

The problem of deepfake technologies has a complex aspect of governance that can no longer be addressed within traditional regulatory frameworks because of its technical complexity, scalability, and dual aspects (Kaludewage, 2025). Compared with previous methods of digital manipulation, deepfakes are highly realistic and can be produced in large quantities, which in turn allows one to create and share synthetic content fast, which can be hard to trace and verify (Farouk & Fahmi, 2024; Ghiurău & Popescu, 2024). This poses a major challenge to policymakers trying to encourage technological innovation and yet be able to reduce harm (Alanazi et al., 2025; Usman, 2025b). The dual use nature of deepfakes also makes it harder to govern, as the very technologies that enable legitimate use in digital storytelling, accessibility tools, and virtual communication can be used to perpetrate other malicious intentions, which include misinformation campaigns, identity fraud, financial fraud, and the creation of non-consensual content, all of which are contributors to the dual use nature of deepfakes (Karnouskos, 2020; Mansoor, 2024). Current legal regulations, especially those pertaining to data protection, intellectual property, and media regulation, tend to fail on these issues since they were not created to consider AI-generated content, which is difficult to distinguish between authenticity and fabrication (Adebiyi & Adeusi, 2025; Khadka, 2025). The issues of liability are especially incomprehensible because it is not always clear if the developers, users, or sites where such material is located should be held responsible (Fischer, 2023). In addition, these governance challenges are exacerbated by the global and decentralized character of digital platforms since deepfakes can easily transcend nation state borders and national regulations have limited efficacy, thus, creating new gaps in enforcement (Couture & Toupin, 2019). In addition to legal and institutional issues, deepfakes present more universal policy-related problems of information integrity and democratic governance in the sense that the popularity of such manipulated media content undermines the integrity of the digital information system and the principles of popular discourse. Deepfakes need to be interpreted, therefore, not only as a technological problem but also as a multilayered governance challenge, which needs to be addressed at multiple levels, with coordinated actions of states, platforms, and international institutions.

1.3 Digital Sovereignty in the AI-Driven Data Economy

Digital sovereignty has become the key term for conceptualizing power, control, and autonomy in the modern digital environment, especially the AI-based data economy (Ishkhanyan, 2025b). It is a general description of the ability of states, institutions, and individuals to control digital infrastructures, data resources, and technological systems in their respective fields (Pohle & Thiel, 2020; Timmers, 2023). Nonetheless, the actualization of digital sovereignty has become more complicated as a result of the transnationality of data flows and the dominance of technology power within a limited set of global companies (Yusuf et al., 2026). AI -generated content exemplifies such tensions on the basis of the existence of large datasets which can include publicly available data in terms of images, videos, and biometric data that are collected and processed across multiple jurisdictions, which questions the ownership of data, consent, and regulatory control (Fischer, 2023). On an individual level, the concept of digital sovereignty is directly associated with the privacy of personal information and control over digital identities, which are undermined by deepfakes that are able to replicate and alter human appearance without permission (Basir et al., 2024; Usman, 2025a). On a state level, governments are highly hindered from controlling those technologies that work across borders because national laws can be limited to international platforms and systems of distributed AI (Hoffmann-Riem, 2019; Ishkhanyan, 2025a). Moreover, the monopoly of major tech corporations in creating and implementing AI systems also makes establishing sovereignty; challenging because such players tend to possess the infrastructure and data resources needed to be innovative (Ishkhanyan, 2025b). This leads to a scenario where data controls are not merely dictated by legal power but also influenced by the interaction of state authority, corporate control, and worldwide data influence. In this context, deepfakes have become an important prism through which the bargaining and contention of control over information and technology in the digital era can be studied.

1.4 Chapter Objectives, Scope, and Structure

This chapter is a critical examination of deepfake technologies as a governance issue that is deeply rooted in the broader concept of digital sovereignty and the data economy as a whole, disaggregating the problems of rights, regulation, and resistance. It seeks to examine how synthetic media transforms the discourse of data control, regulatory powers and digital rights and highlights the weaknesses of the current governance systems. To this end, the chapter addresses three broad goals, namely, conceptualizing deepfakes as sociotechnical systems, which are integrated into data-driven infrastructures; examining the ways in which they intersect with data control, comprising data governance, platform power and cross-border data flows; and finally, assessing the existing regulatory responses and suggesting a way of addressing them more effectively. The chapter also takes an interdisciplinary approach, relying on the policy of digital governance, AI policy, data protection law, and communication studies. On a structural level, it starts with conceptual and technological baselines, and then proceeds to examine the issue of deepfakes in the concept of digital sovereignty. It continues to discuss regulatory frameworks, rights-based and ethical issues, and resistance, and finally, it provides policy suggestions and thoughts on future progress.

1.5 Methodological and Analytical Approach

This chapter assumes a qualitative and interdisciplinary approach to methodology that aims to examine the implications of AI generated content in the digital data economy in terms of governance. The study is based on conceptual analysis, legal-policy analysis, and a political economy perspective, which contrasts primary empirical data with grounding the study on enabling a comprehensive analysis of complex social-technical dynamics. The conceptual analysis aims at defining the central constructs in deepfakes, synthetic media, and digital sovereignty and placing it in the context of the wider scholarly discussion as well as theoretical traditions. The legal-policy discussion analyses the availability of regulatory frameworks, such as established data protection regulations, artificial intelligence governance programs, and policies of the platform, to evaluate how well these can manage the issues that synthetic media technologies present. Additional to these perspectives, the political economy lens offers a critical framework through which the ways in which the digital ecosystem distributes power can be viewed especially with reference to how data are commodified and how technological capabilities are concentrated in the hands of large corporations. Such a view accentuates structural imbalances which can determine the consequences of governance and the impact or success of regulatory interventions. To incorporate these dimensions of analysis, the chapter uses the Data-Technology-Platform-Governance (DTPG) conceptual framework that allows to conduct a systematic analysis of how deepfakes are created, shared and governed at various levels of the digital ecosystem. Through a combination of these methodological perspectives, the chapter presents a multi-layered and subtle analysis of the regulatory gaps concerning the issue of deepfakes that is both theoretically and policy-wise insightful.

2. CONCEPTUALIZING DEEPFAKES AND SYNTHETIC MEDIA

2.1 Defining Deepfakes and Synthetic Media

Building on the definition introduced earlier, deepfakes can be understood not merely as a category of synthetic media, but also as a transformative shift in how audio-visual realism is constructed. Rather than directly capturing reality, deepfake systems algorithmically generate representations that simulate authenticity, thereby reshaping the epistemic status of visual and audio evidence (Farouk & Fahmi, 2024). Deepfakes in the synthetic media category are characterized by the use of deep neural networks to create the appearance, voice, and behavior of a human, thus, allowing the generation of content that can convincingly resemble a real person in some ways, which was not possible previously (Masood et al., 2023; Westerlund, 2019). The idea of deepfakes can be closely linked to the wider change in media production in the era of the digital era, where the products of media production are increasingly mediated by the algorithmic systems of their production and consumption (Lao et al., 2025). Researchers believe that deepfakes have introduced a form of transition to so-called synthetic realism, where digital representations are not directly related to physical phenomena but are formed by means of data -driven processes (Chesney & Citron, 2019; Kalpokas, 2020; Salam et al., 2024). This has enormous epistemological consequences since it erodes the evidential quality that has always been given to visual and audio forms. Additionally, deepfakes are not solitary technological objects but are integrated into complicated sociotechnical systems comprising data mining practices, algorithmic systems, and platform ecosystems (Alanazi et al., 2025; Vasist & Krishnan, 2023). Those systems are driven by the larger environment of the global data economy, whereby user -generated content is used incessantly to train artificial intelligence models. The problems of deepfakes that are beyond technical detection require investigation of their influence on digital power politics, which creates questions of control, responsibility, and trust. Deepfakes intensify issues such as disinformation and nonconsensual content, making it harder to regulate them, which are already unable to respond to them efficiently and are coordinated globally (Birrer & Just, 2025; Lin, 2025). They pose risks to democratic processes by compromising empowered inclusion, the quality of deliberation, and decision legitimacy, through disinformation and hate speech, which requires the governance efforts of social media platforms and regulation agencies (Pawelec, 2022). The law does not align universally, and certain governments demand transparency among the creators of deepfakes and punish malaise usage, however, the harmful effects of deepfakes, including the interference of elections or identity misrepresentation, have yet to be adequately addressed legally (Chawki, 2024; Sloot & Wagensveld, 2022). The optimal governance strategies involve a multidimensional system that includes technological detection tools, legal regulations, media literacy, the ethical development of AI, and international cooperation to reduce risks and avoid negative consequences, while maintaining many positive uses (Diakopoulos & Johnson, 2021; Kopecky, 2024).

Therefore, it is necessary to define deepfakes on the basis of not only technical knowledge of the underlying mechanisms but also an appreciation of their place in the transforming digital power structures. This generalization is necessary to understand the governance issues that come with synthetic media, especially with respect to controlling, accountability, and trust in the digital space.

2.2 Technological Foundations of Deepfake Systems

Deepfake systems are technologically based on the development of machine learning and computational modeling, which makes it possible to create very high-quality synthetic materials (Babaei et al., 2025; Mohammed, 2024). The most important component of these systems is the generative adversarial network, which is a framework proposed by Goodfellow et al. (2014), and has two neural networks that learn to act in opposition to each other to enhance the quality of the generated outputs by training them in a sequence of steps. One network generates fake data, and the other judges whether these data are authentic, which forms a dynamic process that becomes more realistic with time (Akkem et al., 2024; Figueira & Vaz, 2022). In addition to this architecture, deepfake technologies also add autoencoders, convolutional neural networks, and recurrent neural networks to address visual and sound data with increasing accuracy (Kietzmann et al., 2020). Facial mapping and motion capture methods make it possible to align facial expressions and movements precisely, and speech synthesis models make it possible to recreate vocal traits with the help of limited input data (Liao et al., 2023; Lin et al., 2022). The success of these systems is strongly influenced by the availability of large and heterogeneous datasets, which are usually publicly available images and videos gathered on the digital platform and used as a training grounds to take part in algorithmic learning (Naitali et al., 2023; Patel et al., 2023). This dependence on data explains the interdependence of technological development and the availability of data in the digital ecosystem (Alanazi et al., 2025). Moreover, improvements in computational infrastructure, such as cloud computing and special hardware, such as graphics processing units, have made barriers to the creation and deployment of this technology considerably smaller and are no longer exclusive to a dedicated research setting (Karnouskos, 2020). These systems, however, are challenging in terms of transparency and responsibility since, in many cases, there is no easy way to track the way certain outputs are produced or any biases introduced into training data exist (George et al., 2024). These technological features, in addition to making synthetic media evolve quickly, make it more difficult to control their applications and reduce possible injuries.

2.3 Types and Applications of Synthetic Media

Synthetic media encompasses a diverse range of types and applications that reflect its growing integration into various sectors of the digital economy. Among the most notable methods are visual manipulation, facial swapping and facial reenactment, with artificial intelligence being applied to modify or replace facial features in video material, frequently in an entertainment or creative context (Westerlund, 2019). The other notable category is audio synthesis, which involves the recreation of human voices via machine learning models trained on speech data, which may be used in applications such as virtual assistants, automated narration and language translation (Kietzmann et al., 2020). Moreover, text -based generative systems have been developed to be more advanced and generate coherent and contextually appropriate content that can be utilized in journalism, marketing, and communication (Kumar et al., 2024). New technologies are being incorporated into new technologies as well as into virtual reality and augmented reality, where synthetic media also helps create immersive experiences and digital interactions. Commercially, organizations rely on synthetic media to customize advertising, engage with customers, and represent their brands, with the inclusion of virtual influencers, which exist fully in the virtual world (George & George, 2023). Synthetic media can be used in education and training to develop interactive simulations that improve learning outcomes through real-life situations (Cannon-Bowers & Bowers, 2009; Roe et al., 2024). Nevertheless, they come at a very high cost, whereby the same technologies may be deployed to produce misleading or malicious material, such as fake news, identity theft, and nonconsenting media (Kishwar et al., 2025; Mohammed, 2024). The sheer diversity of applications highlights the duality of synthetic media as both an innovation engine and a source of potential ill that governance structures must be devised that can address its complexity without restricting the useful purposes of synthetic media.

2.4 Opportunities and Risks of Synthetic Media Technologies

The rapid growth of synthetic media technologies offers the capabilities of a revolution and serious threats that should be properly balanced in governance systems. On the positive end, these technologies have enormous advantages in terms of efficiency, creativity, and accessibility, which allow the production of high-quality digital content at a lower cost and with more customization. Synthetic media can be used to create new types of storytelling and audience interaction in the entertainment and marketing sector, and facilitate simulation-based learning and training applications that are used in education and healthcare, which may be more effective and accessible (Karnouskos, 2020). Moreover, synthetic media has the potential to strengthen communication through translation into real time and customized content delivery, which increases access to information without language and cultural limitations (Tian, 2024). Nonetheless, the risks of these technologies are also considerable and, in most cases, more challenging to mitigate. The degradation of information integrity is one of the most important issues since an increasing number of synthetic media have become more realistic, and it is difficult to define what is genuine and what is manipulated, thus destroying confidence in digital information systems (Farid, 2022). It has dire consequences for the democracy process since it can be utilized to disseminate fake information and sway the mind (Chesney & Citron, 2019). Moreover, synthetic media also trigger significant concerns with respect to privacy and consent because users can reproduce without their permission, causing reputational damage and infringing upon their rights (Usman, 2025b). These technologies are also more powerful because of their scalability, which allows dangerous content to be spread quickly through digital channels (Keller, 2021). The management of these risks will require a multifaceted solution that involves both technological solutions, the regulatory framework and moral principles to ensure that the advantages of synthetic media can be achieved without violating basic rights or undermining the trustworthiness of society.

2.5 Conceptual Framework: The DTPG Model

To provide a structured understanding of the governance challenges associated with deepfakes, this chapter adopts the data-technology-platform-governance model in Figure 1 as its conceptual framework, which conceptualizes synthetic media as a multilayered sociotechnical system. As discussed earlier, deepfake relies on the massive gathering and processing of user -generated and biometric data at the data level, which casts serious doubts on ownership, consent, and control in the data -driven environment (Mansoor, 2024; Usman, 2025a). The layer indicates the primacy of data in driving artificial intelligence systems and the significance of data governance in determining the outcome of technology. On the technological scale, machine learning algorithms process raw data to produce synthetic media, thus raising the issues of algorithmic transparency, bias, and responsibility (Nikolenko, 2021; Verma, 2026). The platform level addresses how digital platforms are involved in the dissemination and amplification of synthetic content, in which recommendation algorithms are applied to determine who is seen and who interacts with, frequently rewarding content that will most directly capture the attention of users. This layer highlights the increasing strength of platform companies in influencing the development of information ecosystems and controlling content streams. Finally, the governance level includes the types of legal frameworks, interventions, and institutional mechanisms geared toward managing the risks of synthetic media, such as data protection regulations and platform policies (Fischer, 2023). These combined layers enable the DTPG model to offer a powerful analytical framework on which the effects of using deepfakes in the digital ecosystem and the governance solutions can be designed at multiple tiers. Notably, the model has a direct relationship with digital sovereignty since it demonstrates how the ownership of data, technologies and platforms forms the capacity of states, institutions and individuals to exert control over synthetic media and defend digital rights in a more interconnected world.

Figure 1. Conceptual Framework (Data-Technology-Platform-Governance Model)

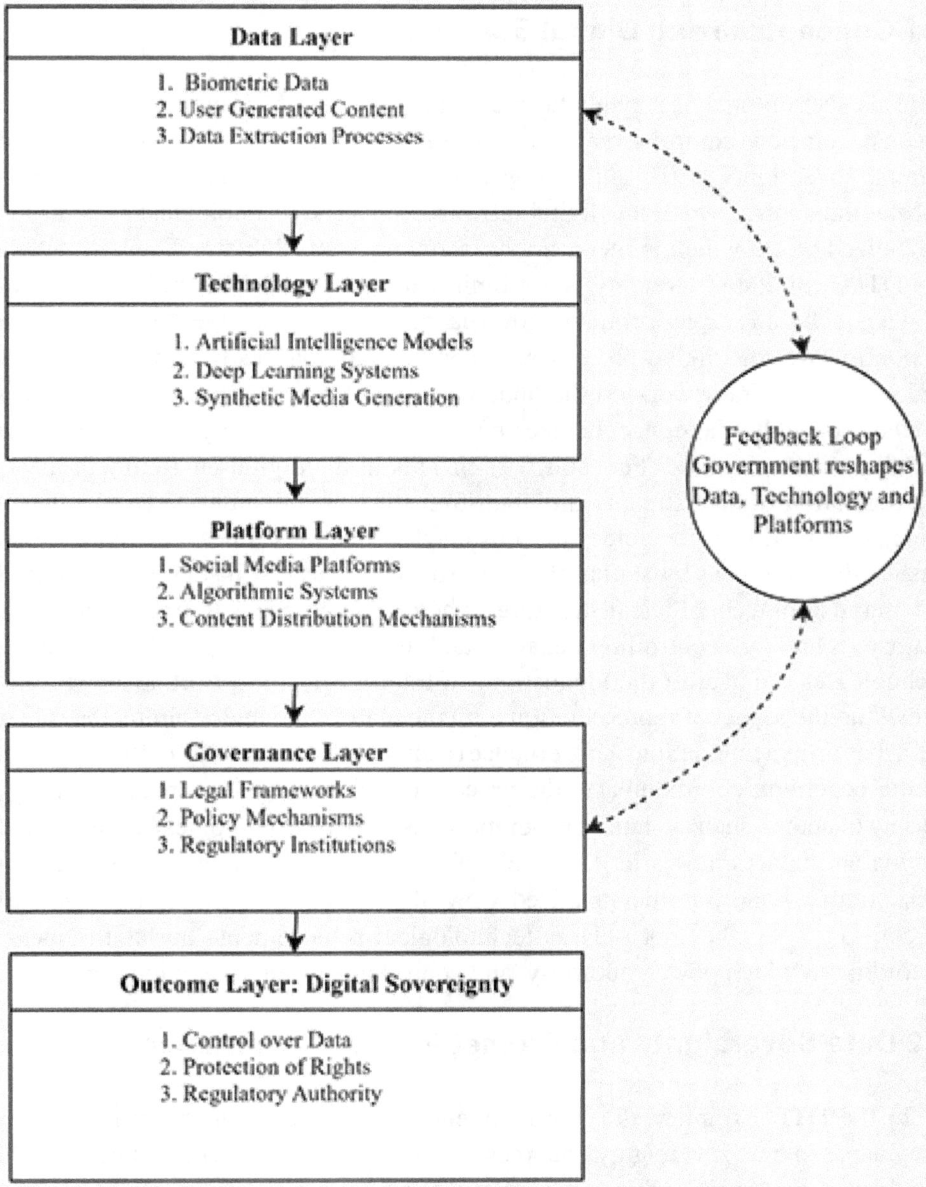

3. DEEPFAKES AND DIGITAL SOVEREIGNTY

3.1 Conceptualizing Digital Sovereignty

This section analyzes synthetic media at the level of sovereignty and power, focusing on how control over data, platforms, and information is reconfigured. Digital sovereignty is the ability of states, institutions and individuals to enjoy substantial control over data, digital infrastructures and technological systems in a globalized world which is increasingly interconnected (Pohle & Thiel, 2020). To the DTPG, digital sovereignty is not limited to one domain, but rather as a result of data, technology, platform, and governance layers that interact to create a layer of control over the digital processes. Theoretical approaches to power give a critical conceptual framework on the understanding of power especially the work of Michel Foucault who conceptualizes power in systems which govern knowledge, visibility, and discourse (Foucault, 1977). This in the digital environment means the regulation of data streams and algorithm structures that define the manner in which information is generated and consumed. Along these lines, Lawrence Lessig pushes this argument by stating that governance is not just instantiated in formal law but also in technological structures where code proceeds to be used as a regulatory technology controlling behavior and interaction (Lessig, 2006). Deepfake technologies run against the foundations of traditional concepts of sovereignty by detaching the aspect of representation with the reality, and undermining the role of information as a foundation of governance (Dahiya & Sharma, 2025). With synthetic media becoming commonplace, the process of sovereignty is dispersed among a variety of actors, such as states, corporations, as well as technological systems, each having an impact on a variety of levels of the digital ecosystem (Pierucci, 2025). This stratified and inter-personalized view of sovereignty points to the necessity to consider deepfakes not only as technological achievements but as the means according to which power, authority, and control alter their face in the digital era.

3.2 Data Sovereignty and Biometric Data Governance

In the DTPG framework, data maintenance is the core of the production of deepfakes, so data sovereignty becomes one of the key issues when addressing the problem of governance. Data sovereignty is the power to regulate the process of data gathering, processing, and harnessing, especially personal and biometric data. Synthetic media systems depend on large scale datasets such as facial images, voice recordings, and behavioral data, which are often sourced from online platforms without explicit consent (Meskys et al., 2020). This reliance raises critical concerns regarding data ownership, consent, and the commodification of personal information within the global data economy (Fischer, 2023; Usman, 2025a). These dynamics may be discussed with the help of the political economy perspective developed by Zuboff (2023) as it emphasizes how personal data are mined and converted into economic output in the system of surveillance capitalism (Zuboff, 2023). In this context, users tend to lose control over their digital inventions, as their information is collected to be used to train artificial intelligence and create more synthetic media. Deepfakes make such concerns even deeper by allowing the reproduction and manipulation of biometric data in a manner that undermines established ideas of identity and consent (He et al., 2025). At the state level, the issue of data sovereignty is further complicated by the transnationality of the flows of data and the lack of protection of national regulations, which leads to inefficiency in enforcing them (Fischer, 2023). Consequently, managing biometric data has emerged as a key concern in managing the responsible utilization of data in addition to individuals having any meaningful control of their digital depictions in the broader data ecosystem.

3.3 Information Sovereignty and Democratic Integrity

Information sovereignty is a situation in which societies and institutions have the capacity to control the production, dissemination, and meaning of information, which is fundamental to democratic integrity (Zozulia et al., 2021). In DTPG, the technology layer and platform layer are closely associated with this dimension, wherein synthetic media are produced and amplified. Deepfake solutions change information sovereignty in a direct way, as they allow the generation of extremely realistic yet fake content that can alter mass discourse and make people question digital informational systems (Farid, 2022). With the help of the theoretical considerations of Michel Foucault, manipulation of information may be viewed as a type of power that shapes the knowledge and determines social reality (Foucault, 1977). In online spaces, this authority is further mediated alongside platform algorithmics, which favor interactions, and tend to promote the sensational or the misleading. This situation forms what has been termed an epistemic crisis, where truth and falsehood have been so hard to separate (Chesney & Citron, 2019). This situation is aggravated by deepfakes, which negatively affect the credibility of the audiovisual evidence, which has been a primary source of credibility in communicating with people. The erosion of trust in this effect is a major implication of the process of democratic processes, since it may affect the masses, destabilize electoral systems and undermine the legitimacy of various institutions (Islam et al., 2024). These problems can be solved not only by the use of technical methods for identifying synthetic media but also by enhancing the media literacy, institutional responsibility and confidence of the general population in information systems.

3.4 Corporate Power and Platform Control in the Data Economy

The platform layer of the framework emphasizes the key part played by the digital platforms in the distribution and influence of the deepfake generated content, and it underlines increased concentration of power in large tech enterprises. These platforms have the effect of mediation by determining the visibility and distribution of content using algorithmic systems that are developed to produce maximum user interactions. This control can be explained in terms of its regulatory implications applying the framework offered by Lawrence Lessig which argues that technological design constitutes an instance of governance because it can influence the way users engage with digital space (Lessig, 2006). Simultaneously, the political economy analysis formulated by Shoshana Zuboff puts a stronger emphasis on how platforms monetize user data and attention, establishing economic impetuses that affect the allocation of content and coerce content moderation (Zuboff, 2023). The deepfakes are especially pertinent in this respect since their ability to draw attention is useful in the context of the engagement based platform economy (Vasist & Krishnan, 2023). puts a strain between business interests and the need to ensure that the information is kept upright since platforms do not have enough incentives to successfully censor malicious content. Moreover, the international nature of these firms restricts the capacity of individual states to impose regulatory sanctions hence defying the traditional ideas of sovereignty. Consequently, platform governance emerges as a focal point of power with far-reaching consequences on data control and governance of synthetic media in terms of decision making on content ownership, algorithmic design, and data usage.

3.5 Cross Border Data Flows and Jurisdictional Challenges

The transnationalism of digital technologies is a feature that is especially challenging for the governance layer of the DTPG framework, as cross-border data flows make it difficult to implement the legal and regulatory framework. Deepfake creation and sharing is a multijurisdictional issue since data might be gathered in one area, manipulated in a different area, and distributed at an international level by digital means. This poses a considerable difficulty with protection and legal enforcement because national legislation should not have the capacity to address cross-border operations (Couture & Toupin, 2019). Digital sovereignty is even more complicated in situations where data and technologies are governed by various actors and different regulatory regimes (Lambach & Monsees, 2025). The legal standards and rights of implementation in various countries might differ, making regulatory gaps in countries, where harmful content flows with minimal control possible. For example, a deepfake generated in one jurisdiction could take advantage of the weaker regulations of another, and then act to prevent the establishment of consistent rules regarding governance. These issues show how global policies and collaborative approaches can be involved in overcoming these difficulties and focus on the globalization of synthetic media technologies without violating the sovereignty of countries. Moreover, they do not mean that creating adaptable governance structures that are able to keep pace with changing technological trends and provide efficient regulation of the various tiers of digital ecosystems is less important.

4. GOVERNANCE AND REGULATORY FRAMEWORKS

4.1 AI Governance and Emerging Regulatory Frameworks

The rapid advancement of artificial intelligence has prompted the development of emerging governance frameworks aimed at addressing the risks associated with technologies such as deepfakes, particularly within the governance layer of the DTPG model. AI governance involves complex principles, policies and institutional procedures that should make artificial intelligence systems developed and deployed ethical, transparent and accountable (Timmers, 2023). Among a large number of important events in the field, the European Union Artificial Intelligence Act follows the risk-based method of controlling AI systems by classifying them on the basis of possible harm to the fundamental rights and safety of society (Kusche, 2024). Deepfake-generated content is high in the risk/ transparency obligation category, and the usage of such synthetic media must be indicated (Sloot & Wagensveld, 2022). In addition to regional efforts, international organizations have even played a role in the governance of AI by providing guidelines that put human-centric principles, accountability, and fairness, which fragment into an increasing agreement on the need to coordinate global action (Floridi et al., 2018). These governance activities, within the framework of DTPG, aim at managing the technological stratum through creating norms of algorithmic transparency and responsible innovation. However, the speed of technological change tends to rise faster than that of regulatory structures, and there is always a mismatch between policy formulation and actual enforcement. This emphasizes the necessity of dynamic and adaptive methodologies of governance that are responsive to changes in risk with the use of synthetic media that balances innovation with the right protection.

4.2 National Legal Responses to Deepfakes

At the national level, governments have begun to introduce legal measures to address the challenges posed by deepfake media content, although these responses vary significantly across jurisdictions. In the US, various states have adopted legislation specifically addressing certain applications of deepfakes, specifically in the context of election interference and non-consensual explicit material, taking the form of a sector-specific regulation (Chesney & Citron, 2019). Instead, the European Union approaches the issue of deepfakes with a more multifaceted regulatory approach where deepfakes are available in the context of digital governance and data protection. Firms like China have also been having more centralized governance by enforcing strict rules that stipulate labeling of synthetic content and creating a sense of responsibility on service providers to curb abuse (Dong & Chen, 2024). These differing legal reactions demonstrate the struggle with building homogenous regulatory frameworks in a globally digitalized world where technologies are conducted across-national boundaries. In the DTPG model, the national laws pursue the governance and platform layers and place responsibilities on the developers and digital platforms to control the risks in the synthetic media. Nevertheless, variations in law and enforcement procedures can lead to inconsistencies that ruin the quality of regulation, and the harmful material may spread among the jurisdictions with less strict regulation. Consequently, the national legal responses, although needed, cannot work on their own because of the global character of this technologies and are more or less forced to be coordinated on the international level.

4.3 Data Protection and Privacy Regulations

Privacy and data protection laws are important for regulating the data layer of the DTPG framework, especially when biometric information is used to train deepfake models. The European Union's general data protection regulation is one of the most wide-ranging laws around the protection of personal data, and has introduced principles and ideas of informed consent, purpose scope, and minimalism of data (European Union., 2016). These ideas are especially applicable to synthetic media systems, where the use of such technologies is frequently based on large datasets of personal information that can be gathered without clear consent. The laws on privacy also cover the rights of the subject of data, such as the ability to access, rectify, and delete their own data, which can be applied when a person is harmed as a result of being exposed to syndrome media usage (Bellovin et al., 2019). The enforcement of such regulations with deepfakes is complicated, however, because it is not always possible to track the source used in training models or even how such data have been processed. Moreover, the international character of data flows makes them more difficult to enforce, because the data can be moved to see various jurisdictions that provide different degrees of protection. Under DTPG, properly handling data governance plays an indispensable role when witnessing the underlying cause of deep fake risk by controlling the manner in which data collection and utilization are performed at its inception. Ensuring that the protective measures of data, including biometric data, are strengthened is thus an important aspect in the overarching processes of the responsible use of artificial intelligence technologies.

4.4 Platform Governance and Content Moderation

Digital platforms can be considered the core of the multiplication of deepfake information, and platform governance is a key element of the overall regulation complex of the DTPG regime. Platform governance involves the policy, practices, and technological structures of digital platforms in terms of how they control user -generated content and how the content can be in line with law and moral principles. Companies in the field of social media have taken numerous steps to address deepfakes, such as labeling content, removing harmful pieces or creating detection technologies that are intended to identify manipulated media (Langa, 2021). Nevertheless, they are mostly reactive and cannot be effective in the same way because of the magnitude and rapid dissemination of content (Gillespie, 2018). Theoretically, platform governance can be represented through the framework offered by Lawrence Lessig, who points out that platforms govern behavior both through formal rules and technological design (Lessig, 2006). Moreover, economic incentives related to activities involving user content may act as a deterrent to platforms engaging in the active moderation of content, especially when some controversial or sensational posts generate users and views of revenue (Zuboff, 2023). This places commercial interests and the need to retain information integrity in a state of tension. In the DTPG model, platforms serve to structure the interface between technology and governance with greater advantages, and risks of synthetic media. Enhancing platform responsibility and transparency consequently involves the need to address the proliferation of deepfakes and the need to make content moderation practices consistent with larger societal objectives.

4.5 Limitations of Current Regulatory Approaches

Despite the growing number of regulatory initiatives aimed at addressing deepfake technologies, significant limitations remain in existing governance frameworks. The first factor is the rate of technological change, which can be a lot faster than the legal and policy frameworks can keep up with and introduces unregulated areas of change and obsolete policies (Timmers, 2023). Moreover, several inconsistencies exist in jurisdictions because of the fragmentation of global governance, and it is hard to apply regulations well in a transnational digital context (Couture & Toupin, 2019). These drawbacks in the DTPG framework are manifested in the characteristics of insufficient control of data collection, deficit of transparency in technological systems, and insufficient mechanisms of digital platforms accountability. The other critical challenge is the inability to impose accountability in the content of deepfakes since the creation and sharing of such content concern several parties, such as developers, users, and the platform, among others (Meskys et al., 2020). This makes it hard to determine and enforce the legal responsibility and control. In addition, current frameworks tend to lean more towards responsive measures as opposed to preemptive ones which would deal with the root causes of the risks of deepfakes. Such restrictions point to the necessity of further integrated and adaptive forms of governance that would be able to act at all levels of the digital environment and integrate legal regulation, technological solutions, and international collaboration in order to adequately cope with the problem of synthetic media.

5. RIGHTS BASED AND ETHICAL LEGAL CHALLENGES

Shifting from structural analysis, this section focuses on individual rights and ethical implications arising from synthetic media.

5.1 Privacy and Biometric Data Protection

Privacy is one of the core digital rights that has been confronted upon by the advent of the synthetic media systems, especially in the data layer of the DTPG framework wherein high volumes of biometric data are generated and handled. Deepfake systems are dependent on the images of the faces, voice recording, and other kinds of personally identifiable information that are extracted through publically available digital platforms without direct permission more than twice, which makes the unauthorized use of data and monitoring a serious concern (Fischer, 2023; Usman, 2025a). Theoretically, the concept of privacy can be perceived as an orientation towards autonomy and dignity of an individual person, which is becoming more jeopardized in data driven environments where data mining occurs regularly. The political economy work by Shoshana Zuboff can show how user data is monetised in the online infrastructure which has changed individual experiences into marketable assets that can be used to develop techno (Zuboff, 2023). Deepfakes exacerbate such dynamics as they allow transforming biometric data into artificial representations that can be moved about and reused without any knowledge or consent of the person (He & Fang, 2024). This poses important ethical issues concerning the extent to which the data can be utilized and the appropriateness of the current data protection paradigms to ensure protection of the personal information. Although laws like the General Data Protection Regulation set up significant safeguards, such as consent and data minimization, their application in the deepfake scenario is difficult because of the lack of ability to trace the origins of those data and identify those responsible (Protection, 2018). Consequently, maintaining privacy amidst synthetic media necessitates the implementation of more stringent legal orders as well as technical measures and structural systems that have the capacity to impose more regulation and control on biometric data.

5.2 Consent, Ownership, and Digital Identity Rights

The emergence of deepfake is a major challenge to consent, ownership, and control of the digital identity, which are core aspects of the digital rights in the modern data economy (Boyd, 2022). These concerns exist in the DTPG framework in the intermediary between the data and technology layers, which turn into synthetic media using artificial intelligence systems. One of the critical ideas in data governance is consent, which is frequently absent or poorly obtained in the context of deepfakes creation since people may know nothing about having their data to create models or create synthetic information (Usman, 2025b). This is a failure to comply with the concept of informed consent and overrides the principle of informational self-determination, that is, they ought to be in control of the way their personal data are gathered and processed. Moreover, the idea of ownership gets even more complicated because with the appearance of digital examples of people, the replication and manipulation of digital objects can be done on their own regardless of their physical identity (Story & Jenkins, 2023; Van Alstyne et al., 1995). Deepfakes deceive the traditional concept of identity through the construction of more than one version of a person, which can be disproportionate to their real activities or intentions, making the question of authorship and responsibility problematic (Verma, 2026). The issues are particularly difficult to adapt within the legal frameworks; in this case, the current laws concerning intellectual property and personality rights might not represent the peculiarities of synthetic media comprehensively (Chesney & Citron, 2019). To overcome these issues, it is necessary to form more resilient legal and ethical frameworks, which will define such phenomenon as digital identity as the right that should be preserved, and people should have the right to control their digital representation.

5.3 Misinformation, Manipulation, and Democratic Rights

Deepfake technologies are also very dangerous to democratic rights because they allow a new type of misinformation and manipulation that can affect the opinions of people and interfere with democratic processes (Pawelec, 2022). These risks in the DTPG framework are directly connected with the technology and platform layers, in which synthetic media is produced and made very prevalent. The growing realism of deepfakes makes differentiating between genuine and fake information challenging and thus discrediting information systems and breaking the principles of informed decision making (Farid, 2022). This has far-reaching effects on the rights to democracy, such as freedom to express oneself, access to information that is true and to take part in societal discussion. Theoretically, the manipulation of information can be interpreted as the type of power that informs knowledge, and social reality, such as that stressed by Michel Foucault (Foucault, 1977). Deepfakes enhance this type of power because they allow actors to develop believable fake stories that can become widespread in digital media in a short period of time (Gregory, 2022). This leads to a scenario where misinformation is more convincing, as well as more difficult to refute, which helps to build what has been referred to as an erosion of epistemic trust (Chesney & Citron, 2019). It has considerable implications for the democratic governance process, whereby, through manipulated information, it is possible to sway elections, ruin reputations, and polarize the masses (Islam et al., 2024). The solution to these challenges is a set of technological, regulatory and educational measures to increase information integrity and safeguard democratic rights in online space.

5.4 Accountability and Responsibility in AI Development

Accountability is a central ethical and legal challenge in the governance of AI -generated content (Lechterman, 2022), particularly within the technology and governance layers of the DTPG framework. It is also difficult to ascertain who is responsible for the development and publication of synthetic media because many actors, such as the developers of artificial intelligence systems, users, and platform providers, are engaged in this process (Erafy, 2023; Karnouskos, 2020). This presents what is commonly referred to as a responsibility gap in which it is not clear who is to be held responsible for illicit results (Floridi et al., 2018). The concept of governance is not simply restricted to legal forms within the digital world, but also resides within the code of technological design, as indicated by Lawrence Lessig, who asserts that the code itself is a regulation (Lessig, 2006). This implies that accountability should be viewed not solely as a legal obligation, but rather with respect to creating and deploying technology systems. This is of special concern to deepfake technologies because these technologies allow the generation of very realistic artificial content that can be applied maliciously. Moreover, artificial intelligence systems require a greater degree of transparency, such as explainability and traceability, to be better monitored and enforced (Balasubramaniam et al., 2022). In the absence of such precautions, it is still difficult to hold anyone accountable and ensure that the creation and utilization of deepfake content are in line with wider societal values.

5.5 Legal Enforcement Challenges in a Global Digital Environment

The application of legal systems that regulate AI generated content is rather problematic as the digital environment is worldwide and decentralized. These issues are most clearly manifested in the layer of governance in the context of DTPG: in this case, regulatory mechanisms are required to act in a variety of jurisdictions with varying and legally binding capacity. Deepfakes are capable of being produced, shared, and viewed internationally and it is hard to say what laws should be applied and how they can be effectively implemented (Couture & Toupin, 2019). This brings loopholes in the law, with actors having chances of evading responsibility by having jurisdictional loopholes. Moreover, the quick advancement of technology tends to be faster than the sphere of law development, and therefore, outdated or inefficient rules that cannot handle the new threats can be observed (Kavanagh, 2022). The fact that deepfakes systems are complex also makes it hard to enforce since in many cases, it is not easy to trace how the synthetic production came up or even to name the people behind the production (Westerlund, 2019). The anonymity provided by online platforms adds to this issue and can make detecting the culprits more difficult and restrict the efficiency of legal interventions. These enforcement issues need to be solved by increased international collaboration and formulation of coordinated regulatory standards that can be used across boundaries. It also requires the incorporation of technological solutions, including the detection and authentication systems, to facilitate the legal procedures and improve the capacity to detect and respond to illegal content. The success of the legal frameworks in regulating AI generated content will not be much successful without such coordinated efforts.

6. RESISTANCE AND CONTESTATION IN THE DATA ECONOMY

6.1 Individual Resistance and Digital Self Defense

Personal opposition is a structural mode of contention within the digital data economy, which is formed at the data level of the DTPG model where individual data is gathered and used to generate deepfakes. With the growing awareness of data exploitation and synthetic media risks, people are developing strategies, which are expected to safeguard their digital identities and reduce the use of data without their consent. These measures involve limiting access to personal information on online platforms, applying privacy enhancing features, and applying data subject rights like data erasure and giving consent with the current legal regulations (Fischer, 2023). On theory, individual resistance can be explained in terms of power relation as defined by Michel Foucault who says that, power is being imposed at the top but it is also being debated through daily resistance exercises (Foucault, 1977). Resistance in the case of deepfakes is manifested through trying to repossess their digital images and reducing their exposure to data mining procedures. The efficacy of such opposition is limited, however, by the structural aspects, such as the ubiquitous quality of information gathering and distribution as well as the power imbalance between the individual and the mass technology site. In spite of these drawbacks, individual actions can contribute significantly to the formation of larger governance processes due to the creation of awareness and demand stronger protections, which are contributing to the development of digital rights and regulation reactions.

6.2 Civil Society and Advocacy Movements

Advocacy movement and civil society organizations are important to oppose the threats posed by deepfake technologies by advocating digital rights, building awareness, and shaping policy-making (Alanazi et al., 2025). These actors work at various levels of the DTPG structure, and their actions include social education, legal advocacy, and research to raise the question of the moral and social consequences of synthetic media. Civil society campaigns have played a central role in defining the problems of privacy, consent, and misinformation as rights issues and setting the tone of the debate and the policy agenda (Chesney & Citron, 2019). In the context of political economy, civil society resistance could be regarded as a reaction to the centralization of power in digital platforms and data driven business models according to Shoshana Zuboff since user data is sold and used to make economic profit (Zuboff, 2023). These practices are commonly questioned by the advocacy groups that demand more transparency, responsibility, and regulation (Goncharenko, 2019). Moreover, they also help to create ethical rules and principles of artificial intelligence that affect national and international regulatory systems. Through influencing opinion and interacting with policymakers, the civil society actors can be a valuable counterbalance to the corporate power, making sure that the regulation of AI generated content is based on the wider values of the society and that the individual rights are not violated (Moon, 2023).

6.3 State Level Resistance and Regulatory Assertion

States can be viewed as one of the primary points of opposition in the governance layer of the DTPG framework because they are striving to establish their control over the digital infrastructures and govern the applications of deepfake technologies within their territories. Resistance at the state level is of different types such as the enactment of data protection legislation, the necessity to label the content, and the invention of the national strategy of the artificial intelligence focused on the restriction of the technological evolution (Andraško et al., 2021; Mitrou, 2018). The attempts are a part of the larger struggle to reassert digital sovereignty amid the global data flows and the control of multinational technological corporations (Timmers, 2023). The state resistance can be perceived as the endeavor to re-establish control over the terms of information production and distribution, which can be related to the definition of governance in the institutional power (Maiguashca, 2003). The success of state level measures is frequently constrained, however, by the transnational character of digital platforms and the speed of technological advancement, which is sometimes far outpacing the regulatory capacity. Moreover, the presence of varying regulations in different nations may cause fragmentation and inconsistency, which lowers the effectiveness of the governance activities (Majone, 1997). Nevertheless, in spite of these issues, state action is one of the crucial elements of resistance, which offers the legal and institutional context that is required to overcome the threats posed by deepfake generated content and safeguard the digital rights in national settings.

6.4 Technological Resistance

The technological resistance is one of the dimensions of contestation of the DTPG framework, which is concerned with the design and implementation of technical means that can reduce the risks of deepfakes. Such solutions encompass detection systems based on artificial intelligence to detect manipulated material, authentication technology such as digital watermarking and content verification software that seek to maintain the integrity of digital data (Farid, 2022). The technological resistance on the platform and technology levels is primarily aimed at countering the functionality of deepfake systems by adding mechanisms to verify and bring transparency to the system (Fraga-Lamas & Fernandez-Carames, 2020). This type of resistance falls into the line of the argument that Lawrence Lessig has put forth where he argues that technological design can become some kind of regulation by influencing the operation of the systems and the ways in which people use it (Lessig, 2006). Technological solutions can be used to strengthen the legal and policy measures by introducing safeguards to digital infrastructures, forming a more extensive governance framework (V. A. Kumar et al., 2024; Linkov et al., 2018). Nonetheless, this type of resistance is marked by a continuous loop of resistance since there has been a constant adjustment of detection methods to newer techniques of deepfake creation. This trend underscores the importance of ongoing innovation and partnership among researchers, industry and policy makers in order to ensure that technological resistance is practical in meeting new threats.

6.5 Contesting Platform Power

The struggle of the platform power is a fundamental aspect of resistance in the DTPG framework, in which the overarching position of digital platforms in the production, distribution, and control of synthetic media is challenged. Digital ecosystems are highly dependent on platforms due to their data, algorithm, and content moderation control, which makes them crucial influencing factors in defining how deepfakes are shared and repressed (Sunkari & Srinagesh, 2024). Platform power resistance comes as a result of regulatory pressure, social criticism and alternative technological models that contest the status quo of power. The political economy critique of Shoshana Zuboff shows the dominance of platforms as an aspect of data extraction and monetization as sources of economic incentives that can lead to the conflict with the necessity to control damaging content (Zuboff, 2023). To this end, there have been more and more demands by policymakers, and civil society actors that there should be more transparency, accountability, and oversight over platform operations. This involves the calls to more clear content moderation policies, the transparency of their algorithm, and the reinvention of the rules that are already in place. Another way of contesting platform power is by considering other forms of governing platforms, including decentralized platforms and community-based moderation systems, which seek to redistribute power and lessen reliance on centralized actors. These resistance activities increase the overall attempt to reform the control of power in digital platforms and reinforce informational autonomy in the digital ecosystem.

7. POLICY IMPLICATIONS AND GOVERNANCE STRATEGIES

Based on the identified regulatory limitations, this section proposes targeted governance strategies.

7.1 Strengthening Regulatory Frameworks for Synthetic Media

The management of deepfake generated content needs to be able to develop multilateral and dynamic regulatory measures to meet the complexities of synthetic media at all levels of the DTPG model (Farouk & Fahmi, 2024). The existing regulatory procedures tend to be ad hoc and reactive and concentrate on particular harms and not on the systemic aspect of the issue (Gangavarapu, 2025; Mania, 2024; Perriello, 2026). The more effective method is risk based regulatory models in which artificial intelligence applications are sorted based on their possible effects on the foundational rights and the stability of society as per the new global models of artificial intelligence governance such as the European Union approach to artificial intelligence governance (Timmers, 2023). These frameworks need to contain explicit transparency and mandatory labeling of synthetic content requirements, along with responsibility mechanisms that establish the roles of the developers, users, and operating platform operators (Esezoobo et al., 2022; Perriello, 2026). Furthermore, the regulatory frameworks must be adaptable enough to meet the fast-changing technological demands, and include a mechanism of constant review as well as revision (Nookala, 2024; Peng, 2019). In the DTPG framework, this strategy fortifies the governance layer besides affecting the design and implementation of technologies in the technology layer. Policymakers can make the regulating of the risks that come with deepfake technologies more effective and coherent by aligning legal requirements with technological realities.

7.2 Data Governance and Biometric Data Protection Policies

Enhancing data governance is needed to help mitigate the underlying causes of deepfake-associated risks, especially the data layer of the DTPG framework, where personal and biometric data are captured and used. The latest policies of data governance focus on the following principles, i.e., informed consent, minimization of data, limitation of purpose, and transparency in data processing, which are based on current policies such as the General Data Protection Regulation (European Union., 2016). As biometric data are central in the production of deepfakes, more security measures, such as consent requirements that are more strict and restrictions on the use of secondary data, are needed. The development of means allowing people to have more control over their data (data access rights and possibilities to demand the deletion of personal information) should also be supported by policies. In a more general sense, data governance must work on the structural imbalances that the political economy of data points to, where big tech firms have unequal access to data resources (Zuboff, 2023). This can include; actions to facilitate the sharing of data on controlled terms, increase transparency in data practices and ensure that the data are utilized in a manner that safeguards individual rights. Policymakers could prevent threats to data security by tightening data management controls to diminish access to unauthorized information to make deepfakes, and by increasing the security of online identity.

7.3 Platform Accountability and Transparency Measures

Considering the key role of digital platforms in the spread of deep fake material, the increase in platform responsibility is an important part of successful governance initiatives in the DTPG framework. The platforms must be compelled to have very transparent and uniform policies on how to detect, label and delete the synthetic media that are harmful, and disclose more information about its content moderation, and algorithmic decision-making processes. It involves revealing the prioritization and the allocation of the content, the criteria applied to identify and deal with deepfake content (Gillespie, 2018). In theoretical terms, platform accountability can be interpreted in connection with the concept of technological systems as regulatory regimes, which dictate the actions of users and the flow of information (Gorwa, 2019; Lessig, 2006). Thus, to make them accountable, it is essential to not only establish legal requirements but also alter the platform design, focusing on accuracy and integrity rather than incentives to engage. Independent oversight mechanisms including audits and reporting mandates can also be an element considered by policymakers to make sure platforms meet the standards of regulatory requirements (MacCarthy, 2020; Ponugoti, 2023). Moreover, the cooperation of platforms, governments and civil society can make the content moderation process more efficient and lead to the evolution of common grounds of the synthetic media management (Gorwa et al., 2020; Sander, 2019). These measures can be used to reduce the risks of the spread of deepfakes and enhance the credibility of the online platform by enhancing transparency and accountability.

7.4 Technological Solutions for Detection and Authentication

Solutions such as technologies can be important to combat the hindrances of deepfake technologies, especially at the technology and platform levels of the DTPG framework. Artificial intelligence has made it possible to create detection systems that may detect the presence of manipulated content through the analysis of discrepancies in visual and audio information, which can also be a possible solution to the proliferation of deepfakes (Farid, 2022). In addition to detection, these authentication methods can be employed to prove the authenticity of digital content, including digital watermarking and cryptographic verification, and users can depend on them as valid signs indicating whether media is manipulated or not (Hajjej et al., 2026; Hurrah et al., 2019). These solutions are consistent with the general idea that technology may be a way of control by introducing protection into digital systems, which is theorized about technological governance (Lessig, 2006). Nonetheless, technological solutions are not as efficient as methods or generating deepfakes continue to evolve and can learn to avoid detection devices (Masood et al., 2023). This forms a loop of constant innovation and counter-innovation, which demands constant investment in R&D. To overcome this challenge, policymakers should encourage the development of partnerships among academia, industry, and the government in the development of detection and authentication technology, and in the development of standards for implementation. The incorporation of these technological solutions in more comprehensive governance systems has the potential to increase the effectiveness of the solutions adopted and help them become part of a more holistic response to the threat of synthetic media.

7.5 International Cooperation and Global Governance

The global nature of deepfake technologies necessitates coordinated international efforts to address policy tensions that extend beyond national boundaries (Dahiya & Sharma, 2025). This dimension is the most related to the governance layer within the DTPG framework where legal and institutional mechanisms have to be used across jurisdictions to control the cross-border data flows and platform activities. The international collaboration may be expressed in the form of the regulatory framework agreements, information exchange systems, and collaborative efforts to fight the abuse of synthetic media. The current initiatives in digital governance on a global scale serve as a basis of such cooperation, as it is necessary to align legal frameworks and share the values of developing artificial intelligence (Floridi et al., 2018). Nonetheless, these efforts may also be complicated by the differences in political structures, priorities in regulation, and technological capabilities, resulting in disjointed actions, which diminish the overall efficiency. These challenges can be addressed through international governance policies that aim to single out common standards of transparency, accountability, and data protection and leave flexibility in application to various situations. Moreover, multilateral organizations may be instrumental in determining dialogue and coordination between the states, industry agencies, and the civil society. Instead of making isolated efforts to combat the threat posed by synthetic media systems at the national level, policymakers can strengthen digital sovereignty through cooperation at the global level to address the transnational risks linked to the use of deepfake.

8. FUTURE TRENDS AND CONCLUSION

8.1 Emerging Trends in Synthetic Media and AI Development

The future of synthetic media is closely tied to ongoing advancements in artificial intelligence, which are expected to further increase the realism, accessibility, and scalability of deepfake (Karnouskos, 2020). The line between genuine and fake content will continue to fade as machine learning models become more advanced, and the validity of digital information and posing new issues to governance will become more challenging. Emerging technologies such as real-time deepfake generation, multimodal artificial intelligence systems, and combinations with immersive technologies such as virtual and augmented environments are likely to increase the use of synthetic media in industries such as entertainment, communication, and education (Kietzmann et al., 2020). Simultaneously, these developments increase the threats associated with misinformation, identity manipulation, and privacy violations, especially due to the increased difficulty of identifying synthetic media. These tendencies, according to the DTPG model, imply that data collection and processing, platform distribution, and governance response pressures will increase, with more stress on the digital system of all layers. Moreover, increased access to generative tools can result in additional democratization of content creation and increase the risk of abuse. To resolve these challenges, regulative frameworks, technological solutions and institutional practices continually adapt so that the benefits of synthetic media can be achieved without the necessity of undermining fundamental rights and societal trust.

8.2 Institutionalization and Standardization of AI Governance

The closer the artificial intelligence technologies are to social and economic systems, the more there is a necessity to institutionalize and standardize the development of governance systems that would effectively regulate their impact (De Almeida et al., 2021). Institutionalization means the creation of consistent regulatory frameworks, legal principles, and practices that regulate the application of artificial intelligence, and standardization implies the creation of shared technical and moral standards by jurisdiction. Under the DTPG mode, the process enhances the governance layer by developing more of the forecastable and predictable data, technology, and platform regulation mechanisms. The emergence of common principles to regulate artificial intelligence, such as principles to promote transparency, accountability, and fairness, are evidence of the fact that people have realized the necessity to act collectively (Floridi et al., 2018). Interoperability can be improved through standardization programs in domains like content authentication and data protection, which will enable cross-border collaboration (Guan, 2025; Jan, 2025). Nevertheless, the effective institutionalization is still difficult to attain because of the variations in the priorities of the regulations, political systems, and technological capabilities of different countries. Besides this, policy and practice are still at a disparity because the pace of technological innovation is accelerating faster than the formal governance structure is (Alanazi et al., 2025; Xi, 2025). The only way to bridge this gap is to continue working together with governments, industry players, and the civil society as well as incorporation of adaptable governance systems that can withstand changing technology situations.

8.3 Limitations and Future Research Directions

The chapter offers an interdisciplinary and conceptual analysis of deepfake technologies in the context of the wider idea of digital sovereignty and the AI-driven data economy; yet, there are also a number of limitations to consider. The debate is mainly based on conceptual interpretation, theoretical integration and policy-oriented analysis but not empirical investigation. Even though this method enables to get a wide picture of governance, regulatory, and ethical issues of synthetic media, it restricts the empirical testing of the suggested Data-Technology-Platform-Governance (DTPG) model in various institutional and sociotechnical contexts. Besides that, the fast pace of artificial intelligence technologies development and synthetic media systems is a natural obstacle to governance studies because technical advancements often surpass regulation adaptation and institutional response strategies. As a result, certain regulatory and technological conversations in this chapter might change over time as the process of deepfake generation, detection, and forms of governance are further developed. Furthermore, the chapter takes a global approach to digital sovereignty, but does not offer a comprehensive comparative study of jurisdiction-specific governance strategies, system of platform moderation, or regionally-differentiated policy responses. The lessen transparency of proprietary platform algorithms and content moderation systems also limits the ability to further analyze how digital platforms operationally handle synthetic media risks within business eco-systems.

Future studies thus ought to go past the conceptual and regulatory discourse and include empirical and behavioral studies, and platform studies on the social consequences of synthetic media technologies. Specifically, future research should examine the impact of deepfakes on consumer trust, perceived authenticity, online buying habits, and brand authenticity in more AI-mediated digital markets. With the increase of synthetic influencers, AI-based endorsements, and deepfake advertisements, scholars ought to examine how consumers perceive authenticity in manipulated online spaces and the impact of deceptive media on trust formation, perceived risk, emotional reaction, and anticipation of behavior. The psychological and social implications of the repeated exposure to synthetic media such as misinformation fatigue, a decrease in institutional trust, distrust of digital information, and emotional manipulation can also be explored in further studies. Also, the role of media literacy, digital awareness, and technological competence in influencing user resistance to synthetic deception in various demographic and cultural settings should be explored in future scholarship. A comparative study across countries would also be valuable in understanding the impact of differences in political systems, regulatory capabilities, and technological infrastructures on the effectiveness of the governance of deepfakes. There is also a greater demand of scholarly focus on Global South views, ethical AI auditing systems, governance of biometric data, accountability mechanisms on platforms, and coordination structures globally that are able to handle the transnational character of synthetic media ecosystems.

8.4 Conclusion

This chapter has discussed deepfake technologies as a complicated governance problem that exists within the broader framework of digital sovereignty and the digital economy, with an emphasis on the interrelated relationships among data, technology, platforms, and governance as operationalized in the DTPG framework. Deep fakes are not only technological breakthroughs but also sociotechnical breakthroughs that change the relations of power, insurmount regulatory frameworks, and cast questions of rights, responsibility, and control in the digital world. The chapter provides an evaluation of the implications of deepfakes on various levels, such as data sovereignty, information integrity, platform power, and cross-border governance, to demonstrate the inadequacy of current methods and regulatory approaches to address this problem. The rights based challenges are discussed to emphasize the need to protect privacy, consent and digital identity, and the analysis of resistance shows how individuals, civil society and states are proactive in challenging the power structures of synthetic media. On the basis of these observations, the chapter suggests a multilayered strategy of governance that integrates legal regulation, technological innovation, and international collaboration to curb the risks inherent in deepfakes and allow their positive uses. Finally, the capacity to govern synthetic media successfully is determined by the ability of stakeholders to manage the tensions between innovation and control, whereby informational autonomy is preserved in such a way that it safeguards individual rights, and fosters a trustworthy digital ecosystem.

REFERENCES

Adebiyi, O. I., & Adeusi, O. C. (2025). Examining legal and ethical frameworks for protecting intellectual property rights in AI-generated content across creative industries. *World Journal of Advanced Research and Reviews, 26*(3), 1553–1561. DOI: 10.30574/wjarr.2025.26.3.2239

Akkem, Y., Biswas, S. K., & Varanasi, A. (2024). A comprehensive review of synthetic data generation in smart farming by using variational autoencoder and generative adversarial network. *Engineering Applications of Artificial Intelligence, 131*, 107881. DOI: 10.1016/j.engappai.2024.107881

Alanazi, S., Asif, S., Caird-Daley, A., & Moulitsas, I. (2025). Unmasking deepfakes: a multidisciplinary examination of social impacts and regulatory responses. *Human-Intelligent Systems Integration*, 1–23.

Andraško, J., Mesarčík, M., & Hamuľák, O. (2021). The regulatory intersections between artificial intelligence, data protection and cyber security: Challenges and opportunities for the EU legal framework. *AI & Society, 36*(2), 623–636. DOI: 10.1007/s00146-020-01125-5

Babaei, R., Cheng, S., Duan, R., & Zhao, S. (2025). Generative artificial intelligence and the evolving challenge of deepfake detection: A systematic analysis. *Journal of Sensor and Actuator Networks, 14*(1), 17. DOI: 10.3390/jsan14010017

Balasubramaniam, N., Kauppinen, M., Hiekkanen, K., & Kujala, S. (2022). Transparency and explainability of AI systems: ethical guidelines in practice. *International Working Conference on Requirements Engineering: Foundation for Software Quality*, 3–18. DOI: 10.1007/978-3-030-98464-9_1

Basir, H., ASMI, F., Arshad, M. U., Khawar, A., Aman, N., Li, P., Zhou, R., & Makki, B. I. (2024). Combatting Deepfakes: Rational Choices, Moral Emotions, and Social Media Literacy. *Moral Emotions, and Social Media Literacy*.

Bellovin, S. M., Dutta, P. K., & Reitinger, N. (2019). Privacy and synthetic datasets. *Stan. Tech. L. Rev., 22*, 1.

Birrer, A., & Just, N. (2025). What we know and don't know about deepfakes: An investigation into the state of the research and regulatory landscape. *New Media & Society, 27*(12), 6819–6838. DOI: 10.1177/14614448241253138

Boyd, P. (2022). Fakes and deepfakes: Balancing privacy rights in the digital age. *Alabama Law Review, 74*, 517.

Cannon-Bowers, J., & Bowers, C. (2009). Synthetic learning environments: On developing a science of simulation, games, and virtual worlds for training. In *Learning, training, and development in organizations* (pp. 229–261). Routledge.

Chawki, M. (2024). Navigating legal challenges of deepfakes in the American context: A call to action. *Cogent Engineering*, *11*(1), 2320971. DOI: 10.1080/23311916.2024.2320971

Chesney, B., & Citron, D. (2019). Deep fakes: A looming challenge for privacy, democracy, and national security. *California Law Review*, *107*(6), 1753–1820. DOI: 10.15779/Z38RV0D15J

Couture, S., & Toupin, S. (2019). What does the notion of "sovereignty" mean when referring to the digital? *New Media & Society*, *21*(10), 2305–2322. DOI: 10.1177/1461444819865984

Dahiya, K., & Sharma, U. (2025). Navigating the Digital Mirage: A Comparative Analysis of Deepfake Challenges and Responses Across BRICS Nations and the Global Arena. In *Navigating the Deepfake Conundrum: A Manager's Roadmap* (pp. 239–261). Springer. DOI: 10.1007/978-3-031-90742-5_16

De Almeida, P. G. R., Dos Santos, C. D., & Farias, J. S. (2021). Artificial intelligence regulation: A framework for governance. *Ethics and Information Technology*, *23*(3), 505–525. DOI: 10.1007/s10676-021-09593-z

Diakopoulos, N., & Johnson, D. (2021). Anticipating and addressing the ethical implications of deepfakes in the context of elections. *New Media & Society*, *23*(7), 2072–2098. DOI: 10.1177/1461444820925811

Dong, H., & Chen, J. (2024). Meta-regulation: An ideal alternative to the primary responsibility as the regulatory model of generative AI in China. *Computer Law & Security Review*, *54*, 106016. DOI: 10.1016/j.clsr.2024.106016

El Erafy, A. N. (2023). Applications of Artificial Intelligence in the field of media. *International Journal of Artificial Intelligence and Emerging Technology*, *6*(2), 19–41. DOI: 10.21608/ijaiet.2024.275179.1006

Esezoobo, S. O., Adebayo, M. E., & Chiobi, N. F. (2022). *Privacy and Legal Guardrails for Deepfake AI in Continuous Delivery Environments: Preventing Misuse and Ensuring Traceability in Generative Media and Security Applications*.

European Union. (2016). Regulation (EU) 2016/679 of the European Parliament and of the Council. *Regulation (Eu)*, *679*, 10–13.

Farid, H. (2022). Creating, using, misusing, and detecting deep fakes. *Journal of Online Trust & Safety*, *1*(4). Advance online publication. DOI: 10.54501/jots.v1i4.56

Farouk, M. A., & Fahmi, B. M. (2024). Deepfakes and media integrity: Navigating the new reality of synthetic content. *Journal of Media and Interdisciplinary Studies*, *3*(9), 47–94. DOI: 10.21608/jmis.2024.275298.1027

Figueira, A., & Vaz, B. (2022). Survey on synthetic data generation, evaluation methods and GANs. *Mathematics*, *10*(15), 2733. DOI: 10.3390/math10152733

Fischer, A. (2023). Data sovereignty and e-governance: The legal implications of national laws on digital government systems. *Legal Studies in Digital Age*, *2*(4), 1–12.

Floridi, L., Cowls, J., Beltrametti, M., Chatila, R., Chazerand, P., Dignum, V., Luetge, C., Madelin, R., Pagallo, U., Rossi, F., Schafer, B., Valcke, P., & Vayena, E. (2018). AI4People—An ethical framework for a good AI society: Opportunities, risks, principles, and recommendations. *Minds and Machines*, *28*(4), 689–707. DOI: 10.1007/s11023-018-9482-5

Foucault, M. (1977). *Discipline and punish: The birth ofthe prison*. Allen Lane.

Fraga-Lamas, P., & Fernandez-Carames, T. M. (2020). Fake news, disinformation, and deepfakes: Leveraging distributed ledger technologies and blockchain to combat digital deception and counterfeit reality. *IT Professional*, *22*(2), 53–59. DOI: 10.1109/MITP.2020.2977589

Gangavarapu, R. (2025). *Mastering AI Governance*. Springer. DOI: 10.1007/978-3-031-93681-4

George, A. S., Baskar, T., & Pandey, D. (2024). Establishing global ai accountability: Training data transparency, copyright, and misinformation. *Partners Universal Innovative Research Publication*, *2*(3), 75–91.

George, A. S., & George, A. S. H. (2023). Deepfakes: The evolution of hyper realistic media manipulation. *Partners Universal Innovative Research Publication*, *1*(2), 58–74.

Ghiurău, D., & Popescu, D. E. (2024). Distinguishing reality from AI: Approaches for detecting synthetic content. *Computers*, *14*(1), 1. DOI: 10.3390/computers14010001

Gillespie, T. (2018). *Custodians of the Internet: Platforms, content moderation, and the hidden decisions that shape social media*. Yale University Press.

Goncharenko, G. (2019). The accountability of advocacy NGOs: Insights from the online community of practice. *Accounting Forum*, *43*(1), 135–160. DOI: 10.1080/01559982.2019.1589901

Goodfellow, I. J., Pouget-Abadie, J., Mirza, M., Xu, B., Warde-Farley, D., Ozair, S., Courville, A., & Bengio, Y. (2014). Generative adversarial nets. *Proceedings. Neurips.CcI Goodfellow, J Pouget-Abadie, M Mirza, B Xu, D Warde-Farley, S Ozair, A CourvilleAdvances in Neural Information Processing Systems, 2014•proceedings. Neurips.Cc.* https://proceedings.neurips.cc/paper/5423-generative-adversarial-nets

Gorwa, R. (2019). What is platform governance? *Information Communication and Society*, *22*(6), 854–871. DOI: 10.1080/1369118X.2019.1573914

Gorwa, R., Binns, R., & Katzenbach, C. (2020). Algorithmic content moderation: Technical and political challenges in the automation of platform governance. *Big Data & Society*, *7*(1), 2053951719897945. DOI: 10.1177/2053951719897945

Gregory, S. (2022). Deepfakes, misinformation and disinformation and authenticity infrastructure responses: Impacts on frontline witnessing, distant witnessing, and civic journalism. *Journalism*, *23*(3), 708–729. DOI: 10.1177/14648849211060644

Guan, C. (2025). Cross-Border Cybercrime Digital Evidence: Current Research and Fundamental Categories. *Modern Law Research, 6*(4).

Hajjej, F., Hamid, M., & Alluhaidan, A. S. (2026). An integrated framework for proactive deepfake mitigation via attention-driven watermarking and blockchain-based authenticity verification. *Scientific Reports*, *16*(1), 9545. DOI: 10.1038/s41598-026-40166-6

He, S., Lei, Y., Zhang, Z., Sun, Y., Li, S., Zhang, C., & Ye, J. (2025). Identity deepfake threats to biometric authentication systems: Public and expert perspectives. *ArXiv Preprint ArXiv:2506.06825.*

He, X., & Fang, L. (2024). Regulatory Challenges in Synthetic Media Governance: Policy Frameworks for AI-Generated Content Across Image, Video, and Social Platforms. *Journal of Robotic Process Automation, AI Integration, and Workflow Optimization*, *9*(12), 36–54.

Hoffmann-Riem, W. (2019). Artificial intelligence as a challenge for law and regulation. In *Regulating artificial intelligence* (pp. 1–29). Springer.

Hurrah, N. N., Parah, S. A., Loan, N. A., Sheikh, J. A., Elhoseny, M., & Muhammad, K. (2019). Dual watermarking framework for privacy protection and content authentication of multimedia. *Future Generation Computer Systems*, *94*, 654–673. DOI: 10.1016/j.future.2018.12.036

Ishkhanyan, A. (2025a). Governing AI across borders: corporate power, state sovereignty and global regulation. *Digital Policy, Regulation and Governance.*

Ishkhanyan, A. (2025b). The sovereignty-internationalism paradox in AI governance: Digital federalism and global algorithmic control. *Discover Artificial Intelligence*, *5*(1), 123. DOI: 10.1007/s44163-025-00374-x

Islam, M. B. E., Haseeb, M., Batool, H., Ahtasham, N., & Muhammad, Z. (2024). AI threats to politics, elections, and democracy: A blockchain-based deepfake authenticity verification framework. *Blockchains*, *2*(4), 458–481. DOI: 10.3390/blockchains2040020

Jan, E. (2025). Mitigating Deepfake Risks in Cloud Data Environments: Privacy and Security Lessons from Cross-Border Data Transfer Case Studies. *Available at SSRN* 5359940. DOI: 10.2139/ssrn.5359940

Kalpokas, I. (2020). Problematising reality: The promises and perils of synthetic media. *SN Social Sciences*, *1*(1), 1. DOI: 10.1007/s43545-020-00010-8

Kaludewage, P. M. W. (2025). *Real-World Challenges and Adoption of Deepfake Detection Technologies in Digital Media Forensics.*

Karnouskos, S. (2020). Artificial intelligence in digital media: The era of deepfakes. *IEEE Transactions on Technology and Society*, *1*(3), 138–147. DOI: 10.1109/TTS.2020.3001312

Kavanagh, C. (2022). *New Tech, New Threats, and New Governance Challenges: An Opportunity to Craft Smarter Responses?* Carnegie Endowment for International Peace.

Keller, D. (2021). Amplification and its discontents: Why regulating the reach of online content is hard. *J. Free Speech L.*, *1*, 227.

Khadka, R. (2025). Navigating the Legal Landscape of AI-Created Content: Intellectual Property, Accountability, and Regulation. *International Scientific Journal of Engineering and Management*, *04*(04), 1–7. DOI: 10.55041/ISJEM03055

Kietzmann, J., Mills, A. J., & Plangger, K. (2020). Deepfakes: Perspectives on the future “reality” of advertising and branding. *International Journal of Advertising*, *40*(3), 473–485. DOI: 10.1080/02650487.2020.1834211

Kishwar, S. D., Tripathi, A., Khatoon, S., Poddar, D., & Khurana, B. (2025). Regulating deep fakes and synthetic media: Privacy, policy and global regulatory challenges. *Journal of Data Protection & Privacy*, *8*(1), 78–96. DOI: 10.69554/HBGG8150

Kopecky, S. (2024). Challenges of deepfakes. *Science and Information Conference*, 158–166.

Kumar, S., Verma, A. K., & Mirza, A. (2024). Digital transformation, artificial intelligence and society. *Springer.* Https://Link. Springer. Com/Book/10, *1007*, 978–981.

Kumar, V. A., Bhardwaj, S., & Lather, M. (2024). Cybersecurity and Safeguarding Digital Assets: An Analysis of Regulatory Frameworks, Legal Liability and Enforcement Mechanisms. *Productivity*, *65*(1), 1–10.

Kusche, I. (2024). Possible harms of artificial intelligence and the EU AI act: Fundamental rights and risk. *Journal of Risk Research*, •••, 1–14. DOI: 10.1080/13669877.2024.2350720

Lambach, D., & Monsees, L. (2025). Beyond sovereignty as authority: The multiplicity of European approaches to digital sovereignty. *Global Political Economy*, *4*(1), 71–88. DOI: 10.1332/26352257Y2024D000000007

Langa, J. (2021). Deepfakes, real consequences: Crafting legislation to combat threats posed by deepfakes. *BUL Rev.*, *101*, 761.

Lao, Y., Hirvonen, N., & Larsson, S. (2025). Everyday encounters with deepfakes: Young people's media and information literacy practices with AI-generated media. *The Journal of Documentation*, *81*(7), 216–235. DOI: 10.1108/JD-01-2025-0007

Lechterman, T. M. (2022). The concept of accountability in AI ethics and governance. *The Oxford Handbook of AI Governance*, 164–182.

Lessig, L. (2006). Code: version 2.0,(Basic Books. *New York.* Liao, X., Wang, Y., Wang, T., Hu, J., & Wu, X. (2023). FAMM: Facial muscle motions for detecting compressed deepfake videos over social networks. *IEEE Transactions on Circuits and Systems for Video Technology*, *33*(12), 7236–7251.

Lin, L. S. F. (2025). Organisational Challenges in US Law Enforcement's Response to AI-Driven Cybercrime and Deepfake Fraud. *Laws*, *14*(4), 46. DOI: 10.3390/laws14040046

Lin, W., Zhu, Y., Guo, D., & Fedkiw, R. (2022). Leveraging deepfakes to close the domain gap between real and synthetic images in facial capture pipelines. *ArXiv Preprint ArXiv:2204.10746*.

Linkov, I., Trump, B. D., Poinsatte-Jones, K., & Florin, M.-V. (2018). Governance strategies for a sustainable digital world. *Sustainability (Basel)*, *10*(2), 440. DOI: 10.3390/su10020440

MacCarthy, M. (2020). *Transparency requirements for digital social media platforms: Recommendations for policy makers and industry*. Transatlantic Working Group.

Maiguashca, B. (2003). Governance and resistance in world politics. *Review of International Studies*, *29*(S1), 3–28. DOI: 10.1017/S0260210503005989

Majone, G. (1997). From the positive to the regulatory state: Causes and consequences of changes in the mode of governance. *Journal of Public Policy*, *17*(2), 139–167. DOI: 10.1017/S0143814X00003524

Mania, K. (2024). Legal protection of revenge and deepfake porn victims in the European Union: Findings from a comparative legal study. *Trauma, Violence & Abuse*, *25*(1), 117–129. DOI: 10.1177/15248380221143772

Mansoor, S. I. U. (2024). Legal implications of deepfake technology: In the context of manipulation, privacy, and identity theft. *Central University of Kashmir Law Review*, *4*, 65–92. DOI: 10.66498/CUKLR.4.2024.65-92

Masood, M., Nawaz, M., Malik, K. M., Javed, A., Irtaza, A., & Malik, H. (2023). Deepfakes generation and detection: State-of-the-art, open challenges, countermeasures, and way forward. *Applied Intelligence*, *53*(4), 3974–4026. DOI: 10.1007/s10489-022-03766-z

Meskys, E., Kalpokiene, J., Jurcys, P., & Liaudanskas, A. (2020). Regulating deep fakes: Legal and ethical considerations. *Journal of Intellectual Property Law & Practice*, *15*(1), 24–31. DOI: 10.1093/jiplp/jpz167

Mitrou, L. (2018). Data protection, artificial intelligence and cognitive services: is the general data protection regulation (GDPR) 'artificial intelligence-proof'? *Artificial Intelligence and Cognitive Services: Is the General Data Protection Regulation (GDPR) 'Artificial Intelligence-Proof.*

Mohammed, A. (2024). Deep Fake Detection and Mitigation: Securing Against AI-Generated Manipulation. *Journal of Computational Innovation*, *4*(1).

Moon, M. J. (2023). Searching for inclusive artificial intelligence for social good: Participatory governance and policy recommendations for making AI more inclusive and benign for society. *Public Administration Review*, *83*(6), 1496–1505. DOI: 10.1111/puar.13648

Naitali, A., Ridouani, M., Salahdine, F., & Kaabouch, N. (2023). Deepfake attacks: Generation, detection, datasets, challenges, and research directions. *Computers*, *12*(10), 216. DOI: 10.3390/computers12100216

Natarajan, S. K., Abdullah, A., Kaur, S., & Natarajan, P. (2025). Advancing Multi-Modal Behavioral Biometric Authentication: A Deep Learning Approach With Synthetic Data Generation. *IEEE Access : Practical Innovations, Open Solutions*.

Nikolenko, S. I. (2021). *Synthetic data for deep learning* (Vol. 174). Springer. DOI: 10.1007/978-3-030-75178-4

Nookala, G. (2024). Adaptive data governance frameworks for data-driven digital transformations. *Journal of Computational Innovation*, *4*(1).

Omogiate, P. M., & Legal, C. A. B. T. (2022). Developing standardized metadata protocols enabling transparent provenance tracking for AI-created media within federal intellectual property regulatory systems nationwide. *International Journal of Computer Applications Technology and Research*, *11*(12), 711–723.

Patel, Y., Tanwar, S., Gupta, R., Bhattacharya, P., Davidson, I. E., Nyameko, R., Aluvala, S., & Vimal, V. (2023). Deepfake generation and detection: Case study and challenges. *IEEE Access : Practical Innovations, Open Solutions*, *11*, 143296–143323. DOI: 10.1109/ACCESS.2023.3342107

Pawelec, M. (2022). Deepfakes and democracy (theory): How synthetic audio-visual media for disinformation and hate speech threaten core democratic functions. *Digital Society : Ethics, Socio-Legal and Governance of Digital Technology*, *1*(2), 19. DOI: 10.1007/s44206-022-00010-6

Peng, S. (2019). The rule of law in times of technological uncertainty: Is international economic law ready for emerging supervisory trends? *Journal of International Economic Law*, *22*(1), 1–27. DOI: 10.1093/jiel/jgy049

Perriello, L. E. (2026). Blurred realities: Legal strategies for the deepfake era. *Maastricht Journal of European and Comparative Law*, 1023263X261433380.

Pierucci, F. (2025). Sovereignty in the digital era: Rethinking territoriality and governance in cyberspace. *Digital Society : Ethics, Socio-Legal and Governance of Digital Technology*, *4*(1), 27. DOI: 10.1007/s44206-025-00189-4

Pohle, J., & Thiel, T. (2020). Digital sovereignty. *Pohle, J. & Thiel.*

Ponugoti, M. (2023). Frameworks for ensuring compliance in digital platform governance. [IJEETR]. *International Journal of Engineering & Extended Technologies Research*, *5*(6), 7575–7586. DOI: 10.15662/IJEETR.2023.0506015

Protection, D. (2018). General data protection regulation. *Intersoft Consulting, Accessed in October, 24*(1).

Roe, J., Perkins, M., & Furze, L. (2024). Deepfakes and higher education: A research agenda and scoping review of synthetic media. *Journal of University Teaching & Learning Practice*, *21*(10), 1–22. DOI: 10.53761/2y2np178

Rostomyan, A. (2026). Used in the Synthetic Media Generations and Applications. *The Convergence of Federated Learning and Healthcare 5.0 and Beyond: A New Era of Intelligent Health Systems*, 301.

Salam, M. A., Rayun, S. M. N., Islam, W., Hasan, R., Firmansyah, E. A., & Kalinaki, K. (2024). Consumer Engagement: Exploring Deepfake Applications in Consumer Marketing Communication. In *Navigating the World of Deepfake Technology* (pp. 397–421). IGI Global.

Sander, B. (2019). Freedom of expression in the age of online platforms: The promise and pitfalls of a human rights-based approach to content moderation. *Fordham Int'l LJ*, *43*, 939.

Story, D., & Jenkins, R. (2023). Deepfake pornography and the ethics of non-veridical representations. *Philosophy & Technology*, *36*(3), 56. DOI: 10.1007/s13347-023-00657-0

Sunkari, V., & Srinagesh, A. (2024). System Architecture for AI-Driven DeepFake Detection and Moderation on Social Media Platforms. *3rd International Conference on Optimization Techniques in the Field of Engineering (ICOFE-2024)*. DOI: 10.2139/ssrn.5065478

Tian, X. (2024). Personalized translator training in the era of digital intelligence: Opportunities, challenges, and prospects. *Heliyon*, *10*(20), e39354. DOI: 10.1016/j.heliyon.2024.e39354

Timmers, P. (2023). Sovereignty in the digital age. In *Introduction to Digital Humanism: A Textbook* (pp. 571–592). Springer.

Usman, S. O. (2025a). *Consent, ownership, and the ethics of using personal data in deepfake creation.*

Usman, S. O. (2025b). *The Role of AI Regulation in Mitigating Deepfake Harms.*

Van Alstyne, M., Brynjolfsson, E., & Madnick, S. (1995). Why not one big database? Principles for data ownership. *Decision Support Systems*, *15*(4), 267–284. DOI: 10.1016/0167-9236(94)00042-4

Van der Sloot, B., & Wagensveld, Y. (2022). Deepfakes: Regulatory challenges for the synthetic society. *Computer Law & Security Review*, *46*, 105716. DOI: 10.1016/j.clsr.2022.105716

Vasist, P. N., & Krishnan, S. (2023). Engaging with deepfakes: a meta-synthesis from the perspective of social shaping of technology theory. In *Internet Research* (Vol. 33, Issue 5). DOI: 10.1108/INTR-06-2022-0465

Verma, A. (2026). Deepfakes and the crisis of digital authenticity: Ethical challenges in the age of synthetic media. *Journal of Information. Communication and Ethics in Society*, *24*(1), 59–76. DOI: 10.1108/JICES-04-2025-0083

Wang, Y. (2023). Synthetic realities in the digital age: Navigating the opportunities and challenges of ai-generated content. *Authorea Preprints*.

Westerlund, M. (2019). The emergence of deepfake technology: A review. *Technology Innovation Management Review*, *9*(11), 39–52. DOI: 10.22215/timreview/1282

Xi, R. (2025). On emerging technologies: The old regime and the proactivity. *Cardozo Int'l & Comp. L. Rev.*, *8*, 75.

Yusuf, M., Rafli, M., & Rahmat, R. (2026). Reassessing State Sovereignty in the Era of Global Digital Governance. *International Legal Dimension Journal*, *1*(1), 49–60.

Zozulia, O. I., Zozulia, I. V, Brusakova, O. V, Kholod, Y. A., & Berezhna, Y. V. (2021). *Information sovereignty as the basis of modern state information security*.

Zuboff, S. (2023). The age of surveillance capitalism. In *Social theory re-wired* (pp. 203–213). Routledge. DOI: 10.4324/9781003320609-27

Chapter 9
African Digital Sovereignty, Cross-Border Cybercrime, and the Future of Networked Governance

Hibah Asiimwe
http://orcid.org/0009-0004-7433-6241
International Islamic University, Malaysia

ABSTRACT

This chapter examines the shifting landscape of African cyber-jurisprudence, moving from the Malabo Convention (AU Convention on Cyber Security and Personal Data Protection) to the complex integration of the 2026 UN Convention Against Cybercrime. The central argument is that Africa faces a "double-edged fragmentation": the external friction between global geopolitical blocs and the internal lack of harmonization between African states. This chapter provides an ecosystem-level analysis of African cross-border cooperation, focusing on the transition from colonial-era Mutual Legal Assistance Treaties (MLATs) to modern, intelligence-led judicial cooperation. It further examines how jurisdictional fragmentation, mobile money ecosystems, and evidentiary challenges enable transnational cybercrime. The chapter concludes by assessing emerging threats posed by artificial intelligence and quantum computing, emphasizing the need for harmonized legal systems, institutional resilience, and collaborative governance to secure Africa's digital future.

DOI: 10.4018/979-8-2600-0288-9.ch009

THE EVOLUTION OF AFRICAN DIGITAL ARCHITECTURE.

Africa's progressive integration into the global digital ecosystem is precipitating a fundamental reconfiguration of its role within international cyber governance. Historically situated at the periphery of technological standard-setting and regulatory influence, African states are increasingly transitioning from passive recipients of externally generated legal frameworks to active participants in the construction of normative and institutional architectures governing cyberspace. This transformation extends beyond technological adoption and reflects a deeper jurisprudential shift toward the articulation of context-sensitive models of digital sovereignty (Maurer, et al. 2022).

At the core of this transition lies a structural tension between inherited legal frameworks and emergent digital realities. Early regulatory responses to cyber threats across African jurisdictions were largely characterized by the transplantation of external legal models, particularly those derived from European and other technologically advanced systems. While such transplants facilitated initial harmonization and normative alignment, they frequently failed to account for disparities in institutional capacity, technological infrastructure, and socio-economic conditions. As a result, a persistent implementation gap emerged, whereby formal legal compliance did not translate into effective enforcement outcomes. This phenomenon reflects a broader critique within post-colonial legal theory, which underscores the limitations of externally imposed normative systems in contexts where institutional ecosystems remain unevenly developed (Mugamba, 2025).

The limitations of this externally oriented regulatory paradigm are particularly evident in the application of the Council of Europe Convention on Cybercrime (Budapest Convention). Although the Convention has played a significant role in promoting global convergence in cybercrime legislation, its operational assumptions are rooted in environments characterized by advanced investigative capacity, institutional coordination, and technological sophistication. In many African contexts, these prerequisites remain underdeveloped, resulting in a disjunction between formal legal adoption and practical enforceability (Chang, 2020). Consequently, the diffusion of the Budapest model has often produced what may be termed "compliance without capacity," wherein legal frameworks exist in form but lack the operational infrastructure necessary for effective implementation.

In response to these limitations, African states have increasingly pursued endogenous approaches to digital governance, culminating in the development of the African Union Convention on Cyber Security and Personal Data Protection (Malabo Convention). The Malabo framework represents a significant normative departure from earlier externally derived models by integrating cybersecurity, data protection, and electronic commerce within a unified regulatory architecture. This integrative approach reflects an understanding of cyber governance as a multidimensional phenomenon, encompassing not only security concerns but also economic development, institutional legitimacy, and public trust (Ewulum, 2023).

From a doctrinal perspective, the Malabo Convention embodies a shift toward contextually grounded norm production, emphasizing regulatory coherence within African socio-economic and institutional realities. Its provisions recognize the centrality of data governance in digital economies, the importance of securing electronic transactions, and the necessity of safeguarding individual rights in increasingly digitized societies. In doing so, the Convention advances a model of development-oriented cyber governance, which situates cybersecurity within broader objectives of economic inclusion and structural transformation (Nhlazane, 2025).

Notwithstanding its normative significance, the operationalization of the Malabo Convention has been uneven across the continent. Ratification and domestication processes have progressed at varying speeds, reflecting differences in political prioritization, administrative capacity, and resource allocation among member states. This implementation asymmetry has given rise to what may be conceptualized as the "Malabo Gap," a structural divergence between continental regulatory aspirations and national-level enforcement realities. The persistence of this gap underscores the broader challenge of translating supranational legal instruments into functionally effective domestic regimes (Emmanuel, et al. 2025).

Concurrently, Africa's role in global cyber governance has undergone a marked transformation, particularly through its collective engagement in multilateral norm-setting processes. The negotiations surrounding the 2026 United Nations Convention Against Cybercrime provide a salient illustration of this shift. Acting through coordinated diplomatic coalitions, African states have contributed substantively to the reorientation of global cybercrime governance frameworks, advocating for greater emphasis on capacity building, technology transfer, and equitable participation. This intervention reflects a strategic deployment of collective bargaining power to address structural asymmetries within the international legal order (de Silva de Alwis, 2024). The implications of this evolving posture are jurisprudentially significant. Traditional conceptions of sovereignty, grounded in territorially bounded authority, are increasingly inadequate in addressing the transnational dynamics of digital networks. In response, African states are experimenting with models of networked sovereignty, wherein regulatory authority is exercised through cooperative, cross-border mechanisms rather than exclusively within territorial confines. This reconceptualization aligns with broader theoretical developments in international law, which recognize the necessity of shared governance arrangements in managing global commons such as cyberspace (Sangwa, 2025).

Within this context, the emergence of Digital Pan-Africanism represents a strategic effort to extend regional integration into the digital domain. Initiatives such as the development of a Single Digital Market under the African Continental Free Trade Area framework exemplify attempts to harmonize regulatory standards, enhance interoperability, and facilitate cross-border digital commerce. These efforts are complemented by institutional mechanisms such as the African Union Mechanism for Police Cooperation (AFRIPOL), which operationalize collaborative security frameworks through intelligence sharing and coordinated enforcement activities (Oloruntoba, 2020).

The transition from fragmented, externally influenced legal systems to more integrated and contextually grounded governance architectures reflect a broader reorientation in African cyber jurisprudence. Rather than merely adapting to pre-existing global norms, African states are increasingly contributing to their evolution, articulating alternative models that prioritize inclusivity, developmental equity, and institutional realism. This shift is not without challenges, particularly in light of persistent capacity constraints and regulatory fragmentation. However, it signals a critical movement toward greater normative agency and strategic autonomy within the global digital order (Farah Hersi, et al. 2024).

I. NETWORK CRIMES VERSUS CONTINENTAL BORDERS.

The rapid digitization of African economies has fundamentally destabilized the territorial foundations upon which conventional legal jurisdiction is constructed. Classical jurisdictional doctrine, grounded in the Westphalian conception of state sovereignty, presumes that regulatory authority is territorially bounded and that criminal conduct can be spatially localized within identifiable national borders. However, the architecture of digital networks disrupts this assumption by enabling the instantaneous transnational movement of data, financial flows, and criminal activity, thereby generating a structural disjunction between territorially anchored legal systems and deterritorialized cyber operations (Li, 2025).

This disjunction is particularly pronounced in African contexts, where accelerated digital adoption has frequently outpaced the harmonization of legal and institutional frameworks. As a result, cybercrime increasingly manifests as a distributed, multi-jurisdictional phenomenon in which discrete components of a single criminal operation are executed across multiple legal systems. Such fragmentation complicates the attribution of criminal liability, disrupts evidentiary continuity, and undermines the effectiveness of enforcement mechanisms (Lambach, 2020). In doctrinal terms, the principle of territorial jurisdiction becomes insufficient when conduct, infrastructure, and harm are dispersed across multiple sovereign domains.

The operational dynamics of contemporary cybercrime further intensify these jurisdictional challenges. Unlike traditional offences, which are typically confined to a single locus, cybercrime is inherently networked, involving layered processes such as intrusion, data exfiltration, financial transfer, and monetization, each of which may occur in different jurisdictions. This distributed structure enables criminal actors to exploit legal discontinuities, thereby reducing the probability of detection and prosecution. From a criminological perspective, this phenomenon aligns with Routine Activity Theory, which posits that crime occurs where motivated offenders encounter suitable targets in the absence of capable guardianship (Schaefer, 2021). In fragmented legal environments, the absence of coordinated cross-border guardianship creates systemic vulnerabilities that transnational actors are able to exploit with relative impunity.

A critical illustration of these dynamics is observable within East Africa's mobile money ecosystem. Platforms such as M-Pesa and analogous financial technologies have significantly enhanced financial inclusion by enabling large segments of the population to participate in digital economies without reliance on conventional banking infrastructure. However, the same structural features that facilitate accessibility, including interoperability, transactional velocity, and decentralized agent networks, also generate exploitable vulnerabilities within the regulatory and enforcement landscape.

From a doctrinal standpoint, mobile money transactions challenge traditional conceptions of jurisdiction by decoupling financial activity from fixed institutional locations. A single transaction may implicate multiple jurisdictions simultaneously, depending on the location of the user, the telecommunications infrastructure, the data storage systems, and the point of cash-out. This multiplicity complicates the determination of applicable law, particularly in cases involving fraud, unauthorized access, or identity manipulation. For instance, SIM-swap fraud, a prevalent form of cyber-enabled financial crime, typically involves the unlawful transfer of a victim's mobile number to a new SIM card, followed by unauthorized access to mobile financial accounts and rapid cross-border fund transfers. Each stage of this process engages distinct legal regimes, including telecommunications regulation, financial crime statutes, and data protection laws, often across different jurisdictions.

The enforcement implications of such fragmentation are significant. Investigative authorities are required to reconstruct evidentiary chains across multiple legal systems, each with distinct procedural requirements, evidentiary standards, and institutional capabilities. Requests for critical data, including subscriber information, transaction logs, and authentication records, are typically processed through Mutual Legal Assistance Treaties (MLATs), which are procedurally rigorous but temporally inefficient. Given the velocity of digital financial transactions, such delays frequently result in the dissipation of evidentiary value and the irreversible movement of illicit funds, thereby undermining prosecutorial viability (Sharma, 2020).

These challenges are further compounded by the extraterritorial location of digital infrastructure. In many instances, data relevant to cybercrime investigations is stored on servers located outside the jurisdiction in which the offence is reported. This raises complex questions of data sovereignty and legal access, particularly where foreign legal regimes impose restrictions on data disclosure or prioritize privacy protections over investigatory access. Consequently, African states often encounter structural constraints in exercising effective jurisdiction over digital evidence, as access is mediated by foreign regulatory frameworks and private sector compliance policies (Rizer, et al. 2022).

At the regional level, the problem of jurisdictional fragmentation is exacerbated by the lack of harmonization across Africa's Regional Economic Communities (RECs), including the East African Community (EAC), the Economic Community of West African States (ECOWAS), and the Southern African Development Community (SADC). While these entities have developed region-specific legal instruments addressing cybercrime and digital governance, their frameworks remain uneven in scope, content, and implementation. This regulatory heterogeneity creates what may be conceptualized as the "REC-Gap," a structural vulnerability arising from the coexistence of multiple, partially aligned legal regimes (Khan, 2023).

The REC-Gap facilitates a phenomenon commonly described as jurisdictional arbitrage, whereby criminal actors strategically distribute components of their operations across jurisdictions with varying levels of regulatory stringency, enforcement capacity, and procedural efficiency. In practice, this may involve initiating fraudulent communications in one jurisdiction, routing digital infrastructure through another, channeling financial flows through intermediary states, and extracting proceeds in yet another. Such fragmentation disperses evidentiary material and complicates legal coordination, thereby reducing the likelihood of successful prosecution. Empirical observations of cross-border fraud schemes within African digital financial systems illustrate the extent to which criminal networks deliberately exploit these regulatory discontinuities (Ndubuisi, 2022).

From a theoretical standpoint, jurisdictional arbitrage within the REC-Gap can be understood through the lens of legal pluralism, which recognizes the coexistence of multiple normative orders within a given geographical space (Malikzada, 2026). While legal pluralism reflects the diversity of legal traditions and institutional arrangements across African states, it simultaneously generates enforcement asymmetries that can be leveraged by transnational criminal actors. The persistence of these asymmetries underscores the limitations of isolated national responses to inherently transnational threats.

Addressing these structural challenges necessitates a paradigmatic shift from territorially bounded enforcement models toward integrated, networked systems of legal cooperation. This includes the development of harmonized legal standards governing cybercrime, digital evidence, and data access, as well as the establishment of mechanisms for real-time information sharing and joint investigative operations. Intelligence-led policing frameworks, supported by regional institutions, offer a viable pathway for enhancing investigative continuity and reducing procedural delays. Such approaches prioritize operational connectivity over formalistic legal sequencing, thereby aligning enforcement mechanisms with the temporal dynamics of cybercrime.

Furthermore, the advancement of a continent-wide digital governance framework, as envisioned within the broader agenda of Digital Pan-Africanism and the African Continental Free Trade Area, presents an opportunity to mitigate jurisdictional fragmentation through regulatory convergence. By establishing common standards for evidence admissibility, cross-border data access, and investigative authority, African states can reduce the structural vulnerabilities currently exploited by transnational criminal networks.

In sum, the tension between networked criminal activity and territorially constrained legal systems represents a central challenge in contemporary African cyber governance. The persistence of jurisdictional fragmentation, infrastructural asymmetries, and procedural inefficiencies continues to undermine enforcement effectiveness. However, through the strategic integration of legal harmonization, institutional capacity building, and transnational cooperation mechanisms, it is possible to recalibrate governance frameworks in a manner that reflects the operational realities of the digital environment. The resolution of this tension will be critical to ensuring both the security and sustainability of Africa's expanding digital economy.

II. MECHANISMS OF AFRICAN CROSS-BORDER CO-OPERATION.

The governance of cybercrime within the African context is increasingly defined by the capacity of states to engage in effective cross-border cooperation. As digital networks transcend territorial boundaries, cyber threats are no longer confined within discrete national jurisdictions but instead manifest as transnational phenomena requiring coordinated legal and institutional responses. This transformation challenges the foundational assumptions of traditional enforcement models, which are primarily structured around territorially bounded sovereignty and bilateral legal assistance frameworks.

Historically, cross-border criminal cooperation has been facilitated through formal mechanisms such as Mutual Legal Assistance Treaties (MLATs) and extradition agreements and while these instruments remain central to international legal cooperation, their procedural rigidity and temporal limitations render them insufficient for addressing the operational realities of cybercrime. Digital evidence is inherently volatile, and cybercriminal activities often unfold in real time across multiple jurisdictions, thereby necessitating more agile and responsive forms of cooperation. The limitations of conventional frameworks have therefore exposed a critical gap between legal formality and enforcement effectiveness within African cyber governance systems.

In response to these challenges, African states have increasingly pursued the development of regional and continental mechanisms aimed at enhancing operational coordination and institutional interoperability. These efforts reflect a broader shift from reactive, state-centric models of cooperation toward more dynamic and networked approaches. Institutions such as the African Union Mechanism for Police Cooperation have emerged as key platforms for facilitating intelligence sharing, joint investigations, and capacity building across national borders. At the same time, collaboration with global enforcement bodies has enabled African jurisdictions to integrate into wider transnational networks of cybercrime prevention and response.

This evolving landscape of cross-border cooperation is not without its complexities. Variations in legal frameworks, disparities in institutional capacity, and concerns relating to sovereignty and data protection continue to shape the contours of collaborative engagement. Moreover, the increasing involvement of private sector actors, particularly technology companies and

Institutional Transformation: From Mutual Legal Assistance to Networked Enforcement

The effectiveness of cybercrime governance in transnational contexts is contingent upon the capacity of legal and institutional systems to operate beyond territorially bounded modes of cooperation. Traditional mechanisms, particularly Mutual Legal Assistance Treaties (MLATs), have historically constituted the primary framework for cross-border criminal investigation. However, these instruments are structurally misaligned with the operational dynamics of cybercrime. Designed for conventional offences characterized by geographic stability and slower evidentiary processes, MLATs rely on formalized, sequential procedures that are inherently time-intensive. In the context of cybercrime, where digital evidence is volatile and financial flows are executed in real time, such procedural latency significantly undermines investigative efficacy (Shami, et al. 2025).

This structural inadequacy has catalyzed a paradigmatic shift toward more adaptive, network-oriented models of cross-border cooperation. Drawing on institutional theory, this transformation can be understood as a process of functional adaptation, whereby governance mechanisms evolve in response to the changing characteristics of the phenomena they regulate. In the African context, this shift is increasingly reflected in the emergence of intelligence-led, networked enforcement architectures that prioritize speed, interoperability, and operational coordination over formalistic legal sequencing.

AFRIPOL and the Institutionalization of Networked Policing

A central institutional expression of this transformation is the African Union Mechanism for Police Cooperation (AFRIPOL), which represents a continental effort to reconfigure law enforcement collaboration within a digitally interconnected environment. Unlike traditional intergovernmental frameworks that operate primarily through diplomatic channels, AFRIPOL is designed as an operational platform facilitating direct engagement among national law enforcement agencies (Evgenii, et al. 2020). Its mandate encompasses intelligence sharing, capacity building, and coordinated responses to transnational threats, thereby embedding cooperation within continuous, rather than episodic, institutional interaction.

From an analytical perspective, AFRIPOL exemplifies a shift toward what may be termed "networked policing," in which authority is distributed across interconnected nodes rather than centralized within individual state institutions. This model enhances responsiveness by enabling real-time information exchange and reducing reliance on hierarchical approval processes. In doing so, it directly addresses the temporal mismatch between cybercrime operations and conventional legal procedures, thereby strengthening the capacity of African states to engage in sustained investigative activity across borders (Modise, 2026).

INTERPOL Integration and Multi-Level Governance

The effectiveness of AFRIPOL is further amplified through its integration with global policing infrastructures, particularly through collaboration with INTERPOL. This partnership facilitates African access to transnational databases, analytical tools, and coordinated operational frameworks, thereby embedding continental enforcement efforts within a broader system of global governance. Institutional arrangements such as INTERPOL's specialized regional coordination mechanisms, including the so-called "African Desk," function as intermediaries that align regional priorities with global enforcement capabilities (Abiodun, et al. 2020).

This multi-level governance structure, linking national, regional, and international institutions, enhances both the scope and depth of enforcement operations. It enables the aggregation of intelligence across jurisdictions, the identification of transnational criminal patterns, and the coordination of simultaneous interventions across multiple states. From a governance perspective, this reflects a transition toward polycentric regulatory systems, in which multiple centers of authority interact dynamically to address complex, cross-border threats (Kanki, et al. 2024).

Operational Shift: From Reactive Enforcement to Intelligence-Led Intervention

A defining feature of contemporary cross-border cooperation mechanisms is the transition from reactive enforcement models to intelligence-led policing frameworks. Traditional approaches to criminal investigation are largely reactive, initiated after the occurrence of an offence and guided by formal evidentiary procedures. In contrast, intelligence-led models emphasize proactive threat identification, continuous monitoring, and anticipatory intervention (Khalfa, et al. 2024).

Within this framework, information functions not merely as evidentiary material but as an operational asset. Law enforcement agencies engage in the continuous exchange of data relating to emerging threat vectors, anomalous transaction patterns, compromised systems, and known criminal networks. This real-time intelligence flow enables authorities to disrupt criminal activities during their execution phase, rather than solely pursuing post hoc prosecution. Empirical observations of coordinated cybercrime operations across African jurisdictions indicate that such approaches significantly enhance detection rates and facilitate the rapid neutralization of transnational criminal networks (Kissorio, 2022).

Public–Private Integration and Data-Centric Enforcement

The evolution of cross-border cooperation mechanisms is also characterized by the increasing integration of private sector actors into enforcement architectures. Digital platforms, financial institutions, telecommunications providers, and cybersecurity firms possess critical datasets and technical expertise that are indispensable for effective cybercrime detection and response. Consequently, contemporary governance models are progressively incorporating these actors into collaborative frameworks, thereby blurring the traditional boundaries between public authority and private capability.

This integration reflects a broader shift toward data-centric governance, in which the capacity to collect, analyze, and act upon digital information becomes a central determinant of enforcement effectiveness. Public–private partnerships facilitate access to real-time transactional data, threat intelligence, and forensic capabilities that are often unavailable within state institutions alone. From an institutional perspective, this represents an expansion of the enforcement ecosystem, in which regulatory authority is exercised through coordinated interaction among heterogeneous actors (Žuvela, et al. 2023).

Capacity Building as an Operational Imperative

Beyond structural coordination, the sustainability of networked cooperation depends on the continuous development of institutional and human capacity. Cybercrime investigations require specialized competencies in digital forensics, data analytics, and cyber threat intelligence, areas in which capacity disparities across African states remain significant (Elijah, 2025). Mechanisms such as AFRIPOL and INTERPOL-supported programs contribute to capacity building not only through formal training initiatives but also through participation in joint operations, which facilitate experiential learning and knowledge transfer.

This operationally embedded capacity building is particularly significant, as it aligns skill development with real-world investigative contexts. Over time, it contributes to the emergence of a transnational community of practice among African law enforcement professionals, characterized by shared standards, methodologies, and operational norms. Such communities enhance institutional interoperability and strengthen the overall coherence of cross-border enforcement efforts (Sibe, et al. 2024).

Constraints and Structural Limitations

Notwithstanding these advances, several structural constraints continue to limit the effectiveness of cross-border cooperation mechanisms. Variations in technical infrastructure, data governance regimes, and institutional trust levels across jurisdictions can impede the seamless exchange of information. Concerns relating to data protection, sovereignty, and the potential misuse of shared intelligence may further constrain cooperation, particularly in politically sensitive contexts.

Additionally, disparities in resource allocation and technological capability risk reproducing asymmetries within the networked enforcement architecture itself. States with more advanced digital infrastructures may dominate information flows, while less-resourced jurisdictions remain peripheral participants. Addressing these imbalances requires deliberate policy interventions aimed at ensuring equitable access to technological tools, training resources, and institutional support systems.

Toward an Integrated Model of Networked Governance

The evolution of mechanisms such as AFRIPOL and their integration with global policing systems reflects a broader transformation in the governance of cybercrime. Rather than relying exclusively on formal legal instruments, contemporary approaches emphasize operational connectivity, institutional adaptability, and multi-actor collaboration (Mahmutovic, et al. 2025). This transition aligns with the concept of networked governance, in which authority is exercised through interconnected systems capable of responding dynamically to complex, transnational challenges.

In the African context, the consolidation of such models holds significant implications for the future of cyber governance. By enhancing real-time cooperation, strengthening institutional capacity, and integrating public and private actors within a unified framework, networked enforcement architectures offer a viable pathway for addressing the structural limitations of territorially constrained legal systems.

III. DIGITAL SOVEREIGNTY, PLATFORM POWER, AND THE GOVERNANCE OF ELECTRONIC EVIDENCE.

The increasing centrality of digital platforms in contemporary economic and social interactions has significantly reconfigured the distribution of regulatory authority within the global digital ecosystem. In the African context, this transformation is particularly pronounced, as states navigate the complexities of governing data, digital infrastructure, and cyber activities within environments heavily mediated by transnational technology corporations. These developments have brought the concept of digital sovereignty to the forefront of legal and policy discourse, raising critical questions regarding the extent to which states can exercise effective control over data and digital processes that transcend territorial boundaries.

At the core of this challenge lies the concentration of data within privately owned platforms that operate across multiple jurisdictions. Such platforms function not merely as intermediaries but as de facto regulators, shaping the rules governing data access, content moderation, and user interactions. This shift complicates traditional notions of sovereignty by introducing corporate actors as central nodes in the governance of digital spaces. Consequently, state authority over electronic evidence is increasingly mediated through private gatekeeping structures, thereby influencing the accessibility, integrity, and admissibility of digital data in legal proceedings.

This section examines the intersection of digital sovereignty, platform governance, and the regulation of electronic evidence within African cyber governance frameworks. It explores the doctrinal and institutional challenges associated with cross-border data access, the evidentiary implications of platform-controlled information, and the broader tensions between state authority and corporate power. Through this analysis, the section seeks to illuminate the evolving contours of sovereignty in a platform-dominated digital environment.

Platformization and the Reconfiguration of Regulatory Authority

The contemporary digital ecosystem is increasingly structured around a limited number of transnational technology corporations whose platforms mediate communication, financial transactions, and data flows at a global scale. This process of platformization has reconfigured traditional distributions of regulatory authority by concentrating infrastructural control within private entities whose operational reach extends beyond the jurisdictional limits of individual states. In the African context, where domestic digital infrastructure remains unevenly developed, reliance on externally owned platforms has intensified the asymmetry between territorial sovereignty and functional control over digital environments (Venske, 2023).

From a governance perspective, this shift challenges the foundational premise that states possess exclusive authority over activities occurring within their territories. Platform operators determine the architecture of data flows, set content moderation standards, and control access to user information, thereby exercising quasi-regulatory functions traditionally associated with public authority (Sampath, et al. 2022). This phenomenon aligns with broader theories of platform governance, which conceptualize large technology firms as private regulators operating within hybrid public–private governance regimes. The resulting configuration produces a diffusion of authority in which state regulation, corporate policy, and transnational norms intersect in complex and often contested ways.

Data Sovereignty and Jurisdictional Complexity

The concentration of data within transnational platforms generates acute challenges for the exercise of data sovereignty, defined as the capacity of a state to regulate and control data generated within or relating to its jurisdiction. In practice, data relevant to cybercrime investigations in African states is frequently stored in data centers located outside the continent, subject to foreign legal regimes and corporate compliance frameworks. This extraterritorial dispersion complicates efforts by domestic authorities to access digital evidence, as such access is mediated by the legal requirements of the host jurisdiction and the internal policies of platform providers (Ishkhanyan, 2026).

Doctrinally, this situation exposes the limitations of territorially grounded jurisdictional principles when applied to digitally distributed data. The conventional bases of jurisdiction, including territoriality and nationality, are increasingly insufficient to capture the multi-sited nature of digital evidence. As a result, states are compelled to rely on mechanisms such as Mutual Legal Assistance Treaties (MLATs) or direct cooperation with service providers, both of which are characterized by procedural constraints and limited responsiveness to the temporal demands of cybercrime investigations.

Efforts to reassert data sovereignty through localization requirements and regulatory mandates have emerged across various jurisdictions. While such measures aim to ensure that data remains subject to domestic legal control, they also raise concerns regarding economic efficiency, cross-border interoperability, and potential fragmentation of the global digital ecosystem. In the African context, the pursuit of data sovereignty must therefore be balanced against the need for integration within transnational digital markets and the practical realities of infrastructural dependency (Saleem, et al. 2025).

Corporate Gatekeeping and the Politics of Data Access

The centrality of private platforms to digital evidence generation and storage positions them as critical gatekeepers in the enforcement of cybercrime laws. Access to essential data, including subscriber information, metadata, and content records, is contingent upon compliance with corporate disclosure policies that are themselves shaped by a combination of legal obligations, reputational considerations, and internal governance frameworks. This intermediation introduces an additional layer of complexity into the evidentiary process, as law enforcement agencies must navigate both legal and corporate procedural requirements to obtain relevant information.

From an analytical standpoint, the role of platforms as gatekeepers reflects a broader shift toward privatized enforcement infrastructures, in which the effectiveness of public law is partially dependent on the cooperation of private actors. This dependency raises important normative questions concerning accountability, transparency, and the balance of power between states and corporations. In particular, disparities in bargaining power between African states and large technology firms may result in unequal access to data, thereby reinforcing existing asymmetries within the global digital order (Tosza, 2021).

Digital Evidence and Doctrinal Challenges of Admissibility

The governance of electronic evidence constitutes a critical interface between digital technology and legal procedure. Unlike traditional forms of evidence, digital data is characterized by its volatility, replicability, and susceptibility to alteration, necessitating specialized standards for its collection, preservation, and authentication. In many African jurisdictions, legal frameworks governing evidence remain anchored in analog paradigms, resulting in doctrinal ambiguities regarding the admissibility and probative value of digital material.

Key evidentiary challenges include the establishment of authenticity, the maintenance of chain of custody, and the verification of data integrity. Courts are often required to assess whether digital evidence has been obtained and handled in a manner that ensures reliability, a determination that depends on the availability of standardized forensic procedures and technical expertise. The absence of harmonized evidentiary standards across jurisdictions further complicates cross-border cases, as evidence deemed admissible in one legal system may not meet the requirements of another (Casino, et al. 2022). These doctrinal uncertainties are exacerbated in cases involving cloud-stored data and platform-generated records, where the evidentiary chain extends beyond the direct control of investigating authorities. The reliance on third-party data custodians introduces additional questions regarding the authenticity and completeness of records, as well as the extent to which corporate certification can substitute for traditional evidentiary safeguards.

Toward Harmonized Frameworks for Digital Evidence Governance

Addressing these challenges requires the development of coherent and harmonized legal frameworks governing the lifecycle of digital evidence, from collection and preservation to transmission and admissibility. At the continental level, initiatives aligned with the African Union's cybersecurity agenda provide a foundation for such harmonization by promoting common standards and facilitating cooperation among member states. The integration of these standards within domestic legal systems is essential to ensuring that digital evidence can be effectively utilized in cross-border investigations.

In parallel, the adoption of streamlined mechanisms for cross-border data access represents a critical priority. Emerging models, including direct cooperation agreements between states and service providers, as well as frameworks enabling expedited data requests, offer potential pathways for overcoming the limitations of traditional MLAT processes (Okolo, et al. 2022). However, the implementation of such mechanisms must be accompanied by robust safeguards to protect fundamental rights, including privacy and due process, thereby ensuring that efficiency gains do not come at the expense of legal legitimacy.

Rebalancing Sovereignty in a Platform-Dominated Ecosystem

The interplay between platform power, data sovereignty, and evidentiary governance underscores the need for a recalibrated understanding of sovereignty within the digital age. Rather than conceptualizing sovereignty as exclusive territorial control, contemporary realities necessitate a more relational model in which authority is exercised through negotiation, coordination, and participation within transnational governance networks (Greven, 2020).

For African states, this entails both the strengthening of domestic regulatory capacity and the strategic engagement with global technology firms and international regulatory processes. By enhancing bargaining power, developing regionally coordinated policy positions, and investing in digital infrastructure, African jurisdictions can mitigate the asymmetries inherent in platform-dominated ecosystems and assert greater influence over the governance of data and digital evidence.

IV. FUTURE TRENDS IN AFRICAN CYBER GOVERNANCE AND DIGITAL REGULATION.

The trajectory of African cyber governance is increasingly shaped by the convergence of technological innovation, regulatory adaptation, and shifting geopolitical dynamics. As digital transformation accelerates across the continent, emerging technologies are not only expanding economic opportunities but also reconfiguring the nature of cyber risks and the institutional responses required to address them. This evolving landscape necessitates a forward-looking regulatory approach that integrates technological foresight, legal adaptability, and institutional resilience.

One of the most consequential developments in this regard is the proliferation of artificial intelligence across both public and private sectors. Artificial intelligence systems are progressively embedded in financial services, security operations, and administrative decision-making processes, thereby enhancing efficiency and predictive capacity. In the domain of cybersecurity, AI-driven tools enable real-time threat detection, anomaly identification, and predictive analytics, significantly strengthening the capacity of law enforcement agencies to anticipate and respond to cyber threats (Sarfraz, et al. 2025). However, these same technologies introduce new vulnerabilities. Malicious actors increasingly deploy AI to automate cyberattacks, generate sophisticated phishing schemes, and exploit system weaknesses with heightened precision. This dual-use character of artificial intelligence produces an escalating cycle of technological competition between defenders and offenders, thereby complicating regulatory intervention. Consequently, governance frameworks must transition from reactive models toward anticipatory approaches that incorporate continuous risk assessment and adaptive regulation (Sanyal, et al. 2024).

Parallel to the rise of artificial intelligence, is the expansion of blockchain technologies and decentralized digital systems. These innovations fundamentally challenge traditional regulatory assumptions by eliminating centralized control points and distributing transactional authority across network participants. Blockchain-based systems, including decentralized finance platforms, operate through protocols that are resistant to unilateral intervention, thereby complicating conventional enforcement mechanisms (Bennet, et al. 2024). Transactions conducted within such systems are often pseudonymous and immutable, characteristics that enhance transparency while simultaneously enabling new forms of illicit financial activity. From a legal perspective, the absence of identifiable intermediaries undermines regulatory strategies that rely on institutional oversight of centralized actors such as banks or payment processors. As a result, African regulatory frameworks must evolve to address decentralized environments through alternative mechanisms, including network-level monitoring, protocol-based regulation, and enhanced international cooperation (Tyagi, 2023).

The increasing centrality of data within digital economies further amplifies the complexity of cyber governance. Data has become a strategic resource, underpinning economic activity, governance systems, and security operations. The integration of advanced analytics and artificial intelligence into data processing introduces critical concerns regarding accountability, transparency, and equity (Bahangulu, et al. 2025). Algorithmic decision-making systems, particularly those utilized in areas such as law enforcement and financial risk assessment, may inadvertently reproduce existing socio-economic biases if not subject to adequate oversight. This raises important normative and legal questions regarding liability, fairness, and the protection of fundamental rights. African states are therefore confronted with the challenge of designing data governance frameworks that simultaneously promote innovation and safeguard individual rights. This requires the establishment of standards for algorithmic transparency, mechanisms for auditing automated systems, and legal provisions addressing harm resulting from algorithmic decision-making.

In addition to technological developments, regional integration initiatives are expected to play a decisive role in shaping the future of African cyber governance. The African Continental Free Trade Area provides a structural foundation for the development of a harmonized digital market, within which regulatory convergence becomes both necessary and advantageous (Agu, 2025). The alignment of legal standards governing cybersecurity, data protection, electronic commerce, and digital evidence is essential for facilitating cross-border digital transactions and reducing regulatory fragmentation. Harmonization not only enhances legal certainty but also strengthens enforcement capacity by enabling coordinated responses to transnational cyber threats. The continued operationalization of continental frameworks, including the Malabo Convention, will be critical in advancing this process and establishing a coherent regulatory architecture across African jurisdictions.

Institutional capacity remains a central determinant of the effectiveness of these evolving governance frameworks. As cyber threats increase in sophistication, the demand for specialized expertise in digital forensics, cybersecurity analysis, and cyber law is expected to intensify. Addressing this demand requires sustained investment in education, professional training, and institutional development. The professionalization of cyber enforcement agencies will facilitate the emergence of highly skilled personnel capable of navigating complex digital environments and conducting sophisticated investigations. Furthermore, the development of transnational communities of practice among cybersecurity professionals is likely to enhance cooperation by fostering shared standards, methodologies, and operational norms. Such communities contribute to institutional interoperability and improve the efficiency of cross-border enforcement mechanisms.

The future of African cyber governance is also closely linked to the continent's evolving role within global regulatory processes. Historically marginalized in international norm-setting, African states are increasingly asserting their presence in multilateral negotiations and contributing to the development of global cybersecurity frameworks. This shift reflects a growing recognition of the need to articulate governance models that are responsive to the specific socio-economic and institutional conditions of African jurisdictions. In particular, African states are likely to advocate for regulatory approaches that prioritize capacity building, equitable access to digital technologies, and the integration of development considerations into cybersecurity policy (Calderaro, et al. 2020). This engagement has the potential to reshape global cyber governance by introducing more inclusive and context-sensitive normative frameworks

Despite these positive developments, significant challenges remain. The rapid pace of technological change continues to outstrip the capacity of legal systems to adapt, resulting in regulatory gaps that can be exploited by malicious actors. Infrastructural disparities across African states further complicate efforts to achieve regulatory harmonization and effective enforcement. Moreover, the dominance of transnational technology corporations within the digital ecosystem introduces additional layers of complexity, particularly in relation to data control and access (Ogundipe, et al. 2023). Addressing these challenges requires a coordinated and multi-dimensional approach that integrates legal reform, institutional strengthening, and technological investment.

Ultimately, the future trajectory of African cyber governance will be defined by the interaction between emerging technologies, regulatory innovation, and institutional capacity building. Artificial intelligence, blockchain systems, and data-driven governance models will continue to reshape the digital landscape, necessitating adaptive and forward-looking regulatory responses. At the same time, regional integration and increased participation in global norm-setting processes provide opportunities for African states to assert greater influence over the development of cyber governance frameworks. By aligning legal systems with technological realities, investing in institutional capacity, and fostering international cooperation, Africa can establish a resilient and coherent cyber governance regime capable of addressing the complex challenges of the digital age.

V. CONCLUSION.

This chapter has demonstrated that the rapid expansion of digital technologies across Africa is fundamentally reshaping the contours of cyber governance, exposing the limitations of territorially bounded legal frameworks in addressing transnational cyber threats. While early reliance on externally derived regulatory models facilitated initial legal harmonization, their effectiveness has been constrained by persistent gaps in institutional capacity and enforcement capability.

The analysis has shown that contemporary cybercrime operates as a networked and multi-jurisdictional phenomenon, thereby complicating traditional approaches to jurisdiction, evidence, and prosecution. In response, African states are increasingly adopting adaptive governance strategies, including the development of continental legal frameworks, the strengthening of cross-border cooperation mechanisms, and the transition toward intelligence-led enforcement models. Institutions such as AFRIPOL, alongside global partnerships, illustrate the emergence of more coordinated and operationally responsive approaches to cybercrime management.

At the same time, the growing dominance of transnational technology platforms and the centrality of data in digital economies have introduced new challenges relating to digital sovereignty and access to electronic evidence. These developments necessitate a reconceptualization of sovereignty as a networked and negotiated form of authority, supported by harmonized legal standards and enhanced institutional capacity.

Looking forward, emerging technologies such as artificial intelligence and decentralized systems will continue to transform both the nature of cyber threats and the regulatory responses required to address them. The effectiveness of future governance frameworks will therefore depend on the ability of African states to integrate legal harmonization, capacity building, and technological adaptation within a coherent and forward-looking strategy.

In sum, the chapter underscores that resilient cyber governance in Africa requires a shift toward integrated, networked, and contextually grounded regulatory approaches capable of aligning legal authority with the realities of an increasingly interconnected digital environment.

REFERENCES

Abiodun, T. F., & Abioro, T. (2020). Roles and challenges of international criminal police organization (Interpol) in investigation of crimes and maintenance of global security. Research Journal of social science and management, 10(3), 12-34.

Agu, C. R. (2025). Legal Analysis of the Implications of Continental Free Trade Area to Africa. Nnamdi Azikiwe UJ Int'l L. &. *Juris.*, *16*, 195.

Bahangulu, J. K., & Owusu-Berko, L. (2025). Algorithmic bias, data ethics, and governance: Ensuring fairness, transparency and compliance in AI-powered business analytics applications. *World Journal of Advanced Research and Reviews*, *25*(2), 1746–1763. DOI: 10.30574/wjarr.2025.25.2.0571

Bennet, D., Maria, L., Sanjaya, Y. P. A., & Zahra, A. R. A. (2024). Blockchain technology: Revolutionizing transactions in the digital age. *ADI Journal on Recent Innovation*, *5*(2), 192–199. DOI: 10.34306/ajri.v5i2.1065

Calderaro, A., & Craig, A. J. (2020). Transnational governance of cybersecurity: Policy challenges and global inequalities in cyber capacity building. *Third World Quarterly*, *41*(6), 917–938. DOI: 10.1080/01436597.2020.1729729

Casino, F., Pina, C., López-Aguilar, P., Batista, E., Solanas, A., & Patsakis, C. (2022). SoK: Cross-border criminal investigations and digital evidence. *Journal of Cybersecurity*, *8*(1), tyac014. DOI: 10.1093/cybsec/tyac014

Chang, L. Y. (2020). Legislative frameworks against cybercrime: The Budapest convention and Asia. The Palgrave handbook of international cybercrime and cyberdeviance, 327-343.

de Silva de Alwis, R. (2024). Gendering the new international convention on cybercrimes and new norms on artificial intelligence and emerging technologies. *Wash. JL Tech. & Arts*, *20*, 1.

Elijah, J. (2025). *Navigating the Legal Challenges of Cybersecurity and Forensic Evidence in the Digital Era*. Law Nectar.

Emmanuel, C. E., & Alofe, O. E. (2025). Technology Regulation in National and International Contexts: Normative Frameworks and Emerging Trends. Law And Social Justice Review, 6(2).

Evgenii, N., & Cocou, M. M. (2020). Unified Digital Law Enforcement Environment-Necessity and Prospects for Creation in the "BRICS Countries". BRICS law journal, 7(2), 66-93.

Ewulum, C. (2023). The legal regime for cross-border data transfer in Africa: a critical analysis. Available at *SSRN* 4546964. DOI: 10.2139/ssrn.4546964

Farah Hersi, M., & Akinola, A. O. (2024). Pan-Africanism and Regional Integration. In *IGAD and Multilateral Security in the Horn of Africa: Through the Lens of the Somali Conflict* (pp. 13–34). Springer Nature Switzerland. DOI: 10.1007/978-3-031-51548-4_2

Greven, M. T. (2020). The informalization of transnational governance: A threat to democratic government. In *Die Erosion der Demokratie: Beiträge von Michael Th. Greven zur kritischen Demokratietheorie* (pp. 107–131). Springer Fachmedien Wiesbaden. DOI: 10.1007/978-3-658-27920-2_6

Ishkhanyan, A. (2026). Governing AI across borders: Corporate power, state sovereignty and global regulation. Digital Policy. *Regulation & Governance*, *28*(3), 280–295.

Kanki, K., & Resch, A. (2024). Strengthening International Law Enforcement Cooperation: INTERPOL and Its Global Fight against Economic and Financial Crime. In Corporate Criminal Liability and Sanctions (pp. 106-126). Routledge.

Khalfa, R., & Hardyns, W. (2024). 'Led by Intelligence': A Scoping Review on the Experimental Evaluation of Intelligence-Led Policing. *Evaluation Review*, *48*(5), 797–847. DOI: 10.1177/0193841X231204588 PMID: 37864492

Khan, M. N. I. (2023). Legal documentation and case management: a systematic review of digitization trends and cybersecurity challenges in legal support roles. Review of Applied Science and Technology, 2(01), 01-25.

Kissorio, T. K. (2022). Effectiveness of Intelligence-Led Policing in Prevention of Crime by the Directorate of Criminal Investigation in Mombasa County, Kenya. An Unpublished Master of Security Management and Police Studies. Thesis, Kenyatta University, Kenya. https://irlibrary. ku. ac. ke/items/6ef854a3-7d68-4b5a-927e-3113f19b08d9.

Lambach, D. (2020). The territorialization of cyberspace. *International Studies Review*, *22*(3), 482–506. DOI: 10.1093/isr/viz022

Li, Z. (2025). On the Fundamental Structure and Flow Framework of Data in Cross-Border Cybercrime. *Mod. L. Rsch.*, *6*, 52.

Mahmutovic, A., & Alsudais, M. (2025). Legal Pluralism and Governance: Redefining Power and Accountability in a Globalized World. *PETITA: JURNAL KAJIAN ILMU HUKUM DAN SYARIAH*, *10*(2), 568–593.

Malikzada, T. (2026). Assessing the Role of International Law in Regulating the Fight Against Cybercrime in the Digital Environment. Futurity Economics&Law, 6(1).

Maurer, T., & Morgus, R. (2022). *Compilation of existing cybersecurity and information security related definitions*. New America.

Modise, J. M. (2026). *An Assessment of Transnational Crime in The African Context: Trends*. Challenges, And Strategic Responses.

Mugamba, E. (2025). Global Data Governance in Digital Law: A Comparative Analysis of EU and Global Approaches to Cybersecurity Legislation. *Journal of Smart Computing and Quantum Technologies*, *1*(1), 10–28. DOI: 10.63456/jscqt-1-1-39

Ndubuisi, A. F. (2022). Cross-border jurisdiction challenges in prosecuting cybercrime syndicates targeting national financial and electoral systems. [IJETRM]. *International Journal of Engineering Technology Research & Management*, *6*(11), 243–261.

Nhlazane, T. N. (2025). *Data Protection and Data Security Standards*. University of Johannesburg.

Ogundipe, F., Bakare, O. I., Sampson, E., & Folorunso, A. (2023). harnessing digital transformation for Africa's growth: Opportunities and challenges in the Technological Era. *African Development Review*, *28*(4), 234–251.

Okolo, F. C., Etukudoh, E. A., Ogunwole, O., Osho, G. O., & Basiru, J. O. (2022). Policy-oriented framework for multi-agency data integration across national transportation and infrastructure systems. Journal name missing.

Oloruntoba, S. O. (2020). Pan-Africanism, regional integration and development in Africa. In *Pan Africanism, regional integration and development in Africa* (pp. 1–14). Springer International Publishing. DOI: 10.1007/978-3-030-34296-8_1

Rizer, A., & Hobson, A. (2022). *Cross-Border Data Requests: Evaluating Reforms To Improve Law Enforcement Access*. R Street Institute.

Saleem, M. S., Imran, Q., & Saghir, A. (2025). DIGITAL SOVEREIGNTY AS A NEW DIMENSION OF POWER POLITICS IN THE GLOBAL SOUTH. *Pakistan Journal of Social Science Review*, *4*(6), 485–503.

Sampath, P. G., & Tregenna, F. (2022). *Digital sovereignty: African perspectives*. DSI/NRF South African Research Chair in Industrial Development.

Sangwa, S. (2025). UN Pact for the Future and Global Digital Compact: A Critical Interdisciplinary Analysis of Global Digital Governance, Digital-ID, and Central-Bank Digital Currencies. Open Journal of Stigmatized Knowledge & Suppressed Discourses (ISSN: 3105-3033), 1(1).

Sanyal, S., Sharma, P., & Dudani, C. (2024). *A complex adaptive system framework to regulate artificial intelligence*. Economic Advisory Council to the PM.

Sarfraz, M., Sumra, I. A., Khalid, B., & Fatima, E. (2025). AI-driven predictive threat detection and cyber risk mitigation: A survey. *Journal of Computing & Biomedical Informatics*, *8*(02).

Schaefer, L. (2021). *Routine activity theory*. Oxford University Press.

Shami, A. Z. A., Saleem, M., & Ashraf, J. (2025). Cybercrime and Digital Evidence: Investigating the Challenges and Opportunities in Prosecuting Cybercrime and Handling Digital Evidence. *Research Consortium Archive*, *3*(2), 401–411.

Sharma, S. (2020). Issues with enforcing Mutual Legal Assistance Treaties (MLATs): Access to cross-border data in criminal investigation. Available at *SSRN* 3815270. DOI: 10.2139/ssrn.3815270

Sibe, R. T., & Kaunert, C. (2024). *Cybercrime, digital forensic readiness, and financial crime investigation in Nigeria*. Springer International Publishing AG. DOI: 10.1007/978-3-031-54089-9

Tosza, S. (2021). Internet service providers as law enforcers and adjudicators. A public role of private actors. *Computer Law & Security Review*, *43*, 105614. DOI: 10.1016/j.clsr.2021.105614

Tyagi, A. K. (2023). Decentralized everything: Practical use of blockchain technology in future applications. In *Distributed computing to blockchain* (pp. 19–38). Academic Press. DOI: 10.1016/B978-0-323-96146-2.00010-3

Venske, T. (2023). Navigating digital sovereignty in Africa: A review of key challenges and constraints. Africa Governance Papers Journal, 1(4).

Žuvela, A., Šveb Dragija, M., & Jelinčić, D. A. (2023). Partnerships in heritage governance and management: Review study of public–civil, public–private and public–private–community partnerships. *Heritage*, *6*(10), 6862–6880. DOI: 10.3390/heritage6100358

KEY TERMS AND DEFINITIONS.

African Cybersecurity Law: encompasses the body of legal instruments, both national and continental, developed to regulate cyber activities, protect digital systems, and address cybercrime within African states.

Artificial Intelligence in Cybersecurity: refers to the application of machine learning and automated systems to detect, prevent, and respond to cyber threats, while also introducing new risks when exploited by malicious actors.

Cross-Border Cybercrime: describes criminal activities conducted through digital networks that span multiple jurisdictions, thereby complicating legal enforcement due to issues of jurisdiction, coordination, and evidence gathering.

Cyber Governance: refers to the systems, legal frameworks, and institutional mechanisms through which states and other actors regulate activities within digital environments, particularly in relation to security, data management, and cross-border interactions.

Data Protection: involves the legal and institutional measures designed to safeguard personal and sensitive information from unauthorized access, misuse, or exploitation within digital systems.

Digital Pan-Africanism: refers to the collective effort by African states to promote regional integration, cooperation, and unified policy approaches within the digital and technological domain.

Digital Sovereignty: denotes the capacity of a state to exercise authority over digital infrastructure, data flows, and technological systems within its jurisdiction, while navigating the constraints imposed by transnational platforms and global networks.

Electronic Evidence: refers to any information or data generated, stored, or transmitted in digital form that can be used to support or refute legal claims in cybercrime investigations and prosecutions.

Institutional Capacity: describes the ability of legal, regulatory, and enforcement bodies to effectively implement laws, manage resources, and respond to cyber threats within their operational environments.

Jurisdictional Fragmentation: describes the existence of multiple, often inconsistent legal frameworks across different regions, which creates gaps and overlaps that can be exploited by transnational cybercriminal actors.

Legal Harmonization: refers to the process of aligning laws and regulatory standards across jurisdictions to ensure consistency, facilitate cooperation, and enhance the effectiveness of cross-border enforcement.

Mobile Money Fraud: involves the exploitation of digital financial platforms, particularly mobile-based payment systems, to conduct unauthorized transactions, identity manipulation, and financial theft.

Networked Policing: refers to a model of law enforcement that relies on continuous collaboration, real-time information sharing, and coordinated operations among multiple agencies across different jurisdictions.

Platform Governance: denotes the regulatory role played by digital platform providers in shaping user behavior, managing data, and enforcing rules within their digital ecosystems, often alongside or in place of state regulation.

Transnational Crime Networks: are organized groups that operate across national boundaries, leveraging digital technologies to coordinate, execute, and conceal criminal activities in multiple jurisdictions.

Chapter 10
Digital Sovereignty and Cross-Border Data Flows:
Legal Fragmentation and Governance Challenges

Hemendra Singh
http://orcid.org/0000-0003-1160-8284
Jindal Global Law School, O.P. Jindal Global University, Sonipat, India

ABSTRACT

This chapter examines the challenges of governing cross-border data flows within a fragmented global legal landscape with a focus on the tension between digital sovereignty and transnational data mobility. It argues that legal fragmentation is a structural feature of contemporary data governance, producing regulatory conflicts and reinforcing power asymmetries between states, corporations and individuals. The chapter analyses how state-led sovereignty strategies and societal as well as technological resistance seek to address these challenges but often reproduce underlying fragmentation. It then explores pathways toward more coherent governance through interoperability, institutional coordination and shared normative principles. In doing so, it highlights the importance of aligning global data governance with broader commitments to inclusive development, accountability and the values reflected in the sustainable development goals.

INTRODUCTION

The expansion of the global data economy has placed cross-border data flows at the center of contemporary legal and governance debates, fundamentally reshaping how states exercise authority in a digitally interconnected world. Data now circulates

DOI: 10.4018/979-8-2600-0288-9.ch010

through complex transnational infrastructures that often operate beyond the effective reach of any single jurisdiction, creating tensions between the global nature of digital systems and the territorially bounded character of law. In this context, digital sovereignty has emerged as a key framework through which states seek to assert control over data, technology, and regulatory space, while remaining embedded in global networks of innovation and exchange (Abdullah et al., 2026). This chapter examines how these competing dynamics are structured by legal fragmentation, arguing that divergent regulatory approaches, infrastructural dependencies, and uneven distributions of power collectively limit the capacity of existing governance models to manage cross-border data flows in a coherent and effective manner.

Scholarship on digital sovereignty and cross-border data flows has evolved in response to the increasing centrality of data in economic and regulatory systems. Early literature primarily engaged with issues of data protection and privacy, focusing on how legal frameworks could safeguard individual rights in an increasingly digital environment (Voss, 2020). This body of work emphasized regulatory obligations of states and the need to control the transfer of personal data across borders, laying the foundation for contemporary governance models. Over time, however, scholars began to recognise that data is not merely a subject of regulation but also a source of economic value and geopolitical influence, leading to a broader understanding of digital sovereignty as encompassing control over digital infrastructures, technological capabilities, and data-driven markets (Pohle & Thiel, 2020).

More recent contributions have examined how different jurisdictions approach data governance in distinct ways, reflecting diverse policy priorities (Opriel et al., 2025). Some frameworks emphasise strong regulatory control and rights-based protections, while others prioritise the free flow of data to support innovation and economic growth. This divergence has been widely discussed in comparative scholarship, which highlights how regulatory choices are shaped by political, economic, and institutional contexts (Ding et al., 2025). At the same time, literature in international economic law has explored the role of trade agreements and cross-border transfer mechanisms in facilitating data flows, often pointing out the tension between commitments to openness and the preservation of domestic regulatory autonomy.

A growing strand of research has also focused on the structural challenges posed by the global data economy, particularly the role of private actors and digital infrastructures. Scholars have pointed out that large technology companies exercise significant influence over how data is stored, processed, and transferred, effectively shaping governance outcomes beyond the reach of traditional state regulation (Damame, 2025). This has led to concerns about dependency, concentration of power, and the limits of state-centric approaches to digital sovereignty. In parallel, there has been increasing attention to the fragmentation of legal frameworks governing data flows, with studies noting how overlapping and sometimes conflicting regulations create uncertainty and complicate compliance (Kaya & Shahid, 2025).

Despite recent advances in scholarship, existing literature continues to examine digital sovereignty, regulatory divergence, and infrastructural power as interconnected yet analytically separate concerns (Fratini et al., 2024). There remains limited sustained engagement with the role of legal fragmentation as the underlying mechanism that links these domains and shapes both the opportunities and constraints of contemporary data governance. This chapter seeks to address that gap by integrating these strands and advancing legal fragmentation as a central analytical lens through which digital sovereignty and cross-border data flows can be more systematically and coherently understood.

At the core of contemporary data governance lies a structural problem that extends beyond mere regulatory divergence. Existing legal frameworks remain territorially anchored, relying on jurisdictional boundaries to assert authority and enforce compliance. However, cross-border data flows operate within a deterritorialized digital environment, where data is continuously generated, processed, and transferred across multiple jurisdictions through globally distributed infrastructures. This creates a fundamental mismatch between the architecture of law and the architecture of data. As a result, legal systems produce fragmented and overlapping regulatory regimes, generate conflicting obligations for transnational actors, and encounter persistent enforcement limitations. The problem, therefore, is not simply one of coordination between different legal systems, but a deeper structural constraint within existing governance models, which struggle to effectively regulate a transnational, technologically complex, and privately mediated data ecosystem.

The Structural Tension between Territorial Law and Global Data Flows

The central problem in governing cross-border data flows lies in the structural mismatch between territorially grounded legal systems and the inherently transnational nature of digital data. Contemporary legal frameworks continue to rely on jurisdictional boundaries to assert authority, enforce compliance, and protect regulatory interests. However, data does not adhere to these boundaries. It moves seamlessly across multiple jurisdictions through cloud infrastructures, platform ecosystems, and global networks, often without clear points of control. This creates a persistent tension in which states seek to regulate activities that are no longer confined within their territorial limits.

This mismatch becomes particularly visible in the context of digital services that operate simultaneously across jurisdictions. For instance, a single transaction on a global platform may involve data collection in one country, storage in another, and processing in multiple locations, each subject to different regulatory regimes. Such arrangements complicate the application of domestic laws, especially where legal standards diverge. Efforts to extend jurisdiction extraterritorially, while necessary in some cases, often lead to conflicts between legal systems, creating uncertainty for both regulators and private actors (AllahRakha, 2024).

The problem is further intensified by the increasing reliance on digital infrastructures controlled by a limited number of global technology firms. These entities design and operate the systems through which data flows, effectively shaping the conditions under which regulation takes place. As a result, the question of control over data is no longer limited to formal legal authority but extends to infrastructural and technological capabilities. States attempting to assert digital sovereignty must therefore navigate not only competing legal regimes but also dependencies embedded in the architecture of the global data economy.

What emerges is not merely a challenge of regulatory coordination but a deeper structural limitation in existing governance models. Legal frameworks are compelled to respond to a deterritorialized environment using tools that remain territorially anchored, leading to fragmentation, overlapping obligations, and gaps in enforcement. This chapter approaches the problem from this structural perspective, examining how the tension between territorial law and transnational data flows shapes the possibilities and limits of digital sovereignty.

Research Methodology

This chapter adopts a doctrinal and comparative research methodology to examine the governance of cross-border data flows through the lens of digital sovereignty and legal fragmentation. It analyses key legal frameworks, regulatory instruments, and judicial developments across jurisdictions to identify patterns of convergence and divergence in data governance approaches. At the same time, the chapter incorporates a structural perspective by situating these legal developments within the broader context of global digital infrastructures and market dynamics, particularly the role of dominant technology firms. By combining legal analysis with comparative and contextual insights, the chapter develops an analytical framework that focuses on fragmentation, jurisdictional limits, and power asymmetries as interconnected dimensions shaping the regulation of cross-border data flows.

CROSS-BORDER DATA FLOWS AND DIGITAL INFRASTRUCTURES

Cross-border data flows are sustained by a complex and often opaque network of digital infrastructures that underpin the functioning of the global data economy. These infrastructures, including cloud computing systems, platform ecosystems, and transnational data networks, enable the continuous movement, storage, and processing of data across jurisdictions, frequently beyond the direct control of any single state. Understanding how these systems operate is essential to analysing the regulatory challenges they pose, as the architecture of data flows not only facilitates economic activity but also shapes the limits of legal authority and enforcement. This section examines the structural features of these infrastructures and their implications for governance, particularly in relation to control, dependency, and the exercise of digital sovereignty.

Architecture of Global Data Flows: Cloud Systems, Platforms and Network Dependencies

The architecture of global data flows is shaped by a layered system of digital infrastructures that enable the continuous movement, storage, and processing of data across jurisdictions. At the core of this system are cloud computing networks, which allow data to be stored and accessed remotely through geographically dispersed data centres (Weber, 2021). These systems are designed for efficiency and redundancy, meaning that data may be fragmented, replicated, and transferred across multiple locations without any fixed territorial anchor. As a result, the physical location of data becomes difficult to determine, complicating the application of jurisdiction-specific legal rules. This is particularly evident in the operations of hyperscale cloud providers, where a single service may involve data routing through multiple countries depending on cost, latency, and system optimization.

Alongside cloud infrastructures, digital platforms play a crucial role in structuring data flows. Platforms that facilitate search, social interaction, e-commerce, and digital services act as central nodes through which vast volumes of data are generated and circulated. For instance, user interactions on a social media platform may generate data that is collected in one jurisdiction, processed in another, and analysed elsewhere for targeted services or advertising. These platform-based ecosystems create dense and continuous flows of data that are integral to business models but remain largely detached from traditional regulatory boundaries. Their global reach and operational integration further blur distinctions between domestic and international data processing activities.

These infrastructures are supported by underlying physical and technical networks, including undersea cables, internet exchange points, and content delivery systems, which facilitate the rapid transmission of data across continents. While these systems are often invisible from a regulatory perspective, they are critical in shaping how data flows are routed and controlled. Importantly, access to and control over these infrastructures is unevenly distributed, with a concentration of ownership and operational capacity in a limited number of actors. This creates dependencies for states and businesses that rely on externally controlled systems to participate in the digital economy.

The cumulative effect of these interconnected systems is the emergence of a data environment that is inherently transnational, dynamic, and difficult to regulate through territorially confined legal mechanisms. Data flows are no longer discrete or easily traceable transactions but part of a continuous and integrated process embedded in global infrastructures. Understanding this architecture is essential for appreciating why regulatory efforts often encounter limitations, as the design of these systems itself constrains the effectiveness of jurisdiction-based governance and shapes the broader challenges of digital sovereignty.

Private Power and Infrastructural dominance in the Data Economy

The governance of cross-border data flows cannot be understood without recognising the central role of private actors that design, control, and operate the infrastructures through which data circulates. A small group of large technology companies has come to occupy a dominant position in the digital economy, not only as service providers but as architects of the systems that structure data movement, storage, and processing (Ingersleben-Seip, 2025). Their control over cloud computing networks, platform ecosystems, and data analytics capabilities allows them to determine how and where data flows, often independently of direct state intervention. This concentration of infrastructural power reshapes traditional notions of sovereignty, as regulatory authority increasingly intersects with privately governed technological systems.

These firms exercise influence through a combination of technical design, contractual arrangements, and standard-setting practices. For instance, cloud service providers determine data storage locations, security protocols, and access conditions through service agreements that are typically non-negotiable for most users. Similarly, digital platforms establish terms of service and algorithmic processes that govern how data is collected, shared, and monetised. Such mechanisms effectively create private regulatory regimes that operate alongside, and sometimes in tension with, public law frameworks. In many cases, compliance with national regulations is mediated through these corporate structures, placing significant interpretative and operational power in private hands.

The dominance of these actors also creates structural dependencies for both states and businesses. Governments increasingly rely on privately owned infrastructures to deliver public services, manage data systems, and support digital economies. For example, public sector data may be hosted on cloud platforms operated by foreign corporations, raising concerns about control, access, and vulnerability. Smaller firms, particularly in developing economies, face similar dependencies, as participation in global markets often requires integration into platform-based ecosystems controlled by dominant players. This asymmetry limits the capacity of less powerful actors to influence governance outcomes or negotiate favourable regulatory conditions.

At the same time, the transnational nature of these corporations enables them to navigate fragmented legal environments more effectively than individual states. They can structure operations across jurisdictions to optimise regulatory compliance, manage risk, and maintain operational flexibility. This ability to adapt to and, in some cases, shape regulatory conditions further reinforces their position within the global data economy. Consequently, the question of governing cross-border data flows is not solely about aligning legal frameworks but also about addressing the concentration of infrastructural and economic power in private hands. This dynamic complicates efforts to assert digital sovereignty, as control over data is increasingly mediated through systems that lie beyond direct state ownership or control.

Regulatory Limitations in governing Transnational Data Systems

Despite the increasing sophistication of legal frameworks aimed at regulating data, the governance of transnational data systems remains constrained by structural and institutional limitations that are deeply embedded in the nature of global data flows. At the core of these limitations is the reliance of regulatory systems on jurisdictional boundaries that are increasingly misaligned with the technical realities of data movement. Laws are typically designed to apply within defined territorial limits, yet data routinely traverses multiple jurisdictions in ways that are neither linear nor easily traceable. This creates significant challenges in determining applicable law, asserting jurisdiction, and ensuring compliance, particularly in cases where multiple legal regimes claim authority over the same data set or transaction.

One of the most persistent difficulties arises in the context of enforcement. Even where legal frameworks assert extraterritorial reach, their practical effectiveness depends on the ability of states to access data, compel compliance, and impose sanctions. In a distributed data environment, these functions are often mediated by private intermediaries who control the infrastructure through which data is stored and transmitted. For instance, a regulatory authority seeking access to data for investigative purposes may encounter barriers if the data is stored in a foreign jurisdiction or managed by a multinational cloud provider subject to conflicting legal obligations (Coche et al., 2024). Mutual legal assistance mechanisms and cross-border cooperation frameworks exist, but they are frequently slow, fragmented, and ill-suited to the speed and scale of digital transactions. This results in enforcement gaps that undermine the credibility and effectiveness of regulatory regimes.

Further complexity arises from the coexistence of divergent legal standards governing similar aspects of data use. Differences in privacy protections, data security requirements, and conditions for lawful access create overlapping and sometimes incompatible obligations for entities operating across borders. A company may be required to comply with strict data protection standards in one jurisdiction while simultaneously being subject to disclosure obligations in another, leading to legal conflicts that are difficult to reconcile. These tensions are not merely theoretical but have material consequences, as they can disrupt data transfers, increase compliance costs, and create uncertainty in digital operations. In such an environment, regulatory strategies often become reactive, focusing on managing conflicts rather than addressing their underlying causes.

Another significant limitation lies in the technological opacity of data systems. The complexity of cloud architectures, algorithmic processing, and data routing mechanisms makes it difficult for regulators to obtain a clear understanding of how data flows operate in practice. This asymmetry of knowledge places regulatory authorities at a disadvantage, as they must rely on disclosures and representations made by private actors who control the relevant infrastructures. While regulatory tools such as audits, reporting requirements, and certification mechanisms attempt to bridge this gap, they often fall short of providing real-time visibility into dynamic data environments. As a result, regulation tends to operate with incomplete information, reducing its precision and effectiveness.

These limitations are further compounded by the global distribution of digital infrastructure, which fragments control and disperses authority across multiple actors and jurisdictions. States may attempt to assert greater control through measures such as data localisation, stricter transfer regulations, or domestic infrastructure development, but such approaches often generate trade-offs between sovereignty, efficiency, and participation in global networks (Deane et al., 2024). In many cases, they also risk deepening fragmentation by creating parallel regulatory systems that are difficult to integrate.

Taken together, these challenges reveal that the limitations of governing transnational data systems are not merely the result of inadequate legal design but are rooted in the structural characteristics of the digital environment itself. The disjunction between legal authority and technological reality, combined with asymmetries in power and information, constrains the capacity of existing frameworks to effectively regulate cross-border data flows. This underscores the need to move beyond incremental regulatory adjustments and toward a more fundamental rethinking of how law engages with the architecture of global data systems.

LEGAL FRAMEWORKS AND REGULATORY DIVERGENCE

The governance of cross-border data flows is shaped by a diverse and often conflicting set of legal frameworks that reflect differing national priorities, institutional capacities, and normative commitments. While all jurisdictions seek to regulate data in some form, the underlying objectives vary significantly, ranging from the protection of individual privacy and national security to the promotion of digital trade and economic growth. These differences have resulted in a fragmented regulatory landscape in which multiple legal regimes coexist, overlap, and at times conflict with one another. Understanding this divergence is essential to analysing the broader challenges of digital sovereignty, as it highlights how legal systems respond differently to the same transnational phenomenon. This section examines key regulatory approaches and the mechanisms developed to facilitate cross-border data transfers, while critically assessing how inconsistencies between them contribute to legal uncertainty and governance complexity.

Comparative Approaches to Data Governance: Privacy, Security and Economic Models

Legal approaches to data governance vary significantly across jurisdictions, reflecting distinct normative priorities and institutional choices regarding the role of the state, the market, and individual rights in the digital economy. Broadly, these approaches can be understood along three interrelated axes: privacy and fundamental rights, national security and state control, and economic efficiency and data mobility. While these categories often overlap in practice, they provide a useful framework for analysing how different legal systems conceptualise and regulate cross-border data flows.

A prominent model is the rights-based approach, which places strong emphasis on the protection of personal data as an extension of individual autonomy and dignity. In such frameworks, data protection is treated as a fundamental legal concern, leading to the development of comprehensive regulatory regimes that impose strict conditions on the collection, processing, and transfer of data (Santana & Ansari, 2023). Cross-border data transfers under this model are typically subject to safeguards designed to ensure that equivalent levels of protection are maintained in receiving jurisdictions. This results in mechanisms such as adequacy assessments and contractual safeguards, which aim to extend domestic standards beyond territorial boundaries. However, the strength of this approach also creates friction in international data flows, as jurisdictions with less stringent protections may be deemed inadequate, thereby restricting transfers and increasing compliance complexity.

In contrast, some jurisdictions adopt a more state-centric model that prioritises national security, public order, and sovereign control over data. Under this approach, data is often viewed as a strategic asset, and regulatory frameworks may include measures such as data localisation requirements, restrictions on cross-border transfers, and enhanced government access to data held by private entities. These measures are justified on grounds of security, economic independence, or political control, but they also have the effect of limiting the openness of data ecosystems. For example, requirements that certain categories of data be stored within national borders can alter the architecture of data flows, forcing companies to restructure their operations and, in some cases, fragment their systems across jurisdictions.

A third approach emphasises economic integration and the free flow of data as a driver of innovation and growth (Arner et al., 2021). In this model, regulatory frameworks are designed to minimise barriers to cross-border data transfers, often through commitments in trade agreements or the adoption of flexible standards that facilitate interoperability. Data is treated primarily as a commercial resource, and the regulatory focus is on enabling digital trade while managing risks through targeted interventions rather than comprehensive restrictions. While this approach supports global connectivity and reduces compliance burdens, it may also raise concerns about the adequacy of protections for privacy and security, particularly when data flows into jurisdictions with weaker regulatory safeguards.

These differing approaches do not operate in isolation but interact within a global system where data flows cut across multiple regulatory environments. This interaction often results in tensions, as the principles underlying one model may conflict with those of another. For instance, a rights-based framework that restricts data transfers to jurisdictions lacking equivalent protections may come into conflict with trade-oriented commitments that seek to ensure the free movement of data. Similarly, state-centric measures such as localisation can disrupt globally integrated systems designed for efficiency and scalability.

The comparative analysis of these models reveals that regulatory divergence is not merely a technical issue but a reflection of deeper disagreements about the nature of data, the scope of state authority, and the balance between control and openness. These divergences shape the legal conditions under which cross-border data flows occur and contribute directly to the fragmentation of the global data governance landscape. Understanding these differences is therefore essential for assessing both the possibilities and limitations of existing frameworks in addressing the challenges of digital sovereignty.

Cross-Border Data Transfer Mechanisms and their Limitations

In response to regulatory divergence, a range of legal and institutional mechanisms has been developed to facilitate cross-border data transfers while attempting to preserve regulatory objectives. These mechanisms are designed to bridge differences between jurisdictions by creating conditional pathways through which data can move, subject to compliance with specified safeguards. Among the most prominent are adequacy determinations, standard contractual clauses, binding corporate rules, and provisions embedded within international trade agreements. While these tools represent important efforts to reconcile competing legal frameworks, their practical operation reveals significant limitations that reflect the underlying fragmentation of the global data governance system.

Adequacy mechanisms, for instance, operate on the premise that data may be transferred to another jurisdiction if it provides a level of protection deemed equivalent to that of the originating system. This approach introduces a form of regulatory recognition, enabling smoother data flows between aligned jurisdictions. However, adequacy assessments are inherently political and context-specific, often influenced by broader considerations such as diplomatic relations and economic interests. They also tend to be limited in scope, applying only to specific jurisdictions that meet the required standards, thereby excluding others and reinforcing divisions in the global data landscape. Moreover, the dynamic nature of legal systems means that adequacy is not static, and changes in domestic law or judicial interpretation can disrupt established transfer arrangements.

Standard contractual clauses and similar instruments attempt to address these limitations by allowing private parties to contractually commit to specific data protection obligations when transferring data across borders. These mechanisms are widely used due to their flexibility and relative ease of implementation (Bradford et al., 2021). However, their effectiveness depends heavily on the ability of parties to actually comply with and enforce these obligations in practice. In complex transnational data environments, where multiple actors and jurisdictions are involved, ensuring consistent adherence to contractual commitments becomes increasingly difficult. Additionally, such mechanisms often place significant compliance burdens on organisations, particularly smaller entities that lack the resources to navigate intricate legal requirements.

Binding corporate rules provide another pathway, particularly for multinational enterprises seeking to manage internal data transfers across different jurisdictions. These rules establish a unified set of standards within an organisation, subject to regulatory approval. While they offer a degree of coherence within corporate structures, their applicability is limited to large organisations with the capacity to develop and maintain such frameworks. They do little to address broader systemic issues affecting data flows between unrelated entities or across diverse regulatory environments.

Trade agreements and international instruments have also sought to facilitate data mobility by incorporating commitments to the free flow of data and restrictions on data localisation. These provisions aim to reduce barriers to digital trade and promote economic integration. However, they often coexist uneasily with domestic regulatory priorities, particularly in areas such as privacy and national security. The result is a complex legal landscape in which trade obligations and domestic regulations may pull in different directions, creating uncertainty and potential conflict.

A key limitation across all these mechanisms is that they operate as overlays on fundamentally divergent legal systems rather than resolving the divergences themselves. They provide procedural solutions to enable data transfers but do not eliminate the substantive differences in regulatory standards and objectives. As a result, they are often reactive and contingent, susceptible to legal challenges, policy shifts, and changes in geopolitical dynamics. The instability of such mechanisms becomes particularly evident when judicial or regulatory interventions disrupt established arrangements, exposing the fragility of the underlying frameworks.

In essence, cross-border data transfer mechanisms function as necessary but incomplete tools within a fragmented system. They facilitate the movement of data in the absence of harmonised global standards but do so at the cost of complexity, uncertainty, and uneven accessibility. Their limitations underscore the broader challenge of governing cross-border data flows through a patchwork of legal instruments, highlighting the need for more coherent and structurally aligned approaches to global data governance.

Conflicts, Inconsistencies and Legal Uncertainty in Global Data Flows

The coexistence of divergent regulatory frameworks governing cross-border data flows inevitably produces conflicts and inconsistencies that undermine legal certainty and complicate compliance. These conflicts arise not only from differences in substantive standards, such as varying thresholds for data protection or state access, but also from competing jurisdictional claims over the same data. In a transnational data environment, a single dataset may simultaneously fall within the regulatory ambit of multiple legal systems, each imposing distinct and sometimes incompatible obligations. This creates a situation in which compliance with one regime may result in the violation of another, placing organisations in structurally irresolvable legal positions.

Such tensions are particularly visible in the interaction between privacy-focused regimes and laws that mandate access to data for law enforcement or national security purposes. For example, a company operating across jurisdictions may be required to restrict the transfer of personal data under one legal framework while being compelled to disclose that same data under another (Handapangoda, 2026). These overlapping obligations are not merely hypothetical but have material consequences, affecting how companies structure their operations, manage risks, and allocate resources. In many cases, firms respond by adopting conservative compliance strategies, such as limiting data transfers or restructuring data storage practices, which can reduce efficiency and hinder innovation.

Inconsistencies also emerge in the interpretation and application of legal standards across jurisdictions. Even where similar principles exist, their implementation may vary significantly due to differences in institutional capacity, regulatory culture, and judicial interpretation. This leads to a lack of predictability, as organisations cannot rely on uniform enforcement or consistent outcomes. For instance, mechanisms designed to facilitate data transfers may be interpreted differently by courts or regulators, resulting in uncertainty regarding their validity and scope. Such unpredictability not only increases compliance costs but also weakens confidence in the stability of legal frameworks governing data flows.

The problem of legal uncertainty is further exacerbated by the dynamic nature of both technology and law. Digital systems evolve rapidly, introducing new forms of data processing and cross-border interaction that outpace existing regulatory frameworks. At the same time, legal regimes are subject to ongoing reform, judicial scrutiny, and policy shifts, which can alter the conditions under which data flows are permitted. The invalidation or modification of established transfer mechanisms, for example, can have immediate and far-reaching effects, disrupting ongoing operations and requiring swift adjustments by affected entities.

Importantly, these conflicts and inconsistencies do not operate in isolation but are embedded within a broader structure of legal fragmentation. They reflect deeper disagreements about the appropriate balance between competing objectives, including privacy, security, economic integration, and state sovereignty. As long as these underlying divergences persist, efforts to harmonise or coordinate regulatory approaches are likely to remain partial and contested. The result is a governance landscape characterised by instability, where legal certainty is difficult to achieve and compliance becomes an ongoing process of negotiation and adaptation.

This environment of uncertainty has significant implications for digital sovereignty. It constrains the ability of states to effectively regulate data flows within their jurisdiction, while also limiting the capacity of organisations to operate seamlessly across borders. More fundamentally, it reveals that the challenge of governing cross-border data flows is not simply one of designing better rules, but of addressing the structural conditions that produce conflict and inconsistency in the first place.

LEGAL FRAGMENTATION AND POWER ASYMMETRIES

The preceding discussion of regulatory divergence and cross-border data conflicts points to a deeper structural condition shaping global data governance: legal fragmentation. This chapter moves beyond describing differences between legal systems to examine fragmentation as an embedded feature of the current regulatory order, arising from competing conceptions of sovereignty, market organisation, and rights protection. Rather than producing a balanced pluralism, this fragmented landscape generates uneven distributions of power, enabling certain actors to navigate, influence, and even exploit regulatory complexity more effectively than others. In this context, fragmentation is not merely a technical challenge but a site where authority, control, and dependency are continuously negotiated. The chapter therefore analyses how fragmentation interacts with power asymmetries between states, corporations, and individuals, and how judicial interventions in transnational data disputes both reveal and intensify these underlying tensions.

Fragmentation as a Structural Feature of Global Data Governance

Legal fragmentation in the context of cross-border data flows is often understood as the by-product of regulatory divergence across jurisdictions. However, such a view understates its depth and persistence. Fragmentation is not merely the result of incomplete harmonization or transitional legal development; rather, it is a structural feature embedded in the architecture of global data governance itself. It arises from the coexistence of multiple, territorially grounded legal systems attempting to regulate a domain that is inherently deterritorialized. This mismatch ensures that fragmentation is continuously reproduced, even as new mechanisms are introduced to manage or mitigate its effects.

At its core, fragmentation reflects fundamentally different regulatory rationalities. Jurisdictions approach data governance through distinct normative frameworks, shaped by varying priorities such as individual privacy, national security, economic competitiveness, and technological innovation (Qiu & Hu, 2025). These priorities are not easily reconcilable, as they are rooted in broader political, constitutional, and institutional contexts. As a result, legal systems develop in parallel rather than converging toward a unified model. Even where common principles appear to exist, their interpretation and application differ significantly, reinforcing rather than resolving fragmentation.

This structural condition is further reinforced by the persistence of territorial sovereignty as the primary organizing principle of law. States assert jurisdiction over data based on factors such as location, citizenship, or market access, extending their regulatory reach beyond physical borders. These overlapping jurisdictional claims create a dense web of legal obligations that intersect and often conflict. Importantly, no single authority exists to reconcile these claims at a global level, leaving fragmentation as the default condition of governance rather than an exception.

Efforts to address fragmentation, such as interoperability frameworks, transfer mechanisms, and international agreements, operate within this structurally fragmented environment rather than transforming it. They provide procedural pathways for coordination but do not eliminate the underlying divergences in legal systems. In many cases, these mechanisms add additional layers of complexity, as organisations must navigate both domestic regulations and transnational compliance instruments simultaneously. This produces a form of managed fragmentation, where coordination is achieved through conditional and often fragile arrangements.

Technological developments also contribute to the persistence of fragmentation. The architecture of digital systems, including cloud infrastructures and platform ecosystems, enables data to be stored, processed, and transferred across multiple jurisdictions simultaneously. This decentralised and dynamic nature of data flows makes it difficult to anchor regulatory authority in a single location, further complicating efforts to impose coherent legal control. As technology evolves, it continuously outpaces regulatory adaptation, reinforcing the structural gap between law and practice.

Understanding fragmentation as a structural feature has important implications. It shifts the focus from seeking complete harmonization, which may be neither feasible nor desirable, to managing and navigating a pluralistic legal environment. At the same time, it highlights that fragmentation is not neutral; it shapes the distribution of power and capacity within the global data ecosystem (Jiang, 2025). By embedding complexity and uncertainty into the system, it advantages actors who possess the resources and expertise to operate across multiple legal regimes, setting the stage for the power asymmetries explored in the following section.

Asymmetries between States, Corporations and Users

The structurally fragmented nature of global data governance does not affect all actors equally. Instead, it produces and reinforces significant asymmetries between states, corporations, and individual users, each of whom occupies a markedly different position within the regulatory landscape. These asymmetries are not incidental but are closely tied to differences in resources, institutional capacity, technological control, and the ability to navigate complex legal environments. As a result, fragmentation becomes a mechanism through which power is unevenly distributed and exercised.

Multinational technology corporations are often the most adept at operating within fragmented legal systems. Their scale, technical expertise, and access to specialised legal resources enable them to interpret, adapt to, and strategically manage diverse regulatory requirements. They can structure their operations across jurisdictions, deploy contractual frameworks, and design technical architectures that accommodate or mitigate legal constraints. In doing so, they are not merely responding to regulation but actively shaping how it is implemented in practice. This capacity allows corporations to maintain a degree of continuity in their operations despite legal divergence, effectively insulating themselves from the full impact of fragmentation.

States, by contrast, face more complex constraints. While they possess formal regulatory authority, their capacity to enforce laws in a transnational digital environment is limited by jurisdictional boundaries, technological dependencies, and economic considerations. Smaller or less technologically advanced states, in particular, may lack the institutional infrastructure and bargaining power required to assert meaningful control over data flows (Lawton et al., 2023). Even larger states encounter difficulties when attempting to regulate entities that operate across multiple jurisdictions or rely on infrastructure located beyond their territorial reach. This creates a paradox in which states retain formal sovereignty but experience practical limitations in exercising it effectively.

The position of individual users is even more constrained. Users are subject to the cumulative effects of fragmented legal regimes without possessing the resources or agency to navigate them. Their rights and protections depend heavily on the jurisdiction in which data is processed or the regulatory framework governing a particular service, often without their knowledge or meaningful consent. Moreover, the complexity of legal arrangements and the opacity of data practices limit the ability of individuals to assert their rights or seek remedies. In this sense, fragmentation contributes to a form of informational and legal asymmetry, where users remain the least empowered actors within the system.

These asymmetries are further reinforced by the interaction between legal and technological infrastructures. Corporations not only operate within regulatory frameworks but also control key elements of the digital environment, including platforms, cloud services, and data architectures. This dual role enhances their influence, enabling them to shape both the conditions under which data flows occur and the practical application of legal rules. States and users, by contrast, are often dependent on these infrastructures, which limits their ability to independently regulate or contest data practices.

Importantly, these power differentials have broader implications for global governance. They affect whose interests are prioritised in the development and interpretation of legal norms, as well as who bears the costs of compliance and regulatory failure. Fragmentation thus becomes more than a technical characteristic of the legal system; it functions as a distributional mechanism that privileges certain actors while marginalising others. Recognising these asymmetries is essential for understanding why existing governance frameworks struggle to achieve equitable and effective regulation of cross-border data flows, and why efforts toward reform must address not only legal divergence but also the underlying imbalances of power.

Judicial Interventions and Transnational Conflicts: Lessons from Data Transfer Disputes

Judicial interventions have played a critical role in exposing and, at times, intensifying the tensions inherent in fragmented data governance systems. Courts, particularly in jurisdictions with strong constitutional or rights-based traditions, have increasingly been called upon to assess the legality of cross-border data transfer mechanisms. In doing so, they do not merely interpret existing frameworks but actively shape the boundaries of permissible data flows. These interventions reveal the limits of regulatory coordination and highlight the deep incompatibilities between different legal orders, especially where fundamental rights and state surveillance practices intersect.

A defining feature of such judicial engagement is its focus on the adequacy and equivalence of legal protections across jurisdictions. Courts are often required to evaluate whether foreign legal systems provide safeguards comparable to domestic standards, particularly in relation to privacy, due process, and state access to data. This evaluative exercise is inherently complex, as it involves assessing not only formal legal provisions but also their practical implementation and enforcement. In many instances, courts have adopted a stringent approach, emphasizing substantive protection over formal assurances, thereby subjecting transnational data arrangements to rigorous scrutiny (Lynskey, 2020).

These judicial decisions have significant systemic consequences. By invalidating or restricting widely used data transfer mechanisms, courts can disrupt established frameworks that underpin global data flows. Such interventions create immediate compliance challenges for organisations and may require the rapid development of alternative arrangements. More fundamentally, they expose the fragility of governance structures that rely on mutual recognition or contractual safeguards without addressing underlying legal divergences. What appears as a functional solution at the regulatory level may be rendered untenable when subjected to constitutional or rights-based review.

At the same time, judicial interventions can intensify transnational conflicts. Decisions grounded in one jurisdiction's constitutional values may have extraterritorial implications, effectively imposing those standards on foreign legal systems or international arrangements. This can generate friction between states, particularly where differing conceptions of privacy, security, and state authority are involved. Courts, in this sense, become key actors in the geopolitics of data governance, influencing not only domestic legal outcomes but also international regulatory dynamics.

However, the role of courts is not solely disruptive. Judicial scrutiny also serves an important accountability function by challenging opaque or insufficiently protective data transfer arrangements. It compels both states and corporations to justify their practices and to align them more closely with articulated legal principles. In this way, courts contribute to the normative development of data governance, even as they expose its structural limitations. Their interventions can prompt regulatory reform, encourage greater transparency, and elevate the importance of rights-based considerations in transnational contexts.

The lessons emerging from data transfer disputes are therefore twofold. On the one hand, they demonstrate that fragmentation cannot be easily managed through technical or procedural mechanisms alone, as deeper legal and constitutional divergences remain unresolved. On the other hand, they highlight the centrality of judicial institutions in shaping the trajectory of global data governance. By bringing underlying conflicts to the surface, courts force a confrontation with the limits of existing frameworks, underscoring the need for more coherent and principled approaches that can withstand both legal scrutiny and transnational complexity.

DIGITAL SOVEREIGNTY AND RESISTANCE IN DATA GOVERNANCE

The persistence of legal fragmentation and the unequal distribution of power within global data governance structures necessitate a closer examination of how different actors respond to these constraints. This chapter shifts the analytical lens from structural diagnosis to strategic response, focusing on the ways in which both states and non-state actors attempt to assert control, reshape governance arrangements, or resist dominant configurations of power. These responses are often articulated through the language of digital sovereignty, yet they unfold within a deeply interdependent and technologically mediated environment that limits the possibility of absolute control. Rather than resolving fragmentation, such strategies frequently reconfigure it, producing new forms of tension between autonomy and interdependence. The chapter therefore examines how state-led assertions of sovereignty and broader societal and technological forms of resistance interact with, and at times reinforce, the fragmented nature of cross-border data governance.

State Assertion and Digital Sovereignty Strategies

In response to the constraints imposed by fragmented data governance frameworks, states have increasingly turned to strategies aimed at reasserting control over data, infrastructure, and digital markets. These efforts are commonly framed under the rubric of digital sovereignty, reflecting a desire to extend traditional notions of territorial authority into the digital domain. At their core, such strategies seek to reduce dependence on external actors, enhance regulatory capacity, and secure greater control over the economic and security dimensions of data flows. However, the pursuit of digital sovereignty is neither uniform nor unambiguous; it encompasses a range of policy tools and reflects differing national priorities and institutional capacities.

One of the most prominent manifestations of this approach is the adoption of data localisation measures, which require certain categories of data to be stored or processed within national borders (Bu, 2026). These measures are often justified on grounds of privacy protection, national security, and economic development, as they enable states to retain jurisdictional control and promote domestic digital industries. Alongside localisation, states have also pursued broader digital industrial policies, investing in domestic infrastructure such as data centres, cloud services, and digital platforms. These initiatives are designed not only to enhance technological self-reliance but also to strengthen a state's position within the global digital economy.

Regulatory assertion forms another key dimension of sovereignty-driven strategies. States increasingly seek to extend the reach of their legal frameworks beyond territorial boundaries, asserting jurisdiction over foreign entities that process data related to their citizens or markets. This extraterritorial application of law reflects an attempt to align regulatory authority with the realities of cross-border data flows. However, it also contributes to overlapping jurisdictional claims and reinforces the very fragmentation that these strategies aim to address. As multiple states assert competing forms of authority, the global data landscape becomes more complex and contested.

Despite their strategic intent, these sovereignty-driven approaches are marked by a fundamental paradox. While they aim to enhance control and autonomy, they often deepen interdependence and fragmentation. Data localisation, for instance, may increase regulatory oversight within a jurisdiction but can also disrupt global data flows, increase costs, and reduce the efficiency of digital services. Similarly, efforts to build domestic technological capacity frequently remain reliant on global supply chains, foreign technologies, and transnational platforms. This reveals the limits of unilateral approaches in a deeply interconnected digital ecosystem.

Moreover, the effectiveness of sovereignty strategies varies significantly across states. Larger economies with greater technological and regulatory capacity are better positioned to implement and enforce such measures, while smaller or less developed states may struggle to do so effectively (Roberts et al., 2021). This uneven capacity further entrenches global inequalities, as only a subset of states can meaningfully exercise digital sovereignty in practice. For others, attempts at assertion may result in symbolic measures that have limited practical impact or unintended economic consequences.

In this context, digital sovereignty emerges not as a stable condition but as a contested and evolving practice. It reflects an ongoing effort by states to negotiate their position within a fragmented and asymmetrical global system, rather than a definitive solution to the challenges of cross-border data governance. The pursuit of sovereignty, while politically and legally significant, thus remains constrained by the structural realities of interdependence, highlighting the need to consider complementary forms of coordination and cooperation alongside unilateral assertion.

Societal and Technological Resistance in Data Governance

Alongside state-led assertions of digital sovereignty, a range of societal and technological responses has emerged to contest dominant structures within the global data ecosystem. These forms of resistance are driven by concerns over privacy, surveillance, corporate concentration, and the erosion of user autonomy (Calzada, 2025). Unlike state strategies, which operate through formal legal and regulatory mechanisms, societal and technological interventions often seek to reshape data governance from below, using advocacy, design, and alternative infrastructures to challenge existing power configurations. In doing so, they introduce new sites of agency within an otherwise asymmetrical system.

Civil society organisations and digital rights movements play a central role in articulating normative critiques of prevailing data governance practices. Through litigation, policy advocacy, and public engagement, these actors seek to hold both states and corporations accountable, particularly in relation to privacy violations, surveillance practices, and opaque data processing systems. Their interventions have contributed to the development of rights-based frameworks and have brought greater visibility to the societal implications of cross-border data flows. However, their influence is often constrained by limited resources, uneven access to institutional processes, and the technical complexity of digital systems.

Technological forms of resistance complement these normative efforts by embedding alternative values directly into the design of digital systems. Encryption technologies, for instance, seek to protect user data from unauthorized access, including by state actors, thereby reconfiguring the balance between security and privacy. Similarly, the development of decentralised platforms and distributed networks aims to reduce reliance on centralised infrastructures controlled by dominant corporations. These technological interventions reflect an attempt to shift control away from concentrated points of authority and toward more distributed models of governance.

Despite their transformative potential, these forms of resistance face significant limitations. The widespread adoption of encryption and decentralised technologies is often hindered by usability challenges, regulatory pressures, and the entrenched dominance of existing platforms. Moreover, states may perceive such technologies as threats to national security or regulatory oversight, leading to attempts to restrict or control their use. This creates a tension between efforts to enhance user autonomy and the regulatory imperatives of states, further complicating the governance landscape.

Additionally, the effectiveness of societal and technological resistance is shaped by the broader structural conditions of the digital economy. Platform dominance, network effects, and infrastructural dependencies limit the ability of alternative systems to scale and compete with established actors. As a result, many resistance strategies operate at the margins, influencing discourse and policy without fundamentally altering the underlying distribution of power. This does not render them insignificant; rather, it highlights the difficulty of achieving systemic change within a deeply entrenched and globally integrated system.

In the end, societal and technological resistance represents an important but partial counterpoint to both state authority and corporate power. It expands the range of actors involved in data governance and introduces alternative visions of how data should be controlled and used. At the same time, its limitations underscore the persistence of structural constraints that cannot be overcome through isolated interventions alone. This reinforces the broader argument that meaningful transformation in data governance requires not only resistance and assertion but also coordinated and systemic approaches capable of addressing fragmentation and power asymmetries at their roots.

TOWARD COHERENT GLOBAL DATA GOVERNANCE

The preceding analysis has demonstrated that cross-border data flows are governed within a structurally fragmented and asymmetrical legal landscape, where neither state-centric assertions of sovereignty nor bottom-up forms of resistance are sufficient to produce stable or equitable outcomes. This final chapter shifts the focus from critique to reconstruction, asking how greater coherence might be achieved without disregarding the diversity of legal systems and regulatory priorities. The challenge is not to impose uniformity, but to develop frameworks that can manage interdependence in a principled and sustainable manner. In this context, coherence must be understood as the outcome of coordination, institutional engagement, and shared normative commitments rather than centralized control. The chapter therefore explores pathways through which legal systems can be aligned functionally, while also identifying the institutional and structural conditions necessary to support such alignment.

Interoperability and Institutional Coordination across Jurisdictions

In the absence of a comprehensive global regulatory authority, interoperability has emerged as a central mechanism for managing the tensions created by legal fragmentation. Rather than seeking full harmonization, interoperability enables different legal systems to coexist while establishing points of connection that allow data to move across jurisdictions under conditions of mutual recognition and functional equivalence. This approach reflects a pragmatic acknowledgment that divergence in regulatory philosophies is likely to persist, and that governance must therefore be built on mechanisms that facilitate coordination rather than eliminate difference.

Institutional coordination plays a crucial role in operationalising interoperability. Regulatory authorities, international organisations, and transnational networks increasingly engage in forms of cooperation that seek to align standards, share best practices, and develop common frameworks for oversight (Berg, 2024). These interactions are not limited to formal agreements but extend to ongoing dialogues, joint initiatives, and informal regulatory convergence. At the same time, private actors, particularly large technology firms and standard-setting bodies, are deeply embedded in these processes, shaping both the technical and normative dimensions of data governance. Their involvement reflects the reality that effective coordination cannot be achieved solely through state action, given the distributed nature of digital infrastructures and the central role of corporate entities in managing data flows.

However, the move toward interoperability and coordination is not without challenges. Differences in legal values, institutional capacities, and geopolitical interests can limit the extent to which alignment is achievable. There is also a risk that coordination mechanisms may privilege dominant jurisdictions or actors, thereby reproducing existing asymmetries under the guise of cooperation. Ensuring that interoperability does not lead to the dilution of regulatory protections or the marginalisation of less powerful stakeholders remains a critical concern.

Despite these limitations, interoperability and institutional coordination represent a shift toward a more relational model of governance, where authority is exercised through interaction rather than isolation. They provide a foundation upon which more coherent and resilient frameworks can be built, setting the stage for the articulation of shared principles that can guide the evolution of global data governance in a fragmented yet interconnected world.

Principles for a Balanced and Inclusive Data Governance Framework

Achieving coherence in global data governance ultimately depends not only on institutional coordination but also on the articulation of shared normative principles that can guide regulatory design and implementation across jurisdictions. A balanced framework must reconcile the competing demands of state sovereignty, economic integration, and individual rights, without allowing any single objective to dominate at the expense of others. Core principles such as transparency, accountability, and proportionality are essential in ensuring that data governance systems remain both effective and legitimate, particularly in contexts involving cross-border data transfers and complex institutional arrangements (Atkinson & Cory, 2021).

At the same time, inclusivity must be treated as a foundational requirement rather than an aspirational goal. This entails recognising the unequal capacities of states, the structural dominance of large corporations, and the limited agency of individual users, and designing governance frameworks that actively address these imbalances. An inclusive approach also requires meaningful participation from diverse stakeholders, including civil society and technical communities, in shaping both regulatory norms and their implementation.

Importantly, these principles must operate within the realities of a fragmented global system. Rather than seeking rigid uniformity, they should provide a flexible yet consistent foundation that can be adapted across different legal and institutional contexts. In this way, principled governance offers a pathway toward coherence that preserves diversity while mitigating conflict, enabling cross-border data flows to function within a more stable, accountable, and equitable global framework.

CONCLUSION

This chapter has examined the increasing tension between the inherently global character of cross-border data flows and the territorially bounded nature of legal and regulatory systems. It has argued that legal fragmentation should not be understood as a temporary or incidental phenomenon, but as a structural feature of contemporary data governance, arising from competing regulatory priorities, overlapping jurisdictional claims, and the absence of a coherent global framework. This fragmentation, in turn, generates significant power asymmetries, enabling certain actors, particularly large technology corporations, to navigate and shape regulatory environments more effectively than states and individual users.

The analysis has further demonstrated that responses to these challenges, whether through state-led assertions of digital sovereignty or societal and technological forms of resistance, remain constrained by the same structural conditions they seek to overcome. Efforts such as data localisation, regulatory expansion, and the development of alternative technological systems reflect important attempts to reclaim control and redistribute power. However, they often reproduce fragmentation, deepen interdependence, or generate new forms of conflict, revealing the limits of unilateral or isolated approaches to governance.

Against this backdrop, the chapter has highlighted the need to move beyond reactive strategies toward more coordinated and principled forms of global data governance. Interoperability and institutional coordination offer pragmatic pathways for managing regulatory divergence, enabling different legal systems to interact without requiring full harmonization. At the same time, the articulation of shared principles, including transparency, accountability, proportionality, and inclusivity, provides a normative foundation for ensuring that such coordination remains both effective and equitable.

The central insight that emerges is that digital sovereignty cannot be meaningfully realised in isolation within a fragmented global system. Instead, it must be reimagined as a relational and cooperative concept, grounded in interdependence rather than absolute control. Achieving this requires not only legal and institutional innovation but also a recognition of the underlying power dynamics that shape the governance of data. A more coherent global framework will therefore depend on the ability to align diverse regulatory approaches while addressing structural inequalities, ensuring that the benefits of cross-border data flows are realised in a manner that is both inclusive and accountable. In this regard, the evolution of global data governance is closely connected with broader international development priorities, particularly those reflected in the United Nations Sustainable Development Goals, including SDG 16: Peace, Justice and Strong Institutions and SDG 17: Partnerships for the Goals.

REFERENCES

Abdullah, A., Alkazraji, S. M. J., Jasim, A. A., Muhsin, A. I., Khazal, F. A. K., & Mykolenko, R. (2026). Sovereignty in the digital age: Social, legal, and governance challenges of global networks. In Z. Molamohamadi, E. Babaee Tirkolaee, A. Mirzazadeh, & G. W. Weber (Eds.), *Optimization and data science in industrial engineering: ODSIE 2025* (Communications in Computer and Information Science, Vol. 2855, pp. 87–104). Springer. https://doi.org/DOI: 10.1007/978-3-032-17023-1_8

Allahrakha, N. (2024). Rethinking digital borders to address jurisdiction and governance in the global digital economy. *International Journal of Law and Policy*, *2*(1). Advance online publication. DOI: 10.59022/ijlp.124

Arner, D. W., Castellano, G., & Selga, E. (2021). The transnational data governance problem. *Berkeley Technology Law Journal*. University of Hong Kong Faculty of Law Research Paper No. 2021/039. https://doi.org/DOI: 10.2139/ssrn.3912487

Atkinson, R. D., & Cory, N. (2021). Cross-border data policy: Opportunities and challenges. In H. Wang & A. Michie (Eds.), *Consensus or conflict?* (*China and globalization*, pp. 351–370). Springer. https://doi.org/DOI: 10.1007/978-981-16-5391-9_20

Berg, C. (2024). Interoperability. *Internet Policy Review*, *13*(2). Advance online publication. DOI: 10.14763/2024.2.1749

Bradford, L., Aboy, M., & Liddell, K. (2021). Standard contractual clauses for cross-border transfers of health data after *Schrems II*. *Journal of Law and the Biosciences*, *8*(1), lsab007. Advance online publication. DOI: 10.1093/jlb/lsab007 PMID: 34164131

Bu, Q. (2026). Data sovereignty in Africa: Steering digital transformation between China and the West. *International Cybersecurity Law Review*, *7*(1), 131–145. DOI: 10.1365/s43439-025-00165-1

Calzada, I. (2025). Decentralizing power? Data sovereignty in the age of AI and Web3. SSRN *Electronic Journal*. https://doi.org/DOI: 10.2139/ssrn.5081504

Coche, E., Kolk, A., & Ocelík, V. (2024). Unravelling cross-country regulatory intricacies of data governance: The relevance of legal insights for digitalization and international business. *Journal of International Business Policy*, *7*(1), 112–127. DOI: 10.1057/s42214-023-00172-1

Damame, L. J. (2025). Digital platforms as supranational regulators: Reconfiguring state power in the digital era. *Beijing Law Review*, *16*(4), 2089–2105. DOI: 10.4236/blr.2025.164105

Deane, F., Woolmer, E., Cao, S., & Tranter, K. (2024). Trade in the digital age: Agreements to mitigate fragmentation. *Asian Journal of International Law*, *14*(1), 154–179. DOI: 10.1017/S204425132300036X

Ding, X., Huang, H., Shi, Z., Li, Y., Chen, M., & Wang, J. (2025). Same text, different meaning: China's risk-based approach to data protection. *Humanities & Social Sciences Communications*, *12*(1), 1821. DOI: 10.1057/s41599-025-06100-3

Fratini, S., Hine, E., Novelli, C., Roberts, H., & Floridi, L. (2024). Digital sovereignty: A descriptive analysis and a critical evaluation of existing models. *Digital Society : Ethics, Socio-Legal and Governance of Digital Technology*, *3*(3), 59. DOI: 10.1007/s44206-024-00146-7

Handapangoda, C. (2026). Cross-border data security and privacy risks in large language models and IoT systems. *arXiv preprint arXiv:2601.06612*. https://arxiv.org/abs/2601.06612

Ingersleben-Seip, N. (2025). A tale of two metaverses: How America, China, and Europe are shaping the "new internet.". *Politics and Governance*, *13*, 10246. Advance online publication. DOI: 10.17645/pag.10246

Jiang, S. (2025). Fragmented rules, global flows: How legal differences shape the cross-border data landscape-Evidence from the EU, US, and China. *Lecture Notes in Education Psychology and Public Media*, *96*(1), 47–57. DOI: 10.54254/2753-7048/2025.BO23772

Kaya, M., & Shahid, H. (2025). Cross-border data flows and digital sovereignty: Legal dilemmas in transnational governance. *Interdisciplinary Studies in Society, Law, and Politics*, *4*(2), 219–233. DOI: 10.61838/kman.isslp.4.2.20

Lawton, T. C., Tonn Goulart Moura, S., Tobin, D., & Silva-Rêgo, B. (2023). Geopolitics of the digital economy: Implications for states and firms. *AIB Insights*, *23*(1). Advance online publication. DOI: 10.46697/001c.67966

Lynskey, O. (2020). Delivering data protection: The next chapter. *German Law Journal*, *21*(1), 80–84. DOI: 10.1017/glj.2019.100

Opriel, S., Möller, F., Strobel, G., & Otto, B. (2025). Data sovereignty in inter-organizational information systems. *Business & Information Systems Engineering*, *67*(6), 833–853. DOI: 10.1007/s12599-024-00893-4

Pohle, J., & Thiel, T. (2020). Digital sovereignty. *Internet Policy Review*, *9*(4). Advance online publication. DOI: 10.14763/2020.4.1532

Qiu, Y., & Hu, Z. (2025). Progress and recommendations in data ethics governance: A transnational analysis based on data ethics frameworks. *Humanities & Social Sciences Communications*, *12*(1), 1354. DOI: 10.1057/s41599-025-05664-4

Roberts, H., Cowls, J., Morley, J., Taddeo, M., & Floridi, L. (2021). Safeguarding European values with digital sovereignty: An analysis of statements and policies. *Internet Policy Review*, *10*(3), 1–28. DOI: 10.14763/2021.3.1575

Santana, P. C., & Ansari, F. A. (2023). Data protection and privacy as a fundamental right: A comparative study of Brazil and India. *Journal of Liberty and International Affairs*, *9*(3), 456–470. DOI: 10.47305/JLIA2393555cs

Voss, W. G. (2020). Cross-border data flows, the GDPR, and data governance. *Washington International Law Journal, 29*, 485–520. https://ssrn.com/abstract=3629348

Weber, R. H. (2021). Global law in the face of datafication and artificial intelligence. In Peng, S., Lin, C.-F., & Streinz, T. (Eds.), *Artificial intelligence and international economic law: Disruption, regulation, and reconfiguration* (pp. 54–69). Cambridge University Press. DOI: 10.1017/9781108954006.004

KEY TERMS AND DEFINITIONS

Cloud Computing: The delivery of data storage, processing, and software services through remote, internet-based servers.

Cross-Border Data Flows: The movement of data across national boundaries through digital networks and infrastructures.

Data Governance: The framework of laws, policies, and practices that regulate the collection, use, storage, and transfer of data.

Data Localization: Regulatory requirement mandating that data be stored or processed within a specific territorial jurisdiction.

Digital Sovereignty: The capacity of a state to exercise control over data, digital infrastructure, and technological systems within its jurisdiction.

Legal Fragmentation: The existence of multiple, overlapping, and often conflicting legal regimes governing the same subject matter.

Platform Economy: An economic system where digital platforms act as intermediaries facilitating data-driven interactions and transactions.

Regulatory Divergence: Variation in legal rules and policy approaches across jurisdictions concerning data governance.

Compilation of References

Aaronson, S. A. (2019). What are we talking about when we talk about digital protectionism? *World Trade Review*, *18*(4), 541–577. DOI: 10.1017/S1474745618000198

Aayog, N. I. T. I. (2021). *Responsible AI for all: Approach document for india, part 2—operationalizing principles for responsible AI.* NITI Aayog. https://www.niti.gov.in/sites/default/files/2021-08/Part2-Responsible-AI-12082021.pdf

Abdullah, A., Alkazraji, S. M. J., Jasim, A. A., Muhsin, A. I., Khazal, F. A. K., & Mykolenko, R. (2026). Sovereignty in the digital age: Social, legal, and governance challenges of global networks. In Z. Molamohamadi, E. Babaee Tirkolaee, A. Mirzazadeh, & G. W. Weber (Eds.), *Optimization and data science in industrial engineering: ODSIE 2025* (Communications in Computer and Information Science, Vol. 2855, pp. 87–104). Springer. https://doi.org/DOI: 10.1007/978-3-032-17023-1_8

Abiodun, T. F., & Abioro, T. (2020). Roles and challenges of international criminal police organization (Interpol) in investigation of crimes and maintenance of global security. Research Journal of social science and management, 10(3), 12-34.

Abraha, H. H. (2019). How compatible is the US 'CLOUD Act' with cloud computing? A brief analysis. *International Data Privacy Law*, *9*(3), 207–215. DOI: 10.1093/idpl/ipz009

Adebiyi, O. I., & Adeusi, O. C. (2025). Examining legal and ethical frameworks for protecting intellectual property rights in AI-generated content across creative industries. *World Journal of Advanced Research and Reviews*, *26*(3), 1553–1561. DOI: 10.30574/wjarr.2025.26.3.2239

African Union Convention on Cyber Security and Personal Data Protection. (2014).

African Union. (2022). *AU data policy framework: An integrated, prosperous and peaceful africa.* African Union. https://au.int/sites/default/files/documents/42078-doc-DATA-POLICY-FRAMEWORKS-2024-ENG-V2.pdf

African Union. (2024). *Continental artificial intelligence strategy: Harnessing AI for africa's development and prosperity*. African Union. https://au.int/sites/default/files/documents/44004-doc-EN-_Continental_AI_Strategy_July_2024.pdf

Agrawal, A. (2023). Web 2.5: The Vision of the Future Needs a Plan for the Now. *Journal of Digital Banking*, *7*(4), 290–300. DOI: 10.69554/ZIGH6972

Agu, C. R. (2025). Legal Analysis of the Implications of Continental Free Trade Area to Africa. Nnamdi Azikiwe UJ Int'l L. &. *Juris.*, *16*, 195.

AI Verify Foundation, & Infocomm Media Development Authority. (2024). Model AI Governance Framework for Generative AI: Fostering a trusted AI ecosystem. https://aiverifyfoundation.sg/wp-content/uploads/2024/06/Model-AI-Governance-Framework-for-Generative-AI-19-June-2024.pdf

Aïmeur, E., Amri, S., & Brassard, G. (2023). Fake news, disinformation and misinformation in social media: A review. *Social Network Analysis and Mining*, *13*(1), 30. DOI: 10.1007/s13278-023-01028-5 PMID: 36789378

Akkem, Y., Biswas, S. K., & Varanasi, A. (2024). A comprehensive review of synthetic data generation in smart farming by using variational autoencoder and generative adversarial network. *Engineering Applications of Artificial Intelligence*, *131*, 107881. DOI: 10.1016/j.engappai.2024.107881

Alahmadi, B. A., Axon, L., & Martinovic, I. (2022). *99% false positives: A qualitative study of SOC analysts' perspectives on security alarms. In 31st USENIX Security Symposium (USENIX Security 22)*. USENIX Association. https://www.usenix.org/system/files/sec22-alahmadi.pdf

Alanazi, S., Asif, S., Caird-Daley, A., & Moulitsas, I. (2025). Unmasking deepfakes: a multidisciplinary examination of social impacts and regulatory responses. *Human-Intelligent Systems Integration*, 1–23.

Allahrakha, N. (2024). Rethinking digital borders to address jurisdiction and governance in the global digital economy. *International Journal of Law and Policy*, *2*(1). Advance online publication. DOI: 10.59022/ijlp.124

Andraško, J., Mesarčík, M., & Hamuľák, O. (2021). The regulatory intersections between artificial intelligence, data protection and cyber security: Challenges and opportunities for the EU legal framework. *AI & Society*, *36*(2), 623–636. DOI: 10.1007/s00146-020-01125-5

Angus, D., Hayden, L., Obeid, A. K., Tan, X. Y., Carah, N., Burgess, J., Parker, C., Andrejevic, M., Fordyce, R., Cellard, L., & Bagnara, J. (2024). Computational methods for improving the observability of platform-based advertising. *Journal of Advertising*, *53*(5), 661–680. DOI: 10.1080/00913367.2024.2394156

Anix. (2026). *U.S. Regulators and Big Tech Compliance Issues.* SIIT. https://siit.co/blog/u-s-regulators-and-big-tech-compliance-issues/50399

Armbrust, M., Fox, A., Griffith, R., Joseph, A. D., Katz, R. H., Konwinski, A., Lee, G., Patterson, D. A., Rabkin, A., Stoica, I., & Zaharia, M. (2010). A view of cloud computing. *Communications of the ACM*, *53*(4), 50–58. DOI: 10.1145/1721654.1721672

Arner, D. W., Castellano, G., & Selga, E. (2021). The transnational data governance problem. *Berkeley Technology Law Journal*. University of Hong Kong Faculty of Law Research Paper No. 2021/039. https://doi.org/DOI: 10.2139/ssrn.3912487

Asimakopoulos, G., Antonopoulou, H., Giotopoulos, K., & Halkiopoulos, C. (2025). Impact of information and communication technologies on democratic processes and citizen participation. *Societies (Basel, Switzerland)*, *15*(2), 40. DOI: 10.3390/soc15020040

Astroulakis, N. 2024. “Nine (+ 1) Milestones in the Adoption of Cryptocurrencies.” https://medium.com/@n.astroulakis/nine-1-milestones-in-the-adoption-of-cryptocurrencies-a492bdbfff21

Atkinson, R. D., & Cory, N. (2021). Cross-border data policy: Opportunities and challenges. In H. Wang & A. Michie (Eds.), *Consensus or conflict?* (*China and globalization*, pp. 351–370). Springer. https://doi.org/DOI: 10.1007/978-981-16-5391-9_20

Autolitano, S., & Pawlowska, A. (2021). Europe’s quest for digital sovereignty: GAIA-X as a case study (IAI Papers 21|14). Istituto Affari Internazionali. https://www.iai.it/en/pubblicazioni/europes-quest-digital-sovereignty-gaia-x-case-study

Babaei, R., Cheng, S., Duan, R., & Zhao, S. (2025). Generative artificial intelligence and the evolving challenge of deepfake detection: A systematic analysis. *Journal of Sensor and Actuator Networks*, *14*(1), 17. DOI: 10.3390/jsan14010017

Bahangulu, J. K., & Owusu-Berko, L. (2025). Algorithmic bias, data ethics, and governance: Ensuring fairness, transparency and compliance in AI-powered business analytics applications. *World Journal of Advanced Research and Reviews*, *25*(2), 1746–1763. DOI: 10.30574/wjarr.2025.25.2.0571

Balasubramaniam, N., Kauppinen, M., Hiekkanen, K., & Kujala, S. (2022). Transparency and explainability of AI systems: ethical guidelines in practice. *International Working Conference on Requirements Engineering: Foundation for Software Quality*, 3–18. DOI: 10.1007/978-3-030-98464-9_1

Banstola, K., Al Faisal, F., & Ou, X. (2026). Experiences of using agentic AI to fill tooling gaps in a security operations center. In Proceedings of the Workshop on SOC Operations and Construction (WOSOC 2026). NDSS Symposium. https://www.ndss-symposium.org/wp-content/uploads/wosoc26-02.pdf

Basir, H., ASMI, F., Arshad, M. U., Khawar, A., Aman, N., Li, P., Zhou, R., & Makki, B. I. (2024). Combatting Deepfakes: Rational Choices, Moral Emotions, and Social Media Literacy. *Moral Emotions, and Social Media Literacy.*

Basu, A. (2021, October 18). *Sovereignty in a datafied world* (Issue Brief No. 501). Observer Research Foundation. https://www.orfonline.org/research/sovereignty-in-a-datafied-world

Beaumont, P., & Sending, O. J. (2012). Governance by indicators and the re-politicisation of expertise. *Review of International Studies*, •••, 1–19.

Belli, L., Gaspar, W. B., & Jaswant, S. S. (2024). Data sovereignty and data transfers as fundamental elements of digital transformation: Lessons from the BRICS countries. *Computer Law & Security Review*, *54*, 106017. DOI: 10.1016/j.clsr.2024.106017

Bellovin, S. M., Dutta, P. K., & Reitinger, N. (2019). Privacy and synthetic datasets. *Stan. Tech. L. Rev.*, *22*, 1.

Bennet, D., Maria, L., Sanjaya, Y. P. A., & Zahra, A. R. A. (2024). Blockchain technology: Revolutionizing transactions in the digital age. *ADI Journal on Recent Innovation*, *5*(2), 192–199. DOI: 10.34306/ajri.v5i2.1065

Benoit, K. (2024). AI and data science for public policy. *LSE Public Policy Review*, *3*(3), 1. DOI: 10.31389/lseppr.115

Berg, C. (2024). Interoperability. *Internet Policy Review*, *13*(2). Advance online publication. DOI: 10.14763/2024.2.1749

Bernal, P. A. (2010). Web 2.5: The Symbiotic Web. *International Review of Law Computers & Technology*, *24*(1), 25–37. DOI: 10.1080/13600860903570145

Berners-Lee, T. J., & Cailliau, R. (1990). WorldWideWeb: Proposal for a HyperText project.

Besson, S. (2011). *Sovereignty.* https://www.merriam-webster.com/dictionary/sovereign

Bhakuni, H., & Abimbola, S. (2021). Epistemic injustice in academic global health. *The Lancet. Global Health, 9*(10), e1465–e1470. DOI: 10.1016/S2214-109X(21)00301-6 PMID: 34384536

Bhanye, J., & Shayamunda, R. (2025). The promise of civic-tech: digital technologies and transparent, accountable governance. In *Digitalisation and public policy in Africa: GovTech and CivicTech innovations* (pp. 93–122). Springer Nature Switzerland., DOI: 10.1007/978-3-031-75079-3_5

Birchall, C. (2017). *Shareveillance: The dangers of openly sharing and covertly collecting data.* U of Minnesota Press. DOI: 10.5749/9781452958347

Birhane, A. (2020). Algorithmic colonization of Africa. *Script-ed, 17*, 389.

Birrer, A., & Just, N. (2025). What we know and don't know about deepfakes: An investigation into the state of the research and regulatory landscape. *New Media & Society, 27*(12), 6819–6838. DOI: 10.1177/14614448241253138

BlackRock. (2025). *Larry Fink's 2025 Annual Chairman's Letter to Investors -The Democratization of Investing: Expanding Prosperity in More Places, for More People.* MKTGM0425U/M-4377239.

Blancato, F. G. (2024). The cloud sovereignty nexus: How the European Union seeks to reverse strategic dependencies in its digital ecosystem. *Policy and Internet, 16*(1), 12–32. DOI: 10.1002/poi3.358

Blaug, M. (1992). *The Methodology of Economics: Or How Economists Explain* (2nd ed.). Cambridge University Press. DOI: 10.1017/CBO9780511528224

Borgogno, O., & Zangrandi, M. S. (2024). *Chinese Data Governance and Trade Policy: From Cyber Sovereignty to the Quest for Digital Hegemony?* Taylor and Francis., DOI: 10.1080/10670564.2023.2299961

Bowen, G. A. (2009). Document analysis as a qualitative research method. *Qualitative Research Journal, 9*(2), 27–40. DOI: 10.3316/QRJ0902027

Boyd, P. (2022). Fakes and deepfakes: Balancing privacy rights in the digital age. *Alabama Law Review, 74*, 517.

Boyer, R. (2022). Platform Capitalism: A Socio-Economic Analysis. *Socio-economic Review, 20*(4), 1857–1879. DOI: 10.1093/ser/mwaa055

Bradford, A. (2019). *The Brussels Effect: How the European Union Rules the World.* Oxford University Press.

Bradford, L., Aboy, M., & Liddell, K. (2021). Standard contractual clauses for cross-border transfers of health data after *Schrems II. Journal of Law and the Biosciences*, *8*(1), lsab007. Advance online publication. DOI: 10.1093/jlb/lsab007 PMID: 34164131

Brähler, N. 2023. "Web2.5: A Clever Term or a Useful Step for Brands Entering Web3?" https://www.brandingmag.com/nathalie-brahler/web2-5-a-clever-term-or-a-useful-step-for-brands-entering-web3/

Braun, D., & Busch, A. (1999). Public policy and political ideas.

Braun, M., & Hummel, P. (2025). Is digital sovereignty normatively desirable? *Information Communication and Society*, *28*(10), 1721–1734. DOI: 10.1080/1369118X.2024.2332624

Braun, V., & Clarke, V. (2006). Using thematic analysis in psychology. *Qualitative Research in Psychology*, *3*(2), 77–101. DOI: 10.1191/1478088706qp063oa

Brazil. (2018). Law No. 13/709, of August 14, 2018 (General Data Protection Law-LGPD). https://www.lgpdbrasil.com.br/wp-content/uploads/2019/06/LGPD-english-version.pdf

Brynjolfsson, E., & McAfee, A. (2014). The second machine age: Work progress and prosperity in a time of brilliant technologies. WW Norton & company.

Buisseret, P., & Van Weelden, R. (2020). Crashing the party? Elites, outsiders, and elections. *American Journal of Political Science*, *64*(2), 356–370. DOI: 10.1111/ajps.12457

Bukht, R., & Heeks, R. (2017). *Defining, Conceptualising and Measuring the Digital*. https://diode.network/wp-content/uploads/2017/08/diwkppr68-diode.pdf.

Bullmann, D., Klemm, J., & Pinna, A. (2019). "In Search for Stability in Crypto-Assets: Are Stablecoins the Solution?" *ECB Occasional Paper Series No 230* 1–55.

Bu, Q. (2026). Data sovereignty in Africa: Steering digital transformation between China and the West. *International Cybersecurity Law Review*, *7*(1), 131–145. DOI: 10.1365/s43439-025-00165-1

Burri, M. (2024). Inequalities in digital trade and digital trade regulation. In Askin, E., & Stoll, H. (Eds.), *Contested equality: International and comparative legal perspectives* (pp. 203–220). Edward Elgar Publishing., DOI: 10.4337/9781035325771.00020

Calderaro, A., & Craig, A. J. (2020). Transnational governance of cybersecurity: Policy challenges and global inequalities in cyber capacity building. *Third World Quarterly*, *41*(6), 917–938. DOI: 10.1080/01436597.2020.1729729

Calzada, I. (2025). Decentralizing power? Data sovereignty in the age of AI and Web3. SSRN *Electronic Journal*. https://doi.org/DOI: 10.2139/ssrn.5081504

Calzada, I. (2024). Decentralized Web3 Reshaping Internet Governance: Towards the Emergence of New Forms of Nation-Statehood? *Future Internet*, *16*(10), 361. Advance online publication. DOI: 10.3390/fi16100361

Cannon-Bowers, J., & Bowers, C. (2009). Synthetic learning environments: On developing a science of simulation, games, and virtual worlds for training. In *Learning, training, and development in organizations* (pp. 229–261). Routledge.

Carlini, N., Tramèr, F., Wallace, E., Jagielski, M., Herbert-Voss, A., Lee, K., Roberts, A., Brown, T., Song, D., Erlingsson, Ú., Oprea, A., & Raffel, C. (2021). *Extracting training data from large language models. In 30th USENIX Security Symposium (USENIX Security 21)*. USENIX Association., https://www.usenix.org/system/files/sec21-carlini-extracting.pdf

Carrapico, H., & Farrand, B. (2025). EU data sovereignty: An autonomy–interdependence governance gap? *Politics and Governance*, *13*, 10331. Advance online publication. DOI: 10.17645/pag.10331

Casino, F., Pina, C., López-Aguilar, P., Batista, E., Solanas, A., & Patsakis, C. (2022). SoK: Cross-border criminal investigations and digital evidence. *Journal of Cybersecurity*, *8*(1), tyac014. DOI: 10.1093/cybsec/tyac014

Catalini, C., & Gans, J. S. (2020). Some Simple Economics of the Blockchain. *Communications of the ACM*, *63*(7), 80–90. DOI: 10.1145/3359552

Catanzariti, M. (2024). *Disconnecting sovereignty: How data fragmentation reshapes the law*. Springer., DOI: 10.1007/978-3-031-60734-9

Cath, C., Wachter, S., Mittelstadt, B., Taddeo, M., & Floridi, L. (2018). Artificial intelligence and the "good society": The US, EU, and UK approach. *Science and Engineering Ethics*, *24*(2), 505–528. DOI: 10.1007/s11948-017-9901-7 PMID: 28353045

Cennamo, C., & Karanovic, J. (2025). Are Social Media Platforms a Threat to Democracy? An Ecosystem Governance Perspective. *Journal of Management Studies*. Advance online publication. DOI: 10.1111/joms.70044

CERT-In. (2022). Directions under sub-section (6) of section 70B of the Information Technology Act, 2000 relating to information security practices, procedure, prevention, response and reporting of cyber incidents. https://www.cert-in.org.in/PDF/CERT-In_Directions_70B_28.04.2022.pdf

Chang, L. Y. (2020). Legislative frameworks against cybercrime: The Budapest convention and Asia. The Palgrave handbook of international cybercrime and cyberdeviance, 327-343.

Charter of Fundamental Rights of the European Union. (2000/C 364/01). (2000). *Official Journal of the European Communities*, C 364, 1–22. https://www.europarl.europa.eu/charter/pdf/text_en.pdf

Chawki, M. (2024). Navigating legal challenges of deepfakes in the American context: A call to action. *Cogent Engineering*, *11*(1), 2320971. DOI: 10.1080/23311916.2024.2320971

Chen, S., Piet, J., Sitawarin, C., & Wagner, D. (2025). *StruQ: Defending against prompt injection with structured queries. In 34th USENIX Security Symposium (USENIX Security 25).* USENIX Association., https://www.usenix.org/system/files/usenixsecurity25-chen-sizhe.pdf

Chesney, B., & Citron, D. (2019). Deep fakes: A looming challenge for privacy, democracy, and national security. *California Law Review*, *107*(6), 1753–1820. DOI: 10.15779/Z38RV0D15J

Chesterman, S. (2021). *We, the robots?: Regulating artificial intelligence and the limits of the law*. Cambridge University Press., DOI: 10.1017/9781009047081

Clarifying Lawful Overseas Use of Data Act, Pub. L. No. 115–141, § 103, 132 Stat. 348, 1213 (2018).

Clayton, R., Murdoch, S. J., & Watson, R. N. M. (2006). Ignoring the great firewall of China. In *Proceedings of the 6th International Workshop on Privacy Enhancing Technologies* (pp. 1–13). PET., https://www.cl.cam.ac.uk/~rnc1/ignoring.pdf DOI: 10.1007/11957454_2

Coche, E., Kolk, A., & Ocelík, V. (2024). Unravelling cross-country regulatory intricacies of data governance: The relevance of legal insights for digitalization and international business. *Journal of International Business Policy*, *7*(1), 112–127. DOI: 10.1057/s42214-023-00172-1

Couldry, N., & Mejias, U. A. (2019). The costs of connection: How data is colonizing human life and appropriating it for capitalism. In *The costs of connection*. Stanford University Press.

Court of Justice of the European Union. (2015, October 6). *Maximillian Schrems v. Data Protection Commissioner* (Case C-362/14), [2015] ECLI:EU:C:2015:650.

Court of Justice of the European Union. (2020, July 16). *Data Protection Commissioner v. Facebook Ireland Ltd and Maximillian Schrems* (Case C-311/18), [2020] ECLI:EU:C:2020:559.

Couture, S., & Toupin, S. (2019). What does the notion of "sovereignty" mean when referring to the digital? *New Media & Society*, *21*(10), 2305–2322. DOI: 10.1177/1461444819865984

Creemers, R. (2022). China's Emerging Data Protection Framework. *Journal of Cybersecurity*, *8*(1), tyac011. Advance online publication. DOI: 10.1093/cybsec/tyac011

Crémer, J., De Montjoye, Y. A., & Schweitzer, H. (2019). *Competition policy for the digital era*. Publications Office of the European Union.

Custodi, J., Trenz, H. J., & Moland, M. (2026). Countering Post-Truth: A Comparative Study of Journalists' Responses to Disinformation Challenges. *Journalism & Mass Communication Quarterly*, *103*(1), 114–133. DOI: 10.1177/10776990251393745

Cybersecurity Law of the People's Republic of China (promulgated by the Standing Comm. Nat'l People's Cong., Nov. 7, 2016, effective June 1, 2017). http://www.npc.gov.cn/englishnpc/c23934/202012/1abd8829788946ecab270e469e13c39c.shtml

Czerniawski, M. (2025). *EU's Digital Sovereignty and the Rights-Based Imperative: Linking Enforcement, Competences and Fundamental Rights*. VerfBlog., DOI: 10.59704/221c82ced6d670b6

Dahiya, K., & Sharma, U. (2025). Navigating the Digital Mirage: A Comparative Analysis of Deepfake Challenges and Responses Across BRICS Nations and the Global Arena. In *Navigating the Deepfake Conundrum: A Manager's Roadmap* (pp. 239–261). Springer. DOI: 10.1007/978-3-031-90742-5_16

Damame, L. J. (2025). Digital platforms as supranational regulators: Reconfiguring state power in the digital era. *Beijing Law Review*, *16*(4), 2089–2105. DOI: 10.4236/blr.2025.164105

Daskal, J. (2018). *Microsoft Ireland, the CLOUD Act, and International Lawmaking 2.0.* SLR. https://www.stanfordlawreview.org/online/microsoft-ireland-cloud-act-international-lawmaking-2-0/

Data Protection Africa. (2026). *Which African Countries Have a Data Protection Law?* https://dataprotection.africa/which-african-countries-have-a-data-protection-law

Data Security Law of the People's Republic of China (promulgated by the Standing Comm. Nat'l People's Cong., June 10, 2021, effective Sept. 1, 2021). http://www.npc.gov.cn/englishnpc/c23934/202112/31728d2983694038879 6593a86377771.shtml

Davidson, S., De Filippi, P., & Potts, J. (2018). Blockchains and the Economic Institutions of Capitalism. *Journal of Institutional Economics*, *14*(4), 639–658. DOI: 10.1017/S1744137417000200

Davis, K. (2012). *Governance by indicators: Global power through classification and rankings*. Oxford University Press. DOI: 10.1093/acprof:oso/9780199658244.001.0001

Davis, K. E. (2019). *Between impunity and imperialism: The regulation of transnational bribery*. Oxford University Press. DOI: 10.1093/oso/9780190070809.001.0001

De Almeida, P. G. R., Dos Santos, C. D., & Farias, J. S. (2021). Artificial intelligence regulation: A framework for governance. *Ethics and Information Technology*, *23*(3), 505–525. DOI: 10.1007/s10676-021-09593-z

de Silva de Alwis, R. (2024). Gendering the new international convention on cybercrimes and new norms on artificial intelligence and emerging technologies. *Wash. JL Tech. & Arts*, *20*, 1.

Deane, F., Woolmer, E., Cao, S., & Tranter, K. (2024). Trade in the digital age: Agreements to mitigate fragmentation. *Asian Journal of International Law*, *14*(1), 154–179. DOI: 10.1017/S204425132300036X

DeFiLlama. (2026). “RWA Protocols.” *DeFiLlama*.

Deighton, J., & Kornfeld, L. (2025). Measuring the Digital Economy. Interactive Advertising Bureau (IAB), 1-179.

DeNardis, L., & Hackl, A. M. (2015). Internet governance by social media platforms. *Telecommunications Policy*, *39*(9), 761–770. DOI: 10.1016/j.telpol.2015.04.003

Desrosières, A. (1998). *The politics of large numbers: A history of statistical reasoning*. Harvard University Press. Eubanks, V. Automating Inequality: How High-Tech Tools Profile, Police, and Punish the Poor. In: HeinOnline.

Diakopoulos, N., & Johnson, D. (2021). Anticipating and addressing the ethical implications of deepfakes in the context of elections. *New Media & Society*, *23*(7), 2072–2098. DOI: 10.1177/1461444820925811

Díaz Vera, L. M. (2023). Non-personal data regulation — A latin american perspective. *GRUR International*, *72*(1), 37–53. DOI: 10.1093/grurint/ikac123

Ding, J. (2018). *Deciphering China's AI Dream.* Future of Humanity Institute, University of Oxford. http://advancedinvestor.com/resources/Research-Materials/China/China_AI_Dream.pdf

Ding, X., Huang, H., Shi, Z., Li, Y., Chen, M., & Wang, J. (2025). Same text, different meaning: China's risk-based approach to data protection. *Humanities & Social Sciences Communications, 12*(1), 1821. DOI: 10.1057/s41599-025-06100-3

Doneda, D., & Zanatta, R. A. F. (2022). *Personality Rights in Brazilian Data Protection Law: A Historical Perspective.* Springer Nature Link. https://link.springer.com/chapter/10.1007/978-3-030-90331-2_3

Dong, H., & Chen, J. (2024). Meta-regulation: An ideal alternative to the primary responsibility as the regulatory model of generative AI in China. *Computer Law & Security Review, 54*, 106016. DOI: 10.1016/j.clsr.2024.106016

Dragomir, M., & Túñez López, M. (2024). How public service media are changing in the platform era: A comparative study across four European countries. *European Journal of Communication, 39*(6), 608–624. DOI: 10.1177/02673231241290062

El Erafy, A. N. (2023). Applications of Artificial Intelligence in the field of media. *International Journal of Artificial Intelligence and Emerging Technology, 6*(2), 19–41. DOI: 10.21608/ijaiet.2024.275179.1006

Elijah, J. (2025). *Navigating the Legal Challenges of Cybersecurity and Forensic Evidence in the Digital Era*. Law Nectar.

Elliot, M., Mandalari, A. M., Mourby, M., & O'Hara, K. (2024). *Dictionary of privacy, data protection and information security*. Edward Elgar Publishing.

Elo, S., & Kyngäs, H. (2008). The qualitative content analysis process. *Journal of Advanced Nursing, 62*(1), 107–115. DOI: 10.1111/j.1365-2648.2007.04569.x PMID: 18352969

Elsheikh, D., Jackson, D., & Jebril, N. (2025). Journalism in transitional context: Societal hostility, self-censorship and the expansion of "one voice journalism". *Journalism Practice, 19*(9), 1921–1939. DOI: 10.1080/17512786.2024.2308526

Emmanuel, C. E., & Alofe, O. E. (2025). Technology Regulation in National and International Contexts: Normative Frameworks and Emerging Trends. Law And Social Justice Review, 6(2).

Esezoobo, S. O., Adebayo, M. E., & Chiobi, N. F. (2022). *Privacy and Legal Guardrails for Deepfake AI in Continuous Delivery Environments: Preventing Misuse and Ensuring Traceability in Generative Media and Security Applications.*

Eubanks, V. (2018). *Automating inequality: How high-tech tools profile, police, and punish the poor.* Macmillan+ ORM.

European Commission. (2022). *Digital Services Package.* Brussels. https://ec.europa.eu/commission/presscorner/api/files/document/print/en/ip_22_4313/IP_22_4313_EN.pdf

European Parliament. (2024). Artificial Intelligence Act (2021/0106(COD))—Procedure document summary (final act) (Regulation (EU) 2024/1689). https://oeil.europarl.europa.eu/oeil/en/procedure-document-summary/pdf?id=1786308

European Union. (2016). Regulation (EU) 2016/679 of the European Parliament and of the Council. *Regulation (Eu), 679*, 10–13.

European Union. (2022). Directive (EU) 2022/2555 of the European Parliament and of the Council of 14 December 2022 on measures for a high common level of cybersecurity across the Union (NIS2). EUR-Lex. https://eur-lex.europa.eu/legal-content/EN/TXT/?uri=CELEX:32022L2555

Evgenii, N., & Cocou, M. M. (2020). Unified Digital Law Enforcement Environment-Necessity and Prospects for Creation in the "BRICS Countries". BRICS law journal, 7(2), 66-93.

Ewulum, C. (2023). The legal regime for cross-border data transfer in Africa: a critical analysis. Available at *SSRN* 4546964. DOI: 10.2139/ssrn.4546964

Falkner, G., Heidebrecht, S., Obendiek, A., & Seidl, T. (2024). Digital sovereignty: Rhetoric and reality. *Journal of European Public Policy*, *31*(8), 2099–2120. DOI: 10.1080/13501763.2024.2358984

Farah Hersi, M., & Akinola, A. O. (2024). Pan-Africanism and Regional Integration. In *IGAD and Multilateral Security in the Horn of Africa: Through the Lens of the Somali Conflict* (pp. 13–34). Springer Nature Switzerland. DOI: 10.1007/978-3-031-51548-4_2

Farid, H. (2022). Creating, using, misusing, and detecting deep fakes. *Journal of Online Trust & Safety*, *1*(4). Advance online publication. DOI: 10.54501/jots.v1i4.56

Farouk, M. A., & Fahmi, B. M. (2024). Deepfakes and media integrity: Navigating the new reality of synthetic content. *Journal of Media and Interdisciplinary Studies*, *3*(9), 47–94. DOI: 10.21608/jmis.2024.275298.1027

Figueira, A., & Vaz, B. (2022). Survey on synthetic data generation, evaluation methods and GANs. *Mathematics*, *10*(15), 2733. DOI: 10.3390/math10152733

Fischer, A. (2023). Data sovereignty and e-governance: The legal implications of national laws on digital government systems. *Legal Studies in Digital Age*, *2*(4), 1–12.

Flensburg, S., & Lomborg, S. (2023). Datafication research: Mapping the field for a future agenda. *New Media & Society*, *25*(6), 1451–1469. DOI: 10.1177/14614448211046616

Flew, T., & Martin, F. R. (2022). *Digital platform regulation: Global perspectives on internet governance*. Palgrave Macmillan., DOI: 10.1007/978-3-030-95220-4

Flonk, D., Jachtenfuchs, M., & Obendiek, A. (2024). Controlling internet content in the EU: Towards digital sovereignty. *Journal of European Public Policy*, *31*(8), 2316–2342. DOI: 10.1080/13501763.2024.2309179

Floridi, L. (2020). The fight for digital sovereignty: What it is, and why it matters, especially for the EU. *Philosophy & Technology*, *33*(3), 369–378. DOI: 10.1007/s13347-020-00423-6 PMID: 35194548

Floridi, L., Cowls, J., Beltrametti, M., Chatila, R., Chazerand, P., Dignum, V., Luetge, C., Madelin, R., Pagallo, U., Rossi, F., Schafer, B., Valcke, P., & Vayena, E. (2018). AI4People—An ethical framework for a good AI society: Opportunities, risks, principles, and recommendations. *Minds and Machines*, *28*(4), 689–707. DOI: 10.1007/s11023-018-9482-5

Foucault, M. (1977). *Discipline and punish: The birth ofthe prison*. Allen Lane.

Foucault, M. (1991). *The Foucault effect: Studies in governmentality*. University of Chicago Press.

Fraga-Lamas, P., & Fernandez-Carames, T. M. (2020). Fake news, disinformation, and deepfakes: Leveraging distributed ledger technologies and blockchain to combat digital deception and counterfeit reality. *IT Professional*, *22*(2), 53–59. DOI: 10.1109/MITP.2020.2977589

Fratini, S., Hine, E., Novelli, C., Roberts, H., & Floridi, L. (2024). Digital sovereignty: A descriptive analysis and a critical evaluation of existing models. *Digital Society : Ethics, Socio-Legal and Governance of Digital Technology*, *3*(3), 59. DOI: 10.1007/s44206-024-00146-7

Fuchs, C., Hofkirchner, W., Schafranek, M., Raffl, C., Sandoval, M., & Bichler, R. (2010). Theoretical Foundations of the Web: Cognition, Communication, and Co-Operation. towards an Understanding of Web 1.0, 2.0, 3.0. *Future Internet*, *2*(1), 41–59. DOI: 10.3390/fi2010041

Gabel, J. M. (2026). *European Union.* https://www.britannica.com/topic/European-Union

Gangavarapu, R. (2025). *Mastering AI Governance.* Springer. DOI: 10.1007/978-3-031-93681-4

Ganz, A., Camellini, M., Hine, E., Novelli, C., Roberts, H., & Floridi, L. (2024). Submarine cables and the risks to digital sovereignty. *Minds and Machines*, *34*(3), 1–23. DOI: 10.1007/s11023-024-09683-z

Gao, R. Y. (2023). A battle of the big three? — Competing conceptualizations of personal data shaping transnational data flows. *Chinese Journal of International Law*, *22*(4), 707–787. DOI: 10.1093/chinesejil/jmad040

Garganas, O. (2024). Digital video advertising: Breakthrough or extension of TV advertising in the new digital media landscape? *Journalism and Media*, *5*(2), 749–765. DOI: 10.3390/journalmedia5020049

Gaweł, H. (2022). "Web 2.5 as a Safe Shift from Web 2.0 to Web 3.0: A Definition of Web 2.5 in Informatological Approach." *Cambridge Open Engage* 1–15. DOI: 10.33774/coe-2022-sj2w3

Gawer, A. (2022). Digital platforms and ecosystems: Remarks on the dominant organizational forms of the digital age. *Innovation (North Sydney, N.S.W.)*, *24*(1), 110–124. DOI: 10.1080/14479338.2021.1965888

George, A. S., Baskar, T., & Pandey, D. (2024). Establishing global ai accountability: Training data transparency, copyright, and misinformation. *Partners Universal Innovative Research Publication*, *2*(3), 75–91.

George, A. S., & George, A. S. H. (2023). Deepfakes: The evolution of hyper realistic media manipulation. *Partners Universal Innovative Research Publication*, *1*(2), 58–74.

Ghiurău, D., & Popescu, D. E. (2024). Distinguishing reality from AI: Approaches for detecting synthetic content. *Computers*, *14*(1), 1. DOI: 10.3390/computers14010001

Giannopoulou, A. (2023). Digital identity infrastructures: A critical approach of self-sovereign identity. *Digital Society : Ethics, Socio-Legal and Governance of Digital Technology*, *2*(2), 18. DOI: 10.1007/s44206-023-00049-z PMID: 37200582

Gillespie, T. (2018). *Custodians of the Internet.* Yale University.

Gillespie, T. (2018). *Custodians of the Internet: Platforms, content moderation, and the hidden decisions that shape social media.* Yale University Press.

Glasze, G., Cattaruzza, A., Douzet, F., Dammann, F., Bertran, M.-G., Bômont, C., Braun, M., Danet, D., Desforges, A., Géry, A., Grumbach, S., Hummel, P., Limonier, K., Münßinger, M., Nicolai, F., Pétiniaud, L., Winkler, J., & Zanin, C. (2023). Contested spatialities of digital sovereignty. *Geopolitics*, *28*(2), 919–958. DOI: 10.1080/14650045.2022.2050070

Goncharenko, G. (2019). The accountability of advocacy NGOs: Insights from the online community of practice. *Accounting Forum*, *43*(1), 135–160. DOI: 10.1080/01559982.2019.1589901

Goodfellow, I. J., Pouget-Abadie, J., Mirza, M., Xu, B., Warde-Farley, D., Ozair, S., Courville, A., & Bengio, Y. (2014). Generative adversarial nets. *Proceedings. Neurips.CcI Goodfellow, J Pouget-Abadie, M Mirza, B Xu, D Warde-Farley, S Ozair, A CourvilleAdvances in Neural Information Processing Systems, 2014•proceedings. Neurips.Cc.* https://proceedings.neurips.cc/paper/5423-generative-adversarial-nets

Gordon, G. (2024). Digital sovereignty, digital infrastructures, and quantum horizons. *AI & Society*, *39*(1), 125–137. DOI: 10.1007/s00146-023-01729-7

Gorwa, R. (2019). What is platform governance? *Information Communication and Society*, *22*(6), 854–871. DOI: 10.1080/1369118X.2019.1573914

Gorwa, R., Binns, R., & Katzenbach, C. (2020). Algorithmic content moderation: Technical and political challenges in the automation of platform governance. *Big Data & Society*, *7*(1), 2053951719897945. DOI: 10.1177/2053951719897945

Government of India, Ministry of Electronics and Information Technology. (2023). The Digital Personal Data Protection Act, 2023. https://www.meity.gov.in/static/uploads/2024/06/2bf1f0e9f04e6fb4f8fef35e82c42aa5.pdf

Government of India. (2023). *The digital personal data protection act, 2023.* https://www.meity.gov.in/static/uploads/2024/06/2bf1f0e9f04e6fb4f8fef35e82c42aa5.pdf

Government of Indonesia. (2019). *Government regulation of the republic of indonesia no. 71 of 2019 on the implementation of electronic systems and transactions.* https://peraturan.bpk.go.id/Details/122030/pp-no-71-tahun-2019

Government of Indonesia. (2022). *Law of the republic of indonesia no. 27 of 2022 on personal data protection.* https://peraturan.bpk.go.id/Details/229798/uu-no-27-tahun-2022

Grand View Research. (2025). *Blockchain Technology Market Size & Outlook, 2030. Horizon Databook.* https://www.grandviewresearch.com/industry-analysis/blockchain-technology-market/dashboard

Green, Leslie. (nd). The *Normativity of Law: What is the Problem?* University of Victoria, Canada. https://www.uvic.ca/victoria-colloquium/assets/docs/Green_Normativity.pdf#

Greenleaf, G. (2025). *Global Data Privacy Laws 2025: 172 Countries, Twelve New in 2023/24.* Macquarie Law School. https://papers.ssrn.com/sol3/papers.cfm?abstract_id=5275559

Gregory, S. (2022). Deepfakes, misinformation and disinformation and authenticity infrastructure responses: Impacts on frontline witnessing, distant witnessing, and civic journalism. *Journalism, 23*(3), 708–729. DOI: 10.1177/14648849211060644

Greven, M. T. (2020). The informalization of transnational governance: A threat to democratic government. In *Die Erosion der Demokratie: Beiträge von Michael Th. Greven zur kritischen Demokratietheorie* (pp. 107–131). Springer Fachmedien Wiesbaden. DOI: 10.1007/978-3-658-27920-2_6

Guan, C. (2025). Cross-Border Cybercrime Digital Evidence: Current Research and Fundamental Categories. *Modern Law Research, 6*(4).

Guerrero, O. A., & Margetts, H. (2024). Are all policymakers data scientists now? data, data science and evidence in policymaking. *LSE Public Policy Review*, *3*(3), 9. DOI: 10.31389/lseppr.116

HACKEN. (2025). "What Is Web2.5? A Builder's Guide to the Web2–Web3 Bridge." https://hacken.io/discover/web2-web3-bridge/

Haenig, M. A., & Ji, X. (2024). A tale of two Southeast Asian states: Media governance and authoritarian regimes in Singapore and Vietnam. *Asian Review of Political Economy*, *3*(1), 4. DOI: 10.1007/s44216-024-00024-6

Hajjej, F., Hamid, M., & Alluhaidan, A. S. (2026). An integrated framework for proactive deepfake mitigation via attention-driven watermarking and blockchain-based authenticity verification. *Scientific Reports*, *16*(1), 9545. DOI: 10.1038/s41598-026-40166-6

Handapangoda, C. (2026). Cross-border data security and privacy risks in large language models and IoT systems. *arXiv preprint arXiv:2601.06612*. https://arxiv.org/abs/2601.06612

Han, S. (2024). Data and statecraft: Why and how states localize data. *Business and Politics*, *26*(2), 263–288. DOI: 10.1017/bap.2023.41

Hastuti, H., Maulana, H. F., Lawelai, H., & Suherman, A. (2025). Algorithmic influence and media legitimacy: A systematic review of social media's impact on news production. *Frontiers in Communication, 10*, 1667471. DOI: 10.3389/fcomm.2025.1667471

Hausman, D. M. (1992). *The Inexact and Separate Science of Economics*. Cambridge University Press. DOI: 10.1017/CBO9780511752032

He, S., Lei, Y., Zhang, Z., Sun, Y., Li, S., Zhang, C., & Ye, J. (2025). Identity deepfake threats to biometric authentication systems: Public and expert perspectives. *ArXiv Preprint ArXiv:2506.06825.*

Helberger, N., Pierson, J., & Poell, T. (2018). Governing online platforms: From contested to cooperative responsibility. *The Information Society*, *34*(1), 1–14.

Helmond, A. (2015). The platformization of the web: Making web data platform ready. *Social Media + Society*, *1*(2), 1–11. DOI: 10.1177/2056305115603080

Hevner, A. R., March, S. T., Park, J., & Ram, S. (2004). Design science in information systems research. *Management Information Systems Quarterly*, *28*(1), 75–105. DOI: 10.2307/25148625

He, X., & Fang, L. (2024). Regulatory Challenges in Synthetic Media Governance: Policy Frameworks for AI-Generated Content Across Image, Video, and Social Platforms. *Journal of Robotic Process Automation, AI Integration, and Workflow Optimization*, *9*(12), 36–54.

Hinsley, F. H. (1986). *Sovereign*. Cambridge University Press.

Hodgson, G. M. (2001). *How Economics Forgot History:The Problem of Historical Specificity in Social Science Economics As Social Theory*. Taylor & Francis Routledge. DOI: 10.4324/9780203519813

Hodgson, G. M. (2013). *From Pleasure Machines to Moral Communities: An Evolutionary Economics without Homo Economicus*. The University of Chicago Press.

Hoffmann-Riem, W. (2019). Artificial intelligence as a challenge for law and regulation. In *Regulating artificial intelligence* (pp. 1–29). Springer.

Hoofnagle, C. J., Van Der Sloot, B., & Borgesius, F. Z. (2019). The European Union general data protection regulation: What it is and what it means. *Information & Communications Technology Law*, *28*(1), 65–98. DOI: 10.1080/13600834.2019.1573501

Horneber, D., & Laumer, S. (2023). Algorithmic accountability. *Business & Information Systems Engineering*, *65*(6), 723–730. DOI: 10.1007/s12599-023-00817-8

Hossin, M. A., Du, J., Mu, L., & Asante, I. O. (2023). Big data-driven public policy decisions: Transformation toward smart governance. *SAGE Open*, *13*(4), 21582440231215123. DOI: 10.1177/21582440231215123

Hsieh, H.-F., & Shannon, S. E. (2005). Three approaches to qualitative content analysis. *Qualitative Health Research*, *15*(9), 1277–1288. DOI: 10.1177/1049732305276687 PMID: 16204405

Hsieh, Y. Y., & Vergne, J. P. (2023). The Future of the Web? The Coordination and Early-Stage Growth of Decentralized Platforms. *Strategic Management Journal*, *44*(3), 829–857. DOI: 10.1002/smj.3455

Huang, V. G. (2024). “BlackRock Launches First Tokenized Fund on Ethereum Blockchain.” *The Wall Street Journal*, March 21.

Hurrah, N. N., Parah, S. A., Loan, N. A., Sheikh, J. A., Elhoseny, M., & Muhammad, K. (2019). Dual watermarking framework for privacy protection and content authentication of multimedia. *Future Generation Computer Systems*, *94*, 654–673. DOI: 10.1016/j.future.2018.12.036

IMF. (2025). “CRYPTO-ASSET MONITOR: 2Q25.” *International Monetary Fund* 1–11.

India, A. I. (2024). *Cabinet approves india AI mission at an outlay of rs 10,372 crore*. https://indiaai.gov.in/news/cabinet-approves-india-ai-mission-at-an-outlay-of-rs-10-372-crore

Infocomm Media Development Authority, & Personal Data Protection Commission. (2020). Model Artificial Intelligence Governance Framework (2nd ed.). https://www.imda.gov.sg/-/media/imda/files/infocomm-media-landscape/sg-digital/tech-pillars/artificial-intelligence/second-edition-of-the-model-ai-governance-framework.pdf

Ingersleben-Seip, N. (2025). A tale of two metaverses: How America, China, and Europe are shaping the “new internet.”. *Politics and Governance*, *13*, 10246. Advance online publication. DOI: 10.17645/pag.10246

International Organization for Standardization. (2023a). ISO/IEC 23894:2023, Information technology—Artificial intelligence—Guidance on risk management. https://www.iso.org/standard/77304.html

International Organization for Standardization. (2023b). ISO/IEC 42001:2023, Information technology—Artificial intelligence—Management system. https://www.iso.org/standard/81230.html

Irion, K. (2012). Government cloud computing and national data sovereignty. *Policy and Internet*, *4*(3–4), 40–71. DOI: 10.1002/poi3.10

Ishkhanyan, A. (2025a). Governing AI across borders: corporate power, state sovereignty and global regulation. *Digital Policy, Regulation and Governance*.

Ishkhanyan, A. (2025b). The sovereignty-internationalism paradox in AI governance: Digital federalism and global algorithmic control. *Discover Artificial Intelligence*, *5*(1), 123. DOI: 10.1007/s44163-025-00374-x

Ishkhanyan, A. (2026). Governing AI across borders: Corporate power, state sovereignty and global regulation. Digital Policy. *Regulation & Governance*, *28*(3), 280–295.

Islam, M. B. E., Haseeb, M., Batool, H., Ahtasham, N., & Muhammad, Z. (2024). AI threats to politics, elections, and democracy: A blockchain-based deepfake authenticity verification framework. *Blockchains*, *2*(4), 458–481. DOI: 10.3390/blockchains2040020

Islam, M. T., & Khan, B. U. (2024). Impacts of data localization policies and lessons for bangladesh. *International Data Privacy Law*, *14*(2), 150–168. DOI: 10.1093/idpl/ipae002

Jamil, S. (2022). Digital transformation in journalism: Implications of media convergence for journalists' work in Pakistan's mainstream news media. In *Die digitale Transformation der Medien: Leitmedien im Wandel* (pp. 443-458). Wiesbaden: Springer Fachmedien Wiesbaden. DOI: 10.1007/978-3-658-36276-8_21

Jan, E. (2025). Mitigating Deepfake Risks in Cloud Data Environments: Privacy and Security Lessons from Cross-Border Data Transfer Case Studies. *Available at SSRN* 5359940. DOI: 10.2139/ssrn.5359940

Jansen, B., Kadenko, N., Broeders, D., van Eeten, M., Borgolte, K., & Fiebig, T. (2023). Pushing boundaries: An empirical view on the digital sovereignty of six governments in the midst of geopolitical tensions. *Government Information Quarterly*, *40*(4), 101862. Advance online publication. DOI: 10.1016/j.giq.2023.101862

Janssen, M., Brous, P., Estevez, E., Barbosa, L. S., & Janowski, T. (2020). Data governance: Organizing data for trustworthy artificial intelligence. *Government Information Quarterly*, *37*(3), 101493. Advance online publication. DOI: 10.1016/j.giq.2020.101493

Janssen, M., Charalabidis, Y., & Zuiderwijk, A. (2012). Benefits, adoption barriers and myths of open data and open government. *Information Systems Management*, *29*(4), 258–268. DOI: 10.1080/10580530.2012.716740

Jean, N., Burke, M., Xie, M., Alampay Davis, W. M., Lobell, D. B., & Ermon, S. (2016). Combining satellite imagery and machine learning to predict poverty. *Science*, *353*(6301), 790–794. DOI: 10.1126/science.aaf7894 PMID: 27540167

Jiang, M. (2024). Models of state digital sovereignty from the global south: Diverging experiences from China, India and South Africa. *Policy and Internet*, *16*(4), 727–738. DOI: 10.1002/poi3.427

Jiang, S. (2025). Fragmented rules, global flows: How legal differences shape the cross-border data landscape-Evidence from the EU, US, and China. *Lecture Notes in Education Psychology and Public Media*, *96*(1), 47–57. DOI: 10.54254/2753-7048/2025.BO23772

JinCheng. Z., & Chuen, D. L. K. (2024). Understanding the Evolution of the Internet: Web 1.0 to Web3. 0, Web3, and Web 3+. In Handbook of Digital Currency (pp. 553-581). Academic Press.

Joris van Hoboken, R. Ó. (2021, July). Fathaigh, Smartphone platforms as privacy regulators. *Computer Law & Security Review*, *41*, 105557. Advance online publication. DOI: 10.1016/j.clsr.2021.105557

Justice K.S. Puttaswamy (Retd.) v. *Union of India* (2017) 10 SCC 1

Kalin, R. P. (2024). *Digital trade and data privacy: Cross-border flows of personal data between data protection and data protectionism*. Springer., DOI: 10.1007/978-3-031-73857-9

Kalpokas, I. (2020). Problematising reality: The promises and perils of synthetic media. *SN Social Sciences*, *1*(1), 1. DOI: 10.1007/s43545-020-00010-8

Kaludewage, P. M. W. (2025). *Real-World Challenges and Adoption of Deepfake Detection Technologies in Digital Media Forensics*.

Kanki, K., & Resch, A. (2024). Strengthening International Law Enforcement Cooperation: INTERPOL and Its Global Fight against Economic and Financial Crime. In Corporate Criminal Liability and Sanctions (pp. 106-126). Routledge.

Karjalainen, T. (2022). The battle of power: Enforcing data protection law against companies holding data power. *Computer Law & Security Review*, *47*, 105742. DOI: 10.1016/j.clsr.2022.105742

Karnouskos, S. (2020). Artificial intelligence in digital media: The era of deepfakes. *IEEE Transactions on Technology and Society*, *1*(3), 138–147. DOI: 10.1109/TTS.2020.3001312

Kavanagh, C. (2022). *New Tech, New Threats, and New Governance Challenges: An Opportunity to Craft Smarter Responses?* Carnegie Endowment for International Peace.

Kaya, M., & Shahid, H. (2025). Cross-border data flows and digital sovereignty: Legal dilemmas in transnational governance. *Interdisciplinary Studies in Society, Law, and Politics*, *4*(2), 219–233. DOI: 10.61838/kman.isslp.4.2.20

Kaye, D. (2019). *Speech Police: The Global Struggle to Govern the Internet.* Columbia Global Reports. https://globalreports.columbia.edu/books/speech-police

Keller, D. (2021). Amplification and its discontents: Why regulating the reach of online content is hard. *J. Free Speech L.*, *1*, 227.

Kenney, M., & Zysman, J. (2016). The Rise of the Platform Economy. *Issues in Science and Technology*, *32*(3). https://issues.org/rise-platform-economy-big-data-work/

Khadka, R. (2025). Navigating the Legal Landscape of AI-Created Content: Intellectual Property, Accountability, and Regulation. *International Scientific Journal of Engineering and Management*, *04*(04), 1–7. DOI: 10.55041/ISJEM03055

Khalfa, R., & Hardyns, W. (2024). 'Led by Intelligence': A Scoping Review on the Experimental Evaluation of Intelligence-Led Policing. *Evaluation Review*, *48*(5), 797–847. DOI: 10.1177/0193841X231204588 PMID: 37864492

Khan, M. N. I. (2023). Legal documentation and case management: a systematic review of digitization trends and cybersecurity challenges in legal support roles. Review of Applied Science and Technology, 2(01), 01-25.

Khanal, S., Zhang, H., & Taeihagh, A. (2026). The rise of Big Tech as super policy entrepreneurs. *Policy and Society*, puag005. Advance online publication. DOI: 10.1093/polsoc/puag005

Khan, L. M. (2017). Amazon's Antitrust Paradox. *The Yale Law Journal.*

Kiberg, H., Olsen, G. R., Krumsvik, A., Kalsnes, B., Kavtaradze, L., & Steensen, S. (2025). Navigating Platform Dependency: Four Strategic Approaches for Social Media News Publishing. *Journalism Studies*, •••, 1–19. DOI: 10.1080/1461670X.2025.2608960

Kietzmann, J., Mills, A. J., & Plangger, K. (2020). Deepfakes: Perspectives on the future "reality" of advertising and branding. *International Journal of Advertising*, *40*(3), 473–485. DOI: 10.1080/02650487.2020.1834211

Kim, H. Y. (2024). What's wrong with relying on targeted advertising? Targeting the business model of social media platforms. *Critical Review of International Social and Political Philosophy*, •••, 1–21. DOI: 10.1080/13698230.2024.2309047

Kim, J., & Ahn, S. (2025). The platform policy matrix: Promotion and regulation. *Policy and Internet*, *17*(1), e414. DOI: 10.1002/poi3.414

Kishwar, S. D., Tripathi, A., Khatoon, S., Poddar, D., & Khurana, B. (2025). Regulating deep fakes and synthetic media: Privacy, policy and global regulatory challenges. *Journal of Data Protection & Privacy*, *8*(1), 78–96. DOI: 10.69554/HBGG8150

Kissorio, T. K. (2022). Effectiveness of Intelligence-Led Policing in Prevention of Crime by the Directorate of Criminal Investigation in Mombasa County, Kenya. An Unpublished Master of Security Management and Police Studies. Thesis, Kenyatta University, Kenya. https://irlibrary. ku. ac. ke/items/6ef854a3-7d68-4b5a-927e-3113f19b08d9.

Knight, J. B. (1977). "Economics: The State of Play." *Social Dynamics. Social Dynamics*, *3*(2), 34–40. DOI: 10.1080/02533957708458201

Knorr, C., & Pentzold, C. (2025). Making sense of "big data": Ten years of discourse around datafication. *Big Data & Society*, *12*(2), 20539517251330181. DOI: 10.1177/20539517251330181

Kokas, A. (2022). *Trafficking data: How china is winning the battle for digital sovereignty*. Oxford University Press., DOI: 10.1093/oso/9780197620502.001.0001

Kokshagina, O., Reinecke, P. C., & Karanasios, S. (2023). To regulate or not to regulate: Unravelling institutional tussles around the regulation of algorithmic control of digital platforms. *Journal of Information Technology*, *38*(2), 160–179. DOI: 10.1177/02683962221114408

Kopecky, S. (2024). Challenges of deepfakes. *Science and Information Conference*, 158–166.

KORIKA. (2020). *Strategi nasional kecerdasan artifisial indonesia 2020–2045*. Kolaborasi Riset dan Inovasi Industri Kecerdasan Artifisial. https://korika.id/wp-content/uploads/2024/07/stranas-ka-2045.pdf

Koskinen, J., Knaapi-Junnila, S., Helin, A., Rantanen, M. M., & Hyrynsalmi, S. (2023). Ethical governance model for the data economy ecosystems. *Digital Policy. Regulation & Governance*, *25*(3), 221–235. DOI: 10.1108/DPRG-01-2022-0005

Kotsios, A., Magnani, M., Rossi, L., Shklovski, I., & Vega, D. (2019). An analysis of the consequences of the general data protection regulation (GDPR) on social network research. *ACM Transactions on Social Computing*, *2*(3), 12. Advance online publication. DOI: 10.1145/3365524

Kou, G., & Lu, Y. (2025). FinTech: A Literature Review of Emerging Financial Technologies and Applications. *Financial Innovation*, *11*(1), 1. Advance online publication. DOI: 10.1186/s40854-024-00668-6

Kramer, D., Rosique, L., Narotam, A., Bursztein, E., Kelley, P. G., Thomas, K., & Woodruff, A. (2025). Integrating large language models into security incident response. In 21st Symposium on Usable Privacy and Security (SOUPS 2025). USENIX Association. https://www.usenix.org/system/files/soups2025-kramer.pdf

Krieger, J. (1993). *The Oxford Companion to Politics of the World*. Oxford University Press.

Kristensen, L. M., & Bro, P. (2024). News values in a digital age-Intra-media, inter-media, and extra-media platforms. *Journalism*, *25*(4), 819–836. DOI: 10.1177/14648849231165855

Krstic, A. (2024). Digital transformation of journalism and media in Serbia: What has gone wrong? *Journalism*, *25*(5), 1014–1030. DOI: 10.1177/14648849231151798

Kuang, Y., Zheng, J., Sun, M., & Xu, X. (2025). The Role of Algorithmic Fairness, Accountability, and Transparency in Shaping User Satisfaction on Digital Platforms: A Quantitative Study in China. *International Journal of Human-Computer Interaction*, •••, 1–17. DOI: 10.1080/10447318.2025.2546663

Kuhn, T. S. (1970). *The Structure of Scientific Revolutions* (2nd ed.). University of Chicago Press.

Kumar, S., Verma, A. K., & Mirza, A. (2024). Digital transformation, artificial intelligence and society. *Springer*. Https://Link. Springer. Com/Book/10, *1007*, 978–981.

Kumar, V. A., Bhardwaj, S., & Lather, M. (2024). Cybersecurity and Safeguarding Digital Assets: An Analysis of Regulatory Frameworks, Legal Liability and Enforcement Mechanisms. *Productivity*, *65*(1), 1–10.

Kuner, C., Bygrave, L. A., & Docksey, C. (Eds.). (2020). *The EU General Data Protection Regulation (GDPR): A commentary*. Oxford University Press., DOI: 10.1093/oso/9780198826491.001.0001

Kusche, I. (2024). Possible harms of artificial intelligence and the EU AI act: Fundamental rights and risk. *Journal of Risk Research*, •••, 1–14. DOI: 10.1080/13669877.2024.2350720

Kuzio, J., Ahmadi, M., Kim, K. C., Migaud, M. R., Wang, Y. F., & Bullock, J. (2022). Building better global data governance. *Data & Policy*, *4*, e25. DOI: 10.1017/dap.2022.17

Kwet, M. (2019). Digital colonialism: US empire and the new imperialism in the Global South. *Race & Class*, *60*(4), 3–26. DOI: 10.1177/0306396818823172

Lakatos, I. (1978). *The Methodology of Scientific Research Programmes. Philosophical Papers* (Worrall, J., & Currie, G., Eds.). Vol. 1). Cambridge University Press. DOI: 10.1017/CBO9780511621123

Lambach, D. (2020). The territorialization of cyberspace. *International Studies Review*, *22*(3), 482–506. DOI: 10.1093/isr/viz022

Lambach, D., & Monsees, L. (2025). Beyond sovereignty as authority: The multiplicity of European approaches to digital sovereignty. *Global Political Economy*, *4*(1), 71–88. DOI: 10.1332/26352257Y2024D000000007

Landesberg, M. K., Levin, T. M., & Curtin, C. G. Lev, Ori., (1998). *Privacy Online: A Report To Congress*. Federal Trade Commission.

Langa, J. (2021). Deepfakes, real consequences: Crafting legislation to combat threats posed by deepfakes. *BUL Rev.*, *101*, 761.

Lao, Y., Hirvonen, N., & Larsson, S. (2025). Everyday encounters with deepfakes: Young people's media and information literacy practices with AI-generated media. *The Journal of Documentation*, *81*(7), 216–235. DOI: 10.1108/JD-01-2025-0007

Lawo, D., Neifer, T., Esau, M., & Stevens, G. (2023). Digital sovereignty: What it is and why it matters for HCI. In *Extended Abstracts of the 2023 CHI Conference on Human Factors in Computing Systems* (Article 317). ACM. DOI: 10.1145/3544549.3585834

Lawson, T. (1997). *Economics and Reality*. Routledge. DOI: 10.4324/9780203195390

Lawson, T. (2003). *Reorienting Economics*. Routledge.

Lawton, T. C., Tonn Goulart Moura, S., Tobin, D., & Silva-Rêgo, B. (2023). Geopolitics of the digital economy: Implications for states and firms. *AIB Insights*, *23*(1). Advance online publication. DOI: 10.46697/001c.67966

LCX. (2023). "Introduction to Web 2.5." https://lcx.com/en/introduction-to-web-2-5

Lechterman, T. M. (2022). The concept of accountability in AI ethics and governance. *The Oxford Handbook of AI Governance*, 164–182.

Lei Geral de Proteção de Dados Pessoais [General Personal Data Protection Law], Lei No. 13.709, de 14 de agosto de 2018 (Braz.). https://www.lgpdbrasil.com.br/wp-content/uploads/2019/06/LGPD-english-version.pdf

Leiner, B. M., Kahn, R. E., Postel, J., Cerf, V. G., Kleinrock, L., Roberts, L. G., Clark, D. D., Lynch, D., & Wolff, S. (2009). A Brief History of the Internet. *Computer Communication Review*, *39*(5), 22–31. http://www.acm.org. DOI: 10.1145/1629607.1629613

Lessig, L. (2006). Code: version 2.0,(Basic Books. *New York*. Liao, X., Wang, Y., Wang, T., Hu, J., & Wu, X. (2023). FAMM: Facial muscle motions for detecting compressed deepfake videos over social networks. *IEEE Transactions on Circuits and Systems for Video Technology*, *33*(12), 7236–7251.

Lin, W., Zhu, Y., Guo, D., & Fedkiw, R. (2022). Leveraging deepfakes to close the domain gap between real and synthetic images in facial capture pipelines. *ArXiv Preprint ArXiv:2204.10746*.

Lin, Y., Gao, Z., Tu, Y., Du, H., Niyato, D., Kang, J., & Yang, H. (2022). A blockchain-based semantic exchange framework for web 3.0 toward participatory economy. arXiv preprint arXiv:2211.16662.

Lindahl, H. (2001). Sovereignty and the Institutionalisation of Normative Order. *Oxford Journal of Legal Studies*, *21*(1), 165–180. Advance online publication. DOI: 10.1093/ojls/21.1.165

Lindquist, J., & Weltevrede, E. (2024). Authenticity governance and the market for social media engagements: The shaping of disinformation at the peripheries of platform ecosystems. *Social Media + Society*, *10*(1), 20563051231224721. DOI: 10.1177/20563051231224721

Linkov, I., Trump, B. D., Poinsatte-Jones, K., & Florin, M.-V. (2018). Governance strategies for a sustainable digital world. *Sustainability (Basel)*, *10*(2), 440. DOI: 10.3390/su10020440

Lin, L. S. F. (2025). Organisational Challenges in US Law Enforcement's Response to AI-Driven Cybercrime and Deepfake Fraud. *Laws*, *14*(4), 46. DOI: 10.3390/laws14040046

Linsi, L., & Mügge, D. K. (2019). Globalization and the growing defects of international economic statistics. *Review of International Political Economy*, *26*(3), 361–383. DOI: 10.1080/09692290.2018.1560353

Li, S. C., Chen, Y. C., Chen, Y. W., & Huang, Y. (2022). Predicting advertisement revenue of social-media-driven content websites: Toward more efficient and sustainable social media posting. *Sustainability (Basel)*, *14*(7), 4225. DOI: 10.3390/su14074225

Lischka, J. A., & Garz, M. (2023). Clickbait news and algorithmic curation: A game theory framework of the relation between journalism, users, and platforms. *New Media & Society*, *25*(8), 2073–2094. DOI: 10.1177/14614448211027174

Lis, D., Gelhaar, J., & Otto, B. (2023). Data strategy and policies: The role of data governance in data ecosystems. In *Data governance: From the fundamentals to real cases* (pp. 27–55). Springer Nature Switzerland., DOI: 10.1007/978-3-031-43773-1_2

Liu, Y., Jia, Y., Geng, R., Jia, J., & Gong, N. Z. (2024). Formalizing and benchmarking prompt injection attacks and defenses. In 33rd USENIX Security Symposium (USENIX Security 24). USENIX Association. https://www.usenix.org/system/files/usenixsecurity24-liu-yupei.pdf

Li, Z. (2025). On the Fundamental Structure and Flow Framework of Data in Cross-Border Cybercrime. *Mod. L. Rsch.*, *6*, 52.

Longworth, J. (2021). Benjamin Ruha (2019) Race After Technology: Abolitionist Tools for the New Jim Code. Medford: Polity Press. 172 pages. eISBN: 9781509526437. *Science & Technology Studies*, *34*(2), 92–94. DOI: 10.23987/sts.102639

Lundahl, O. (2022). Algorithmic meta-capital: Bourdieusian analysis of social power through algorithms in media consumption. *Information Communication and Society*, *25*(10), 1440–1455. DOI: 10.1080/1369118X.2020.1864006

Lynskey, O. (2020). Delivering data protection: The next chapter. *German Law Journal*, *21*(1), 80–84. DOI: 10.1017/glj.2019.100

MacCarthy, M. (2020). *Transparency requirements for digital social media platforms: Recommendations for policy makers and industry*. Transatlantic Working Group.

Mäder, A., & Rinsdorf, L. (2023). Constructive journalism as an adaptation to a changing media environment. *Journalism Studies*, *24*(3), 329–346. DOI: 10.1080/1461670X.2022.2159859

Mahmutovic, A., & Alsudais, M. (2025). Legal Pluralism and Governance: Redefining Power and Accountability in a Globalized World. *PETITA: JURNAL KAJIAN ILMU HUKUM DAN SYARIAH*, *10*(2), 568–593.

Maiguashca, B. (2003). Governance and resistance in world politics. *Review of International Studies*, *29*(S1), 3–28. DOI: 10.1017/S0260210503005989

Majone, G. (1997). From the positive to the regulatory state: Causes and consequences of changes in the mode of governance. *Journal of Public Policy*, *17*(2), 139–167. DOI: 10.1017/S0143814X00003524

Makady, H. (2023). To interact or not to interact with news posts: The role of algorithmic awareness & self-monitoring in Facebook news consumption. *Electronic News*, *17*(4), 223–246. DOI: 10.1177/19312431231166933

Malikzada, T. (2026). Assessing the Role of International Law in Regulating the Fight Against Cybercrime in the Digital Environment. Futurity Economics&Law, 6(1).

Mania, K. (2024). Legal protection of revenge and deepfake porn victims in the European Union: Findings from a comparative legal study. *Trauma, Violence & Abuse*, *25*(1), 117–129. DOI: 10.1177/15248380221143772

Mansoor, S. I. U. (2024). Legal implications of deepfake technology: In the context of manipulation, privacy, and identity theft. *Central University of Kashmir Law Review*, *4*, 65–92. DOI: 10.66498/CUKLR.4.2024.65-92

Mantelero, A. (2017). From group privacy to collective privacy: Towards a new dimension of privacy and data protection in the big data era. In Taylor, L., Floridi, L., & van der Sloot, B. (Eds.), *Group privacy: New challenges of data technologies* (pp. 139–158). Springer., DOI: 10.1007/978-3-319-46608-8_8

Masiero, S., & Das, S. (2019). Datafying anti-poverty programmes: Implications for data justice. *Information Communication and Society*, *22*(7), 916–933. DOI: 10.1080/1369118X.2019.1575448

Masood, M., Nawaz, M., Malik, K. M., Javed, A., Irtaza, A., & Malik, H. (2023). Deepfakes generation and detection: State-of-the-art, open challenges, countermeasures, and way forward. *Applied Intelligence*, *53*(4), 3974–4026. DOI: 10.1007/s10489-022-03766-z

Mattern, J., Mireshghallah, F., Jin, Z., Schölkopf, B., Sachan, M., & Berg-Kirkpatrick, T. (2023). Membership inference attacks against language models via neighbourhood comparison. In Findings of the Association for Computational Linguistics: ACL 2023 (pp. 11330–11343). Association for Computational Linguistics. DOI: 10.18653/v1/2023.findings-acl.719

Maurer, T., & Morgus, R. (2022). *Compilation of existing cybersecurity and information security related definitions*. New America.

Mayer-Schönberger, V., & Cukier, K. (2013). *Big data: A revolution that will transform how we live, work, and think.* Houghton Mifflin Harcourt.

McNally, N., & Bastos, M. (2025). The news feed is not a black box: A longitudinal study of facebook's algorithmic treatment of news. *Digital Journalism (Abingdon, England), 13*(7), 1209–1228. DOI: 10.1080/21670811.2025.2450623

Mellado, C., Blanchett, N., Stępińska, A., Mothes, C., Lecheler, S., Blanco-Herrero, D., & Zhao, X. (2024). Does news platform matter? Comparing online journalistic role performance to newspaper, radio, and television. *Digital Journalism (Abingdon, England), 12*(3), 376–399. DOI: 10.1080/21670811.2023.2191332

Meskys, E., Kalpokiene, J., Jurcys, P., & Liaudanskas, A. (2020). Regulating deep fakes: Legal and ethical considerations. *Journal of Intellectual Property Law & Practice, 15*(1), 24–31. DOI: 10.1093/jiplp/jpz167

Micheli, M., Ponti, M., Craglia, M., & Berti Suman, A. (2020). Emerging models of data governance in the age of datafication. *Big Data & Society, 7*(2), 1–15. DOI: 10.1177/2053951720948087

Mindel, V., Mathiassen, L., & Rai, A. (2018). The sustainability of polycentric information commons. *Management Information Systems Quarterly, 42*(2), 607–631. DOI: 10.25300/MISQ/2018/14015

Ministério da Ciência. Tecnologia e Inovação. (2024). *Plano brasileiro de inteligência artificial (PBIA).* MCTI. https://www.gov.br/mcti/pt-br/acompanhe-o-mcti/transformacaodigital/plano-brasileiro-de-inteligencia-artificial-pbia-_vf.pdf

Ministério da Ciência. Tecnologia e Inovações. (2021). *Estratégia brasileira de inteligência artificial (EBIA).* MCTI. https://www.gov.br/mcti/pt-br/acompanhe-o-mcti/transformacaodigital/arquivosestrategiadigital/copy_of_RelatoriofinalEBIA_Eixo6V2.4.pdf

Ministry of Electronics and Information Technology. (2025). *Digital Personal Data Protection Rules, 2025.* Government of India. https://pib.gov.in/PressReleasePage.aspx?PRID=2090271

Ministry of Information, Communications and the Digital Economy, Kenya. (2025). *Kenya national artificial intelligence strategy 2025–2030.* Government of Kenya. https://ict.go.ke/sites/default/files/2025-03/Kenya%20AI%20Strategy%202025%20-%202030.pdf

Mishra, N., & Agarwal, B. (2026). The emerging framework for non-personal data protection in India: Perils, promises, and lessons for the developing world. *International Journal of Law and Information Technology*, *34*(1), eaaf025. Advance online publication. DOI: 10.1093/ijlit/eaaf025

Misra, S., Barik, K., & Kvalvik, P. (2025). Digital sovereignty in the era of industry 5.0: Challenges and opportunities. *Procedia Computer Science*, *254*, 108–117. DOI: 10.1016/j.procs.2025.02.069

Misra, S., Barik, K., & Kvalvik, P. (2025). Trust in digital sovereignty: A review of security, privacy, and governance challenges. *Public Organization Review*. Advance online publication. DOI: 10.1007/s11115-025-00968-0

Mitchell, A. D., & Samlidis, T. (2022). Cloud services and government digital sovereignty in Australia and beyond. *International Journal of Law and Information Technology*, *29*(4), 364–394. DOI: 10.1093/ijlit/eaac003

Mitrou, L. (2018). Data protection, artificial intelligence and cognitive services: is the general data protection regulation (GDPR) 'artificial intelligence-proof'? *Artificial Intelligence and Cognitive Services: Is the General Data Protection Regulation (GDPR) 'Artificial Intelligence-Proof.*

Modise, J. M. (2026). *An Assessment of Transnational Crime in The African Context: Trends*. Challenges, And Strategic Responses.

Mohammed, A. (2024). Deep Fake Detection and Mitigation: Securing Against AI-Generated Manipulation. *Journal of Computational Innovation*, *4*(1).

Montalbano, K. (2022). Reimagining section 230 and content moderation: Regulating incivility on anonymous digital platforms. *Communication Law and Policy*, *27*(3-4), 187–219. DOI: 10.1080/10811680.2022.2136442

Moon, M. J. (2023). Searching for inclusive artificial intelligence for social good: Participatory governance and policy recommendations for making AI more inclusive and benign for society. *Public Administration Review*, *83*(6), 1496–1505. DOI: 10.1111/puar.13648

Mugamba, E. (2025). Global Data Governance in Digital Law: A Comparative Analysis of EU and Global Approaches to Cybersecurity Legislation. *Journal of Smart Computing and Quantum Technologies*, *1*(1), 10–28. DOI: 10.63456/jscqt-1-1-39

Müller, J. (2024). *Turning Point: How IT Is Changing Our World*. Springer. DOI: 10.1007/978-3-658-46079-2

Murphy, J., & Roser, M. (2019). "Internet." https://ourworldindata.org/internet

Musiani, F. (2022). Infrastructuring digital sovereignty: A research agenda for an infrastructure-based sociology of digital self-determination practices. *Information Communication and Society, 25*(6), 785–800. DOI: 10.1080/1369118X.2022.2049850

Naitali, A., Ridouani, M., Salahdine, F., & Kaabouch, N. (2023). Deepfake attacks: Generation, detection, datasets, challenges, and research directions. *Computers, 12*(10), 216. DOI: 10.3390/computers12100216

Nakamoto, S. (2008). Bitcoin: A peer-to-peer electronic cash system.

Nanni, R., Bizzaro, P. G., & Napolitano, M. (2024). The false promise of individual digital sovereignty in europe: Comparing artificial intelligence and data regulations in china and the european union. *Policy and Internet, 16*(4), 711–726. DOI: 10.1002/poi3.424

Natarajan, S. K., Abdullah, A., Kaur, S., & Natarajan, P. (2025). Advancing Multi-Modal Behavioral Biometric Authentication: A Deep Learning Approach With Synthetic Data Generation. *IEEE Access : Practical Innovations, Open Solutions.*

National Institute of Standards and Technology. (2023). Artificial Intelligence Risk Management Framework (AI RMF 1.0) (NIST AI 100-1). https://nvlpubs.nist.gov/nistpubs/ai/nist.ai.100-1.pdf

National Institute of Standards and Technology. (2023). *Artificial intelligence risk management framework (AI RMF 1.0).* NIST. https://nvlpubs.nist.gov/nistpubs/ai/nist.ai.100-1.pdf

National Institute of Standards and Technology. (2024). Secure software development practices for generative AI and dual-use foundation models: An SSDF community profile (NIST Special Publication 800-218A). DOI: 10.6028/NIST.SP.800-218A

National Privacy Authority. (2024). *Federal Privacy Framework Overview.*

Ndubuisi, A. F. (2022). Cross-border jurisdiction challenges in prosecuting cybercrime syndicates targeting national financial and electoral systems. [IJETRM]. *International Journal of Engineering Technology Research & Management, 6*(11), 243–261.

Nguyen, D., & Hekman, E. (2024). The news framing of artificial intelligence: A critical exploration of how media discourses make sense of automation. *AI & Society, 39*(2), 437–451. DOI: 10.1007/s00146-022-01511-1

Nhlazane, T. N. (2025). *Data Protection and Data Security Standards*. University of Johannesburg.

Nikolenko, S. I. (2021). *Synthetic data for deep learning* (Vol. 174). Springer. DOI: 10.1007/978-3-030-75178-4

Nookala, G. (2024). Adaptive data governance frameworks for data-driven digital transformations. *Journal of Computational Innovation*, *4*(1).

O'neil, C. (2017). *Weapons of math destruction: How big data increases inequality and threatens democracy*. Crown.

Oduro, S., Moss, E., Metcalf, J., & Narayanan, A. (2022). Obligations to assess: Recent trends in AI accountability regulations. *Patterns (New York, N.Y.)*, *3*(11), 100608. Advance online publication. DOI: 10.1016/j.patter.2022.100608 PMID: 36419454

OECD. (2019). *OECD AI principles*. https://www.oecd.org/en/topics/ai-principles.html

OECD. (2020). *The Tokenisation of Assets and Potential Implications for Financial Markets*. https://www.oecd.org/content/dam/oecd/en/publications/reports/2020/03/the-tokenisation-of-assets-and-potential-implications-for-financial-markets_370f9853/83493d34-en.pdf

OECD. (2024a). *OECD Digital Economy Outlook 2024 (Volume 2):Strengthening Connectivity, Innovation and Trust*. OECD Digital Economy Outlook. OECD Publishing, Paris.

OECD. (2024b). *OECD Digital Economy 2024 (Volume 1): Embracing the Technology Frontier*. OECD Digital Economy Outlook. OECD Publishing, Paris.

Office of Management and Budget. (2025a, April 3). M-25-21: Accelerating federal use of AI through innovation, governance, and public trust. The White House. https://www.whitehouse.gov/wp-content/uploads/2025/02/M-25-21-Accelerating-Federal-Use-of-AI-through-Innovation-Governance-and-Public-Trust.pdf

Office of Management and Budget. (2025b, April 3). M-25-22: Driving efficient acquisition of artificial intelligence in government. The White House. https://www.whitehouse.gov/wp-content/uploads/2025/02/M-25-22-Driving-Efficient-Acquisition-of-Artificial-Intelligence-in-Government.pdf

Ogundipe, F., Bakare, O. I., Sampson, E., & Folorunso, A. (2023). harnessing digital transformation for Africa's growth: Opportunities and challenges in the Technological Era. *African Development Review*, *28*(4), 234–251.

Okolo, F. C., Etukudoh, E. A., Ogunwole, O., Osho, G. O., & Basiru, J. O. (2022). Policy-oriented framework for multi-agency data integration across national transportation and infrastructure systems. Journal name missing.

Oloruntoba, S. O. (2020). Pan-Africanism, regional integration and development in Africa. In *Pan Africanism, regional integration and development in Africa* (pp. 1–14). Springer International Publishing. DOI: 10.1007/978-3-030-34296-8_1

Oloyede, A. A., Faruk, N., Noma, N., Tebepah, E., & Nwaulune, A. K. (2023). Measuring the Impact of the Digital Economy in Developing Countries: A Systematic Review and Meta- Analysis. *Heliyon*, *9*(7), 1. DOI: 10.1016/j.heliyon.2023.e17654 PMID: 37501966

Omogiate, P. M., & Legal, C. A. B. T. (2022). Developing standardized metadata protocols enabling transparent provenance tracking for AI-created media within federal intellectual property regulatory systems nationwide. *International Journal of Computer Applications Technology and Research*, *11*(12), 711–723.

Opara-Martins, J., Sahandi, R., & Tian, F. (2016). Critical analysis of vendor lock-in and its impact on cloud computing migration: A business perspective. *Journal of Cloud Computing (Heidelberg, Germany)*, *5*(1), 4. Advance online publication. DOI: 10.1186/s13677-016-0054-z

Opriel, S., Möller, F., Strobel, G., & Otto, B. (2025). Data sovereignty in inter-organizational information systems. *Business & Information Systems Engineering*, *67*(6), 833–853. DOI: 10.1007/s12599-024-00893-4

Osorio, C. P., & Gojo Cruz, J. I. (2025). Promoting free flows via competition law: An AI industry blueprint for southeast asia. *Telecommunications Policy*, *49*(5), 102953. DOI: 10.1016/j.telpol.2025.102953

Paik, S. (2025). Journalism ethics for the algorithmic era. *Digital Journalism (Abingdon, England)*, *13*(4), 696–722. DOI: 10.1080/21670811.2023.2200195

Papaevangelou, C. (2023). The role of citizens in platform governance: A case study on public consultations regarding online content regulation in the European Union. *Global Media and China*, *8*(1), 39–56. DOI: 10.1177/20594364221150142

Parasol, M. (2021). *AI development and the "fuzzy logic" of chinese cyber security and data laws*. Cambridge University Press., DOI: 10.1017/9781009064804

Patel, Y., Tanwar, S., Gupta, R., Bhattacharya, P., Davidson, I. E., Nyameko, R., Aluvala, S., & Vimal, V. (2023). Deepfake generation and detection: Case study and challenges. *IEEE Access : Practical Innovations, Open Solutions*, *11*, 143296–143323. DOI: 10.1109/ACCESS.2023.3342107

Pawelec, M. (2022). Deepfakes and democracy (theory): How synthetic audio-visual media for disinformation and hate speech threaten core democratic functions. *Digital Society : Ethics, Socio-Legal and Governance of Digital Technology*, *1*(2), 19. DOI: 10.1007/s44206-022-00010-6

Peffers, K., Tuunanen, T., Rothenberger, M. A., & Chatterjee, S. (2007). A design science research methodology for information systems research. *Journal of Management Information Systems*, *24*(3), 45–77. DOI: 10.2753/MIS0742-1222240302

Peitz, M., & Motta, M. (2020). Big Tech Mergers. *Information Economics and Policy*.

Peng, S. (2019). The rule of law in times of technological uncertainty: Is international economic law ready for emerging supervisory trends? *Journal of International Economic Law*, *22*(1), 1–27. DOI: 10.1093/jiel/jgy049

Perriello, L. E. (2026). Blurred realities: Legal strategies for the deepfake era. *Maastricht Journal of European and Comparative Law*, 1023263X261433380.

Personal Information Protection Law of the People's Republic of China (promulgated by the Standing Comm. Nat'l People's Cong., Aug. 20, 2021, effective Nov. 1, 2021). http://www.npc.gov.cn/englishnpc/c23934/202112/1bed4cd1443340a2aabc94e391bd35e0.shtml

Peters, C., Schrøder, K. C., Lehaff, J., & Vulpius, J. (2022). News as they know it: Young adults' information repertoires in the digital media landscape. *Digital Journalism (Abingdon, England)*, *10*(1), 62–86. DOI: 10.1080/21670811.2021.1885986

Pierucci, F. (2025). Sovereignty in the digital era: Rethinking territoriality and governance in cyberspace. *Digital Society : Ethics, Socio-Legal and Governance of Digital Technology*, *4*(1), 27. DOI: 10.1007/s44206-025-00189-4

Pileggi, S. F., Fernandez-Llatas, C., & Traver, V. (2012). When the Social Meets the Semantic: Social Semantic Web or Web 2.5. *Future Internet*, *4*(4), 852–864. DOI: 10.3390/fi4030852

Plikynas, D., Rizgelienė, I., & Korvel, G. (2025). Systematic review of fake news, propaganda, and disinformation: Examining authors, content, and social impact through machine learning. *IEEE Access : Practical Innovations, Open Solutions*, *13*, 17583–17629. DOI: 10.1109/ACCESS.2025.3530688

Png, M.-T. (2022). At the tensions of south and north: Critical roles of global south stakeholders in AI governance. *Proceedings of the 2022 ACM Conference on Fairness, Accountability, and Transparency*, 1434–1445. DOI: 10.1145/3531146.3533200

Pohle, J., & Thiel, T. (2020). Digital sovereignty. *Pohle, J. & Thiel.*

Pohle, J., & Thiel, T. (2020). Digital sovereignty. *Internet Policy Review*, *9*(4). Advance online publication. DOI: 10.14763/2020.4.1532

Polanyi, K. (2001). *1944. The Great Transformation The Political and Economic Origins of Our Time*. Beacon Press.

Ponugoti, M. (2023). Frameworks for ensuring compliance in digital platform governance. [IJEETR]. *International Journal of Engineering & Extended Technologies Research*, *5*(6), 7575–7586. DOI: 10.15662/IJEETR.2023.0506015

Popa, D. M. (2025). Frontrunner model for responsible AI governance in the public sector: The Dutch perspective. *AI and Ethics*, *5*(3), 2789–2799. DOI: 10.1007/s43681-024-00596-2

Poyton, D. (2023). The role of regulation in facilitating new business models driven by digital platforms: Creating regulatory ecosystems. *International Review of Law Computers & Technology*, *37*(3), 227–251. DOI: 10.1080/13600869.2022.2136934

Presidency of the Republic of Brazil. (2018). *Lei no. 13.709, de 14 de agosto de 2018 (lei geral de proteção de dados pessoais)*. https://www.planalto.gov.br/ccivil_03/_ato2015-2018/2018/lei/l13709.htm

Protection, D. (2018). General data protection regulation. *Intersoft Consulting, Accessed in October, 24*(1).

PWC. (2025). *PwC Global Crypto Report 2025: Navigating the Global Landscape*. https://legal.pwc.de/content/services/global-crypto-regulation-report/pwc-global-crypto-regulation-report-2025.pdf

Qiu, Y., & Hu, Z. (2025). Progress and recommendations in data ethics governance: A transnational analysis based on data ethics frameworks. *Humanities & Social Sciences Communications*, *12*(1), 1354. DOI: 10.1057/s41599-025-05664-4

Rafaelof, E., Webster, G., Tai, K., Neville, K., Creemers, R., & Sacks, S. (2020). *Translation: China's 'Data Security Law (Draft)'*. New America. https://www.newamerica.org/insights/translation-chinas-data-security-law-draft/

Raji, I. D., Smart, A., White, R. N., Mitchell, M., Gebru, T., Hutchinson, B., Smith-Loud, J., Theron, D., & Barnes, P. (2020). Closing the AI accountability gap: Defining an end-to-end framework for internal algorithmic auditing. In *Proceedings of the 2020 Conference on Fairness, Accountability, and Transparency* (pp. 33–44). Association for Computing Machinery. DOI: 10.1145/3351095.3372873

Ray, P. P. (2023). Web3: A Comprehensive Review on Background, Technologies, Applications, Zero-Trust Architectures, Challenges and Future Directions. *Internet of Things and Cyber-Physical Systems*, *3*, 213–248. DOI: 10.1016/j.iotcps.2023.05.003

Regulation (EU) 2016/679 of the European Parliament and of the Council 27 April 2016.

Regulation (EU) 2022/1925 of the European Parliament and of the Council of 14 September 2022.

Regulation (EU) 2022/2065 of the European Parliament and of the Council of 19th October 2022.

Republic of Kenya. (2019). *Data protection act, 2019*. https://new.kenyalaw.org/akn/ke/act/2019/24/eng@2022-12-31

Reserve Bank of India. (2018). *Storage of payment system data*. https://www.rbi.org.in/Scripts/NotificationUser.aspx?Id=11244&Mode=0

Rizer, A., & Hobson, A. (2022). *Cross-Border Data Requests: Evaluating Reforms To Improve Law Enforcement Access*. R Street Institute.

Roberts, H. (2024). Digital sovereignty and artificial intelligence: A normative approach. *Ethics and Information Technology*, *26*(4), 1–10. DOI: 10.1007/s10676-024-09810-5

Roberts, H., Cowls, J., Morley, J., Taddeo, M., & Floridi, L. (2021). Safeguarding European values with digital sovereignty: An analysis of statements and policies. *Internet Policy Review*, *10*(3), 1–28. DOI: 10.14763/2021.3.1575

Roberts, H., Hine, E., & Floridi, L. (2023). Digital sovereignty, digital expansionism, and the prospects for global AI governance. In Timoteo, M., Verri, B., & Nanni, R. (Eds.), *Quo vadis, sovereignty? New conceptual and regulatory boundaries in the age of digital China* (pp. 51–75). Springer., DOI: 10.1007/978-3-031-41566-1_4

Roe, J., Perkins, M., & Furze, L. (2024). Deepfakes and higher education: A research agenda and scoping review of synthetic media. *Journal of University Teaching & Learning Practice*, *21*(10), 1–22. DOI: 10.53761/2y2np178

Rone, J. (2024). The sovereign cloud in Europe: Diverging nation state preferences and disputed institutional competences in the context of limited technological capabilities. *Journal of European Public Policy*, *31*(8), 2343–2369. DOI: 10.1080/13501763.2024.2348618

Rosenbaum, S. (2010). Data governance and stewardship: Designing data stewardship entities and advancing data access. *Health Services Research*, *45*(5 Pt 2), 1442–1455. DOI: 10.1111/j.1475-6773.2010.01140.x PMID: 21054365

Rostomyan, A. (2026). Used in the Synthetic Media Generations and Applications. *The Convergence of Federated Learning and Healthcare 5.0 and Beyond: A New Era of Intelligent Health Systems*, 301.

Rothmann, C. C. (2024). *Modernizing U.S. Commercial Privacy Standards for a Digital Economy.* https://www.csis.org/analysis/modernizing-us-commercial-privacy-standards-digital-economy

Salam, M. A., Rayun, S. M. N., Islam, W., Hasan, R., Firmansyah, E. A., & Kalinaki, K. (2024). Consumer Engagement: Exploring Deepfake Applications in Consumer Marketing Communication. In *Navigating the World of Deepfake Technology* (pp. 397–421). IGI Global.

Saleem, M. S., Imran, Q., & Saghir, A. (2025). DIGITAL SOVEREIGNTY AS A NEW DIMENSION OF POWER POLITICS IN THE GLOBAL SOUTH. *Pakistan Journal of Social Science Review*, *4*(6), 485–503.

Samiha, Y. T., Handayani, T., Razaq, A., Fithriyah, M., Fitri, A., & Anshari, M. (2022, March). Implementation of Education 4.0 as sustainable decisions for a sustainable development. In *2022 International conference on decision aid sciences and applications (DASA)* (pp. 846-850). IEEE. DOI: 10.1109/DASA54658.2022.9765080

Sampath, P. G., & Tregenna, F. (2022). *Digital sovereignty: African perspectives.* DSI/NRF South African Research Chair in Industrial Development.

Sander, B. (2019). Freedom of expression in the age of online platforms: The promise and pitfalls of a human rights-based approach to content moderation. *Fordham Int'l LJ*, *43*, 939.

Sangwa, S. (2025). UN Pact for the Future and Global Digital Compact: A Critical Interdisciplinary Analysis of Global Digital Governance, Digital-ID, and Central-Bank Digital Currencies. Open Journal of Stigmatized Knowledge & Suppressed Discourses (ISSN: 3105-3033), 1(1).

Santana, P. C., & Ansari, F. A. (2023). Data protection and privacy as a fundamental right: A comparative study of Brazil and India. *Journal of Liberty and International Affairs*, *9*(3), 456–470. DOI: 10.47305/JLIA2393555cs

Santaniello, M. (2025). Attributes of digital sovereignty: A conceptual framework. *Geopolitics*, *31*(2), 1–22. DOI: 10.1080/14650045.2025.2521548

Santos, A., Cazzamatta, R., & Napolitano, C. J. (2025). Holding platforms accountable in the fight against misinformation: A cross-national analysis of state-established content moderation regulations. *The International Communication Gazette*, *87*(8), 729–750. DOI: 10.1177/17480485251348550

Sanyal, S., Sharma, P., & Dudani, C. (2024). *A complex adaptive system framework to regulate artificial intelligence*. Economic Advisory Council to the PM.

Sarfraz, M., Sumra, I. A., Khalid, B., & Fatima, E. (2025). AI-driven predictive threat detection and cyber risk mitigation: A survey. *Journal of Computing & Biomedical Informatics*, *8*(02).

Schaefer, L. (2021). *Routine activity theory*. Oxford University Press.

Schaetz, N. (2024). Journalism & audience datafication: How audience data practices shape inequity. *Digital Journalism (Abingdon, England)*, *12*(8), 1184–1204. DOI: 10.1080/21670811.2023.2171894

Schaetz, N., Lischka, J. A., & Laugwitz, L. (2025). Datafication of journalism: How data elites and epistemic infrastructures change news organizations. *Digital Journalism (Abingdon, England)*, *13*(4), 677–695. DOI: 10.1080/21670811.2023.2235601

Schär, F. (2021). Decentralized Finance: On Blockchain-and Smart Contract-Based Financial Markets. *Review - Federal Reserve Bank of St. Louis*, *103*(2), 153–174. DOI: 10.20955/r.103.153-74

Schneider, G. (2024). Stakeholder engagement in EU digital platform regulations: Ways forward and persisting gaps. In *Repositioning Platforms in Digital Market Law* (pp. 125–153). Springer Nature Switzerland., DOI: 10.1007/978-3-031-69678-7_6

Schrepel, T. (2023). The Complex Relationship between Web2 Giants and Web3 Projects. *Computer Law & Security Review*, *50*, 1–11. DOI: 10.1016/j.clsr.2023.105845

Schwab, K., Marcus, A., Oyola, J., Hoffman, W., & Luzi, M. (2011). Personal data: The emergence of a new asset class. An Initiative of the World Economic Forum, Scott, J. C. (2020). *Seeing like a state: How certain schemes to improve the human condition have failed*. yale university Press.

Shami, A. Z. A., Saleem, M., & Ashraf, J. (2025). Cybercrime and Digital Evidence: Investigating the Challenges and Opportunities in Prosecuting Cybercrime and Handling Digital Evidence. *Research Consortium Archive*, *3*(2), 401–411.

Sharma, S. (2020). Issues with enforcing Mutual Legal Assistance Treaties (MLATs): Access to cross-border data in criminal investigation. Available at *SSRN* 3815270. DOI: 10.2139/ssrn.3815270

Shirkoohi, S. M., & Mohiuddin, M. (2025). Developing sustainable global value chain: Role of multi-stakeholder collaborations and digitalization. *Cleaner Logistics and Supply Chain, 100271*, 100271. Advance online publication. DOI: 10.1016/j.clscn.2025.100271

Sibe, R. T., & Kaunert, C. (2024). *Cybercrime, digital forensic readiness, and financial crime investigation in Nigeria*. Springer International Publishing AG. DOI: 10.1007/978-3-031-54089-9

Simon, F. M. (2022). Uneasy bedfellows: AI in the news, platform companies and the issue of journalistic autonomy. *Digital Journalism (Abingdon, England)*, *10*(10), 1832–1854. DOI: 10.1080/21670811.2022.2063150

Sinha, A. (2017). *India's Data Protection Framework Will Need to Treat Privacy as a Social And Not Just an Individual Good.* EPW. https://www.epw.in/engage/article/for-indias-data-protection-regime-to-be-efficient-policymakers-should-treat-privacy-as-a-social-good

Spalević, Ž., & Vićentijević, K. (2022). Spalević, žaklina and Vićentijević, Kosana. (2022). *GDPR And Challenges of Personal Data Protection. The European Journal of Applied Economics*, *19*(1), 55–65. Advance online publication. DOI: 10.5937/EJAE19-36596

Srnicek, N. (2017). *Platform Capitalism*. Polity Press.

Stockmann, D. (2023). Tech companies and the public interest: The role of the state in governing social media platforms. *Information Communication and Society*, *26*(1), 1–15. DOI: 10.1080/1369118X.2022.2032796

Story, D., & Jenkins, R. (2023). Deepfake pornography and the ethics of non-veridical representations. *Philosophy & Technology*, *36*(3), 56. DOI: 10.1007/s13347-023-00657-0

Su, C., & Tang, W. (2023). Data sovereignty and platform neutrality: A comparative study on TikTok's data policy. *Global Media and China*, *8*(1), 57–71. DOI: 10.1177/20594364231154340

Sunkari, V., & Srinagesh, A. (2024). System Architecture for AI-Driven DeepFake Detection and Moderation on Social Media Platforms. *3rd International Conference on Optimization Techniques in the Field of Engineering (ICOFE-2024)*. DOI: 10.2139/ssrn.5065478

Swindle, O. (2002). The Effectiveness of Privacy Protection in Economic Systems. The Italian Garantì©'s International Conference. https://www.ftc.gov/news-events/news/speeches/effectiveness-privacy-protection-economic-systems

Swire, P., & Hemmings, J. D. (2016). *Mutual Legal Assistance in An Era of Globalised Communications: The Analogy to the Visa Waiver Program.* NYU Annual Survey of American Law. https://annualsurveyofamericanlaw.org/wp-content/uploads/2017/04/71-4_swirehemmings.pdf

Szabo, N. 1997. "The Idea of Smart Contracts." https://www.fon.hum.uva.nl/rob/Courses/InformationInSpeech/CDROM/Literature/LOTwinterschool2006/szabo.best.vwh.net/smart_contracts_idea.html

Tallberg, J., Erman, E., Furendal, M., Geith, J., Klamberg, M., & Lundgren, M. (2023). The global governance of artificial intelligence: Next steps for empirical and normative research. *International Studies Review, 25*(3), viad040. Advance online publication. DOI: 10.1093/isr/viad040

Tanchangya, T., Sarker, T., Rahman, J., Islam, M. S., Islam, N., & Siddiqi, K. O. (2025). Mapping Blockchain Applications in FinTech: A Systematic Review of Eleven Key Domains. *Information (Basel), 16*(9), 1–33. DOI: 10.3390/info16090769

Tapscott, A. (2023). *Web3: Charting the Internet's Next Economic and Cultural Frontier*. Harper Business.

Tapscott, D. (2014). *The Digital Economy: Rethinking Promise and Peril in the Age of Networked Intelligence*. McGraw-Hill Education.

Taylor, L., & Broeders, D. (2015). In the name of development: Power, profit and the datafication of the global south. *Geoforum, 64*, 229–237. DOI: 10.1016/j.geoforum.2015.07.002

Taylor, R. D. (2020). "Data localization": The internet in the balance. *Telecommunications Policy, 44*(8), 102003. Advance online publication. DOI: 10.1016/j.telpol.2020.102003

The Times. (2009). "Chancellor on Brink of Second Bailout for Banks." *The Times*, January 3.

Thomson, T. J., Angus, D., Dootson, P., Hurcombe, E., & Smith, A. (2022). Visual mis/disinformation in journalism and public communications: Current verification practices, challenges, and future opportunities. *Journalism Practice, 16*(5), 938–962. DOI: 10.1080/17512786.2020.1832139

Tian, X. (2024). Personalized translator training in the era of digital intelligence: Opportunities, challenges, and prospects. *Heliyon, 10*(20), e39354. DOI: 10.1016/j.heliyon.2024.e39354

Timmers, P. (2023). Sovereignty in the digital age. In *Introduction to Digital Humanism: A Textbook* (pp. 571–592). Springer.

Titanium Ventures. (n.d). "Web 2.5 Is a Bridge to a New Digital Era."

Toonders, J. (2014). *Data is the new oil of the digital economy.* Wired, July.

Topor, L. (2024). *Cyber sovereignty: International security, mass communication, and the future of the internet.* Springer., DOI: 10.1007/978-3-031-58199-1

Topscott, A., & Topscott, D. (2016). Blockchain revolution: How the technology behind bitcoin and other cryptocurrencies is changing the world.

Tosza, S. (2021). Internet service providers as law enforcers and adjudicators. A public role of private actors. *Computer Law & Security Review*, *43*, 105614. DOI: 10.1016/j.clsr.2021.105614

Tyagi, A. K. (2023). Decentralized everything: Practical use of blockchain technology in future applications. In *Distributed computing to blockchain* (pp. 19–38). Academic Press. DOI: 10.1016/B978-0-323-96146-2.00010-3

U.S. Congress. (2018). Clarifying Lawful Overseas Use of Data Act, Pub. L. No. 115-141, div. V, 132 Stat. 1213. https://www.law.cornell.edu/topn/clarifying_lawful_overseas_use_of_data_act

U.S. Government Accountability Office. (2025). Artificial intelligence: Generative AI use and management at federal agencies (GAO-25-107653). https://www.gao.gov/products/gao-25-107653

UK Government. (2022). National Cyber Strategy 2022. https://www.gov.uk/government/publications/national-cyber-strategy-2022

UK Government. (2023). AI regulation: A pro-innovation approach. https://www.gov.uk/government/publications/ai-regulation-a-pro-innovation-approach/white-paper

UN Trade and Development (UNCTAD). (2021). *Digital economy report 2021: Cross-border data flows and development—for whom the data flow.* UNCTAD. https://unctad.org/system/files/official-document/der2021_en.pdf

UNESCO. (2021). *Recommendation on the ethics of artificial intelligence.* https://www.unesco.org/en/articles/recommendation-ethics-artificial-intelligence

United Nations Conference on Trade and Development (UNCTAD). (2024). *Digital Economy Report 2024: Shaping an Environmentally Sustainable and Inclusive Digital Future.* https://unctad.org/system/files/official-document/der2024_en.pdf?utm_source=chatgpt.com

United States v. Microsoft Corp., 584 U.S. _ 2018 https://supreme.justia.com/cases/federal/us/584/17-2/

Usman, S. O. (2025a). *Consent, ownership, and the ethics of using personal data in deepfake creation.*

Usman, S. O. (2025b). *The Role of AI Regulation in Mitigating Deepfake Harms.*

Vaile, D. (2014). The Cloud and data sovereignty after Snowden. *Journal of Telecommunications and the Digital Economy.*, *2*(1), 60. DOI: 10.18080/jtde.v2n1.317

Van Alstyne, M., Brynjolfsson, E., & Madnick, S. (1995). Why not one big database? Principles for data ownership. *Decision Support Systems*, *15*(4), 267–284. DOI: 10.1016/0167-9236(94)00042-4

Van der Sloot, B., & Wagensveld, Y. (2022). Deepfakes: Regulatory challenges for the synthetic society. *Computer Law & Security Review*, *46*, 105716. DOI: 10.1016/j.clsr.2022.105716

Van Dijck, J., de Winkel, T., & Schäfer, M. T. (2023). Deplatformization and the governance of the platform ecosystem. *New Media & Society*, *25*(12), 3438–3454. DOI: 10.1177/14614448211045662

van Dijck, J., Poell, T., & de Waal, M. (2018). *The Platform Society*. Oxford University Press. DOI: 10.1093/oso/9780190889760.001.0001

Varian, H. (2018). *Artificial Intelligence, Economics, And Industrial Organisation.* NBER Working Paper Series. https://www.nber.org/system/files/working_papers/w24839/w24839.pdf

Vasist, P. N., & Krishnan, S. (2023). Engaging with deepfakes: a meta-synthesis from the perspective of social shaping of technology theory. In *Internet Research* (Vol. 33, Issue 5). DOI: 10.1108/INTR-06-2022-0465

Venske, T. (2023). Navigating digital sovereignty in Africa: A review of key challenges and constraints. Africa Governance Papers Journal, 1(4).

Verma, A. (2026). Deepfakes and the crisis of digital authenticity: Ethical challenges in the age of synthetic media. *Journal of Information. Communication and Ethics in Society*, *24*(1), 59–76. DOI: 10.1108/JICES-04-2025-0083

Visa. (2026). "Average Stablecoin Supply, All Stablecoins." https://visaonchainanalytics.com/

von Scherenberg, F., Hellmeier, M., & Otto, B. (2024). Data sovereignty in information systems. *Electronic Markets*, *34*(1), 15. Advance online publication. DOI: 10.1007/s12525-024-00693-4

Voss, W. G. (2020). Cross-border data flows, the GDPR, and data governance. *Washington International Law Journal, 29*, 485–520. https://ssrn.com/abstract=3629348

Wang, Y. (2023). Synthetic realities in the digital age: Navigating the opportunities and challenges of ai-generated content. *Authorea Preprints*.

Weber, R. H. (2021). Global law in the face of datafication and artificial intelligence. In Peng, S., Lin, C.-F., & Streinz, T. (Eds.), *Artificial intelligence and international economic law: Disruption, regulation, and reconfiguration* (pp. 54–69). Cambridge University Press. DOI: 10.1017/9781108954006.004

Webster, M. (March 2026). *Sovereign*. https://www.merriam-webster.com/dictionary/sovereign

Werbach, K. (2018). *The Blockchain and the New Architecture of Trust*. The MIT Press. DOI: 10.7551/mitpress/11449.001.0001

Westerlund, M. (2019). The emergence of deepfake technology: A review. *Technology Innovation Management Review*, *9*(11), 39–52. DOI: 10.22215/timreview/1282

Wicki, D. (2020). The Budapest Convention and the General Data Protection Regulation: Acting in concert to curb cybercrime? *International Cybersecurity Law Review*, *1*(1-2), 63–72. DOI: 10.1365/s43439-020-00012-5

Woods, A. K. (2016). *Against Data Exceptionalism*. Stanford Law Review. https://www.stanfordlawreview.org/wp-content/uploads/sites/3/2016/04/68_Stan_L._Rev._729_-_Woods.pdf

Wunderlich, U. (2025). *Can the EU become a Strategic-normative Power in a Fractured World?* London School of Economics. https://blogs.lse.ac.uk/europpblog/2025/07/03/can-the-eu-become-a-strategic-normative-power-in-a-fractured-world/

Xiangjuan, J., Fang, X., Zhang, Y., Heng, Y., Chen, X., Ge, W., Liu, W., & Huang, F. (2025). Integration and Innovation of Blockchain in Web3.0: Current Status and Standardization Prospects. *World Wide Web (Bussum)*, *28*(1), 7. Advance online publication. DOI: 10.1007/s11280-024-01319-7

Xi, R. (2025). On emerging technologies: The old regime and the proactivity. *Cardozo Int'l & Comp. L. Rev.*, *8*, 75.

Xu, J., Ma, M., Wang, F., Xiao, C., & Chen, M. (2024). Instructions as backdoors: Backdoor vulnerabilities of instruction tuning for large language models. In *Proceedings of the 2024 Conference of the North American Chapter of the Association for Computational Linguistics: Human Language Technologies* (Volume 1: Long Papers) (pp. 3421–3438). Association for Computational Linguistics. DOI: 10.18653/v1/2024.naacl-long.171

Yakovleva, S. (2024). *Governing cross-border data flows: Reconciling EU data protection and international trade law*. Oxford University Press., DOI: 10.1093/oso/9780192899248.001.0001

Yaraghi, N. (2018). *A Case against the General Data Protection Regulation*. Brookings. https://www.brookings.edu/articles/a-case-against-the-general-data-protection-regulation/

Yusuf, H., Fitri, A., & Razzaq, A. (2026). Using artificial intelligence for human-AI collaboration in knowledge management systems to improve organizational efficiency and learning. In *Driving Organizational Transformation Through Human-Robotic Collaboration* (pp. 35–48). IGI Global Scientific Publishing.

Yusuf, M., Rafli, M., & Rahmat, R. (2026). Reassessing State Sovereignty in the Era of Global Digital Governance. *International Legal Dimension Journal*, *1*(1), 49–60.

Zander, U., Lu, L., & Chimenti, G. (2025). The Platform Economy and Futures of Market Societies: Salient Tensions in Ecosystem Evolution. *Journal of Business Research*, *189*, 115037. Advance online publication. DOI: 10.1016/j.jbusres.2024.115037

Zeng, J., & Kaye, D. B. V. (2022). From content moderation to visibility moderation: A case study of platform governance on TikTok. *Policy and Internet*, *14*(1), 79–95. DOI: 10.1002/poi3.287

Zhang, W., Ong, L. M., & Findlay, M. (2023). Digital self-determination: An alternative paradigm for emerging economies. In M. Findlay, L. M. Ong, & W. Zhang (Eds.), *Elgar companion to regulating AI and big data in emerging economies* (pp. 158–179). Edward Elgar Publishing. DOI: 10.4337/9781785362408.00016

Ziegert, R. F., & Sotirov, M. (2024). Regulatory politics and hybrid governance: The case of Brazil's Amazon Soy Moratorium. *Global Environmental Change*, *88*, 102916. DOI: 10.1016/j.gloenvcha.2024.102916

Zozulia, O. I., Zozulia, I. V, Brusakova, O. V, Kholod, Y. A., & Berezhna, Y. V. (2021). *Information sovereignty as the basis of modern state information security*.

Zuboff, S. (2015). Big other: Surveillance capitalism and the prospects of an information civilization. *Journal of Information Technology*, *30*(1), 75–89. DOI: 10.1057/jit.2015.5

Zuboff, S. (2023). The age of surveillance capitalism. In *Social theory re-wired* (pp. 203–213). Routledge. DOI: 10.4324/9781003320609-27

Zukis, B. (2022). Digital and cybersecurity governance around the world. *Annals of Corporate Governance*, *7*(1), 1–92. DOI: 10.1561/109.00000032

Žuvela, A., Šveb Dragija, M., & Jelinčić, D. A. (2023). Partnerships in heritage governance and management: Review study of public–civil, public–private and public–private–community partnerships. *Heritage*, *6*(10), 6862–6880. DOI: 10.3390/heritage6100358

Zygmuntowski, J. O. (2023). Data governance in a trilemma: A qualitative analysis of rights, values, and goals in building data commons. *Digital Society : Ethics, Socio-Legal and Governance of Digital Technology*, *2*(2), 30. Advance online publication. DOI: 10.1007/s44206-023-00058-y

About the Contributors

Muhammad Anshari is an Associate Professor of Business Information Systems at the Universiti Brunei Darussalam School of Business and Economics (UBDSBE). After completing his PhD at the Faculty of Business, Economics and Policy Studies, Universiti Brunei Darussalam, he served as a Research Fellow at National Taiwan University, following an earlier research fellowship at King Saud University, Saudi Arabia. He has completed eight research grant projects and three industry research consultancies. Since 2022, Dr. Anshari has been listed among Stanford University's Top 2% World Scientists in the fields of ICT and Business and Management. He received two Outstanding Paper Awards at the Emerald Literati Awards 2023, and his work has been cited in three U.S. patents. In 2024, he was awarded the Research Excellence Award for Senior Academic Career (Social Sciences) at Universiti Brunei Darussalam. His research primarily contributes to the United Nations Sustainable Development Goal 9 (Industry, Innovation, and Infrastructure), with interests spanning Business Information Systems, Knowledge Management Systems, Digital Business, Digital Humanities, Digital Governance, and Digital Health.

Mohammad Nabil Almunawar is currently a professor at the School of Business and Economics, Universiti of Brunei Darussalam (UBDSBE), Brunei Darussalam. Hwe was the former dean of UBDSBE. He received his bachelor's degree in 1983 from Bogor Agricultural University, Indonesia, master's degree (MSc) from the Department of Computer Science, University of Western Ontario, London, Canada in 1991, and Ph.D in Computer Science/Information Systems from the University of New South Wales in 1998. Dr. Almunawar has published more than 250 papers in refereed journals, books, book chapters, encyclopedias, and international conference proceedings. He has more than 30 years of teaching experience in the area of information systems. His overall research interests include applications of IT in management, e-business/commerce, digital marketplace/

platform, digital business ecosystem, health informatics, information security, and cloud computing. Currently, he focuses his research on digital transformation, digital marketplace, digital platform, and digital business ecosystem.

Hazri Kifle is the Vice-Chancellor of Universiti Brunei Darussalam (UBD), and is recognized for his leadership in higher education, public sector innovation, and digital transformation. His vision aligns UBD with Brunei's Vision 2035, emphasizing sustainability, global partnerships, and preparing graduates for future industries. He has contributed significantly to e-Government development, focusing on ICT's role in governance and service delivery, and has published research on teacher professionalism, youth leadership, and innovation in education. Beyond academia, he actively promotes regional cooperation and has delivered keynote addresses on AI literacy, maritime governance, and strategic trust. His expertise spans public sector innovation, digital transformation, higher education leadership, and youth development, making him a pivotal figure in shaping Brunei's academic and policy landscape while positioning UBD as a hub for sustainability and innovation.

***

Azamat Ali is an Associate Professor in the School of Liberal and Creative Arts (Journalism and Mass Communication) at Lovely Professional University, Punjab, India. He earned his Ph.D. from the Central University of Gujarat, Gandhinagar, and a M.Sc. in Science Communication from Devi Ahilya Vishwavidyalaya, Indore. His research interests span emerging technologies, development communication, public policy, and health and science communication. Dr. Ali research is directed toward bridging the divide between scientific innovation and societal application, with a particular focus on harnessing the transformative potential of emerging technologies to drive innovation, address developmental challenges, and enhance societal wellbeing.

Asiimwe Hibah is currently a Master's candidate in Computer Science and Information Technology (research mode) at the International Islamic University Malaysia. Her research focuses on cybersecurity governance, with particular emphasis on digital sovereignty and cross-border cybercrime. She is presently engaged in advanced research examining the capacity of existing cybersecurity laws to combat cybercrime in Uganda, contributing to ongoing debates on the intersection of law, technology, and development. Professionally, she has served within the Liaisons and Partnerships Department of the Afro-Arab Youth Council, where she has been actively involved in initiatives promoting youth engagement, digital awareness, and transnational collaboration. Her work has included organizing policy dialogues and contributing to thought leadership on issues such as digital transformation, youth empowerment, and regional cooperation. Her academic contributions span emerging areas including African digital governance, cybersecurity law, and the role of technology in socio-economic development. She has authored and contributed to analytical writings on digital sovereignty, youth employment in the digital economy, and the implications of global cyber governance frameworks for developing regions.

Abdelraouf M. Ishtaiwi is an Associate Professor of Artificial Intelligence and Data Science at the University of Petra, Jordan, with over 22 years of academic and research experience in AI. He earned his Master's and Ph.D. degrees in Artificial Intelligence from Griffith University, Australia, where he focused on heuristic optimization techniques for satisfiability problems. His research expertise spans machine learning, hybrid metaheuristic optimization, associative classification, and AI applications in cybersecurity and emerging technologies like the metaverse. Dr. Ishtaiwi has developed innovative AI algorithms, such as ACRIPPER and hybrid crayfish-DE models, and contributed significantly to areas like phishing detection, blockchain security, and smart IoT defense. As a former Head of the Department of Data Science and AI at Petra University, he led academic reforms and accreditation initiatives. He has also been a visiting scholar at Griffith University and Universitat Pompeu Fabra, reflecting his international academic engagement.

Waziha Islam is a graduate student at Noakhali Science and Technology University, has dedicated four years to academic research, contributing to multiple projects. Her expertise was recognized with the Best Presenter Award at the International Conference on Embracing Industry 4.0 for Sustainable Business Growth in 2024. Her research interests include technology adoption, cashless tourism, technology adoption in tourism, and smart tourism.

Jikku Susan Kurian is an Assistant Professor (Senior Grade) at Symbiosis Institute of Business Management Bengaluru with over two decades of combined experience in industry and academia. She holds a Ph.D. in Management from Bharathiar University and specializes in Organizational Behaviour, Human Resource Management, leadership development, employee wellbeing, and behavioral training. Her academic and professional expertise spans teaching, research, consulting, executive development, and corporate training. Dr. Kurian has published research in reputed Scopus-indexed and ABDC-listed journals in areas including gig economy workforce wellbeing, artificial intelligence in HRM, blockchain adoption, sustainable branding, and supply chain analytics. She has also authored business case studies published through Economic Times Cases and presented research at national and international conferences. In addition, she serves as an approved doctoral research guide and is currently supervising doctoral scholars. Prior to academia, she gained extensive industry experience in corporates across training, recruitment, organizational development, and human resource management functions. She has also conducted executive development programs for leading organizations in areas such as leadership, emotional intelligence, team building, cross-cultural perspectives, and interpersonal effectiveness. Dr. Kurian is a member of professional bodies such as the American Psychological Association (APA), and the National Institute of Personnel Management (NIPM). Her interdisciplinary approach integrates behavioral sciences, management research, and industry practice to enhance organizational and individual effectiveness.

N. Bindu Madhavi is working as Associate Professor in KLEF Centre for Distance & Online Education. She has academic and administrative experience covering the past 25 years with 24 years of teaching Post Graduate Management students and 1year industry experience. She received her MBA degree with Marketing, specialization from Acharya Nagarjuna University and M.Com in Banking from Annamalai University. She received her Ph.D. degree from Acharya Nagarjuna University. She got qualified in UGC NET (National Eligibility Test) and APSET (AP State level Eligibility Test). She is contributing to the University level administration as Deputy Director, KL Centre for Distance & Online Education. She is a Senior Lifetime Member of professional societies like the "International Society for Research and Development" & "World Economics Association". She has presented papers in more than 50 national and international conferences. She delivered Invited Lectures on Management related topics in various Management Institutions. Besides, she has a number of research papers and book chapters published in reputed National and International journals.

Muhammad Abdus Salam known professionally as "Salam Shadhin", is an award-winning academic and researcher.

Hemendra Singh is an Assistant Professor of Law at Jindal Global Law School, situated within O.P. Jindal Global University, Sonipat. He pursued his LL.M. in Intellectual Property Rights from National Law University, Jodhpur, following his graduation with a B.A. LL.B. (Hons.) from Rajiv Gandhi National University of Law, Punjab. With a focus on environmental law, intellectual property law, criminal law and constitutional law, he has authored numerous research articles and book chapters published in both national and international journals and books.

Amit Verma has been a teacher, career counselor, and career counselor for eighteen years. He has a Ph.D. from Ranchi University, a Master's in Technology from MDU University in Rohtak, and a Bachelor of Technology in Computer Science from IET in Lucknow. Additionally, he holds a Ph.D. in Management from Panama's Swahili University. He most recently served as the ICSSR Project Director for the collaborative short-term empirical research project "Digital Transformation of Health Services: A Comparative Study of Bhopal and Lucknow." The Communication Institute of Greece, located in Athens, Greece, has nominated him as an Academic Member. Additionally, he received an invitation to speak as the chief speaker at the Media Management Seminar from Saint Augustine University of Tanzania (SAUT), located in Mwanza, Tanzania, East Africa. Dr. Verma has held positions as a lecturer, senior lecturer, assistant professor, and associate professor at prestigious institutions in Delhi NCR, Uttar Pradesh, and Uttarakhand. He has been accepted as a faculty member for the M. Com. and B. Com. programs offered by Lucknow University and is currently an assistant professor at Kalicharan PG College. He teaches management information systems, advertising management, and marketing management. He also gets ready for his career and takes part in seminar activities. His values have influenced Dr. Verma, based on the philosophy of Swami Vivekananda, and he attempts to impart his principles of good character and ethics during his teachings. He is the author of 20 papers in peer-reviewed journals, including 10 in ABDC, SSCI, and SCOPUS-indexed journals. He has also reviewed a large number of research papers. His publications encompass edited volumes that bridge the gap between academia and industry. His publications include edited books that cater to both academic and industrial audiences.

Index

A

B

C

D

E

G

I

J

L

M

N

P

S

www.ingramcontent.com/pod-product-compliance
Lightning Source LLC
LaVergne TN
LVHW081539300926
849161LV00006B/1493

9798260002889